John Wimber

His Life and Ministry

Praise for John Wimber: His Life and Ministry

Dr. Connie Dawson has taken on the exhilarating yet challenging task of writing an inspiring and comprehensive biography of a great Christian leader. In his lifetime, Wimber envisioned thousands of pastors and leaders like myself, and now he will inspire you with his life, insights, and teachings.

John Arnott,
Former Pastor, Toronto Airport Vineyard

I have read Connie Dawson's biography on John Wimber carefully and slowly and will read it again and again. It touches me so much that I have been brought to tears a number of times. She has served Jesus and the body of Christ well in the hundreds of hours it must have taken her to research and write this comprehensive biography of a great Christian leader. I am amazed that a researcher could get such accurate nuance with so many details. I love this book beyond measure. I tell so many leaders that this is a MUST read. A new generation needs to know about this man who so powerfully impacted the church in the second half of the twentieth century. I encourage everyone to read it, and get ready to be inspired!

Mike Bickle
Founder of International House of Prayer Kansas City

In Brooklyn, New York, in the late seventies, my then new wife and I lived in an apartment owned by a graduate of Fuller Theological Seminary. This landlord, who was involved in church growth initiatives in the greater New York City area, brought in Peter Wagner, whom he had studied with previously, to address pastors and cell-group leaders. Peter, in turn, had brought someone with him named John Wimber. That night, John slept in the basement bedroom of our three-story apartment. Little did I know how much a part this man would play in what would become known, because of his seminal influence, as the Third Wave movement.

This narrative of John's journey by Dr. Connie Dawson both draws you in as a reader and gives you a front-row seat to the unfolding of a life that has impacted millions for Christ and the kingdom of God. Connie's writing brilliance shines as she carefully and faithfully takes the reader from John's beginnings all the way through his sustained and arduous journey as a pioneer and father in a movement whose impact continues to this day, even after his homegoing. Connie tells the whole story, including the sufferings and challenges John faced both as a preacher of the gospel and as one who saw many healed, while he himself was beleaguered with much physical suffering.

Connie's work is masterful, historically faithful, and theologically insightful. For the lay reader and the academic scholar alike, there is much here to glean and contemplate. Connie is indeed a scholar, and yet her writing makes this work accessible to all who are hungry and interested in an important part of Pentecostal history. My prayer is that the emerging generation will take time to become acquainted, through the pages of her book, with the life of one of the twentieth century's most compelling and cogent voices in the kingdom of God.

Mark J. Chironna, D.Min.
Mark Chironna Ministries
Church on the Living Edge, Longwood, Florida

I am so pleased to see Dr. Connie Dawson's book, *John Wimber: His Life and Ministry,* enter the public market. It is an important read. Important for those in the Vineyard who did not have the great privilege of knowing Wimber; important for those not in the Vineyard to gain an understanding of this vessel of honor made of clay. For those of you who have wished you could have known him, I encourage you to get to know him by reading this book. Thank you, Dr. Dawson, for the years of work and research you have spent on this labor of love.

Randy Clark, D.Min.
Founder and President, Global Awakening

I met John Wimber in Pasadena, California in 1985, while I was attending Fuller Theological Seminary. In fact, I went to Fuller because of the "Signs and Wonders" course that John initiated at Fuller. A few weeks before my departure from Fuller, John had dinner with Barbara and me and it was an amazing time of encouragement and impartation. It was the last time I would have an encounter with him. I believe biographies of great people should be written by people who love and admire the persons about who they are writing. This does not require unbridled adulation that ignores human flaws, but places them in crucible of life and delivers a sane estimate of the person. My friend, Dr. Connie Dawson has done just the kind of project that gives us the needed perspective of a person who carried a "glorious treasure" in "common clay jars." (Passion Translation) I needed this book, it answered questions about Wimber, to which I needed answers. The Church needs this book, it will yield insights into Wimber's life, work and ministry. Dr. Dawson's work is scholarly, and honoring and I believe it will bring glory through a life that impacted so many for the kingdom.

Bishop Joseph L. Garlington Sr., Ph.D.
Senior Pastor of Covenant Church of Pittsburgh

I had the privilege of meeting John Wimber on more than one occasion during my tenure as editor of *Charisma* magazine. People treated the man like a celebrity, but I could tell Wimber did not view himself that way. He was humble and aware of his flaws. Yet he was one of the most passionate Christians I've ever met. He was hungry for the reality of the Holy Spirit, and his desire to see that power demonstrated in the modern church was inspiring to me and to a whole generation of leaders. I was sad when Wimber died, because I didn't want to see that passion wane.

I was thrilled when I learned that Rev. Connie Dawson was carefully studying Wimber's life so that she could write a sensitive biography of him. There is so much to learn from his multifaceted life: Wimber had childlike faith, yet he was a thinker as well. He was also willing to experiment because he didn't want our experience of God to be limited to what we have been able to fit into a small box. He read the New Testament and wanted to see the book of Acts repeated. He would lay hands on the sick for days and months, with no results, because he knew his faith was growing. In the end, he was used by God to stir modern revival movements—even though they were fraught with problems and challenges.

Connie Dawson writes with grace and sensitivity—which is the only way I would want anyone to treat Wimber's exemplary life. This book should be read by anyone who is hungry for more of God's power. And it should be read especially by leaders who are willing to take the risks associated with spiritual revival.

> J. Lee Grady
> Former Editor, *Charisma* magazine
> Author, *Set My Heart on Fire* and other books
> Director, The Mordecai Project

Few ministers in the last quarter of the twentieth century have had the impact and influence on the North American church like John Wimber. Who was he? Dr. Connie Dawson has delivered a well-research tome that, at last, pulls back the curtain on this man's life and ministry. This engaging, readable, and inspirational volume on Wimber is well-worth the time and effort to come to a greater understanding and appreciation of the man and his impact on the church domestically and globally.

> Rev. Paul W. Lewis, Ph.D.
> Associate Dean
> Assemblies of God Theological Seminary

Connie Dawson has done a great service in producing the first full-length biographical treatment of the life of John Wimber. Paying close attention to detail without losing track of the bigger story, she introduces readers to the fascinating life of a humble leader who had a profound effect on the western church in the second half of the twentieth century. Students of Wimber's life and legacy—and any who hunger for ongoing charismatic renewal in the church—will not want to miss this book!

> Caleb J. D. Maskell, Ph.D.
> Founder, Society of Vineyard Scholars

This excellent biography, *John Wimber: His Life and Ministry*, seeks to present an objective overview of the major events of Wimber from the perspective of one outside the Vineyard. It also attempts to better understand this man, who has been called one of the most important and controversial figures in North American evangelicalism in the twentieth century. Well written and highly documented, it presents a comprehensive picture of Wimber's life. It should stand the test of time as the definitive biography of Wimber.

Vinson Synan, Ph.D.
Scholar in Residence, Oral Roberts University
Dean Emeritus, Regent University School of Divinity

In *John Wimber: His Life and Ministry*, Dr. Connie Dawson recounts the steps God took my father through and shows him as a man, obediently trusting to see "God's Ministry" and not build his own. For those who never met my dad this book gives background for a lot of what the Vineyard movement believes and a theology for supernatural ministry.

Tim Wimber
John Wimber's son

I really appreciate Dr. Dawson's book on John Wimber. I very seldom read any book but the Bible. That's the way I've been for five decades. I might read one book a year on average but some years I won't read any. That's neither good nor bad, it's just the way it is. But I felt led to read this book, and I'm so glad I did. It really impacted me. I knew virtually nothing about John Wimber, but this book was enlightening and inspiring. I was totally blessed and also warned about potential ways the devil could attack me. I know it was the Lord that led her to write this book. It has been a blessing. I believe many will be impacted by this book.

Andrew Wommack
Founder of Gospel of Truth
Andrew Wommack Ministries
Founder of Charis Bible College

John Wimber

Foreword

By Vinson Synan

I have known Connie since she came to Regent University as a Ph.D. student in 2006. During her weeks of residency, she stayed in our home and became like a member of our family. Connie was one of the outstanding students at Regent and was presented with the J. Rodman Williams Award for her academic achievements and commitment to excellence in the study of theology. She was also the first woman to graduate from the PhD program at the Regent University School of Divinity.

Connie's work, *John Wimber: His Life and Ministry,* is the biography of John Wimber's life and ministry in the context of the events of his day. It is the account of a man who grew up fatherless and yet fathered an organization and movement that has impacted multiplied millions around the globe. Wimber's story leads the reader through his early life and ministry to discover his encounter with the Holy Spirit that ultimately formed his understanding of power healing and power evangelism. This is followed by an account of the development of Vineyard Ministries and of the issues surrounding his controversial MC510 Signs and Wonders and Church Growth class at Fuller Theological Seminary. We also get a view of his evangelical doctrine with a Pentecostal experience and the impact of George Ladd's kingdom of God theology. Next, there is an interaction with Wimber's most vocal critics and the Vineyard's response, his involvement with the Kansas City prophets, and the circumstances surrounding the Toronto Blessing and the controversy of his disfellowshipping the Toronto Vineyard. The decline of his health and his death then round out the narrative, followed by a tribute to his life.

This work relies heavily on Wimber's own books, articles, audio recordings, and other extant materials as well as on books and articles written by both his critics and close friends, on personal interviews, and on Carol Wimber's personal account of his life in *John Wimber: The Way it Was.* In addition, Connie had the great advantage of having Wimber's colleague at Fuller, C. Peter Wagner, on her dissertation committee.

As a biography, this project seeks to present an objective overview, from the perspective of one outside the Vineyard, of the major events of John Wimber's life, and it attempts to better understand this man, who has been called one of the most important and controversial figures in North American evangelicalism in the twentieth century.

Well written and highly documented, *John Wimber: His Life and Ministry* presents a comprehensive picture of Wimber's life. It should stand the test of time as the definitive biography of Wimber.

Vinson Synan, Ph.D.
Scholar in Residence, Oral Roberts University
Dean Emeritus, Regent University School of Divinity

His Life and Ministry

Connie Dawson

John Wimber: His Life and Ministry
Copyright © 2011, 2020, 2021 by Connie Dawson

All Rights Reserved. Printed in the United States of America. No part of this book may be used or reproduced in any manner, electronic, mechanical, photocopying, recording, stored in a retrieval system, transmitted in any form without prior permission of the author except in the case of brief quotations for academic documentation or use in critical articles and reviews.

Printed by Amazon Kindle Direct Publishing.
United States.

Requests for information should be addressed to:
The Wimber Project
740 North 70th Street
Lincoln, NE 68505
www.conniedawson.com

First edition August 2020. Second edition March 2021. Third edition November 2021.
Materials used by permission.

Cover design by Rachel Gaarder. Cover photo from the Regent University Library Wimber Collection. Photo used by permission.

Contents

Contents

Acknowledgments

Preface

Introduction

1. The Making of a Fool for Christ
2. The Birth of an Equipping Healer
3. The Birth of the Vineyard Movement and International Ministry
4. MC510: Signs and Wonders and Church Growth
5. A Practical Theology
6. The Pain of Criticism
7. The Prophetic Years
8. The Father's Blessing
9. The Closing Years and a Tribute

Appendixes

A. A Timeline of Wimber's Life and Ministry
B. An Overview of the MC510 Syllabus
C. A Five-Step Healing Model
D. Critical Characteristics of the Bible
E. An Overview of the Fuller Committee Report
F. Joint Statement from the Leadership of the Full Faith Church of Love Ministries and the Metro Vineyard Fellowship of Kansas City
G. Letters Regarding Toronto
H. Wimber's Conference Schedule
I. Ministry Emphasis and Themes
J. Songs Written by Wimber

Bibliography

To Bruce, my wonderful husband, who is my
constant source of encouragement and strength.

I would also like to dedicate this book to the late Dr. Vinson Synan,
my friend and mentor, who lovingly
and meticulously guided my research on this project.
Words cannot express my love and gratitude.

Foreword

By Randy Clark

My life changed when I met John Wimber. My very first impartation came within twelve hours of first seeing and hearing him. When he laid his hands on me, this Baptist pastor fell under the power of God for the first time in his life. The prophecy John gave me just before laying hands on me would become an anchor tied to my personal destiny. He said I had an apostolic call on my life and that I would have an international ministry. It took exactly ten years after this event for this prophecy to come to pass.

Thereafter, I learned from the live teachings and books of John Wimber and his associate, Blaine Cook, and my faith increased. I was inspired, as well, by their stories and testimonies. But the most powerful change came through the impartations of the Holy Spirit that occurred in my life through their meetings.

John Wimber has impacted my life the most in regard to practical theology and the theology of the kingdom. This being the case, I have tried to be a spiritual son who has honored his spiritual father, John Wimber. It is not difficult to see my indebtedness to Wimber in my conferences, training schools, certification programs, and seminary courses. My foundational messages are from him.

I am so pleased to see Dr. Connie Dawson's book, *John Wimber: His Life and Ministry,* enter the public market. I met Dr. Dawson for the first time to give an interview that was to be part of her doctoral dissertation on Wimber. Since then, she became a professor in the Global Awakening Seminary where she is loved for her three dynamic courses on church history, with an emphasis on revival and renewal.

John Wimber: His Life and Ministry is an important read. Important for those in the Vineyard who did not have the great privilege of knowing Wimber and important for those not in the Vineyard, to gain an understanding of this vessel of honor made of clay. He was humble, teachable, passionate for God, a worshiper more than a theologian (as in the orthodox churches, where the theologians were first of all worshipers). He was a pioneer. He was apostolic and a strong leader.

He was also human, impacted by being raised in a dysfunctional home in regard to father figures; therefore, most of all, in my opinion, he is an example of God's grace enabling one to become powerfully used even with brokenness and shortcomings. John continues to be my hero, not because he was perfect, but because he was a model of hope, epitomizing the message that God could use me too—that I, too, could be used with my brokenness and weaknesses.

I will never forget one of my first experiences with John. He had told me to be his shadow in several meetings, to follow him around, observing what the Father was doing and then, at the end of the meeting, asking John questions. During one such night of shadowing at a Methodist church, I observed that everyone he prayed for was healed. I was amazed! The next night, everyone he prayed for was not healed. I was perplexed! When I started to ask John why, he stopped me and said, "Let me tell you what your question is." He then told me correctly what I was about to ask and proceeded to give me his answer. "I had no more faith last night than I did tonight. I had no more sin in my life tonight than last night. Both nights I prayed, "Come, Holy Spirit," and blessed what God was doing. Last night everyone was healed, but I didn't go to bed thinking I was a great man of faith or a great man of God; tonight no one was healed, and I am not going to bed feeling like a great failure of God. Tomorrow I will get up and do it all over again." In that moment of seeing John in weakness, I truly understood his utter dependence upon God and how he was able to stand on his "rug of peace" when ministering. I learned that his rug of peace consisted of God's grace, and later renamed it the "rug of grace" in my teachings.

I have been traveling the world for the past twenty-five years, growing and changing and developing my own voice for what God has been teaching me but, most of the time, also being an echo of John Wimber. And in my ten years of teaching before I began international ministry, I still sounded the echo of his voice. I hope to be a son who brings honor to John's memory and joy to his heart, as he watches from among the great crowd of witnesses his teachings—about the kingdom, about everyone getting to play, about the gifts, and especially about healing—continuing to be taught.

I know that as he witnesses what God is continuing to do, he will be well pleased to hear the echoes of his voice calling in the wilderness of evangelicalism, of Roman Catholicism, and of Pentecostalism, echoes regarding the Coming One and advancing the kingdom through *power evangelism*. May he rejoice to hear evangelicals, Catholics, Pentecostals, and Holiness leaders echoing his teachings to their spiritual families. May he be thrilled to see his teaching confirmed by its fruit, as millions are born into the kingdom as a result of seeing the power of God in signs and wonders and healings and miracles, and as, from these millions of salvations, scores of thousands of new churches are planted.

For those of you who wish you could have known him, I encourage you to get to know him by reading *John Wimber: His Life and Ministry*. Thank you, Dr. Dawson, for the years of work and research you have spent on this labor of love.

Randy Clark, D.Min.
Founder, Global Awakening
President, Global Awakening Theological Seminary

Acknowledgments

Several people deserve special recognition for their contributions to this project. First, I would like to thank Dr. Vinson Synan, who has been a mentor and father figure in my life. And a special thanks to Carol Lee, his beautiful wife, for opening their home and adopting me as a member of their own family. Our conversations around the breakfast table will always be treasured memories. Thank you both for your love and encouragement. Thank you also for the times you read this manuscript and helped guide me through the process. Yours is a labor of love.

A special thank you also to Dr. Graham Twelftree who helped direct my research and meticulously read through my original manuscript. He also worked with the Wimber family to donate John Wimber's personal library collection to Regent University, thus making accessible many primary sources for this project. Thanks also to the late Dr. C. Peter Wagner, who was a personal friend and colleague of Wimber, for his valuable input as the external reader of my research.

I also want to thank Rachel Gaarder, my administrative assistant, for her technical expertise, support, encouragement, and hard work in helping to bring this manuscript to its present form. You are a treasure.

Many thanks go to Lynn Everett for her expert editing of the final draft of this book. You were a joy to work with.

Loving appreciation also goes to all of my friends and church family who prayed and supported me throughout this process. I especially want to thank my husband, Bruce, who was and has always been my greatest source of encouragement.

Finally, I thank Jesus, who assigned me this project. Through the discipline of this research you introduced me to this amazing man, John Wimber, who, through I never met him, has tremendously impacted my life. Thank you, Jesus, for this experience, which was exceedingly, abundantly above all I could ask or imagine. I praise you with all of my heart.

Preface

While this work was initially written as a dissertation for my PhD at Regent University, I have subsequently rewritten the manuscript to appeal to a wider audience. There are still two chapters: A Practical Theology and The Pain of Criticism that may be a bit tedious for some readers. I encourage you to not get bogged down in these areas but press through because the final chapters of Wimber's life are fascinating.

Chapter one begins with an introduction of Wimber's early years in Kirksville, Missouri, and his subsequent move to California, where he met Carol, his future wife and mother of their four children. This chapter covers John and Carol's radical Christian conversion and their joining the Quaker Church. It tells about the influence of their spiritual mentor, Gunner Payne, and about Wimber's relationship with C. Peter Wagner, and his work with Fuller Theological Seminary as a church growth consultant.

In chapter two, John and Carol's experience with the Holy Spirit moves us into the next phase of Wimber's spiritual journey, as he resigns from Fuller to plant a church under the covering of Chuck Smith and Calvary Chapel. We also see the "watershed experienced" when the "hippie preacher" Lonnie Frisbee said, "Come, Holy Spirit," and spiritual pandemonium launched them into their power evangelism ministry.[1]

The third chapter reveals the story of the birth of the Vineyard movement and Wimber taking a team of freshly trained young people and leaders from his church to the United Kingdom and South Africa to field-test his new model of training and equipping the saints for power evangelism. Wimber's model eventually became the material for his famous MC510 Signs and Wonder and Church Growth class at Fuller Theological Seminary.[2] This material is covered in chapter four, and details and format of Wimber's lectures, the controversy the class caused among the Fuller faculty, and the success of the class—which ultimately became its demise.[3]

Chapter five offers a brief overview of Wimber's practical theology and reveals the paradigm shifts Wimber went through on his healing journey; the impact of George Ladd's "already-and-not-yet" theology of the kingdom of God, which eventually became the harbinger for his own ministry and theology of power evangelism;[4] and how power healing and power evangelism are to be a normal part of the Christian life.[5]

Chapter six takes a look at the negative criticism surrounding Wimber's ministry and theology and the responses of the men who rose to defend him and his Spirit-empowered ministry.[6]

Chapter seven then investigates Wimber's association with Mike Bickle, Paul Cain, and the Kansas City prophets, and their attempt to "cross-pollinate" the Kansas City prophetic and intercession with the Vineyard's compassion and worship. As the controversy surrounding the Kansas City prophets escalated, Wimber was asked to step in and provide leadership and spiritual covering; however, this resulted in a parting of the two ministries for reasons revealed in this chapter.[7]

The "Toronto Blessing," which erupted in January 1994 at the Toronto Airport Vineyard Christian Fellowship under the leadership of John Arnott, is covered in chapter eight. Wimber's reaction to the exotic and extrabiblical manifestations, along with his attempts to bring correction, resulted in his withdrawing Vineyard support and disfellowshipping the Toronto Vineyard.[8]

Chapter nine, following the Toronto controversy, reveals a tired and physically sick Wimber facing his final battle—the fight for his life. During this season, he reevaluated his theology of suffering and nonhealing, while at the same time struggling with releasing the reins of the Vineyard to others. His ultimate homegoing is then honored in chapter eight with a final tribute from family and friends.[9]

The goal of this work is not to produce a critical analysis or evaluation. Rather it seeks to present a research-based, chronological biography, offering information that tells the story of Wimber's life and ministry. The narrative genre attempts to carry the reader from one event in Wimber's life to the next, telling the story through interviews and primary-source literature while attempting to interact with the events surrounding his life. The culmination of these stories aims to validate Wimber's ministry and recognize him as a significant forerunner in the current renewal movement, who will continue to impact both present and future generations.

Volumes more could have been written and still not adequately represent all that Wimber contributed to the body of Christ and the impact he had on so many leaders in the church today. It is with great humility that I offer this particular work, which I pray will be a blessing to the Body of Christ.

[1] Carol Wimber, "A Hunger for God," in *Power Encounters among Christians in the Western World*, 12; Ronald M. Enroth, Edward Erickson, and C. Breckenridge Peters, *The Jesus People: Old-Time Religion in the Age of Aquarius* (Grand Rapids: Eerdmans, 1972). Also see C. M. Robeck Jr., "Calvary Chapel," in *NIDPCM*, 453; and Jackson, *Quest for the Radical Middle*, 392–405. Jackson states that Frisbee became a controversial figure in Calvary Chapel and the Vineyard movement. He was converted from a homosexual lifestyle to be used in a powerful signs-and-wonders ministry, only to lapse back into homosexuality and die of AIDS. At his funeral, which was held in Robert Schuller's Crystal Cathedral, with thousands in attendance, Frisbee was called a modern-day Samson. His story, hidden by many in the movement out of embarrassment, is now coming to light and is currently available on DVD: David Sabatino, *Frisbee: The Life and Death of a Hippie Preacher*, DVD (Truly, CA: Jester Media and KQED, 2006).

[2] Accounts of these trips and their events are documented in the following books and articles: Kevin Springer, ed., *Riding the Third Wave*, (Hants, U.K.: Marshall Morgan and Scott, 1987); Wimber and Springer, *Power Evangelism* and *Power Healing* (San Francisco, CA: Harper and Row, 1987); David Pytches, ed., *John Wimber: His Influence and His Legacy* (Guildford, Surrey: Eagle, 1998); Anne Watson, "Third Wave Has Only Begun," in *Power Encounters among Christians in the Western World*, 16; Carol Wimber, *John Wimber*, 150–65; and Margie McClure, "A Diary of the South African Mission, October 1980," unpublished document in John Wimber Special Collections, Regent University Library, Virginia Beach, Virginia.

[3] Wagner, "God Wasn't Pulling My Leg," 51; Carol Wimber, *John Wimber*, 167; C. Peter Wagner, "MC520: Genesis of a Concept," *Signs and Wonders Today*, ed. C. Peter Wagner (Altamonte Springs, FL: Creation House, 1987), 41–2. In 1982, *Christian Life Magazine* published a complete issue about the MC510 course at Fuller. Christian Life Missions later reprinted this publication in conjunction with Wagner under the title *Signs and Wonders Today*. The magazine articles published in book form were expanded and organized into sessions, with study questions and material added at the end of each session. In 1987, Wagner edited the material, added three new chapters, and published it through Creation House as a book with the same title, but he eliminated the magazine pictures and study materials. Kevin Springer, "Applying the Gifts," 26–34; John Wimber and Kevin Springer, "John Wimber Calls It Power Evangelism," *Charisma*, September 1985, 35–8; Steven Lawson, "The Vineyard: Where Spiritual Gifts Blossom," *Charisma*, September 1985, 39; Majorie Lee Chandler, "Fuller Seminary Cancels Course on Signs and Wonders," *Christianity Today*, February 21, 1986, 48; Lewis B. Smedes, ed., *Ministry and the Miraculous: A Case Study at Fuller Theological Seminary* (Pasadena: Fuller Theological Seminary, 1987); Jackson, *Quest for the Radical Middle*, 124; C. Peter Wagner, *The Third Wave of the Holy Spirit*; C. Peter Wagner, *How to Have a Healing Ministry without Making Your Church Sick* (Ventura, CA: Regal Books, 1988). Charles Kraft, *Christianity with Power: Your Worldview and Your Experience of the Supernatural* (Manila, Philippines: OMF Literature, 1989); Don Williams, *Signs, Wonders and the Kingdom of God* (Ann Arbor, MI: Vine Books, 1989); John White, *When the Spirit Comes with Power: Signs & Wonders among God's People* (Downers Grove, IL: InterVarsity, 1988).

[4] Carol Wimber, *John Wimber*, 65–9; John Wimber and Kevin Springer, *Power Evangelism* (San Francisco: Harper & Row, 1986), x; Kevin Springer, "Applying the Gifts to Everyday Life," *Charisma*, September 1985, 29; C. Peter Wagner, "God Wasn't Pulling My Leg," in *Power Encounters among Christians in the Western World*, ed. Kevin Springer (San Francisco: Harper & Row, 1987), 50; Carol Wimber, *John Wimber*, 97–8; Tim Stafford, "Testing the Wine from John Wimber's Vineyard," *Christianity Today*, August 18, 1986, 18; Wimber and Springer, *Power Evangelism*, 12. George Eldon Ladd's works include *Crucial Questions about the Kingdom of God* (Grand Rapids: Eerdmans, 1954); *Jesus and the Kingdom* (Waco: Word Books, 1964); *The Pattern of New Testament Truth* (Grand Rapids: Eerdmans, 1968); *Gospel of the Kingdom* (Grand Rapids: Eerdmans, 1973); *The Presence of the Future* (Grand Rapids: Eerdmans, 1974); *A Theology of the New Testament* (Grand Rapids: Eerdmans, 1975); and *The Last Things* (Grand Rapids: Eerdmans,

1978).

[5] Wimber, *Power Evangelism*, 16, 61–2; Vernon L. Purdy, "Divine Healing," in *Systematic Theology*, ed. Stanley M. Horton (Springfield, Missouri: Legion, 2007), 207–12, 489–522; Steve S. Carter, "Demon Possession and the Christian," *Asian Journal of Pentecostal Studies* 3, no. 1 (January 2000): 19–31; Morris Williams, "Can a Christian Have a Demon?" in *Power Encounter: A Pentecostal Perspective*, ed. Opal Reddin (Springfield, Missouri: Central Bible College Press, 1999), 160–73; Kevin Springer, ed. *Power Encounters* (San Francisco: Harper and Row, 1988); and John Wimber and Kevin Springer, *Power Points*.

[6] Dave Hunt and T. A. McMahon, *The Seduction of Christianity: Spiritual Discernment in the Last Days* (Eugene, Oregon: Harvest House, 1985), 171–88; Robert Doyle, John Woodhouse, Paul Barnett, and John Reid, *Signs and Wonders and Evangelicals: A Response to the Teachings of John Wimber* (Randburg: Fabel Distributors, 1987); James R. Coggins and Paul G. Hiebert, eds., *Wonders and the Word: An Examination of Issues Raised by John Wimber and the Vineyard Movement* (Winnipeg, MB: Kindred Press, 1989), 12; "Signs and Wonders: Wimber Breaks Silence to Answer Vineyard Critics," *Christianity Today*, March 9, 1992, 66–8. Also see Jackson, *Quest for the Radical Middle*, 152–4; the Vineyard position papers at www.vineyardusa.org/publications/positionpapers.aspx; Philip Jensen and Tony Payne, "John Wimber: Friend or Foe?" *Briefing*, April 1990, 4–48; Jack Deere, "The Vineyard's Response to the Briefing," *Position Paper #2* (Anaheim, CA: Association of Vineyard Churches, May 1992), 1–31; Wayne Grudem, "The Vineyard's Response to the Standard," *Position Paper #3* (Anaheim, CA: Association of Vineyard Churches, June 1992), 1–37; Jackson, *Quest for the Radical Middle*, 158–9; Wayne Grudem, "Power and Truth: A Response to the Critiques of Vineyard Teaching and Practice," *Position Paper #4* (Anaheim, CA: Association of Vineyard Churches, March 1993), 2–61; Charles Colson, J. I. Packer, R. C. Sproul, et al., *Power Religion: The Selling Out of the Evangelical Church?* (Chicago: Moody Bible Institute, 1992); Rich Nathan, "A Response to Charismatic Chaos: The Book Written by John F. MacArthur, Jr.," *Position Paper #5* (Anaheim CA: Association of Vineyard Churches, April 1993), 1-27. John MacArthur, *Charismatic Chaos* (Grand Rapids, MI: Zondervan, 1992).

[7] Jackson, *Quest for the Radical Middle*, 216. Also see Carol Wimber, *John Wimber*, 167–80; Ernie Gruen, "Kansas City Prophets Exposed." Accessed March 12, 2010, http://www.birthpangs.org/articles/kcp/kcp-gruen.html; Michael G. Mauldin, "Seers in the Heartland: Hot on the Trail of the Kansas City Prophets," *Christianity Today*, January 14, 1991, 18–22; David Pytches, *Some Said It Thundered* (Nashville: Oliver Nelson, 1991); G. W. Gohr, "Kansas City Prophets," in *NIDPCM*, 816–7.

[8] Synan, *Century of the Holy Spirit*, 379–80; Synan, *Holiness-Pentecostal Tradition*, 277.

[9] Carol Wimber, *John Wimber*, 167–8, 177; John Wimber, *Living with Uncertainty: My Bout with Inoperable Cancer* (Anaheim, CA: Vineyard Ministries International), 8. Also see John Wimber, "Signs, Wonders, and Cancer," *Christianity Today*, October 7, 1996, 51; Jackson, *Quest for the Radical Middle*, 275; Carol Wimber, *John Wimber*, 190; John Wimber, *The Way In is the Way On* (Norcross, GA: Ampelon, 2006).

Introduction

C. Peter Wagner, professor of church growth at Fuller Theological Seminary School of World Mission, called John Wimber "a molder of an entire generation," and christened him the "fountainhead" of the Third Wave renewal movement in the twentieth century.[1] Wagner coined the term "third wave" to designate the most recent wave of renewal among evangelicals, which is connected to the tradition of the Pentecostal and charismatic movements but has unique features separating it from the preceding waves.[2]

The first wave, classic Pentecostalism, originated with the outpouring of the Holy Spirit at the turn of the twentieth century and can be traced back to Charles Parham's Bible School in Topeka, Kansas, and the Azusa Street Revival of 1906 with William Seymour. This movement, born out of both the Holiness and Keswick Movements, was different from classic evangelicalism in a couple of ways. First, Pentecostals believe the baptism in the Holy Spirit is a second work of grace, subsequent to conversion, confirmed by the initial physical evidence of speaking in tongues. They also believe the gifts of the Spirit are operational for today, and they have historically promoted divine healing.[3]

The second wave of the Spirit originated with the mid-century charismatic movement and gained inroads into both the traditional evangelical and Catholic churches. Charismatics advocate glossolalia and Holy Spirit baptism but not as a subsequent work of grace. Charismatics also believe the gifts of the Spirit are for today, thus rejecting the cessationist view held by many traditional evangelical churches.[4]

The third wave of the Spirit has its origins in Wimber's Signs and Wonders class, at Fuller Theological Seminary between 1982 and 1985, and in the formation of the Vineyard Christian Fellowship.[5] Third wavers, also known as Neo-charismatics, embrace the miraculous, and believe in divine healing and casting out demons as did the previous two waves, but a few doctrines set them apart. First, while those in the third wave believe in the baptism of the Holy Spirit, they advocate neither a post-conversion experience of Spirit baptism nor the necessity of speaking in tongues. This segment of the renewal movement believes the Holy Spirit is received at the time of conversion and that the gifts of the Spirit, including tongues, simply need to be activated at some point in the believer's life.[6]

Unlike traditional Pentecostals, third wavers believe a Christian can be demonized. They also believe in inner healing—something normally rejected by classic Pentecostals but frequently accepted by charismatics.[7] Today the third wave renewal represents one of the largest segments of the Christian population under the umbrella of Pentecostalism in the world.[8] The impact Wimber made upon the renewal movement can be seen by telling his life story. As such, it is the goal of this biography to present the life and ministry of John Wimber, a man with an evangelical theology and a Pentecostal experience who embodied a model for renewal that impacted millions around the globe. As you read through it, however, note that while Wagner and others credit Wimber as the founder and father of this movement, Wimber himself resisted the title or, at most, held it lightly.[9]

John Wimber was an evangelical with a pneumatological, experiential theology.[10] He was an exegetical teacher and preacher who took the words of Jesus in the Gospels literally. For John, evangelicals had only two choices: they could embrace the cessation theory and relegate the works and power of Jesus to the ancient past, or they could take him literally and obey his commission to heal the sick and cast out demons. Wimber believed there was no choice: one had to decide whether to offend God or man. He chose to be "a fool for Christ."[11] For him, an emphasis on the Gospels brought the Word back into balance with the Spirit, thus allowing every Christian to experience the kingdom of God and to do the works of Jesus.[12]

Rarely has a single man touched so many people and been involved in so many things in such a short lifespan. Although Wimber's life and ministry had global impact, due to the constraints of this work, his international ministry will be only briefly mentioned here, in the overall story of his life. Documenting the full impact of his international ministry will remain the challenge of another research project. In addition, although Wimber was the founder of the Vineyard movement, this work makes no attempt to tell the complete story of the Vineyard, since that has been covered extensively in Bill Jackson's book *The Quest for the Radical Middle: A History of the Vineyard Movement,* and in Douglas Erickson's book *Living in the Future: The Kingdom of God & the Holy Spirit in the Vineyard Movement.*

From the beginning of his ministry, Wimber attracted believers across the Christian spectrum. He appealed to Pentecostals and charismatics because of his openness to the Holy Spirit and gifts of the Spirit, and he appealed to Catholic charismatics because he embraced the mystical and was unguarded and willing to dialogue.[13] Many evangelicals accepted his ministry because it was scripturally based, yet it presented the Holy Spirit in such a way that allowed conservatives to embrace the Pentecostal experience while avoiding the sometimes controversial aspects of traditional Pentecostalism.

His ministry experienced explosive growth as he emphasized the proclamation of the gospel in conjunction with the demonstration of signs, wonders, and miracles that revealed the presence of the kingdom of God. He attempted to represent the supernatural ministry of Jesus in a way that brought the experience of the Holy Spirit into mainstream evangelicalism, and, in so doing, he helped shape the ethos of a new generation of Spirit-filled believers. His emphasis on the Holy Spirit and success in reaching into the evangelical churches at large, however, also made him a lightning rod for debate. R. A. N. Kydd recognized Wimber as "one of the most controversial figures in North American evangelicalism during a fifteen-year span that started in the 1980s."[14] What follows is his story.

[1] Interview by the author with C. Peter Wagner, August 10, 2011. Also see Bill Jackson, *The Quest for the Radical Middle: A History of the Vineyard* (Cape Town, South Africa: Vineyard International, 1999), 44; G. B. McGee and B. A. Pavia, "Charles Peter Wagner," in *The New International Dictionary of Pentecostal and Charismatic Movements*, ed. Stanley M. Burgess and Eduard M. Van Der Mass (Grand Rapids, MI: Zondervan, 2002), 1181 (hereafter cited as *NIDPCM*); and Vinson Synan, *The Holiness-Pentecostal Tradition: Charismatic Movements of the Twentieth Century* (Grand Rapids, MI: William B. Eerdmans, 1997), 285. Also see Stanley Burgess, "Introduction," in *NIDPCM*, xxi; Nigel Wright, "The Theology and Methodology of 'Signs and Wonders,'" in *Charismatic Renewal* (London: Society for Promoting Christian Knowledge, 1995), 71; Wayne Grudem, ed. *Are Miraculous Gifts for Today? Four Views* (Grand Rapids, MI: Zondervan, 1996), 12; and McGee, "Charles Peter Wagner," in *NIDPCM*, 1181.

[2] C. Peter Wagner, *The Third Wave of the Holy Spirit: Encountering the Power of Signs and Wonders Today* (Ann Arbor, MI: Vine Books, 1988), 16.

[3] Synan, *Holiness-Pentecostal Tradition*, x, 85–106; William W. Menzies, *Anointed to Serve: The Story of the Assemblies of God, Vol. 1* (Springfield, MO: Gospel Publishing, 1971), 24–6, 34–59.

[4] Vinson Synan, *The Century of the Holy Spirit* (Nashville: Thomas Nelson, 2001), 396; Burgess, "Introduction," xxi.

[5] Synan, *Holiness-Pentecostal Tradition*, 285. Also, Burgess, "Introduction," xxi; Wright, "The Theology and Methodology of 'Signs and Wonders,'" 71; Grudem, *Are Miraculous Gifts for Today?* 12.

[6] Rich Nathan, "A Response to Charismatic Chaos: The Book Written by John F. MacArthur, Jr.," *Position Paper #5* (Anaheim, CA: Association of Vineyard Churches, 1993); Burgess, "Introduction," xxi; and Synan, *Century of the Holy Spirit*, 396.

[7] Burgess, "Introduction," xxi; Synan, *Century of the Holy Spirit*, 396; Morris Williams, "Can Demons Invade Believers?" in *Power Encounters: A Pentecostal Perspective*, ed. Opal Reddin (Springfield, MO: Central Bible College Press, 1999), 160–72.

[8] Synan, *Century of the Holy Spirit*, 396; McGee and Pavia, "Wagner," in *NIDPCM*, 1181. David Barrett, "Global Statistics," in *NIDPCM*, 284, reports the statistics as of 2000 AD being as follows: classic Pentecostals number 65 million, charismatics represent 175 million, and Third Wavers or Neo-charismatics constitute 295 million of the total 523 million people globally who associate with the Holy Spirit renewal that started at the turn of the twentieth century.

[9] Rich Nathan, "A Response to Charismatic Chaos."

[10] Interview by the author with Bob Fulton, Wimber's brother-in-law and lifelong ministry partner, in Anaheim, California, on February 11, 2010; Todd Hunter, "The Leader," in *John Wimber: His Influence and Legacy*, ed. David Pytches (Surrey, U.K.: Engle, 1998), 190.

[11] John Wimber, *I'm a Fool for Christ, Who's Fool Are You?*, DVD (Stafford, TX: Vineyard Music, 1987).

[12] Rich Nathan, "The Bible Teacher," in *John Wimber: His Influence and Legacy*, 96–7.

[13] Charles Whitehead, "A Catholic Evaluation," in *John Wimber: His Influence and Legacy*, 220.

[14] Kydd, "Healing in the Christian Church," in *NIDPCM*, 701.

Chapter 1

The Making of a Fool for Christ

John Richard Wimber was born on February 25, 1934, in Kirksville, Missouri, to Genevieve Martin and Basil Wimber.[1] His seventeen-year-old parents had crossed state lines, with the aid of Basil's parents, and married.[2] Baby John, the Martins' first grandson, was born a few months later on the Martins' farm.[3] John's mother, whom he later called "Sissy," had returned to live with her parents, Claude and Maude Martin, because of her new husband's terrible temper and drinking. When John's dad showed up with his new girlfriend to see the baby the night Wimber was born, Genevieve's father ran him out of town at gunpoint.[4] As an adult, Wimber reflected on this day as the time the seeds of severe rejection and abandonment were planted in his heart.[5]

When John was four, the Martins lost their farm in Kirksville to the bank during the Great Depression, and the family moved to Peoria, Illinois.[6] Wimber deeply admired his adventurous mule-skinning, horse-taming grandfather. Claude, who was half Pawnee Indian, and made a living making whiskey and working as a rumrunner during the time of Prohibition.[7] He also worked on a horse farm in Illinois, where he trained Tennessee trotting horses, which are horses with a unique, high-strutting gait. If his grandfather had a horse with a problem gait, he would hitch it to one with a proper gait, and within a few days, the problem horse would be walking like the pacer horse. Years later this method of training would become the seed of Wimber's evangelistic model.[8]

By Wimber's own admission, his family was anything but religious. He said he grew up as a fourth-generation "pagan" who knew Jesus only as a "cuss word."[9] Carol said John's unbelief was shaken, however, when his grandfather, who by now had done jail time, was visited by a Baptist minister and "gloriously saved" just six months before he died of a stroke in 1953. On the night of his death, Grandfather Martin had a dramatic vision of Jesus coming to receive him—a picture he emotionally articulated to his family as they looked on. Many members of the family thought he had been hallucinating, but John, who was only nineteen, was visibly shaken. Carol Wimber believed it was at this moment that a desire for salvation was instilled in John's heart.[10]

While his grandparents were influential in his formative years, his confidence and sense of responsibility is said to have derived from his mother, who showered him with unconditional love and acceptance.[11] From an early age, John had loved music. When he was six, he set his heart on a saxophone he saw in a music store window. His mother, who worked at a liquor factory earning a dollar a day, somehow managed to finance the instrument and purchase music lessons.[12] The horn was so large for his small frame that he had to sit on a chair to play it. His appetite for music was seasoned with jazz on the radio, which he listened to in secret because of his grandfather Martin's disapproval.[13]

John grew up knowing very little about his biological father and his Wimber heritage. He only knew he had inherited his father's red hair and freckles—which earned Basil the nickname Red. In his mid-twenties, John had a disastrous reunion with his father, who asked him if he could hold his liquor like his old man. This event seemed to solidify the pain of rejection and the void associated with his father's absence throughout his life.[14] In his adult years, Wimber reflected on his childhood and believed that being raised as an only child without a strong father figure in the home had a negative impact on his relationship with his heavenly Father. He realized that these same rejection issues had also handicapped his interactions with other authority figures and had created barriers to relationships in his adult life.[15] When John became a minister, these issues were further compounded when his father-like demeanor attracted young men seeking leadership and ministry role models: some believe that at times, because of this own father-figure issues, he unintentionally wounded those who looked to him as a surrogate father figure.[16]

Years later, John's youngest daughter, Stephanie, contacted Basil's sister, Juanita Wimber, and obtained more information about her grandfather—John's dad. It seems that at age fourteen, Basil, who hated farming, had run away to Arizona. There, he took up boxing and, at the age of seventeen, won the state Golden Gloves Boxer Award. Riding the crest of his victory, he returned to his parents' farm in Missouri where he met and married Genevieve. Following John's birth and Basil's subsequent separation from the family, Basil remarried, sired two sons, and spent time in prison for statutory rape.[17] After a great deal of searching, John was able to meet his two half-brothers, George and Bill, just a few years before his death.[18]

The Making of a Fool for Christ

John was twelve when his mother Genevieve married Earl Bearce, who worked as the headwaiter of the Crown Royal Hotel in Peoria. Friends and family members recall that, in Wimber's early years, the only thing he would say about his stepdad was simply that "he was a good man."[19] However, several years later, a more reflective Wimber said,

> I grew up without a father. My father left the night I was born. So, until I was seven or eight, we did not have anyone in the family. Then my mother remarried, and my relationship with my stepfather was extremely difficult for about ten years until I left home. After I left home, we started developing a relationship. I was no longer a threat to him. We have become close, I love him, and he knows about this, so I am not telling stories on him. But let me say this: for years, I had great difficulty understanding the fatherhood of God because I never knew a father.[20]

In 1946, John's mother and stepdad packed everything they owned into a pickup truck and moved to California, just a few miles from Disneyland, in the same neighborhood where Wimber would one day pastor the Anaheim Vineyard.[21] With both his parents working, the family was able to purchase a home, and for the first time in his life he had his own room.[22] With his parents working, he was left alone for long periods of time, and he filled the hours with music. By the time he was seventeen, he could play twenty musical instruments. He was an introverted melancholy youth with a keen intellect and a nearly photographic memory.[23] Throughout his life he was described as a mature and responsible person who made educated rather than emotional decisions. Years later, when he was a pastor, people who worked with him became familiar with his famous words: "If you need an answer now, before God makes it clear to me, then the answer is 'no.'"[24]

Love and Music

Wimber's love for music was evident in his ability to play almost any musical instrument and in the many music awards he earned in high school. His first job as a musician was in 1949, when he was fifteen, working in a burlesque house called the Dixie Castle.[25] John grew up loving jazz. In the late 1950s and early 1960s he made the transition to rock and roll, but black jazz always remained his first love.[26] While waiting for his break with a big band, he worked in a bank during the day and played at high school proms and private parties on weekends. In particular, 1955 was a big year for him. He not only won the award for the best composer and arranger at the Lighthouse All Stars Jazz Festival, he also met his future bride, Carol Kay Evans.[27] In May that year, John's band played for her high school prom, and Carol said they "fell madly in love at first sight."[28] He was twenty-one, and she was seventeen. They were married seven months later in the home of a Baptist minister in Riverside, California. It was December 23, 1955, one month after Carol turned eighteen.[29]

Years later, reflecting back on his time alone as an adolescent and the hours he spent with his music, he quipped, "You can't learn much about intimacy with a horn in your mouth." He lovingly credited Carol as being the person who taught him how to have intimacy with another human being. Filling this love void also helped him believe that God "liked" him and wanted to be his "friend."[30]

In 1962, it was by accident that John helped form the Righteous Brothers. That year, John introduced Bobby Hatfield to Bill Medley and scheduled their first performance at the Black Derby in Orange County, where he was working. They had previously formed a group called the Paramours, but after they finished playing that night, a black member in the audience yelled out, "That was righteous, brother!" The name stuck.[31] Wimber played saxophone for them and composed most of their arrangements in the early years.[32]

Wimber's music skills also proved valuable when he became the leader of the Vineyard, where he wrote many of the soft-rock worship songs that became its hallmark. As a musician, John understood a musician's heart and was able to develop worship leaders. He also helped them realize that music was for the purpose of exalting Jesus and leading people into worship and not for putting their own talents on display. In fact, one of Wimber's earliest decisions was that worship music was to be sung *to* God and not *about* God. This dramatic change became another unique feature of Vineyard songs that have now been sung by millions of Christians around the globe.[33]

Cry for Help

Wimber's successful music career with the Righteous Brothers took him on the road and away from his young family, which now consisted of three red-headed boys. Christopher Earl was born in 1957, Timothy Charles followed quickly in 1958, and Sean Richard arrived in 1961. During this time Wimber recalled that his life seemed to be out of control. He was drinking heavily, doing drugs, and smoking five packs of cigarettes a day. He had a soaring career, but his relationship with Carol had deteriorated to the point that Carol asked him to file for a no-fault divorce while he was in Las Vegas.[34]

Leaving Carol and the children at their Westminster, California, home, he headed to Vegas, where he worked with the Righteous Brothers on a ten-to twelve-week contract. Overwhelmed with the feeling of failure from his broken marriage, he followed the advice of a friend to go out into the desert to be alone, think, and have a "religious experience" watching the sunrise. Late at night, while driving to the desert, he suddenly began to weep as he became aware of "someone or something" in the car with him. Not knowing what else to do, he pulled the car to the side of the road, got out "cussing and kicking the cactus," and tried to pull himself together. Then he looked up into the night sky and, for the first time in his life, he saw the stars and constellations as emanating from someone. Awestruck, he cried out in desperation, "Hey! If You're up there, if Anybody's up there, could you give me a little help here?"[35] Even though no one was with him, he embarrassed himself and thought, "Oh no, now I'm talking to the dark. I'm going crazy!"[36]

At the same time John was in the desert, Carol was having a sleepless night in California. Alone in the dark with her three little sleeping boys, the idea came into her head that she was in the process of destroying her life and the family she loved. Even though she had very little spiritual understanding at that time, she thought that if there were a devil, they were playing into his hands. Then she thought that if there were a devil, there must also be a God who was willing and able to help them. With this simple revelation, she prayed the sincerest prayer she knew: "Jesus, help me!" After this brief prayer, she decided to call John and give their marriage one more chance.[37]

When John returned to his hotel room from his desert experience, he was totally surprised to find a message from Carol, requesting he call home. He returned the call, and Carol asked him to forgive her and to come get her and the children so they could try one more time to make their marriage work. Without hesitation, he made the 350-mile trip back to their home in California in record time—talking to the someone or something he had shouted out to in the desert for the entire ride home.

Carol had been adamant about getting a divorce, and now she had suddenly changed her mind. So with a slight touch of pride, he smugly concluded that he was somehow in touch with the "supernatural," and that this "force" had answered his prayer by getting Carol to change her mind. That was how his prayer life began, but he was soon to realize he had a lot to learn about prayer—and about marriage.[38]

Back in Las Vegas, John and Carol wanted to know more about God, so they decided to purchase a Bible. Drawing from her Catholic background, Carol explained to John that a Bible was big and black with the words "Holy Bible" written on the front. So John went to the casino shops searching for a Bible, but instead of a black book, the clerk offered him a green one and told him it was the Bible. When he objected, she assured him, saying it was "a new testament." When he asked her what "a new testament" was, she told him it was "half a Bible." Hesitant about buying half a Bible, he returned to Carol with a *New English Bible* version of the *New Testament*, and they began their spiritual journey together.[39]

After this, every night when John went to work, he would take his Bible with him and, during breaks, would read it at the bar where there was better light. Then one night a bartender asked him what he was reading. John told him what seemed obvious—that he was reading the Bible. The bartender informed him that this was not a Bible because Bibles are black and have "Holy Bible" written on the cover. Hearing these words, John slammed the book closed and said, "I knew it! This is *not* the Bible!" The bartender told him he could buy a "real" Bible at the Bible bookstore, and he gave John a piece of paper to give to the clerk. With this paper, the bartender assured him that he would get the real thing.[40] Early the next day, John and Carol found a Bible bookstore, where they discovered there were many kinds, sizes, and shapes of Bibles. John handed the clerk the note written by his bartender friend and told her he wanted "this Bible." She opened the note that read, "King James Virgin." While they didn't understand why she laughed, they were excited to be in possession of a large, black Holy Bible that even had thumb tabs.[41]

Reflecting on this time, Wimber recalled that his choice to reach out to God was not an intellectual response to information but, rather, was due to his desperate need: his life and marriage were in shambles, but he somehow believed God could help. This launched him, along with Carol, on a journey that would ultimately heal their failing marriage, free them from guilt and the fear of death, and even give them a new purpose for living.[42]

While John and Carol were still living in Las Vegas, Dick Heying, John's friend since high school, and his wife Lynn drove down from Yorba Linda, California, to visit them. Dick had been a drummer in several bands and done a lot of partying with John. The Heyings came with the intent of sharing their newfound faith in Christ with John and Carol, but their plans were foiled when, during the trip, the temperature dropped and, in an attempt to stay warm, they consumed the entire bottle of expensive Scotch they had bought as a gift for their friends. When they arrived in Las Vegas, the couple was too intoxicated and embarrassed to share their Christian testimony. Even though Dick and Lynn were inebriated, however, John and Carol noticed a visible change that caused them to wonder what had taken place in their friends' life.[43]

Settling into a New Life

Four months later, after fulfilling the Vegas contract with the Righteous Brothers, John decided that being on the road was too taxing on his family so he left the bright lights of Las Vegas to find work in the Los Angeles, Orange County, area. Carol, now pregnant with their fourth child and only daughter Stephanie, packed up their belongings, and the family headed back to California with the goal of settling into a normal family life. Since they had struggled in their marriage, they also decided to get married all over again, and since Carol had grown up Catholic, they decided to renew their vows in a Catholic church. Before the ceremony, Carol had to attend confession, and although at the time she did not understand the significance of this event, she later recalled that, for the first time in her life, she truly felt forgiven. And she recalled that after the wedding ceremony, she felt "really married" for the first time.[44] Realizing the need for spiritual training for the children, they began attending Mass every Sunday but were very dissatisfied with the services. It was at this time that Dick and Lynn Heying asked them to attend their Protestant church, and they gladly accepted.

The Heyings attended the Yorba Linda Friends Quaker church, which had its roots in the Holiness tradition and was culturally far from anything John had previously experienced. John said he had been in and out of bars for years and seen a lot of stuff, but nothing had prepared him for what he was to experience in this church. When they arrived, John was still smoking a cigarette, but not finding an ashtray inside the church, he went outside and crushed it on the steps—something the guy with the flower on his jacket did not seem to appreciate. When they entered the church, someone asked if she could take their baby, but not knowing what the "nursery" was all about, they decided to keep Stephanie with them in the service. Another man with a flower walked them all the way to the front. John wondered why the back of the church was full and they had to sit on the front row. But there they sat with four children—ages six, four, two, and six months—who were wiggling and asking questions, while John punctuated sentences with cuss words. Someone handed him a church bulletin, which John thought was a menu. After a brief prayer, the choir led in congregational singing. To John's trained musician's ears, the sound was horrid. He said the man behind him began singing but was not anywhere near a note on the page. John looked over his shoulder because he figured surely one of the men with a flower would soon come and bounce that man right out of there for the noise he was making. John also knew the choir had to be a "pick-up group" because no one could sound that bad after practicing. Reflecting back on this time, Wimber said, "Now don't get me wrong. These were really lovely people, but this was my impression that first day."[45]

Obviously, John did not immediately "fit" into the church scene. Years later he said,

> I came from a slightly altered worldview than the average evangelical. Keep in mind, being a musician, I was more into drugs, a pre-hippie hippie. Though not a baby boomer, I identified with that generation. I had written music to it and been involved in entertaining it for years. Being around people much younger than myself made me more attuned to this generation more than my own. As a result, when I became a Christian, because I had a pagan background and because I was enculturated along with the baby boom people—a media person, saturated with media from the time I was a young person, writing for movies, writing for shows, writing for records from a young age. All of that altered my worldview significantly from the general populace.[46]

He remembered, early in his Christian experience, thinking, "I gave up drugs for this?"[47] From the very beginning, some of the Christian terms he heard really bothered him. He was particularly worried about the day they would require him to be "washed in the blood!"[48] All of these initial experiences in the Christian faith made a strong impact on Wimber and helped form his opinion of how church appeared to the unchurched. Later, when he had the opportunity to create a church culture of his own choosing, he said he consciously removed the traditional religious barriers that made newly saved people feel like outsiders, which included making a concerted effort to avoid "Christianese" when sharing the Scriptures with new believers.[49]

This Guy is Really Hungry

Dick and Lynn Heying were also instrumental in integrating John and Carol into a weekly Bible study group that would set the course for their life and ministry. When Dick called and invited John and Carol to the study group, John thought he could get off the hook by saying he only had Monday nights off from work, because the Bible study was on Tuesday nights. After talking for a while, Dick hung up but called back a few minutes later with the good news that the group had agreed to move the meeting to Monday nights so John and Carol could attend. They were so touched by the kindness of the group that they decided to attend the following week.[50]

The first night they attended the Bible study, John did not appear to be their most promising student. When he arrived, he "fell into a chair in the corner of the living room, lit up a cigarette, and announced" that he had a few questions before they got started.[51] Then he plunged into questions he had asked before: How do you know the Bible is true? And how do you know there is a God? The Bible study leader, Lawrence Gunner Payne—affectionately called Gunner—patiently answered all Wimber's questions. Because of his obvious spiritual hunger, from time to time, Gunner would comment, "This guy is really hungry," but John, not understanding what he was talking about, would think, "No, I'm not hungry, I ate before I came."[52] The Bible study went on for several weeks until one night, Gunner seemed to go on and on about Jesus and his death on the cross. John became annoyed and asked why he kept talking about Jesus, when all he wanted was to learn about was God. So for weeks, Gunner patiently taught through the Old Testament to reveal to John's satisfaction that Jesus was the predicted Messiah.[53]

Signing Up to Be a Fool for Christ

Then one evening, John and Carol both knew "something" needed to happen. John finally asked how someone could "join this thing." Gunner told them that a child born too soon is not healthy, that an apple would fall when it was ripe—a metaphor that meant they were not quite ready. Finally, in June 1963, Carol blurted out, "Something's got to happen. We believe all this. Can we sign up somewhere or something? Please?"[54] That was the moment Gunner finally admitted it was time to pray. Carol immediately fell to her knees, praying the only Catholic prayer she could remember from childhood. Then John looked around the room and, being a stage entertainer for years, realized "his act was up next."[55]

Later he could not remember if he had been pushed or if he fell, but suddenly he found himself on the floor beside Carol, sobbing uncontrollably. John tells it this way:

> To this day I cannot fully account for how I got out of that chair. All I know is that I ended up on the floor, sobbing, nose running, eyes watering, every square inch of my flesh perspiring profusely. I had this overwhelming sense that I was talking with Someone who had been with me all my life, but whom I had failed to recognize. Like Carol, I began talking to the living God, telling him that I was a sinner. I was trying to pray the 'Sinner's Prayer,' but all I could do was to blub the Sinner's Blub: 'Oh, God! Oh, God! Oh, God!'[56]

While praying, John had a flashback of a man he had seen years earlier walking down the street wearing a sandwich board—the kind with a sign on the front and a sign on the back and straps over the shoulders. On the front of the sign was written, "I'M A FOOL FOR CHRIST," and on the back, "WHOSE FOOL ARE YOU?" At the time, he thought it was the stupidest thing he'd ever seen, but from that moment in Gunner's living room onward, John knew he would live the rest of his life as a fool for Christ.[57] It were as if God had given him a prophetic picture of his apostolic calling as seen in 1 Corinthians 4:9-10. While John never embraced this apostolic title for himself, many in the body of Christ who knew him recognized this calling and anointing on his life. Over the years John often said he was just change in God's pocket, and it was up to God how he spent his life. His life message became the kingdom of God, which, to Wimber, meant Jesus's right to rule and reign in his life and in any situation.[58]

Learning from the Master

The impact that this fifty-year-old man, Lawrence "Gunner" Payne, made on John and Carol's lives cannot be overestimated. From the beginning, Wimber had realized there was something different about Gunner.[59] He was patient, intelligent, and a gifted teacher, but these qualities were not what arrested Wimber's attention. What impressed him most was Gunner's character, which was something more important to John than his knowledge of the Bible. For Gunner, nothing seemed to matter except living for God, and the peace of Jesus seemed to permeate his being. At this stage in Wimber's spiritual development, he needed a trustworthy witness, and in Wimber's eyes, Gunner embodied the gospel. His very life was revelation.[60] It was also through Gunner that John and Carol were exposed to a "lay down your life" Christianity and a spiritual understanding of suffering.

After getting to know Gunner, Wimber discovered the source of this teacher's strength and spiritual maturity: eleven years prior, Gunner's sixteen-year-old daughter, Ruby Ann, was brutally murdered in an attempted rape. This tragic event was followed by a trial that dragged on for six months and drew national attention. The young man who had been accused in her murder was eventually sentenced to death, but before he was executed, Gunner had the opportunity to lead him to the Lord. After this traumatic ordeal, Gunner laid aside his personal life and made the commitment to knock on the door of every home in Yorba Linda to tell them about Jesus Christ.[61]

Then, the year before Wimber met Gunner, Gunner's twenty-two-year-old son, Preston, was in an automobile accident and suffered massive injuries that left him requiring constant care. The night Ruby Ann had been killed, Gunner had told God that although he did not understand, he would not question but trust. He prayed the same prayer the night Preston was injured, and he prayed it many times since. Gunner didn't know why these things had to happen, but he was convinced that God was in control. So when Wimber met Gunner, it was the mature character of Christ that attracted him more than his teaching skills. For Wimber, this man who was forged through suffering was someone who deserved his attention.[62]

In time, Gunner started taking John with him as he went from house to house to evangelize. Through this experience, John realized in practice what he had learned years before from his horse-training grandfather: you can take a young horse and team it with an old, mature horse, and soon the immature horse will walk just like the mature one. John became Gunner's shadow, going everywhere he went, doing what he did, talking like him, quoting the same Scriptures, and even telling Gunner's stories.[63] It was through Gunner that Wimber realized, in order to win someone to your Lord, you must win that person to yourself.[64] This became the foundation of his evangelism model. Within a short amount of time, through Gunner's training, he became a successful soul-winner, leading hundreds of people into the kingdom.

John and Carol lived for their weekly times with Gunner and asked probing questions that overflowed from their rigorous personal study of the Scriptures.

Eventually, they decided to move from their home in Westminster to Yorba Linda, just so they could be closer to the Bible study group and the Friends' church.

The Pearl of Great Price

Shortly before Wimber's life-changing conversion, Gunner had taught on the "pearl of great price" found in Matthew 13:45-46. Until now John's source of income had been the jazz-rock music industry; now he was being confronted with the possibility of giving up the only livelihood he had known.[65] Sitting in Gunner's living room listening, John posed a hypothetical question to Gunner, saying, "If a guy was only good at one thing and made his living doing it, would God ask that person to give it up?" Gunner, knowing John was referring to himself, thoughtfully responded that the guy had to be willing if God had asked it of him. John looked down and said, "I thought so."[66]

Until this point things had been going pretty smoothly. He had been learning about God and getting close to making the commitment. But this was a big obstacle. The night he became a fool for Christ, however, he also knew he had found "the pearl," and he was now ready to lay down his music career to buy it.[67] In response to this revelation, John said good-bye to his music friends, and then loaded up his life's work as a musician—which included boxes of albums and music arrangements—and took them to the city dump. Then he found a job working in a shop with heavy equipment. Suddenly he went from working nights in a soaring music career under the bright lights of a Vegas stage to being awoken early by an alarm clock, doing physical labor in broad daylight, and ending the day with his hands covered in black oil. It was a humiliating process.[68]

In one particularly painful experience, an old partner from the music industry paid him a visit at the factory. He had a recording contract Wimber had signed that was worth a lot of money, and Wimber needed to sign the release of his portion of the contract before it could be fulfilled. With his head inside the oil drum he had been assigned to clean that day, Wimber heard his partner say, "Where's John Wimber's office?" He pulled his head out of the oil drum just in time to see the disgust in his friend's eyes at his oil-covered condition. His friend said, "What are you doing here?" Wimber realized how ridiculous he looked, and at that moment, he certainly did not feel like he owned the Pearl. After looking at his friend, back at himself, and then to his friend again, he blurted out, "God did this to me." Wimber said his friend's eyes narrowed as if to say, "He's never going to do that to me."[69]

John wondered why this God of love was treating him this way. He felt ashamed. But years later a more mature Wimber articulated a different perspective:

> From time to time the Lord challenges us to make new commitments. He lets us know that he wants us to give up something we are successful at and begin doing something we don't yet know anything about—maybe something we don't like. The economy of the kingdom of God is quite simple. Every new step in the kingdom costs us everything we have gained to date. Every new step may cost us all the reputation and security we have accumulated to that point. The disciple is always ready to take the next step. If there is anything that characterizes Christian maturity, it is the willingness to become a beginner again for Jesus Christ. It is the willingness to put our hand in his hand and say, 'I'm scared half to death, but I'll go with you, Lord. I'll risk everything to go with you. You're the pearl of great price.[70]

Pondering this time in Wimber's life, Carol said, "What I find interesting is that he did not lay down his career for something else. He laid it down because Jesus asked him to. And there was no promise of ministry in the future to soften the decision. It was a sacrifice born out of obedience, and that is the key to understanding what motivated John Wimber his whole Christian life."[71] This was the beginning of John's life philosophy of just being "change in God's pocket," to be spent anyway the Lord might choose.[72]

Naturally Supernatural

From the outset of his spiritual journey, John seemed to have a predisposition to the supernatural. He took the Bible literally and expected the same supernatural experiences he saw in the Scriptures to occur today. Believing this, he and Carol would pray for their refrigerator when it was broken and for their car when it needed repair. And when they needed money, they would simply ask the Lord and he would send it to them. They just assumed this was the New Testament norm. It wasn't until later that he realized they were living in what some considered an altered state, significantly different from other Christians around him—at least according to the church they were attending. As a result, John and Carol struggled to fit into the church scene. They didn't seem to speak the same language as Christians around them, and they found it difficult to relate to the church culture and value system; however, they were too preoccupied with winning the lost to notice that their attitudes and experiences were quite different from those of the general church population. During the first three years after their conversion, they led between four hundred to five hundred people to the Lord. Years later Wimber realized he was doing this largely through supernatural means. He said he was accustomed to knowing in advance when people were going to come visit him, and he would know the sin they were struggling with and the condition of their lives before they arrived.[73]

It was about three years into his walk with the Lord that he had gotten enough exposure to the larger church population to figure out that he had been living in what others believed to be a "naïve world." That is, the way they were living was not considered by their church a "valid" Christian experience. He was told that if he had sound doctrine, he would not live in such a "flighty, flimsy, foolish way." So for the next twelve years, he tried to live like the rest of the evangelicals, ignoring the supernatural aspects of what he saw in the Bible and was experiencing in his own life.[74] But it seemed odd, he thought, because "when I worked for the devil, he let me *do* things," but Christians only wanted to sing about, talk about, and pray about things.[75]

With the pressure to conform, he attempted to suppress the supernatural in his life, but he continued periodically to receive words of knowledge from God. One example he frequently shared was the time he was on an airplane and looked at the man sitting across the aisle and saw the word ADULTERY written across the man's forehead. When he saw this, he also heard the name "Janet." The man noticed Wimber staring at him and indignantly wanted to know what he was looking at. Wimber leaned over and asked if the name "Janet" meant anything to him. The man turned white and asked John to meet him in the airplane lounge, where Wimber had the opportunity to explain what he was seeing, after which he led the man to the Lord. At that time Wimber found it difficult to explain what was happening in his life because he did not yet have a theological grid to it. At times, in his college evangelism classes, he would attempt to discuss his experiences, but they were so foreign to others' religious worldviews that they would stare at him in disbelief.[76] Eventually he started calling these experiences "divine appointments," which later became one of the foundations for his teaching on Power Evangelism.

The Devil's Got You

Sometime after John and Carol's conversion, Gunner moved away from Yorba Linda, causing John to become overwhelmed with concern for who would lead Gunner's evangelistic efforts and the Bible study group. His heart was so burdened, he decided to go for a long walk along an irrigation ditch near his home to pour his concern out in verbal conversation to the Lord. Suddenly he realized he could no longer understand what he was saying because he was praying in some language he didn't recognize. Shortly after this experience, his three-year-old son, Sean, was attacked by a swarm of bees. As red spots began to appear all over Sean's body, John frantically prayed in this new language, punctuated by intermittent pleas of "Heal him, Jesus!" As his prayer burden lifted, the red spots vanished before their very eyes, and Sean fell into a restful sleep. When the baby awoke a few hours later, only one red spot remained, and Wimber took that as evidence of answered prayer.[77] This was John's first experience with divine healing.[78]

By this time in their Christian experience, Carol had become thoroughly indoctrinated to believe that speaking in tongues was of the devil. She had been teaching against this charismatic experience in her women's Bible study, so when she heard John praying in tongues that afternoon, she said to him, "Oh no. The devil's got you."[79] Sheepishly, John apologized and told her he had not meant to let the devil get him. It had just happened when he'd been walking along and talking to the Lord. Carol then tried to reassure him that it would go away, but she said that, just in case, he should go to their Quaker pastor for counsel.[80]

Their pastor, who was both a dispensationalist and cessationist, agreed with Carol's assessment and told John that the charismatic gifts of healing and speaking in tongues were divisive and that he should "repent of speaking in tongues and turn away from it."[81] John was obedient, but over the next few years, he periodically checked to see if he could still pray in tongues, wondering if the devil still had him—and sure enough, he did. John thought, "Boy, once the devil gets you, it's hard to get rid of him."[82]

In 1982, when he relayed this story to students in his MC510 Signs and Wonders and Church Growth class at Fuller, he said,

> About a year and a half into my conversion, I was introduced to a new relationship, a new experience, that the Pentecostals call the Baptism in the

Holy Spirit. Now, I did not know what I was being introduced to. I did not have any theological background for understanding. All I knew is that a gentle, loving businessman that I knew laid hands on me and within a day or two I spoke in tongues and began prophesying on a regular basis and the manifestations of spiritual gifts accelerated very rapidly. I began having visions and all. About two years later I was indoctrinated out of it. I became a dispensationalist. I became exposed to evangelicalism hardcore, and a fundamentalist. And within three years I was not speaking in tongues, I wasn't prophesying, I wasn't healing the sick, I wasn't as effective in evangelism as I had been before, and I was literally inundated as to my effectiveness in my early Christian life.[83]

Then again, in 1984, as he was teaching on "repentance in the body of Christ," he shared how he used to experience the presence of Christ in those early years. It wasn't something he frequently talked about, but with deep emotion in his voice, he said,

There was a time when I was a young Christian. The first year or so when I was a Christian [emotion in his voice], the Lord Jesus would come in the room at night. He would just light up the room. It would just light up all over the room. I never saw a figure. I never saw a face. I never heard an audible voice. But he would tell me what he wanted me to do. He would tell me what it was going to be like. And he prophesied this church. And he prophesied this revival to me in those days. And he told me that it would affect the whole earth. That churches, the church all over the world would be touched by it. The fragrance of Jesus. I can remember falling asleep in his presence with the room all aglow. I would wake up in the morning and think, 'Oh, he's gone.' Then there would be that witness. 'No, he's not gone. You just cannot see the glow in the daylight.' Hallelujah![84]

Through the years, he would shy away from talking about such encounters with the Lord whenever people asked him if the reason he had a healing ministry was because he'd had some divine "visitation." It wasn't that he had not had the experiences. It was just that he wanted to point people to the Scriptures, which could guide everyone into the supernatural ministry of Jesus, whether they had an experience or not. So he would hold up the Bible and say, "It's simple. I've been reading the Book. It's all in here."[85]

The Quaker Influence

Because John and Carol had come to faith through the Quaker Friends church, its doctrine and theology formed their foundational beliefs. It was perhaps unsurprising, then, that John had an aversion to "professional" ministry, an opinion he'd inherited from Gunner, who believed it was ordinary people who were most effective in the "real work" of soul-winning. This belief originated with George Fox, the founder of the Quaker church in the mid-1600s, who rejected outward sacraments and professional paid clergy, instead embracing the priesthood and democracy of all believers and promoting a faith devoted to simple living.[86]

Nonetheless, Wimber still felt God was leading him in the direction of full-time ministry. So on August 15, 1970, just four years after joining the church, John reluctantly assumed the role of associate pastor of the Friends church in Yorba Linda. In the fall of the same year, he also enrolled at Azusa Pacific University to complete a degree in biblical studies.[87] As such, between 1963 and 1970, the Yorba Linda Friends church grew to become the largest in the denomination. Wimber had personally led several hundred people to Christ, creating an influx of "strange and unholy young people" that caused some older church members to complain that John had "ruined their church."[88]

Wimber's Quaker roots also significantly influenced his understanding of Scripture. Robert Barclay, who wrote the defining theology of the Quaker faith, stated that Quakers have a slightly different perspective of Scriptures than do traditional evangelicals.

[Quakers] alone of the surviving groups insisted on the primacy of the Holy Spirit as the authority and source of revelation . . . which all Christians ultimately appeal for guidance. Most Protestants insist that Scriptures have meaning because of the response invoked in the hearts and minds of readers by the Spirit. Quakers go a step further and say that it is the Spirit who reveals to us both the Word and the Son, and they point out, as is sometimes forgotten, that Christ himself, not the Scriptures, was the Word.[89] Years later, when Wimber's critics scrutinized his interpretation of Scripture, the significance of these Quaker ideas became critical.

Quiet and stillness were additional aspects that John carried over from the Quaker church into the Vineyard movement. In 1652, Fox had had a vision that profoundly changed his life and caused him to believe that God could speak directly to any person. In Quaker meetings, therefore, participants practice a form of group mysticism, in which they sit in silence waiting for the Spirit of God to speak. Tim Wimber, John and Carol's youngest son, remembers, as a child, sitting for long periods on hard wooden pews at the Yorba Linda church as the congregation waited to receive a "word" from God. He said the stillness was so intense, he could hear the clock ticking on the wall.[90] This Quaker influence would later be evidenced in Wimber's ministry, as he taught people to "dial down" their emotions in order to be more sensitive to the Spirit as they ministered.[91]

Reflecting on this tradition of "listening" for God to speak, Bob Fulton, Wimber's brother-in-law and lifelong ministry associate, said that in the Yorba Linda church, they would wait for words of prophecy and words of knowledge, although Quakers would never call it that.[92] Because of this Quaker understanding, it seemed natural for John when he began receiving words of knowledge. He was comfortable standing behind the keyboard for long periods, waiting to hear the Lord speak. This no-hype, low-key way of ministering was attractive to traditional evangelicals, who were turned off by the high-energy and loud-volume characteristics of traditional Pentecostal church meetings.

Regarding the Quakers' understanding of miracles, Barclay wrote, "We do not need miracles, because we preach no new gospel but only what has already been confirmed by the numerous miracles of Christ and his apostles."[93] This Reformed doctrine of dispensational cessationism was something Wimber would confront as he entered into his next phase of spiritual development.

Flunking Out of the System

Becoming assimilated into the evangelical holiness church was very slow for John. He acknowledged that he came from a slightly altered worldview than the average evangelical. Regarding traditional church, he said, "I never made it. I actually failed. I flunked out of the system. I just could not get there from where I was. I tried. I loved the people. I affirmed them and they affirmed me, but I could not get there."[94] But it wasn't just the church culture Wimber struggled with; he also experienced frustration that new converts were unable to stay in the church. Reflecting on these struggles, he said:

> All I was trying to do was reach my kind of people, people I had come to know as I was in and out of the record business. I invited them to a church

that even I did not fit into but none-the-less was going to because I believed that commitment to God meant commitment to that church because that was where I was converted. But, our church was unable to receive them and they were unable to relate to the church. The music, dress, lifestyle, policies, and values were literally nonverbally communicating to the people 'don't come in, we don't want you.'[95]

After twelve years, he felt like a failure. And though he continued his struggle to fit into the religious system, he knew something had to change. Fortunately, the winds that would dramatically alter his future were beginning to blow.

Get Me Out of Here

Even though John was experiencing success as a minister, Carol remembered that, by 1974, the "magic" had somewhat faded from their Christian experience. She did not know if it was because John was sitting under what she termed "unbelieving-believing" professors in the Bible college or if the responsibility of the pastorate was too draining for him. All she knew was that John had changed.[96] They didn't understand what was happening at the time, but he was nearing burnout. He'd become a licensed family counselor, and for seven years he had a large marriage and family practice that he had integrated into the church. He carried a heavy load and became progressively frustrated in his inability to effectively help people with their problems.[97] During these years, an underlying rebellion against God began to grow in his heart. He gained fifty pounds in one year and continued to gain until he had put on a total of one hundred. He said his heart had become hard. He was mad at the people he was pastoring, and he was starting to turn away from God to do his own thing.[98]

One day a young man in the church approached him about a personal sin problem. John rebuked the man, telling him he just needed to attend church more often. But as he walked away, the Lord asked him, "John, would you go to this church if you weren't paid to?" His own gut-level reaction was, "No way, I wouldn't come here. I don't really like this place." He said this even as he recognized that he had personally led many in the congregation to the Lord and had left his own fingerprints all over the church. With this realization, he ran to his office, fell on his face, and sobbed, "How did I get this way, God?" The Lord was merciful to his servant's cry and quickly answered, saying the problem was that he had given himself to the things that *looked* like God rather than to the things *of* God. In anguish of that intense realization, John cried, "God, get me out of here."[99]

Fuller and the Puzzle Coming Together

While all this was going on, Wimber had been enrolled in the doctor of ministry program at Fuller Theological Seminary and was taking a class on church growth under C. Peter Wagner.[100] Wagner had heard of John's success for instigating church growth in the Yorba Linda Friends church and recognized his name on the student roster.[101]

In addition to his teaching responsibilities, Wagner was also the director of the Fuller Evangelistic Association and was in the process of establishing the Charles E. Fuller Institute of Evangelism and Church Growth. He knew that, in himself, he was a good church-growth "theoretician" but that he lacked the skills of a church-growth "practitioner"—someone who could apply the principles of church growth at the grassroots level. In class, Wagner recognized "John's gift as an evangelist, his talent for clear analysis and his practical comprehension of the principles of church growth," so he asked John to be the founding director of the institute.[102] This invitation came just three weeks after Wimber laid on his office floor and cried for God to get him out of there.

John accepted Wagner's offer and resigned his pastoral position to begin traveling to evangelical churches throughout the United States as a church growth consultant.[103] According to Wagner, even though he and John both spoke in tongues, they were both still traditional straight-line evangelicals. Wagner used his "prayer language" from time to time, and John had spoken in tongues early in his Christian experience but had stopped when his pastor told him he shouldn't continue this practice.[104] Additionally, they had mutual respect for one another professionally, and eventually, they became close friends.[105]

Between 1975 and 1978 Wimber worked with twenty-seven denominations, nine parachurch organizations, and over forty thousand pastors in America and Canada.[106] He went from the small pond of their Quaker church to being exposed to almost the whole of Christendom. Carol said it was almost like Galileo's discovery that the planets did not revolve around the earth—it was as if they suddenly realized they were not the center of the universe.[107]

John fell in love with all of the expressions of the church, and he seemed to have caught the lovebug from Wagner. No matter what church they attended, he would lean over to John and whisper, "John, you know, if I lived here, I would go to this church. Isn't this a wonderful group?"[108] Years later, John would say that Vineyard was just one vegetable in the pot of stew. He had learned from his travels and exposure to the larger church world that God had people in every denomination and church, and he loved the variety. For John, it didn't matter what denominational flag you flew over your building, the important issue was that "we see one another as the objects of God's love," as "members of the Body of Christ" coming together "in the Spirit."[109]

During one of his trips, John met an old Church of God evangelist who preached a message that powerfully impacted his life. The man had preached so hard through the years that he'd blown his vocal cords and could hardly rasp out the message. In this particular sermon, he called the people back to their first love and caring for the poor. Wimber said the power of the Spirit was so heavy upon the preacher's words and brought such conviction that the congregation groaned and sighed under the weight. The people swayed back and forth in one accord like wheat driven by the wind. After the meeting, John called Carol and told her about the service. On the phone, with tears streaming down his face, he prayed and made the commitment that if God ever allowed him to pastor again, he would have a church that was committed to caring for the poor.[110] Time proved him faithful to this pledge, and caring for the poor became an integral part of the Vineyard's spiritual DNA.[111]

A third influence that shifted Wimber's worldview and inspired a vision for church-planting occurred when he and Wagner attended a funeral—not for the death of a person but of a church. The funeral lasted all day, and approximately twenty thousand people filed through in groups of one thousand, which were made up largely of people of Puerto Rican descent. This mother church had given birth to fifty-six churches, and like an old "bitch dog" she produced so many offspring congregations that she eventually died. John said later, "That day burned a passion into my soul for renewal and growth. I knew then that whatever God called me to do, it had to be marked by a willingness to give everything away. I prayed, 'Lord, if you ever call me to minister in another church, I promise it will be a sending church.'"[112] Again, time proved him faithful to this commitment.

Another piece of the puzzle that fell into place during this season of John and Carol's life was their understanding of evangelism. Ever since their conversion, John and Carol had followed Gunner's model and poured themselves into personal evangelism, but John had noticed a marked difference in Carol's approach to evangelism compared to his own. While Carol was more of an intellectual in her evangelistic efforts, John relied more on his "spiritual intuition." Whereas Carol believed that a person had to first receive a clear, logical presentation of the gospel to come to a saving knowledge of Christ, John believed that, with minimal information, a person could enter a relationship with Jesus.[113] John just seemed to rely on his "intuition—a spiritual guidance system that told [him] when people were ready to give their lives to Christ."[114] All during his tenure as a pastor at the Yorba Linda Friends church, he wrestled with this tension between the intellectual and intuitive aspects of evangelism, and he continued to wrestle with it until this fourth piece of his puzzle fell into place. After joining the Fuller Institute of Evangelism, John discovered the Engel Scale, which is a model that describes the various stages and attitudes people generally go through in their conversion experience.[115] Through James F. Engel, John came to understand that he and Carol were both correct—there must be an effective presentation of the gospel message (Rom. 10:17) *and* the timing must be right.

What he was beginning to realize was that the Western way of presenting the gospel focused almost exclusively on the intellectual aspect and largely ignored the intuitive portion of the evangelism equation.[116] Further, John realized that this Western focus produced disciples who came to know Christ only through an intellectual assent but did little to transform their lives.[117] This caused him to reflect on some of the "insights" into other people's lives that he had experienced during his own times of personal evangelism. Eventually, he began to understand that such "intuitions" were actually a spiritual gift. This revelation came to him one day as he was watching the *700 Club*. When Pat Robertson or Ben Kinchlow would call out problems in the lives of people who were watching the program, he would know and see these things before they were spoken. It was through this experience that he suddenly understood he was operating in the words of knowledge.[118]

Another aspect of John and Carol's spiritual formation came together through his contact with Pentecostal churches, which he noticed were the ones experiencing significant vitality and church growth compared to mainline evangelical churches. During this time, he was also reading Wagner's book *Look Out! The Pentecostals Are Coming*, which was filled with testimonies of how miracles, deliverance, and healings had resulted in mass evangelism and church growth in South America. Wagner suggested in his book that miraculous encounters and charismatic gifts were responsible for the explosive church growth and immense spiritual harvest the developing countries were experiencing.

The impact of Wagner's book on Wimber was followed by the impact of Donald Gee's book *Concerning Spiritual Gifts* and Morton Kelsey's *Healing and Christianity*. John then also became acquainted with Fuller professors such as Donald McGavran, the founder and first academic dean of the Fuller Theological Seminary School of World Mission and the author of several books and articles on mission and church growth; Paul Hiebert, a Mennonite, missiologist, and missionary to India who authored numerous books and articles and taught missions and anthropology at Fuller; Russell Spittler, an Assemblies of God minister and New Testament scholar and theologian who was a leading expert in the field of Pentecostal spirituality and a professor in Fuller's School of Theology during the time Wimber served as adjunct faculty; and Charles Kraft, who taught anthropology and intercultural studies. In the years to come, Kraft would become one of Wimber's strongest supporters and a proponent of his burgeoning supernatural ministry. In addition to learning from the testimonies of these credible professors, John met students from developing countries who shared with him their personal experiences of charismatic gifts of healing and miracles, revealing how these experiences resulted in rapid church growth in their nations. Wimber said the witness and testimonies of these people served to soften his heart toward the Holy Spirit and divine healing.[119]

All of these personal encounters and experiences drove Wimber to the Scriptures in search of the truth regarding the gifts of the Spirit. He struggled with these theological concepts because he was an evangelical dispensationalist who had been taught that miracles had ceased with the apostles and that he should avoid all aspects of Pentecostal or charismatic ministry. Now, confronted with such credible witnesses, he was forced to rethink his positions. His heart was being stirred, and this launched him into an intense study of the ministry of Jesus in the Gospels. As he reread the Gospel accounts, he saw for the first time that Jesus coupled the *proclamation* of the gospel of the kingdom with *demonstrations* of healing the sick, casting out demons, and raising the dead.

A final shift in John's perspective came when he discovered the writings of George Eldon Ladd. Ladd was a Baptist minister and New Testament scholar who had been a professor at Fuller in the 1950s. His books *Jesus and the Kingdom* and *A Theology of the New Testament* challenged Wimber's dispensationalist views and provided theological moorings for his emerging model of supernatural ministry. More will be said about these later.

I've Seen Your Ministry

For nearly four years, John worked with Wagner as the director of the Fuller Institute of Church Growth. He said, "I examined the underbelly of the church in America, and frankly, it was not that attractive." He developed many wonderful relationships and believed it was one of the "most educational and expansive experiences" of his life but also one of his lowest places spiritually.[120] Although he experienced what many would define as success, John was becoming increasingly disillusioned. Later he said, "There was a lot of action that was called the work of the Holy Spirit, but it was nothing more than human effort in which the Holy Spirit was asked to tag along. I felt it turned the stomach of God. It certainly did mine, and it wore me out."[121]

Then one evening in 1977, overweight and sick in spirit and body, his family was home in California while he traveled to yet another conference in a city where he knew no one. Leaning his head against the plane window and peering out at the approaching lights of Detroit, he cried out again from the poverty of his own spirit, saying, "God, what's wrong with me?"[122] Once he landed and was settled into his hotel room, he knelt beside his bed and opened his Bible for some much-needed devotional reading—something he had not done for a long time. He fell asleep in this position, and sometime during the night, he awoke to what seemed to be an audible voice—a voice saturated with compassion and empathy that said simply, "I've seen your ministry; now I will show you mine." With these words, the weight of the world seemed to be lifted off his shoulders, and he quietly sobbed. "Oh, God, that's all I've ever wanted."[123] Soon he drifted off to sleep again, and he slept like a baby cradled in the arms of his heavenly Father, filled with a peace he had not felt for a long time.

The next morning, in the light of a new day and a busy schedule, the experience of the previous night quickly faded, and the divine visitation was pushed to the back of his mind. But God had spoken, and a new chapter in the book of Wimber's life and ministry was about to begin.

Shortly after this event, John was having a conversation with Wagner and was surprised when he uncharacteristically suggested that maybe John should return to Yorba Linda and start a church. Then a few days later, at another conference, a Lutheran pastor, quite embarrassed and apologetic about the situation, handed Wimber a note, saying it was a message from God. The note contained two simple words: "Go home."[124]

The final confirmation God used to lead John in a new direction came in the fall of the same year, at a Friend's Quaker Leadership Retreat camp meeting in northern California. The host pastor told Wimber that a well-respected woman in his congregation had a "word" for him. Wimber was hesitant, but because of the minister's insistence, he finally relented and met the woman in a quiet place on the campground. They sat together in uncomfortable silence as the woman just sat and cried—cries that eventually turned to sobs. After half an hour or so, John became irritated and asked the woman what God wanted to say because he had a busy schedule and an afternoon class to teach. The woman looked up and said, "That's it." Then she got up and walked back down the hill.[125] He instantly knew he had wounded the heart of God, and when he realized God was weeping for him, it "hit his heart like a sledgehammer."[126] Later during the conference, the woman gave him several additional words from God, one in which God asked when he was going to "use his authority." At this point in his life, he had no idea what "authority" she was talking about.[127]

Just a few weeks before that, God had promised to show John "his ministry." Wimber had no idea what that ministry would look like, but he would soon learn it was very different from anything he had encountered in his past fourteen years of Christian experience.[128] This is the story for the next chapter.

[1] Wimber and Springer, *Power Points*, 60. Also, Carol Wimber, *John Wimber*, 8, 26.

[2] Interview by the author with Tim Wimber on February 10, 2010, in Mission Viejo, California. Tim, John Wimber's youngest son, said the family was uncertain which state they had crossed into to marry. Of the legal age requirements of the adjoining states of Illinois and Iowa, however, Iowa's law is more lenient, making this state the most likely location of the union; http://law.findlaw.com/state-laws/marriage-age-requirements/iowa/ and http://law.findlaw.com/state-laws/marriage-age-requirements/iowa/. Accessed May 31, 2010.

[3] Carol Wimber, *John Wimber*, 26. After Carol's book was published, the family received feedback from several living relatives who believed Genevieve was not pregnant at the time of the marriage but became pregnant shortly thereafter. Interview by the author with Tim Wimber.

[4] Interview by author with Tim Wimber.

[5] Wimber and Springer, *Power Points*, 60.

[6] Interview by the author with Tim Wimber.

[7] Carol Wimber, *John Wimber*, 10, 40. In an interview with Tim Wimber, he said he believed it was more of a family rumor that his grandfather Claude was half Pawnee who made his living as a Rum Runner during Prohibition, but it seemed to be a story the family enjoyed telling.

[8] John Wimber, "No Shortcuts to Maturity," *Equipping the Saints* 1, no. 4 (July/August 1987): 2; Wimber and Springer, *Power Evangelism*, 195.

[9] Wimber and Springer, *Power Evangelism*, 7; Kevin Springer, "Applying the Gifts," 26.

[10] Carol Wimber, *John Wimber*, 10.

[11] Carol Wimber, *John Wimber*, 18.

[12] Carol Wimber, *John Wimber*, 16.

[13] Carol Wimber, *John Wimber*, 16.

[14] Wimber and Springer, *Power Points*, 60.

[15] Wimber and Springer, *Power Points*, 61.

[16] Interview by author with Carl Tuttle on February 8, 2010, Palm Springs, California.

[17] Carol Wimber, *John Wimber*, 23.

[18] Carol Wimber, *John Wimber*, 20.

[19] Interview by the author with Tim Wimber.

[20] John Wimber, "The Way On: Repentance in the Body of Christ," vol. 2, cassette tape 5 (Anaheim, CA: Vineyard Ministries International), 1985.

[21] Carol Wimber, *John Wimber*, 18–9; Wimber, *I'm a Fool for Christ*, DVD.

[22] Carol Wimber, *John Wimber*, 19.

[23] Carol Wimber, *John Wimber*, 19.

[24] Carol Wimber, *John Wimber*, 32–3.

[25] Carol Wimber, *John Wimber*, 31.

[26] Interview by the author with Tim Wimber.

[27] The Lighthouse All Stars Jazz Festival was held at the Lighthouse Café at 30 Pier Avenue, Hermosa Beach, California, where, in the 1950s, an inter-colligate Jazz competition was sponsored; http://en.wikipedia.org/wiki/Lighthouse_Cafe. Accessed May 31, 2010.

[28] Carol Wimber, *John Wimber*, 34.

[29] Carol Wimber, *John Wimber*, 31, 35.

[30] John Wimber, "Prayer: Intimate Communication," cassette tapes (Anaheim, CA: Vineyard Ministries International), 1985.

[31] Rock and Roll Hall of Fame Museum, http://www.rockhall.com/inductee/righteous-brothers. Accessed January 5, 2010.

[32] Carol Wimber, *John Wimber*, 34. The Righteous Brothers had two hits in the Top 10. Their first hit was in 1964—"You've Lost That Lovin' Feeling," written by Mann and Cynthia Weil (http://www.oracleband.netLyrics/you've-lost-that-lovin-feeling.htm. Accessed January 4,

2010). The second song, "Unchained Melody," written by William Stirrat (a.k.a., Hy Zaret), was first released in 1955. The Righteous Brothers later recorded their own version, which went to the top of the rock music charts in 1965. Both songs were hits after Wimber left the group (http://newstranscript.gmnews.com/news/2003/1203/Front_Page/047.html. Accessed January 4, 2010).

[33] Carol Wimber, *John Wimber*, 116.

[34] Wimber and Springer, *Power Evangelism*, 7; Wimber and Springer, *Power Points*, 17; in this account Wimber remembers it as 1961, but correlating material places it in 1962. Carol Wimber, *John Wimber*, 49; Wimber, *I'm a Fool for Christ*, DVD.

[35] Carol Wimber, *John Wimber*, 50.

[36] Wimber, *I'm a Fool for Christ*, DVD; Wimber and Springer, *Power Points*, 17–8.

[37] Carol Wimber, *John Wimber*, 50; Wimber and Springer, *Power Points*, 18.

[38] Wimber and Springer, *Power Points*, 18; Wimber, *I'm a Fool for Christ*, DVD.

[39] Wimber and Springer, *Power Points*, 22.

[40] Wimber, *I'm a Fool for Christ*, DVD.

[41] Wimber, *I'm a Fool for Christ*, DVD.

[42] Wimber and Springer, *Power Evangelism*, 7.

[43] Carol Wimber, *John Wimber*, 54–5; Wimber, *I'm a Fool for Christ*, DVD.

[44] Carol Wimber, *John Wimber*, 55–7; Wimber and Springer, *Power Points*, 22.

[45] Wimber, *I'm a Fool for Christ*, DVD.

[46] John Wimber, *MC510 Signs and Wonders and Church Growth*, cassette tape 1A (Pasadena, CA: Fuller Theological Seminary, 1982). The original set of sixteen cassette tapes can be found in the John Wimber Special Collections, Regent University Library, Virginia Beach, Virginia.

[47] Wimber, *I'm a Fool for Christ*, DVD.

[48] Wimber, *I'm a Fool for Christ*, DVD.

[49] Graham Cray, "The Communicator," in *John Wimber: His Influence and Legacy*, 145–7.

[50] Carol Wimber, *John Wimber*, 57; Wimber and Springer, *Power Points*, 23.

[51] Wimber and Springer, *Power Points*, 23.

[52] Wimber, *I'm a Fool for Christ*, DVD.

[53] Wimber, "The Cross," *Equipping the Saints* 2, no. 2 (Spring 1988): 2.

[54] Carol Wimber, *John Wimber*, 64–5.

[55] Carol Wimber, *John Wimber*, 65.

[56] Wimber and Springer, *Power Points*, 116.

[57] Carol Wimber, *John Wimber*, 65; Wimber, *I'm a Fool for Christ*, DVD; I Corinthians 4:9-10.

[58] Carol Wimber, *John Wimber*, 78.

[59] Carol Wimber, *John Wimber*, 57; Wimber and Springer, *Power Points*, 23.

[60] Wimber and Springer, *Power Points*, 24.

[61] Carol Wimber, *John Wimber*, 68.

[62] Carol Wimber, *John Wimber*, 69.

[63] Wimber, "No Shortcuts to Maturity," 2.

[64] Carol Wimber, *John Wimber*, 69.

[65] Springer, "Applying the Gifts," 29.

[66] Wimber and Springer, *Power Points*, 118–9; Carol Wimber, *John Wimber*, 65–6.

[67] Wimber and Springer, *Power Points*, 118–9.

[68] Carol Wimber, *John Wimber*, 71.

[69] Wimber and Springer, *Power Points*, 119. Years later, Wimber had a new revelation of the pearl of great price. In his more mature understanding, he realized that Jesus came to redeem people. Those who would say yes to Jesus were the pearl of great price, for whom he was willing to give all he had, including his life, to purchase them for his own; http://www.youtube.com/watch?v=fqxGVCH9qH4.

[70] John Wimber, "Utter Obedience," *Pastoral Renewal* 12, no. 2 (September 1987): 12.

[71] Carol Wimber, *John Wimber*, 72.

[72] Carol Wimber, *John Wimber*, 68, 78.
[73] Wimber, *MC510*, cassette tape 1A.
[74] Wimber, *MC510*, cassette tape 1A.
[75] David Hall, "Signs and Wonders," *Today*, October 1984, 20.
[76] Wimber and Springer, *Power Evangelism*, 75: Wimber, *MC510*, cassette tape 1B.
[77] Wimber and Springer, *Power Healing*, 3–4.
[78] Carol Wimber, *John Wimber*, 74–6.
[79] Springer, "Applying the Gifts," 30, 32. Also James R. Coggins and Paul G. Hiebert, "The Man, the Message and the Movement" in *Wonders and the Word: An Examination of Issues Raised by John Wimber and the Vineyard Movement* (Winnipeg, MB: Kindred, 1989), 17; Carol Wimber, *John Wimber*, 74, 77.
[80] Carol Wimber, *John Wimber*, 74.
[81] Springer, "Applying the Gifts," 30.
[82] John Wimber, "Church Planting: God's Heart for Expansion," cassette tape, vol. 1 (Anaheim, CA: Vineyard Ministries International, 1985).
[83] Wimber, *MC510*, cassette tape 1A. Wimber's teaching experience at Fuller will be covered in a later chapter.
[84] John Wimber, "The Way On," cassette tape 7.
[85] Carol Wimber, *John Wimber*, 167.
[86] Dandelion Pink, *An Introduction to Quakerism* (Cambridge, U.K.: Cambridge University Press, 2007), 13–4; J. E. Johnson, "Society of Friends," in *Evangelical Dictionary of Theology*, ed. Walter A. Elwell (Grand Rapids, MI: Baker Academic, 2001), 470–1.
[87] Carol Wimber, *John Wimber*, 90; Wimber and Springer, *Power Evangelism*, 83; Wimber and Springer, *Power Healing*, 23; C. P. Wagner, "Wimber, John," in *NIDPCM*, 1199. Also Jackson, *Quest for the Radical Middle*, 51.
[88] Wimber, *I'm a Fool for Christ*, DVD; Carol Wimber, *John Wimber*, 90.
[89] Robert Barclay, *Barclay's Apology in Modern English*, ed. Dean Freiday (Elberon, NJ: Sowers, 1967), xxii–xxiii.
[90] Interview by the author with Tim Wimber.
[91] Telephone interview by the author on January 14, 2010, with Linda Spicer, a member of the Yorba Linda Friends church, a ministry associate of Vineyard, and lifelong friend of the Wimber family.
[92] Interview by the author with Bob Fulton on February 10, 2010 in Anaheim, California. Fulton is John Wimber's brother-in-law and lifelong ministry associate.
[93] Barclay, *Barclay's Apology*, 189–90.
[94] Wimber, *MC510*, cassette tape 1A.
[95] Wimber, *MC510*, cassette tape 1A.
[96] Wimber and Springer, *Power Healing*, 27. Carol Wimber, *John Wimber*, 90. Carol remembers the date being 1975, but Wimber consistently refers to the date as 1974.
[97] Wimber, *MC510*, cassette tape 11A.
[98] John Wimber, "The Way On," cassette tape 8.
[99] Wimber, *I'm a Fool for Christ*, DVD; Springer, "Applying the Gifts," 30.
[100] Carol Wimber, *John Wimber*, 92, 97.
[101] Wagner, *Third Wave of the Holy Spirit*, 19.
[102] Wagner, "God Wasn't Pulling My Leg," 50–1; Wimber and Springer, *Power Evangelism*, 84; Pytches, "A Man Called John," in *John Wimber: His Influence and Legacy*, 23.
[103] Wimber, *I'm a Fool for Christ*, DVD; Springer, "Applying the Gifts," 30.
[104] Wagner, "God Wasn't Pulling My Leg," 50.
[105] Wagner, "God Wasn't Pulling My Leg," 50.
[106] Wimber, *I'm a Fool for Christ*, DVD.
[107] Carol Wimber, *John Wimber*, 101.
[108] Carol Wimber, *John Wimber*, 101.
[109] Wimber, "The Way On," Vol 1, cassette tape 6.

[110] Carol Wimber, *John Wimber*, 104–5.

[111] Interview by the author with Tino Suffi on February 10, 2010, at the Vineyard Christian Fellowship in Anaheim, California. Suffi is the director of the clothing and distribution center, Anaheim Vineyard. Suffi said the Anaheim Vineyard continues to feed and clothe hundreds of people each week.

[112] John Wimber, "Sent into the Harvest Field," *Equipping the Saints*, 1, no. 5 (September/October 1987): 2.

[113] Wimber and Springer, *Power Evangelism*, 8.

[114] Wimber and Springer, *Power Evangelism*, 8.

[115] Wimber and Springer, *Power Evangelism*, 9.

[116] Wimber and Springer, *Power Evangelism*, 10.

[117] Wimber and Springer, *Power Evangelism*, 10.

[118] Interview by the author with Bob Fulton.

[119] Wimber and Springer, *Power Evangelism*, 29–30.

[120] Wimber, *MC510*, cassette tape 1A.

[121] Stafford, "Testing the Wine from John Wimber's Vineyard," 19.

[122] Wimber, *I'm a Fool for Christ*, DVD.

[123] Wimber, *I'm a Fool for Christ*, DVD.

[124] Wimber, *I'm a Fool for Christ*, DVD.

[125] Carol Wimber, *John Wimber*, 112.

[126] Carol Wimber, *John Wimber*, 112.

[127] Carol Wimber, *John Wimber*, 112.

[128] Springer, "Applying the Gifts," 31–2.

Chapter 2

The Birth of an Equipping Healer

Carol was familiar with the charismatics, and she strongly opposed the movement by doing everything she could to keep new converts from falling into the error of charismatic practice.[1] The problem was that there were two charismatic bastions dangerously close to their Quaker church. One was Melodyland, a large revival center located in Anaheim, where Ralph Wilkerson hosted weeklong "charismatic clinics," attracting people from around the world.[2] The other major concern was Chuck Smith's Calvary Chapel, which was popular among the Jesus People and was now experiencing charismatic-type meetings.

Out of dread for losing many of their new converts to this charismatic heresy, the Friend's Ministry Council appointed Carol, who had continued to serve as an elder and board member of their church after John resigned as pastor, to teach and warn the people against this powerful seduction. Carol took her assignment seriously and became, in John's words, a "self-appointed Pharisee" who had a religious zeal equal to that of the apostle Paul.[3] In her passion for truth, Carol doubled her previous crusading efforts, and by 1976 she was leading several women's Bible study groups around Orange County, using them as a platform to spread her anti-charismatic message.[4] At that time, John had little to say about the situation, and she assumed his silence was a confirmation of his agreement, but later she would realize the painful truth.

While John was traveling with Wagner and going through his own paradigm shifts, God was also working on Carol. In September of 1976, she had a dream that she was standing on a soapbox at the end of her street, preaching her well-rehearsed seven-point sermon against the gifts of the Holy Spirit, when suddenly she experienced a sensation like hot electricity hitting her head, traveling down her body, and then shooting out her mouth. When she woke up, she was speaking in tongues.[5] It was a very troubling dream that caused her to feel less confident about her previous position on charismatic issues. Bewildered by what she believed God was showing her, Carol resigned from the church board and closed herself in her bedroom, crying out in deep repentance. She felt like a blind and naked Pharisee who had measured everyone's relationship with God by her own standards, and her heart was broken. She had gone to God asking what was wrong with the church, and now she realized the problem was her.[6]

During this time, Carol said she came to understand several things. Her first and possibly most painful revelation was that she had influenced John to lay aside his experience with the Holy Spirit. Fifteen years earlier he had spoken in tongues during prayer, when Sean had been healed of bee stings, but later, because of her insistence, John had laid aside his God-given gift. Her second revelation was that God had wanted John to move out in faith and power, but she had stopped him—and as a result, John had been deeply wounded. Finally, she understood that "God had a pattern, a blueprint for renewal, and John was a key in what God wanted to do," but she had stood in the way.[7]

Carol spent three weeks in prayer and repentance, sleeping and eating little, anguishing before God because she believed she had wounded God's heart with her attitudes and prejudices. She had what she called a "personality meltdown," in which her self-will was broken, resulting in total transformation.[8] When her mourning came to an end, she went out and made restitution with approximately thirty people, asking them to forgive her misguided zeal.[9] John later said that it was Carol's brokenness that actually birthed the renewal movement. He said, "It created a ripple of revival and repentance through the entire community, and over the next few months literally hundreds of people were touched by the power of God. Some of them were brought into conversion and some into Holy Spirit baptism, but all of them were brought into renewal."[10]

Burned-Out Cessationists

After Carol came out of seclusion, she started meeting with a group of leaders from the Friends church who had been gathering in the home of Candice Chendori Wickwire, Carl Tuttle's sister. John had led Carl to the Lord when he was only eleven. Consequently, Carl grew up in their Quaker church and was a close friend of the family. Carl had become the worship leader of the small group because he was the only one with a guitar, and he would gradually

The Birth of an Equipping Healer

mature as a worship leader and travel around the world with Wimber. Bob Fulton, who was married to Carol's younger sister Penny, facilitated the home prayer groups. Years later, Fulton described the group as a bunch of "tired, burned-out, and somewhat disillusioned" people who were just hungry for more of God.[11]

When they came together, there was no planned music. Tuttle simply led choruses he had learned from the Jesus movement or new songs released by Maranatha! Music, and the others joined in. They would worship for hours and then break up into small groups and pray for one another.[12] No one taught in those days. They only worshiped and prayed. Fulton said they were not interested in hearing what the others had to say. They just wanted to draw close to God.[13]

One evening, while Carol was praying, the word "worship" appeared in her mind like a newspaper headline, and she realized God was trying to reveal to her something more about worship than she had known from her evangelical experience. And indeed, as the Holy Spirit ministered in their home fellowship, drawing them into intimacy, they all learned lessons that would later form their philosophy of worship and guide the new Vineyard movement.

When Carol first joined the home group, she had just come out of her intense encounter with the Holy Spirit, and because the group was theologically cessationist, she cautiously placed the "charismatic" issues in the Lord's hands and waited to see what would happen. She said that, in the end, they fell so in love with Jesus that when the gifts of the Spirit were eventually introduced, they forgot their cessationist theology and sweetly received their gift of tongues.[14] The group had been praying for renewal, and it seemed to be falling like a gentle California rain.

When John returned home after his most recent ministry trip, he entered into a significantly different spiritual climate than the one he'd left a few weeks earlier. Although Carol had not immediately told him about her encounter with the Holy Spirit, her transformation was visible to him.

Then in January 1977, four months after Carol's dream experience, John started attending the home meetings whenever he was in town. By March, attendance had reached 125, but John told Carol it would never last because the group lacked leadership.[15] Later Wimber reflected on how negatively he had responded to the idea of the group meeting:

> By the time I started attending the meetings they were already running over 100. The people were gathered in a small room—just packed tight as you could possibly get them. They would worship for hours—three and four hours just pouring their heart out to God. They came together for one purpose and that was to make contact with God. And the result was a harmonization, a new warmth, a new exuberance about the person of Jesus, a new caring for one another, a gentling of attitudes, a putting away of prejudices and biases, a unity began manifesting around the person of Jesus Christ. They forgot about the things they had been at tension with in the past and just began loving one another.[16]

This is what Wimber later remembered, but at the time it was all happening, he had a completely different perspective:

> My first exposure to the group, I just thought, 'This is ridiculous.' I already know how to sing. I don't like sitting in a hot room for four hours with sweaty people. So I went home thinking, 'This is absurd.' I thought, 'I don't get it.' And I really didn't. It demonstrated to me how superficial, how blasé, and how blind I was to the work of God. I didn't know it when I saw it. And yet, there it was happening in front of me.[17]

Knowing how John felt about the meetings at the time, Carol reservedly approached him and let him know that if he ever felt called to reenter the pastorate, she would support him—something she had adamantly refused to entertain earlier.[18]

Passive Healing

After Carol experienced the power of the Holy Spirit, she remembered how Sean had been healed of the bee stings when John prayed for him, and she became convinced that he had the gift of healing. For years she had been suffering from rheumatoid arthritis in her shoulder, and so one night while John was asleep, she took his hand and put it on her shoulder and said, "Okay, Lord, now do it." Remarkably, a surge of heat flowed from his hand into her shoulder, and she was immediately healed. The experience awakened John from his sleep, and he wondered why his hand was hot. When Carol told him what had happened, he was glad she was healed, but he thought nothing more about it.[19]

While Carol had come through her spiritual transformation and was doing quite well—John, on the other hand, was still struggling. He had to admit that something had happened to Carol because there was such a transformation. One day, for example, he confronted her about her temper outburst when she discovered one of their sons had washed his greasy carburetor in the kitchen sink. But instead of retaliating with more anger, as she normally did, she received John's correction with love and then went off to the home meeting. After she left, John went to his room and began to pray. He admitted to the Lord that Carol had changed and then cried the familiar refrain, "Lord, what's wrong with me?" That night, Wimber, now forty-three years old, experienced his own healing, as he cried and prayed in tongues for hours.[20] This was his turning point. Shortly afterward, he began providing the pastoral leadership that the growing home group needed.

The Quaker Kick-Out

It did not take long for the ministry council of their Quaker church to hear about the charismatic overtones of their home fellowship. From the outset, it was never their intention to make tongues or spiritual gifts an issue. The only issues they were actually experiencing were brokenness, repentance, and a deep hunger for God. Speaking in tongues was only a peripheral matter, but it quickly became the central concern. The Friends Church had recently dealt with an associate pastor with a "tongues problem," so the leaders decided to take immediate action. The denominational leader called John to his office, asked him some questions, and then gave him an ultimatum: either stop the tongues or leave the church. John chose the latter, severing the thirteen-year relationship that he and Carol had with the Yorba Linda Friends church. The remaining members in the home fellowship were also told that if they remained in the home group, their names would be removed from the church roll. Sixty people, most between the ages of sixteen and twenty-five, chose to leave, many whose family roots went all the way back to George Fox.[21]

Introduction to Calvary Chapel

Now that the fellowship was without a church affiliation, John wondered where God would lead them. It was at this time that Don McClure, a long-time friend and pastor, suggested they connect with Calvary Chapel. Calvary Chapel had originated as an evangelical congregation out of Costa Mesa, California, under the leadership of Chuck Smith, who became famous for his involvement with the Jesus People movement in the early 1970s.[22] Smith, once a pastor with the Four Square church, had become disenchanted with the hype he had observed in his denomination and decided to pioneer an independent church free of denominational control.[23] After successfully building the Corona Christian Center, which he pastored for several years in the 1960s, he received a call to pastor a church of only twenty-five members in Costa Mesa. Reluctantly, he assumed the position. The church grew steadily under his leadership and the visibility he had through his weekly radio broadcasts, but it was not until the hippie element was introduced that the church's growth really exploded.[24]

Although Wimber had now become a part of the traditional Quaker church structure, he had never forgotten his hippie roots and his love for southern California rock music. In those early years the Calvary Chapel church was informal, and it was open to charismatic expressions without the Pentecostal hype. They had integrated a worship-music style with a soft-rock sound that attracted a younger crowd. They were evangelical, scripturally centered, and displayed minimal "Christianese"—something that had been a major turn-off for Wimber in his early Christian experience. All of these things created a palatable combination easily embraced by Wimber, the evangelist and church growth expert who well understood the need to remove as many obstacles as possible for people to come to faith. As such, the Calvary Chapel model fit well with the emerging church he was now leading. Since no one in the group desired to be "independent," they all agreed to join with Calvary. So on Mother's Day 1977, they had their first church service as Yorba Linda Calvary Chapel, now meeting in the Mason Lodge. The group of 150 people installed Wimber as their pastor, a role he filled while continuing to work full time at Fuller as a church growth consultant.[25]

The church services were casual and the dress code was informal, both carryovers from the house meetings. Even as the church grew, John remained true to his "casual" roots. It was not unusual for him to lead a church service in Bermuda shorts, a Hawaiian shirt, and bedroom slippers.[26] Tim, Wimber's son, recalled another tradition born of the early days. Because it was hot in southern California and their meeting place had no air-conditioning, the body heat generated when they laid hands on one another for prayer was oppressive. Wimber suggested that, rather than everyone touching the person being prayed for, they simply extend their hands in that direction while only one person actually touched the recipient of the prayer.[27] This became a model for prayer that seeped into the Pentecostal and charismatic churches and is now practiced around the globe.

The worship team was equally casual and unpretentious. Wimber played the keyboard, Carl Tuttle the guitar, Jerry Davis the bass, and Dick Heying the drums. Cindy Reithmeier periodically joined the team when a female voice was needed. According to Tuttle, the only reason she was not a regular vocalist was because their eight-by-sixteen-foot portable stage was too small to accommodate another singer.[28]

The week after they joined Calvary Chapel, they had their first baptismal service. Since Quakers do not baptize or participate in communion, John asked Chuck Smith to help him baptize 120 new believers in Wimber's backyard pool. A week later, 40 more were immersed. The elements for their first communion service consisted of pita bread and wine.[29]

The Healing Journey Begins

Wimber was still working full time for Fuller and was frequently on the road during the week; therefore, he asked John Amstrutx, a professor from Life Bible College in Los Angeles, to teach some of the Wednesday night classes at his church. For the Sunday services, Wimber was teaching through the book of Luke, while Amstrutx was teaching about the gifts of the Spirit on Wednesday nights. There were so many accounts of Jesus healing the sick in Luke that Wimber was forced to also talk about divine healing. As a consequence of the combined teachings, many people in his congregation gained an interest in divine healing and started praying for the sick. In addition, after teaching from the gospel of Luke for four months, John had also started to wonder if praying for the sick was something the church was supposed to do today. He was not sure what to make of this at the time, but since God had promised to show him his ministry, he decided to keep an open heart and follow the Lord's leading.[30] Then, one Wednesday night when he was home from his travels, he went to church and listened to Amstrutx's teaching, and as he did, he experienced a major paradigm shift.

At this time, they had been a part of Calvary Chapel for approximately a year, and Wimber said their church culture was a typical Bible church. They emphasized preaching through the Word, worship, and fellowship—basically the same things he'd done before as a pastor without much significant difference. But that night, as John sat listening to Amstrutx's teaching he was drawn into a mental dialogue with God. The Lord brought to his mind Matthew 9:1-8 which tells the story of the paralytic who was let down through the roof by his friends. Jesus told the man his sins were forgiven, and for this saying, the Pharisees became indignant and said he was blaspheming. In response, Jesus asked them which was easier, to forgive sins or to heal the body? As he read this passage, Wimber, the soul winner, suddenly wondered if his "attitude about praying for the sick was supposed to be like [his] attitude toward personal evangelism." In response to this thought, he sensed the Lord say, "Yes, Christians are called to heal the sick in the same way as they are called to evangelize." As a matter of fact, to John, it seemed as if Jesus was saying healing the sick was actually *easier* than forgiving sins.[31]

This thought prompted a second question in Wimber's mind, and the dialogue continued. "Lord . . . are most people (myself included) afraid to pray for the sick because their understanding of your nature—who you are and how you work—inhibits them?" Again, he sensed the Lord respond, "Yes, most people are hesitant, even fearful, to pray for other's healing because they misunderstand my compassion and mercy. They know about me, but they do not always know me."[32] In this Matthew 9 passage, Jesus seemed to be saying that the mind of the religious teachers was so clouded by religious pride that they could not even recognize it when God healed the sick. And it was at that moment John realized he had not prayed for the sick both because he had a theology that denied divine healing and also that this belief was a façade for the evil unbelief and skepticism in his own heart.

John then asked his final question in his mental dialogue with God. "Do you mean that we are supposed to pray for the sick?" To which God responded, "Yes. Just as I give authority to preach the gospel for forgiveness of sins, in a similar way I give authority to heal the sick."[33]

A few years later when he recounted this story, he said the whole concept of God intending for him to actually pray for the sick was incredible to him at the time. As an evangelical, he had been taught that the gifts of the Spirit had ended with the apostolic church. He had believed this was a well-documented fact. Now he was carrying on a dialogue with God and discovering that the Lord had another opinion on the subject. "Lord, what about the people who don't get healed?" He'd asked and sensed an immediate response saying, "What about the people who don't get saved?" Suddenly, Wimber realized that in the average evangelical church today, the opposite would be true: few people would doubt God's willingness to forgive a person of sin, but if that same person asked for prayer for cancer, few people would believe God would provide healing. The proposition God seemed to put before him that night was, "How can you believe for the forgiveness of sin, which you cannot measure, if you cannot believe in my power to heal what you can measure and see?"[34] Jolted with this flash of insight, Wimber, the evangelist who had personally led hundreds of people to Christ, quickly realized that Christians have the same authority and responsibility to pray for the sick as to evangelizing the lost. He realized that both preaching and healing were normal activities of the kingdom and that Christians have been called and commissioned to pray for the sick just as they have been called and commissioned to evangelize. In just a few moments, in this brief conversation with God, he realized that all Christians, including himself, were commissioned by God to heal the sick.[35]

A short time later, as he was speed-reading the Scriptures while eating lunch and relaxing in the shade on the patio at Fuller, he came to a full stop when he read John 14:12, "If you have faith in me, you will do what I have been doing." In that instant, the text seemed to explode with meaning before his eyes. He was quickly encouraged to read Matthew 4:23-24, where the ministry of Jesus was described as preaching the good news of the kingdom, healing every disease and sickness, delivering the demonized, and alleviating all sorts of suffering and pain. At that moment, he began to weep as he realized he had preached the gospel but had never healed any kind of sickness or disease. He'd not done the works of Jesus; therefore, his walk was incomplete. That day he wrote in the margin of his Bible, "I must learn to believe everything Jesus believed and learn to do everything Jesus did."[36] These two revelations created a paradigm shift that totally transformed his life, and from that moment on, divine healing became one of the core messages of Wimber's signs and wonders ministry.

Preach It or Get Out

Over the next several months, almost every sermon Wimber preached was related to divine healing, and eventually the Lord led him to have altar calls and pray for the sick. The only way he knew how to pray for the sick in those days was using the Pentecostal one-man model, where the minister prayed as the healer and others stood with him. At this point, he did not yet understand that everyone could be used in the gift of healing. After several months of praying, with no one healed, John was hurt, frustrated, and despondent. People started leaving the church, not because he was *teaching* on healing but because he was actually attempting to *practice* it. And not only were the sick not getting healed, but the people praying were also getting sick from the ones they were praying for. So one day, out of total exasperation, Wimber told the Lord he was not going to teach on healing again. Immediately he sensed the Lord say, "Either preach my word or get out." John thought, "Out? Out of the what? Out of the ministry? Out of the Kingdom? How far out?" Again, that familiar voice responded, "Preach my word, not your experiences." *Now that was a new twist*, he thought. Normally evangelicals chided charismatics for preaching their "experience," and now God was telling him not to preach the experience of his *non*-experience. After again feeling gently chastened by the Lord, he was more determined than ever teach the example of Christ that he saw in the Gospels.[37]

"It's Not Fair!"

He forged on for another ten months, praying for the sick with no success. Then he experienced his darkest night before the day of his healing ministry dawned. His church had continued to grow and was now meeting in a school gymnasium. They had a curtain on the stage, and anytime someone wanted prayer, they went behind the curtain—a model they had learned from Calvary Chapel. The gym was not air-conditioned, and this night in southern California was particularly hot and humid. After two hours of John and a few other men praying for a sick man who was not healed, he fell on his face in total frustration, beating the floor and crying, "It's not fair, God! You tell us to teach what your book says, but you don't back up your act. Here we were doing the best we can, and nothing happens. You tell us to believe in healing and pray for healing, but you're not doing anything. Oh, God, it's not fair!" Months of pent-up frustration continued to pour out. "Lord, it's a farce to ask for healing if it doesn't happen. It's misleading; its hypocrisy to say, 'Your sins are forgiven in Jesus name' if I cannot also say, 'Be healed in Jesus name.'"[38]

After he had poured out all of his frustration and regained his senses, he looked around, and there on the floor beside him were the other men, also sobbing with the same unbridled passion. He later said this was one of the most precious and encouraging moments in his life, when he realized these men had the same intense feelings he did. One man that night, named Jim, was so frustrated, he told the group that he was "never going behind that damn curtain again." As Jim walked out of the church that night, God gave him a Scripture verse from the Old Testament, but he waited until he arrived home to look it up. The text read, "God dwells behind the curtain."[39] He deeply repented. That night, they all had experienced the agony of bitter defeat.

"We Got One!"

The next morning Wimber received a phone call from a new family in the church. The man explained that his wife was sick, they had small children, and he needed to go to work. He asked if John would come and pray for his wife to be healed. When Wimber hung up, he recalled being very angry that people were actually beginning to believe what he was teaching. He stormed out of the back door, and though he didn't exactly shake his fist at God, he threw his hands in the air, "palms inward, like an Italian merchant who had just taken delivery of a shipment of damaged goods."[40] When he arrived at the couple's home, the lady was lying in bed with a red, swollen face and a fever. He walked over to the bed, mumbled a quick faithless prayer, and then turned to explain to her husband why God does not always heal—an excuse he had perfected over the past few months. Suddenly, John noticed the man was looking over his shoulder and smiling. When he turned, he saw the woman making the bed, and he blurted out, "What happened to you?" She responded that he had healed her. Wimber was so stunned by the healing that he refused the couple's offer for coffee and hurried out the door. As he crossed the lawn on his way to the car, the past months of frustration washed away as the reality of this healing sank in. In genuine exhilaration, he danced a quick jig and yelled, "We got one!"[41]

The Sweetness of God's Mercy

He drove home rejoicing and thinking, "This stuff really works." Then suddenly, he saw an incredible vision. He thought at first it was a cloud bank, but then he realized it was a vision of what looked like honeycomb. Intrigued, he parked the car to get a better look at what he was visualizing with his mind's eye. This honeycomb was dripping honey, and the people standing below the honeycomb were responding in different ways. Some were receiving it with thanksgiving and entreating others to enjoy it, and the more they gave away, the more they received. Others, however, were indignant, annoyed with the sticky substance, and they were complaining about the mess. God told Wimber that the honey was representative of his mercy. Wimber sensed the Lord say, "My mercy endures forever. My mercy is healing and the salvation of man.

Mercy is poured out for everyone, and for some it is a blessing but others will reject it. There's plenty for everyone. Never beg for my mercy again. The problem is not on this end but down there."[42] From this point on, he never viewed healing the same again. He realized that Jesus's disciples could not heal the boy in Mark 9 because of unbelief, and the same principle was true today. He also realized that the "key to experiencing God's healing mercy was belief, belief in the God who heals."[43] He said God never spoke to him about healing again after that. In Wimber's mind, there was no need for further dialogue on the subject. God had made it apparent to him that it was his will to heal. John still had unanswered questions, but from this point on, he was fully committed to the belief that "God had tied into salvation the healing and wholeness of people . . . body, soul, and spirit."[44]

Through this paradigm shift, Wimber had gone from the belief that God *could* heal the sick to the conviction that Christians were actually *commissioned* to pray for the sick. He had been humbled through his lack of success, and now his faith was grounded in the mercy and grace of God. Regarding this process, he later said,

> This period of failure was a learning experience, a time in which I was purged of my pride and self-sufficiency. I was humiliated and I was humbled. God had first to cleanse a vessel before it was fit to fill with his precious oil of healing. I believe God began healing the sick through me only after I came to a place of total dependence on his grace and mercy. I also learned about obedience to God's Word. In the past I had been able to get some good results without God's help. But praying for the sick was different. I realized that I could get no results without God's anointing. My job was to obey, pray, and rely on his sovereign mercy; his part was to heal.[45]

He had learned experientially that he could do nothing without God's anointing, and he was finally a surrendered vessel, ready to believe God's word and place his faith squarely in God's sweet grace and mercy.[46]

Holy Spirit Baptism Begins

In April 1978, John started another home Bible study where he taught on Holy Spirit baptism, and people started asking him to pray for them to be filled with the Spirit. As he moved around the room laying his hands on people, there was incredible power, like electricity, coming from his hands, which at times caused people to fall to the floor. Since these people had not had previous

Pentecostal exposure, there was no way they could have been preprogrammed to fall over—or why would they even want to? For John, this was the first time he actually *felt* the power of God flow in this way.[47]

Although Wimber had experienced the Holy Spirit and had spoken in tongues, he always considered himself an evangelical and not a Pentecostal or charismatic. But contrary to most evangelicals, tongues was not an issue for him. In his understanding, the Holy Spirit came at the time of conversion, and subsequent experiences were simply additional "fillings."

In 1985 he clarified his position, saying that when he prayed for evangelicals, he would ask them if they had received the Spirit when they believed. If they answered affirmatively, he would tell them they simply needed to actualize what the Spirit had already given them. Then he would lay his hands on them and say, "Speak in tongues or prophesy." He always referred to these two initiatory gifts because he believed this was the New Testament pattern.[48] Wimber had a problem with evangelicals who taught that the Acts 2 account was the birth of the church, because if that were true, the gifts of the Spirit should still be operational in the church. He believed the reason people didn't receive the gifts of the Spirit was because they had not been taught this experience was still available for them today.

Show and Tell

One night during a home study group, Wimber taught from the gospel of John on the healing of the crippled man at the Pool of Bethesda. At the meeting that night, there was a young woman who had a shortened leg because of a childhood accident, and she asked if John would pray for her leg to be lengthened. When he did, her leg shook violently for some time, and then to everyone's amazement her leg was visibly longer, evidenced by her pant leg now being excessively short.[49]

Later that evening, John and Carol were discussing the events of the evening and marveling at how teaching on healing from the Scriptures had produced the miraculous. As John was getting a glass of milk from the refrigerator, he turned to Carol and commented that it was like show-and-tell—he would tell them what the Scripture said and then show them the miraculous working of the word. When he said this, the power of God hit him, his knees buckled, he lost his balance, and the milk in his glass shot up into the air. In astonishment he looked at Carol and said, "I think we're onto something here,

Carol Kay."[50] From this point forward, Wimber began formulating his understanding that the ministry of Jesus was both *proclamation* and *demonstration*. Jesus used his words to *illuminate* and then did miraculous works to *illustrate* God at work in the world. He realized that both proclamation and demonstration were needed to present a complete message of Jesus.[51] This combination eventually became the basis for his Power Evangelism model.

Don't Just Read the Menu

As John became convinced that the role of the pastor and teacher was to train and equip the body of Christ to do the works of Jesus, he began using the Bible as an instruction manual.[52] He believed that *reading about* the works of Jesus and *doing* these same works today were inseparable.[53] Studying the Scriptures was not enough; we had to do what Jesus did. To illustrate, he would hold up a menu from a restaurant and say, "This is a menu. It is not the meal. It describes the meal, but you must order and eat before the transaction is complete! Don't be satisfied with just studying the menu!"[54] Then he would hold up the Bible and declare that reading the Bible without doing the works described in it was like reading a menu without eating the meal. Both the word and the works were necessary if the message of Jesus Christ was to be complete.[55] This, he believed, was the good news of the kingdom of God. Jesus came in power to heal the sick, cast out demons, raise the dead, and set captives free. This meant it was the responsibility of every believer to face the enemy with the authority of Jesus, proclaim the kingdom of God, and do the works of Jesus—by doing these things, believers would defeat Satan's kingdom and advance the kingdom of God.[56] John's understanding of power healing and power evangelism was coming into focus.

At times in his later ministry, some complained that he was not feeding them enough meat from the Scriptures. This often came from people with a strong evangelical-word background who had missed his point of equipping the saints to do the work of the ministry. He would simply tell the people who wanted more meat that "the meat is in the street." By this he meant that the church needed to go outside the prayer meetings and into the marketplace—exercising the gifts of the Spirit in the public square, the workplace, and the wider community. This was the meat of the gospel.[57]

Wimber's concern was always for the church. He wanted to see what God could do through a group of people who were willing to obey the commands of Jesus. From this vision grew his goal to develop a body of mature Christians who could be equipped and trained to function as ministers. His motive was never to learn only how to effectively pray for the sick himself; rather, his goal from the beginning was to train and equip every member of his congregation to be healers.[58] He did not want to build an audience; he wanted to build an army.[59] These concepts were the foundation of Wimber's vision for equipping the saints and became the underlining emphasis of his ministry.

Passing on the Anointing

In the early days of his ministry, as healings began occurring through John, people would come only to him for prayer to be healed. This bothered him because he had never wanted to have a one man-healing ministry. He was committed to the Ephesians 4:11-13 text of training and equipping the body to do the work of the ministry. So, during one Sunday night service, he decided to call his church together and to anoint the elders and anyone who desired to minister to the sick. The plan was to read the text in Exodus pertaining to Moses anointing Aaron and his sons for ministry, but he accidentally read the passage in Leviticus related to leprosy. No one seemed to notice, and John proceeded to anoint everyone's right earlobe, right-hand thumb, and right big toe, commissioning them to heal the sick. According to Carol, that was their first and only anointing service, and as far as she knew, everyone who had leprosy that night was healed![60]

Meeting His First Demon

In 1978, Wimber had his first encounter with a demon. Late one evening he received a pastoral call from a young man asking for help. He and his girlfriend Melinda were in a pickup truck parked in a field. Although eighteen-year-old Melinda weighed only about a hundred pounds, she was thrashing about in the truck, causing it to rock back and forth violently. The frightened young man broke free and called Wimber from a phone in a nearby garage. When Wimber arrived on the scene, the demon began to speak through the girl. In a deep, growling, eerie voice, the demon informed John that he knew who he was, that the girl belonged to the demon, and that Wimber did not know what he was doing. John knew the demon was right on the last account—he did not know what he was doing—but by now he had started to understand that he had some authority, and he felt it was his responsibility to use this authority to set the girl free. Wimber described what happened next, as follows:

> Then began ten hours of spiritual warfare during which I called on the forces of heaven to overcome Satan. I thumbed through the Gospels, looking for passages on [the] casting out of demons. During this time, I smelled putrid odors from the girl and saw her eyes roll back and her profuse perspiration. I heard blasphemy and saw wild physical activity that required more strength than a slight girl operating under her own power could possibly possess. I was appalled and very afraid, but I refused to give up the fight. In the end I think the demon left because I wore it out, certainly not because I was skilled at casting out evil spirits.[61]

As he studied the Scriptures, he came to the conclusion that deliverance—or setting the demonized free—represented a large part of Jesus's ministry. From experience, he also developed an understanding that Christians could be demonized, though not possessed, and that believers and unbelievers alike could suffer varying degrees of demonization.[62]

His theology regarding demonization, informed by both Scripture and experience, became a major portion of his ministry, but this perspective that Christians could be demonized would eventually draw sharp criticism from those within both evangelical and Pentecostal camps. He agreed that the Scriptures were too ambiguous on the subject to be dogmatic, but he said that experience had taught him that Christians could at times suffer from demonization.[63] Subsequently, he believed the kindest and most loving thing he could do was to set the demonized person free. For this reason, even when he was severely criticized, he refused to back down from his position.

With his new theology regarding healing and deliverance now firmly established, he was about to experience one more revelation of the ministry God had promised to show him, which would transform his life and ministry forever.

"Come, Holy Spirit!"

In 1980, while attending a Calvary Chapel minister's conference, Chuck Smith introduced Wimber to Lonnie Frisbee.[64] Frisbee was an ex-hippie who had been a prominent leader in the Jesus movement and had made a major impact on Smith and Calvary Chapel.[65] In the late 1960s and early 1970s, Smith was concerned about the lost condition of the hippies he saw around Costa Mesa, but he had never had a personal encounter with a hippie until his daughter's boyfriend brought Lonnie to Smith's house. Smith was instantly impressed with Frisbee's walk with the Lord and asked him to share his testimony with his congregation. There were approximately thirty to forty people present on the Wednesday night Frisbee spoke. The hippie crowd was immediately attracted to Lonnie, so Smith eventually asked him to join his staff.

Smith later ordained Frisbee, and he became the regular Wednesday night speaker, consistently packing the house. Within six months, Smith's church grew from two hundred to two thousand members, and soon Calvary Chapel churches began springing up all across the southwestern United States. However, as Calvary Chapel grew, Smith started to shift his emphasis away from the Pentecostal/charismatic expressions of worship to a more concentrated focus on Bible teaching. Because Frisbee was more prophetic and had a flair for the charismatic, his relationship with Smith eventually became strained. As a result, Frisbee left Calvary and moved to Florida, where he became involved with the Shepherding Movement. After four years, however, he contacted Smith and asked if he could return to Calvary Chapel, and Smith graciously extended an open hand to the hippie preacher once again.[66]

When John first met Lonnie Frisbee, he invited Lonnie over to their house for dinner.[67] Although he was a bit cautious of the hippie phenomenon, at the end of their time together, he felt comfortable enough to invite Frisbee to share his testimony at the Sunday evening church service. By that time, the church was meeting in the Canyon High School gymnasium in Anaheim and had approximately seven hundred people.[68] The church at this point was open to receiving words of knowledge and it had experienced healings, but it was still quite traditional, characterizing the reserve of its Quaker roots.

At the Mother's Day evening service on May 11, 1980, John introduced the twenty-nine-year-old ex-hippie as a preacher who had been part of the Jesus movement. Because of his reservations regarding Lonnie, John decided to remain on the platform, seated at the keyboard, in case something happened that required him to take control of the service. After a while, however, he relaxed as Lonnie shared his story with skill and humor. Then it happened. At the close of the meeting, Lonnie invited everyone under the age of twenty-five, which was about three-quarters of the people, to come forward for prayer. As the young people crowded around, Lonnie announced, "For years now the Holy Spirit had been grieved by the church, but he's getting over it. 'Come,

Holy Spirit!'"[69] Then he waved his hand across the congregation, and as he did, holy bedlam broke out. Young people started speaking in tongues and began falling like dominoes all across the building, without anyone touching them. Several of them knocked over chairs as they went down.[70]

One young man, Tim, who was on the platform at the time, became tangled in a microphone cable as he fell, and the microphone landed next to his mouth. His voice was broadcast over the intercom system as he prayed loudly in tongues, but no one silenced it because the people in the sound booth had also been knocked down.[71]

Bob Fulton, Carol's brother-in-law, said they had heard of this kind of thing happening before, but until then, they had never seen it.[72] Carol remembered not being able to hear anything above the roar of the crowd, as hundreds were filled with the Holy Spirit and speaking in tongues. She excitedly moved among the fallen bodies in what now looked like a battlefield, believing this was the answer to their prayers for a move of God. Although it was not what she had expected, she was convinced it must be God, because how else could all these young people, who had never seen such manifestations, all be displaying the same actions in unison? Wimber was also stunned, but his reaction was more of anger than joy. All he could think about was how his church was being destroyed, and he cringed as he heard the sound of Bibles slamming and watched upset people walk out of the building.[73]

That night John was unable to sleep, so he spent the night praying, studying Scripture, and reading books on church history and the history of revivals.[74] Early the next morning, Tom Stipe, a Calvary Chapel pastor from Denver, called and said the Lord had awoken him with instructions to call John Wimber and say, "John, this is of me."[75] Stipe had no idea what this meant; he was simply acting out of obedience. Right there, John made the decision of his career to embrace this as a move of the Holy Spirit and to allow God to have his way. After all, hadn't God promised to show him "his" ministry?

John went into his office the next morning to find a disgruntled staff awaiting his arrival. After quietly listening to their complaints, he took off his glasses, leaned forward, and quietly but firmly said, "I understand how you feel. What happened last night may result in people leaving, but there is something you need to understand about me if we are to continue to work together. If there is ever a choice between the smart thing to do and the move of the Holy

Spirit, I will always land on the side of the Spirit. You need to know that."[76] Carol remembered this as the defining moment of the Vineyard movement.

Moving On

Many people who left the church that night never came back, but the church continued to grow, and revival seemed to be underway. After being powerfully touched by the Spirit, young people from the church started sharing their testimonies and seeing people healed in the schools, restaurants, and on the streets, witnessing the same manifestations they were experiencing in the church and leading hundreds of souls to Christ. As word spread of this outpouring of the Holy Spirit, people poured into the church, and in a few short months the church attendance went from seven hundred to a soaring two thousand. It was then that Wimber began to make a connection between "signs and wonders" and church growth—something that would eventually catapult him into another level of ministry.

The No-Hype Model for Ministry

Although he was willing to accept this Mother's Day outpouring as a genuine move of the Spirit, Wimber normally sought to curtail overt emotionalism in his church. He not only remained true to his evangelical doctrine but also embodied his quiet Quaker roots and employed a no-hype model for ministry. For example, music, for John, was for the purpose of worship, and he refused to use it as a means of elevating the atmosphere to stir people's emotions. Typically, he would not allow music to be played when he prayed for the sick, insisting that increased emotionalism actually blocked the move of the Holy Spirit. On the other hand, if people became "too religious" when praying for the sick, he would call for a coffee break and let people "dial down" before proceeding.[77]

In like manner, if someone became wobbly while receiving prayer, he would have them sit in a chair so they could rest in the Spirit. He saw no benefit in someone being "slain in the Spirit."[78] As for a healing model, he gravitated toward the ministry of Francis MacNutt. Though Wimber did not thoroughly embrace all of MacNutt's Catholic-rooted theology, he appreciated his "naturally supernatural" approach to healing. He liked MacNutt's model of quiet, soaking prayer, of simply praying and then waiting on the Lord without flash or drama.[79] By incorporating this no-hype model, he was able to minister in the power of the Spirit to people who would normally be turned off by the more emotional model historically identified with Pentecostalism.

"Doin' the Stuff" and Equipping the Saints

When John was a young believer reading the Gospels and observing the works of Jesus, he had asked his church leader when he could "do the stuff." When asked what "stuff" he was referring to, he replied, "You know, the stuff they did in the Bible." When the leader told him these gifts were no longer for today, he was discouraged but accepted this as the truth.[80] Now that the Holy Spirit was being poured out in his church, he was witnessing firsthand how the power of the Holy Spirit could transform lives and bring people quickly to Jesus[81]—and he was once again confronted with the truth about "the stuff" of the Gospels and the ministry of Jesus. Only now he was convinced that everyone not only *could*, but *should*, do the works that Jesus did, including praying for the sick. As a result, he set out to learn not only how to be an effective healer himself but also how to train and equip *every* member of his congregation to pray effectively for the sick and to do the works of Christ.[82]

Everything Wimber did flowed from his heart as a personal evangelist who had won multitudes of souls to Christ. He understood that the purpose of signs and wonders, which he translated into power evangelism and everybody "doin' the stuff," was not to build a ministry but to advance the kingdom of God. (In fact, he didn't believe mass evangelism was effective and thus rarely gave altar calls in his meetings; rather, he focused on training and equipping the saints to win the lost.) Thus, a key to understanding Wimber's ministry is realizing his goal was not to make converts, but to make disciples who could proclaim the word and demonstrate the works of Jesus, and thereby building an army of effective soul-winners. Perhaps one of the greatest contributions he made in his ministry was to re-remind the church of the priesthood of all believers and to make it possible for everyone to do the works of Jesus.

It was with this heart and mindset that John set to work. He knew from experience that the most effective way to equip people was to provide an effective model by which they could learn and practice, and he found this model in the "show and tell" ministry of Jesus.[83] Bob Fulton said that from this point on, John was constantly "formulating" and "tinkering" to learn and develop a training-and-equipping model.[84] He made many mistakes, tried new things, and when he discovered something that worked, he taught others to do it. They all learned together through trial and error. He would minister to the sick, ask questions, make adjustments, and teach as he went. This was the procedure that eventually became the "clinic" model he used to "equip the saints" and that ultimately developed into the format for his famous Signs and Wonders and Church Growth conferences.

In the process of ministering, modeling, and doing, John also realized that people learned faster and became more efficient at healing when teaching was coupled with experiential learning.[85] As such, terms such as "everyone gets to play" and "doin' the stuff" became synonymous with his ministry.

Just a few years earlier, when Carol had gone through her spiritual meltdown, she had come to realize that God had a blueprint for renewal and that John was a key component of that plan. Indeed, God was now building something through him. As a builder, John understood there were steps involved in the process, and he believed the first step was to excavate and lay a foundation. The depth and width of the foundation would determine the height and width of the structure, so for years, he labored to lay the groundwork. Now it was time to build up and out. It appeared that the promise God had made to Wimber in Detroit to "show you my ministry" was starting to unfold.

[1] Carol Wimber, *John Wimber*, 98.

[2] Ralph Wilkerson founded the Melodyland in 1960. In 1963, the Melodyland Theater, which was famous for its Broadway musicals and concerts and had a seating capacity of 3,200, went up for sale. Wilkerson purchased the property and turned the facility into a church. The church became known as Melodyland Christian Center. Eventually, they added Melodyland School of Theology, with J. Rodman Williams serving as the first president. Although the school closed in 1981, it influenced other schools, one of which was Regent University in Virginia Beach where Williams held the distinguished role of renewal systematic theologian.

[3] Carol Wimber, *John Wimber*, 113.

[4] Carol Wimber, *John Wimber*, 98; Carol Wimber, "A Hunger for God," in *Power Encounters*, ed. Kevin Springer (San Francisco: Harper & Row, 1988), 3.

[5] Carol Wimber, "A Hunger for God," 4; Carol Wimber, *John Wimber*, 110–1; Springer, "Applying the Gifts," 26.

[6] Carol Wimber, "A Hunger for God," 4.

[7] Carol Wimber, "A Hunger for God," 5. Also see Wimber and Springer, *Power Healing*, 31.

[8] Carol Wimber, "A Hunger for God," 5. This article was also recorded in the Vineyard Newsletter 2, no. 3 (Fall 1987).

[9] Wimber and Springer, *Power Healing*, 31; Wimber stated that many of these people later joined the home fellowship and became members of the church.

[10] John Wimber, "Wimber's Personal Testimony," cassette tape 1. Original tapes from the John Wimber Special Collections, Regent University Library, Virginia Beach, Virginia.

[11] Interview by the author with Bob Fulton.

[12] Interview by the author with Carl Tuttle. Also see "Vineyard Worship—The Early Years—Part 1" at http://www.carltuttle.com/wimber-years/2009/1/31/vineyard-worship-the-early-years-part-1.html. Accessed 1/05/10. Tuttle recalled that they did not have any idea what a "worship leader" was back then. He said he just happened to be the only one with a guitar, so he simply led them in some familiar courses. Also see Carol Wimber, "A Hunger for God," 7–8.

[13] Interview by the author with Bob Fulton.

[14] Carol Wimber, *John Wimber*, 115.

[15] Carol Wimber, *John Wimber*, 116. In *Power Evangelism*, Wimber stated that he firmly believed in the need for organization. This is something his critics would later question him on, as they observed the seeming lack of organization in his meetings. What they interpreted as "lack of organization" was his attempt to allow the Holy Spirit freedom to minister to the people without his control. From his experience with church growth, he learned that "the right kind of order is necessary for a church to develop to maturity and fulfill its task." He went on to say, "The church is an organism, a living body. A corpse is highly organized, but it is dead—it has no spirit within it. Many congregations are like corpses: well-ordered but lacking the life of Christ. On the other hand, the one-celled amoeba, which certainly lacks organization and complexity, has life but can accomplish little. Prayer groups and other Christian organizations that reject the need for leadership are often like amoebas: they have life but are not able to accomplish much." Wimber and Springer, *Power Evangelism*, 64.

[16] Wimber, *MC510*, cassette tape 1B.

[17] Wimber, *MC510*, cassette tape 1B; also John Wimber, "Power Healing and a Vision of God's Compassion," *Renewal*, no. 127 (December 1986): 9.

[18] Carol Wimber, *John Wimber*, 118; Wimber and Springer, *Power Healing*, 45.

[19] Wimber and Springer, *Power Healing*, 30–3.

[20] Carol Wimber, *John Wimber*, 117, 126.

[21] Carol Wimber, *John Wimber*, 118–20.

[22] Robeck Jr. "Calvary Chapel," 453.

[23] Donald E. Miller, *Reinventing American Protestantism* (Los Angeles: University of

California Press, 1997), 32.

[24] Miller, *Reinventing American Protestantism*, 32–3.

[25] Carol Wimber, *John Wimber*, 122.

[26] Carol Wimber, *John Wimber*, 122.

[27] Interview by the author with Tim Wimber on February 10, 2010.

[28] Interview by the author with Carl Tuttle on February 8, 2010.

[29] Carol Wimber, *John Wimber*, 139–40.

[30] Wimber and Springer, *Power Healing*, 46.

[31] Wimber and Springer, *Power Healing*, 47.

[32] Wimber and Springer, *Power Healing*, 48.

[33] Wimber and Springer, *Power Healing*, 48.

[34] Wimber, *MC510*, cassette tape 1A. Also see Wimber and Springer, *Power Healing*, 48.

[35] Wimber and Springer, *Power Healing*, 48.

[36] John Wimber, *Witness for a Powerful Christ* (Anaheim, CA: Vineyard Ministries International, 1996), 35–6.

[37] Wimber and Springer, *Power Healing*, 48–50; Wimber and Springer, *Power Evangelism*, 90; Wimber, *I'm a Fool for Christ*, DVD; Wimber, *MC510*, cassette tape 1B.

[38] Wimber, *MC510*, cassette tape 1B.

[39] Wimber, *MC510*, cassette tape 1B.

[40] John Wimber, *Kingdom Ministry* (Anaheim, CA: Servant Publication, 1987), 8.

[41] Wimber and Springer, *Power Healing*, 51–2; Wimber, *I'm a Fool or Christ*, DVD; Wimber, *MC510*, cassette tape 1B.

[42] Wimber and Springer, *Power Healing*, 54; also Wimber, *MC510*, cassette tape 1B.

[43] Wimber and Springer, *Power Healing*, 53.

[44] Wimber, *MC510*, cassette tape 1B.

[45] John Wimber, "Power Healing and a Vision of God's Compassion," 12.

[46] Wimber and Springer, *Power Healing*, 54.

[47] Carol Wimber, "A Hunger for God," 10.

[48] Wimber and Springer, "John Wimber Calls It Power Evangelism," 35.

[49] Wimber, *MC510*, cassette tape 1B; also Wimber, *I'm a Fool for Christ*, DVD.

[50] Carol Wimber, *Back to Our Roots: Stories of the Vineyard*, DVD (Vineyard Music, USA, 2006); Carol Wimber, "A Hunger for God," 10; and Carol Wimber, *John Wimber*, 134.

[51] Wimber and Springer, *Power Evangelism*, 34, 86; John Wimber, "Signs and Wonders Conference," (Anaheim, CA: Anaheim Vineyard, 1985), http://www.youtube.com/watch?v=aFzHHfwX7Xc.

[52] Carol Wimber, *John Wimber*, 133.

[53] Carol Wimber, *John Wimber*, 133.

[54] Carol Wimber, *John Wimber*, 133.

[55] John Wimber, "John Wimber Signs and Wonders Conference—Westernized Churches," (Anaheim, CA: Anaheim Vineyard, 1985), http://www.youtube.com/results?search_query=signs+and+wonders+-+westernized+churches&aq=f. Accessed on June 6, 2010.

[56] Wimber and Springer, *Power Healing*, 101–2.

[57] Nathan, "Bible Teacher," 97. Note John 4:34 (KJV): "Jesus saith unto them, My meat is to do the will of him that sent me, and to finish his work."

[58] Wimber, "Power Healing and a Vision of God's Compassion," 12.

[59] John Wimber, "Zip to 3,000 in Five Years," *Christian Life* 44, no. 6 (October 1982): 20.

[60] Carol Wimber, *John Wimber*, 132.

[61] Wimber and Springer, *Power Evangelism*, 51–2.

[62] Wimber and Springer, *Power Healing*, 97–8, 114.

[63] John Wimber, *Spiritual Warfare*, CD, part 2 no. 3.

[64] In early writings, Frisbee is referred to only as a "young man" rather than by his name. Carol identifies Frisbee by name in Carol Wimber, *John Wimber*, 145. Also see Carol Wimber,

"A Hunger for God," 12; Wimber and Springer, *Power Evangelism*, 61.

65 Lonnie Frisbee's life story is told in *Frisbee: The Life and Death of a Hippie Preacher,* DVD by David Di Sabatino (Jester Media, 2006). This is a documentary of Lonnie Frisbee who had a troubled childhood, was sexually molested as a child, went heavily into the drug and hippie scene, and then was saved and delivered out of drugs and a gay lifestyle. He was called into ministry through a vision of a sea of lost humanity worshiping God. He was recognized as a modern-day Samson at his funeral because, after living a life manifesting the power and presence of the Holy Spirit in ministry, he died of AIDS. Frisbee was a native of southern California, born June 16, 1949. His marriage to Connie Bremer ended in divorce. Although Frisbee lapsed periodically into homosexual sins, Wimber was unaware of Frisbee's struggle when he invited him to minister in his church. Once Wimber was informed of Frisbee's lifestyle, he severed ties with Frisbee and, for several years, omitted his name from Vineyard's history. Some ridiculed Wimber for doing this, but Ken Fish believes Wimber did this because of his concern that Frisbee's story would negatively impact the growth of the Vineyard movement. In an interview with Bob Fulton, Wimber expressed regret that they had allowed Frisbee to become involved with the Vineyard ministry without knowing about his homosexual lifestyle.

66 Sabatino, *Frisbee*, DVD. Prior to this, Frisbee was very nontraditional, wearing Hippie clothes resembling the attire of Jesus's day along with long hair and a beard.

67 Wimber, "Seasons of New Beginnings," *Vineyard Reflections: John Wimber's Leadership Letter* (May/June 1994), 1–2; Sabatino, *Frisbee*, DVD.

68 Sabatino, *Frisbee*, DVD. Carol Wimber, *John Wimber*, 146–7; Carol Wimber, "A Hunger for God," 12.

69 Lonnie Frisbee, "Mother's Day Service, May 1980, Anaheim, CA," cassette tape; also see Carol Wimber, "A Hunger for God," 3. Wimber's testimony is available at http://www.youtube.com/watch?v=44VDUicRk-A.

70 Carol Wimber, *John Wimber*, 147; Wimber, "Season of New Beginnings," 2; Sabatino, *Frisbee*, DVD.

71 Wimber and Springer, "John Wimber Calls It Power Evangelism," 35; Carol Wimber, "A Hunger for God," in *Power Encounters,* 12.

72 Sabatino, *Frisbee*, DVD.

73 Carol Wimber, *John Wimber*, 148; Carol Wimber, "A Hunger for God," 12; Wimber and Springer, *Power Evangelism,* 62–3. Carol's account states that John also read Scripture, but in John's account he talks only about reading books on church history to find something to validate these experiences. The fact that he did not mention searching Scripture for his answer would become an issue for which his critics would condemn him in the coming years.

74 Wimber, "Zip to 3,000 in 5 Years," 21; Wimber and Springer, *Power Evangelism*, 61–4.

75 Carol Wimber, *John Wimber*, 148.

76 Carol Wimber, *John Wimber*, 148–49.

77 Wimber and Springer, *Power Healing*, 174. See also Sandy Millar, "A Friend's Recollections," *Equipped: A Vineyard Magazine*, October 1997.

78 John Wimber, "Signs and Wonders Conference," http://www.youtube.com/watch?v=aFzHHfwX7Xc.

79 John Wimber, "Witness for a Powerful Christ," *Equipping the Saints,* Third Quarter 1996, 42.

80 Wimber, *I'm a Fool for Christ*, DVD.

81 Wimber, "Witness for a Powerful Christ," 43.

82 Wimber and Springer, *Power Healing*, 50; Wimber, "Zip to 3,000," 20 and 23; Interview by the author with Tim Wimber.

83 Wimber and Springer, *Power Healing*, 169.

84 Interview by the author with Bob Fulton.

85 Wimber, *MC510*, cassette tape 6A.

Chapter 3

The Birth of the Vineyard Movement and International Ministry

Coming into the Christian faith under the mentorship of Gunner Payne, who drilled into him the scriptural responsibility of personally leading people to the Lord, John had become a successful evangelist. Later, he became the pastor of his Quaker church, where he personally led hundreds of people to the Lord and consequently grew the church into one of the largest in the denomination. God then gave John the opportunity to field-test what he had learned by working with C. Peter Wagner as a church growth consultant for Fuller. Now, becoming a prominent leader in the emerging church growth movement seemed the next natural step in his spiritual journey.

Becoming a Church Planter

In 1979, Wimber's Calvary Chapel, which now had approximately two thousand people in attendance, was ready to launch its first church-planting team. Todd and Debbie Hunter, who had served as interns with John for two years, sensed God leading them to plant a church. After seeking the Lord, they decided Wheeling, West Virginia, was the place they were to put down roots.[1]

A few years prior to sending the Hunters out on the church's first planting mission, John received a "supernatural" vision. He described the vision in the *First Fruits* magazine, the same issue that carried an article by Hunter regarding his experience of planting their church in West Virginia. Wimber described his vision as follows:

> Several years ago God spoke to me in a vision concerning the planting of 10,000 fellowships. In this vision I saw a map of the United States with

thousands of little lights all across the country. Some in the Mid-West, Denver, Chicago, Kansas City, etc.: a large number across the Sun-Belt from Los Angeles to Phoenix to Houston and on into Florida. The New England states from Maine to New York City were covered as well as the Pacific Northwest clear down to Southern California. Thousands of little flashing lights! I asked God what this meant. He told me that each light represented a new fellowship that He wanted to start. I thought I had gone berserk. It must be me. I am only making this up. As usual, God was persistent and patient and I was slow and resistant. I am now convinced that God has called me to encourage the planting of these 10,000 fellowships.

Where will they come from? Some will adopt (i.e., existing churches who wish to become Vineyards.) To some we will be foster parents to (i.e., they will stay who they are, and we will provide assistance as requested). Others we will give birth to. It is in this latter group that most fellowships will be planted. God has initiated; now it is up to us to follow.[2]

From the conception of the church-planting movement, Wimber purposefully instilled church planting into the congregation's spiritual DNA, and as time would prove, he faithfully executed his promise to be a sending church. His personal philosophy was that "when a church is planted, we have actually set up camp in the enemy's territory to bring the kingdom of God to bear down against the kingdom of darkness."[3]

Leaving Calvary and Becoming a Vineyard

The first church-planting endeavor, led by the Hunters, occurred while they were still part of Calvary Chapel. But that was soon to change. As Calvary Chapel continued to experience robust growth, Chuck Smith shifted his focus further from the charismata and the accompanying charismatic manifestations and put a stronger emphasis on Bible teaching. As this shift occurred, the relationship between Wimber and Smith became progressively strained. Both men were strong leaders, and Smith was growing increasingly uncomfortable with the charismatic manifestations in Wimber's ministry.[4] As the relationship between Smith and Wimber became more intense, another significant man came into their life.

Meeting Kenn Gulliksen

Smith called Kenn Gulliksen the "pastor of love," not only because he had written the song "Charity," which was an exposition of 1 Corinthians 13, but also, and more importantly, because no matter whom Gulliksen talked to, he had the uncanny ability to convince them of the reality of God's love.[5] Gulliksen was ordained by Calvary Chapel in 1971 and maintained a loose-knit relationship with Smith as he planted Calvary-style churches around the southwestern part of the United States. After Kenn and his wife, Joanie, worked for a while with the Jesus Chapels in El Paso, Texas, they returned to California in 1974, where for the next eight years Kenn planted churches around the state, including in Los Angeles, Newport Beach, San Fernando Valley, and Beverly Hills. Gulliksen's churches were all similar in doctrine and format to Smith's Calvary Chapels, but he placed a greater emphasis on intimate worship and the gifts of the Spirit than Calvary Chapel.[6]

By the end of the 1970s, Gulliksen's ministry was attracting such well-known people as Randy Stonehill, Debbie Boone, Bob Dylan, Hal Lindsay, Priscilla Presley, Eldridge Cleaver, Frank Peretti, and Keith and Melody Green.[7] At one point he had two house churches, one that met in the home of Larry Norman and the other in the home of Chuck Girard, both recognized figures in the early development of contemporary Christian music.[8] (Larry Norman has since been credited with introducing Christian rock music to the church,[9] and, at that time, Girard was recording songs with Maranatha! Music, which was a part of Chuck Smith's Calvary Chapel.)[10] Then in 1975, Gulliksen combined the two home groups and formed a church.[11]

During those early days, Gulliksen said they planted churches more "by accident" than through strategic planning, but he realized God's blessing upon their efforts, and before long they had planted churches. As the group of churches pondered what to call themselves, the passage in Isaiah 27:2-3 jumped out at Gulliksen. It read, "In that day—sing about a fruitful vineyard: I, the Lord, watch over it; I water it continually. I guard it day and night so that no one may harm it." He felt God was saying, "You're the vineyard. Everything the Father wants to do in the life of the church can be seen in a vineyard. Ground preparation, sowing, husbandry, pruning, the production of fruit, grafting, beauty, the joy of wine. . . . "[12] Later Gulliksen wrote, "God [was] a faithful gardener," who "watered and guarded" the planting of the Vineyard even though we made "more mistakes than summer has ticks."[13] Gulliksen was skilled in planting churches, but he knew he did not possess the organizational skills to grow a church movement. Wimber, on the other hand, was an expert in church growth.

Separation from Calvary Chapel

In April of 1982, Smith called a meeting of Calvary's pastors, during which some raised concerns about the charismatic emphasis in Wimber's church. Regarding this meeting, Bill Jackson wrote, "When John Wimber began to promote in the front room what Calvary was doing only in the back room, tension began to mount."[14] Wimber's church, with its new emphasis on the gifts of Spirit, did not fit well with the Calvary Chapel model of downplaying the charismata and focusing primarily on teaching. So it was suggested that Wimber align himself with Gulliksen's Vineyard churches, since both groups had a strong charismatic focus.[15] Smith was pleased with the recommendation and blessed the union. At that point, Smith assumed the Vineyard churches would remain affiliated with Calvary Chapel and simply operate under a different name and slightly different spiritual expression. But this was not to be the case.[16]

A month later, the Vineyard pastors, along with some Calvary Chapel pastors, met with Gulliksen and Wimber. At the meeting, Gulliksen suggested he relinquish his leadership position and transfer the reins of his fledgling Vineyards to Wimber. Reflecting back on this decision, Gulliksen wrote,

> We were in way over our heads—drowning. God in his incredible mercy, sent John Wimber to us, who was to become the pastor to these Vineyard pastors, who was to teach us how to cooperate with God in the process of pastoring and church planting. We began to see planning in the Spirit was far more efficient than accidental birthing.[17]

Maybe it was Gulliksen's love for God and people, combined with his humility and a sense of personal inadequacy, that caused him to make this move. He also recognized in John someone who was a trained expert in church growth, a leader with strategic insight and planning skills, and a man who could be trusted.

Wimber agreed with the transition but also impressed upon Gulliksen that if he assumed the name "Vineyard," the name would remain a permanent part of Wimber's organization. His group had gone from Quaker, to Calvary

Chapel, and now to Vineyard, so changing their name again would not be an option. They all agreed that, even if Gulliksen later changed his mind and chose to leave, the name "Vineyard" would remain with the newly forming organization.[18]

When Wimber disengaged from Calvary, thirty Calvary Chapel pastors immediately merged with the eight Vineyard fellowships (including Wimber's church), and several more Calvary Chapel pastors followed a few years later.[19] So while the idea of separation was initially amiable, the timbre changed when pastors left Calvary to align with Wimber, and a painful rift developed between the groups.[20] In addition, aside from the initial personal differences between Smith and Wimber, several other factors contributed to the tension between the two groups.

First, there was a conflict regarding the focus on intimacy in worship. (More will be said about this later.) Second, there was a basic difference in the way Smith and Wimber approached church growth. Wimber believed church growth was a result of both strategic planning and evangelism through the supernatural ministry of signs and wonders. Smith, conversely, resisted the signs-and-wonders phenomenon and held that church growth was a direct result of the sovereignty of God.

The third rub between the two groups related to eschatology. Calvary Chapel had always embraced a pre-tribulation rapture as their central doctrine. Wimber, on the other hand, had been influenced by George Ladd's post-tribulation theology and displayed a greater flexibility in his doctrine regarding the time of the rapture. Another aspect was the move of the Holy Spirit in Wimber's church, where there were physical manifestations such as people shaking, singing, and being slain in the Spirit—all of which made Smith uncomfortable. Carol believed the final straw that broke the back of their relationship was when John started ministering deliverance and inner healing to professing Christians, while Smith firmly maintained that a Christian could not be demonized.[21]

All these issues contributed to severing the relationship between Wimber and Smith and ultimately resulted in Vineyard becoming an independent organization. It was a painful break, and wounds were inflicted on both sides. Years later John called the Vineyard church to repentance and expressed grief over the Christian fellowship lost as a result of the break with Calvary Chapel.[22]

Initially, he appointed Kenn Gulliksen as the overseer of the Vineyard churches in the United States, but after ten years Kenn became restless with the denominational structure and once again became an independent church pioneer.[23] The name "Vineyard" remained with Wimber's organization.

By 1985, the Vineyard movement had three megachurches. These included the two-thousand-member Vineyard church in West Los Angeles, pastored by Jim Kermath; Tom Stipe's four-thousand-member church in Denver, Colorado; and Wimber's Anaheim Vineyard, attended by approximately six thousand people.[24]

Building a Movement

In September 1983, Wimber moved his original Yorba Linda congregation to 5340 East La Paloma Avenue in Anaheim and changed the name to Vineyard Christian Fellowship. They rented 65,000 square feet of the Pacific Stereo warehouse and later occupied an additional 30,000 square feet of the same building, with a total seating capacity of 3,000.[25] The facility was modest and simply decorated, the only extravagance being a life-size bronze statue of Christ washing the disciple's feet in the main entry, which was a gift to the church from the artist.[26]

To facilitate this rapidly expanding ministry and the burgeoning church-planting efforts, two separate entities were organized. In May of 1983, Vineyard Ministries International (VMI) was established to facilitate John's international conference ministry. VMI also distributed Wimber's teaching tapes as well as Vineyard's music and printed materials, assisted associate conference speakers, and oversaw Vineyard's church planting within the United States. In addition, VMI developed its own magazine publication, called *Equipping the Saints*, which emphasized renewal in churches outside the Vineyard movement.[27] In the summer of 1985, VMI added another arm to its ministry, called Mercy Media, to produce John's thirty-minute radio program *Walk in the Word*. Then in 1986, the Association of Vineyard Churches was incorporated to license pastors, oversee the church-planting movement, help independent churches that wished to affiliate with Vineyard, and direct Vineyard fellowships.[28]

As John was building an organizational infrastructure, he was also growing in his understanding of ministry, and one of the greatest contributions he made to the church was his gift of music.

From Garage Bands to Worshipers

In the early 1980s, Chuck Smith founded Maranatha! Music, which produced contemporary soft-rock Christian music evolving from the Jesus movement. Although Smith produced this type of music for widescale distribution, in his own church he allowed contemporary worship music only during Saturday evening services, while traditional hymns were sung in the Sunday morning services.

John, on the other hand, had grown up on rock and roll. He was more in tune with the emerging hippie culture and had entertained this generation before becoming a Christian. He had never grown comfortable with choirs and organ music, and the words to hymns seemed archaic. He said he sang "Beulah Land" for years without having a clue what it meant. Further, his entire generation had grown up on rock and roll—it was who they were—and he believed the emerging Christian soft-rock music was a sound this baby boom generation could easily embrace.[29]

One day, driving on the Los Angeles freeway, he suddenly had a picture of young kids playing instruments in their garage and heard what he described as a "horrible sound" to his trained musical ears. At this, he pulled over to the side of the road and began to weep. He said, "Lord, if they [meaning Calvary Chapel] don't want this music, I want it. I'll take it. I'll train these young people to be worshipers." (Later, Bob Fulton said he believed the reason so many worship leaders were raised up within the Vineyard fellowship was because John had this vision and made this commitment.)[30]

This is when Wimber made the decision that what Calvary sang only on Saturday nights, they would sing on Sunday morning. He personally took charge of the worship music and began applying his secular experience to creating a level of professionalism in Vineyard recordings that would set the standard for the industry.[31] He set up a twenty-four-track studio in his Anaheim church that produced a creative and contemporary style of worship music that was cutting edge, and out of this grew Vineyard's Mercy Music industry. Wimber was a role model who inspired many young musicians and attracted talented artists such as Carl Tuttle, Brian Doerksen, Andy Park, David Ruis, Eddie Espinosa, Kevin Prosch, Matt Redman, and others. Eventually Chris Wimber, John and Carol's oldest son, who had a background in Christian music, assumed the role of studio manager and engineer.[32]

God Gave Wimber Songs

John wrote a total of sixteen Christian worship songs during his life that were produced by Mercy Music.[33] Carol liked to call them his "airport songs," because he often received them as he was driving to or from the airport. She remembered him scratching out the words of *Spirit Song* on the back of an envelope on the way home from the airport, exhausted from a "grueling" trip.[34]

But the song he may best be remembered for is *Isn't He*. This song also came to him on the way to the airport—after he had unjustly reprimanded his son, Tim. John had just gotten home from an exhausting day's work when Tim informed him that a man had called and was expecting John to pick him up from the airport. John, with a "shoot the messenger" attitude, railed at Tim for not telling the "uninvited visitor" he had no plans of picking him up from the airport. Tim had only answered the phone, but John showed no mercy. He stormed out of the house into the pouring California rain and begrudgingly headed to the airport. On the way, he began to weep and ask God to forgive him for the way he had spoken to his son. Suddenly, the presence of the Lord filled the car, and he was overwhelmed with God's love and grace. Words began to flow:

> Isn't he beautiful? Beautiful, isn't he?
> Prince of Peace, Son of God, isn't he?
> Isn't he wonderful? Wonderful, isn't he?
> Counselor, Almighty God, isn't he? Isn't he?[35]

Carol said the royalties from this song still puts food on her table. He taught the song to his congregation the following Sunday, and soon it was being sung around the globe.[36]

The Heart of Worship

The worship sound of Vineyard contributed to the transformation of Christian music. During this era, choruses viewed from overhead projectors began replacing hymn books, and electric keyboards, drums, and guitars took center stage as the traditional piano and organ were pushed aside.

Additionally, John also developed a theology of worship that placed it at the top of Vineyard's priorities. And intimacy—singing songs *to* God rather than *about* God—became the hallmark of Vineyard music. This was because

John saw worship as an opportunity to touch the heart of God and to give love back to him.[37] Tim Wimber said songs like "Jesus, I love you" in those early days seemed so intimate that he had to close his eyes because it was almost embarrassing to sing such words to the Lord.[38] For John, however, worship was not just about singing words; it was something that involved offering your entire being to God through getting on your knees, raising your hands, and laying prostrate before God.

Reinforcing this experience, Carol said the revelations they received about worship eventually led to their corporate understanding that true worship was the expression of their love to God that flowed out of their own personal and intimate relationship with Him.[39] Carol summed up Vineyard worship, saying that John . . .

> taught us that worship is not a vehicle to warm up the congregation for the preacher, or to soften people up for an offering. Worship comes from Jesus and goes back to Jesus from us. Jesus gives us everything, but worship belongs to him. We do not make stars of worship leaders. Worship is not for anything, but just for him: that is what he gets. He gives everything else to us, and what he gets back from us is worship. John taught us that.[40]

Jack Deere believed that Wimber restored true worship to the church, saying that "now churches everywhere have worship leaders and music directors."[41] For John, worship expressed through music was at the heart of his vision for his growing Vineyard. This was a major paradigm shift that changed worship in the early 1980s.

Kinship Groups

In addition to emphasizing intimacy with God, John stressed the importance of intimacy with one another, and this emphasis found specific expression in their small assemblies called "kinship groups." Wimber, the church growth expert, had seen firsthand that the fastest growing churches were the products of their successful small groups. He also saw the "kinship groups" as a place where safe relationships could be nurtured, broken hearts could be healed, and people could grow in their spiritual walks. In these groups, the body could minister to one another and people could learn to operate in their spiritual gifts.[42]

Loving God and caring for one another were two important aspects of the church he was building. And as they grew in their understanding of these two aspects, they became ready to take the next step in their spiritual development—caring for the poor.[43]

Caring for the Poor

Caring for the poor was not a new idea to Wimber. His commitment and vision to care for the less fortunate had been birthed in his spirit in the mid-1970s, when he had still been traveling with Wagner. The two men had attended a regional meeting for the Church of God denomination, where an old evangelist, hoarse from years of preaching, pleaded with the people to remember their roots and not forget to clothe the naked and feed the hungry. The message was simple, but the conviction of the Holy Spirit was so strong that the people moaned under the weight of it. The next morning John called Carol and told her he had been up all night reading Isaiah 58 about the true fast God had chosen. He sobbed as he told her the story of the previous night, and right there on the phone, he prayed and made the commitment to live out God's heart for the poor.[44]

Wimber never forgot his promise. Later, when he started pastoring again, one of the first things he did was institute caring for the poor as one of the church's core values, which led to the formation of Compassionate Ministries. At the time of this writing, this ministry was feeding and clothing over 35,000 individuals a year. They hosted a total of nine events between Tuesday and Sunday, serving up to 830 individuals and 2,700 families and distributing over 5,000 bags of groceries each month. They also served up to 250 families twice a week through their Mobile Food Pantry, ministered to over 500 people in four prisons, and had programs to care for the elderly.[45] Because of his teaching and heart for the poor, the church has continued to live out in practical ways its responsibility to the poor and needy. For example, just before Wimber died, his church needed to raise $500,000 to refinance a loan on their buildings. It was announced up front that the first $250,000 would be given to the poor, and as a result, a total offering of $750,000 came in in just one week![46]

Women in Ministry

In the spring of 1994, Wimber issued a statement regarding the Vineyard's position on women in ministry. He said that "to relegate a gifted believer to a desolate place in the body of Christ because of gender would be an injustice." However, he went on to say that he did not "favor ordaining women as elders in the local church." He encouraged women to participate in preaching, teaching, evangelism, healing, prophesying, counseling, nurturing, administration, and building up the flock of God—as well as ministering to men, with the caveat that they be under the authority of a man. He believed that such texts as 1 Timothy 2:12, which says women should be silent in the church, were situational and did not apply today; however, this did not take away from the fact that he personally did not believe women should be elders.[47] In 2006, nine years after his death, the National Board amended the Vineyard policy and empowered women to serve at all levels of leadership. According to Bert Waggoner, national director of Vineyard USA, there is a growing number of women pastoring in the Vineyard movement today.[48]

Charisma magazine printed an article saying that Happy Leman, regional overseer of the Midwest Vineyard, led the way in ordaining women as senior pastors, something Wimber had refused to do. The article went on to say, "Wimber affirmed women in ministry, but his position was that he could not ordain women if ordination is concerned with governing, not ministering." Leman told *Charisma* that Wimber "had a couples focus—a woman eventually could be ordained as a pastor so long as her husband was the senior pastor."[49]

Beginning an International Ministry

Simultaneous to John growing the Vineyard movement at home, an international ministry was about to be birthed. Due to the magnitude of his international influence and the limitations of this work, what follows serves only as an introduction to this aspect of his ministry.

Just two months after the Mother's Day outpouring of the Holy Spirit in 1980, which later became known as the launching of "power evangelism," John launched the international phase of his ministry.[50]

The door into the United Kingdom was actually set up two years prior, in January 1978, when Eddie Gibbs, a visiting faculty member from the United Kingdom, came to Fuller to teach a two-week intensive course on church growth in the School of World Mission. Gibbs was introduced to Wimber, who was teaching a class on church growth with Wagner. Gibbs was impressed with Wimber's knowledge of church growth, but he was especially impressed with Wimber as an evangelist.

Before Gibbs had left for his trip, David Pytches, the vicar of St. Andrew's Anglican Church in Chorleywood, suggested that if Gibbs discovered anyone who could help their church grow, he should talk with them about the possibility of coming to visit. So during this particular trip in 1978, Gibbs broached the subject with Wimber but made no immediate plans. Then in 1980, David Watson went to Fuller to teach a class on renewal. Watson was the recognized harbinger for renewal in the United Kingdom as well as an internationally known evangelist and author. During his visit to Fuller, he asked Gibbs, who was also at Fuller at that time, where he should attend church the following Sunday. Gibbs suggested he visit Wimber's church, which at that time was meeting in the Yorba Linda Canyon High School gymnasium.[51] Watson paid them a visit and was deeply touched by what he saw.

Watson was impressed by the fact that, in just a few short years, John's church had grown from a small home gathering to over 3,000 people, most of whom were previously unchurched or newly converted. What impressed him more than the numbers was the spiritual atmosphere he sensed in the meeting. When he arrived, he took a seat on what he called "terraced benches." (Since he did not know they were called "bleachers," when someone later asked him how he liked the bleachers, he thought they were referring to the name of a singing group, so he responded that he thought they were great!)[52]

Watson was impressed with the casual atmosphere, including the attire of the people, and described the "whole event" as being "wonderfully relaxed and low-key, with nothing of the showbiz performance common in many of the big American churches."[53] He described Wimber as a patriarchal figure with a twinkle in his eye, who led the service from his position behind the electric piano—where he also rested his Bible and sermon notes. Although the worship songs were new to Watson, he found them easy to learn and was soon caught up in an atmosphere of intimate worship and heartfelt praise. He said he was overwhelmed by the "incredible sense of genuine caring love" that pervaded the entire church. Watson recalled Wimber teaching from the Scriptures, after which an altar call drew approximately a hundred people forward into a side room to receive Christ or receive prayer for healing.

Watson believed the most powerful attraction to Wimber's church was the "signs and wonders," in which remarkable healings took place. He witnessed blind eyes seeing, deaf ears hearing, bodies crippled by arthritis becoming straight, satanic power being broken, and testimonies of barren wombs being healed.[54] Watson was excited because he believed that, in Wimber and his

Vineyard, he had found the "indisputable evidence of God's power to heal, coupled with a lot of biblical wisdom and human sanity."[55] These people did not claim to have all the answers—they experienced failure and were just as puzzled as others as to why some people were not healed—but they stuck with it. Watson, himself an agent of renewal in the United Kingdom, had seen some healings in his own ministry, but he had never found "such a wholesome and powerful healing ministry" as he experienced in Yorba Linda.[56]

Because of their common interest in evangelism and church renewal, Wimber and Watson quickly became friends.[57] After returning to the United Kingdom, Watson told his friend, David Pytches, that he would never be the same. Then, upon Watson's recommendation, Pytches and Watson decided to partner in inviting Wimber to minister in both of their churches in the United Kingdom.[58]

Carol believed that it was not until they took their first ministry trip to England that they began to grasp the transformation that had taken place in their life. That realization happened in October 1980, when Watson asked John to come speak about the kingdom of God.[59] John agreed and gathered a team of ministers from his church—including John and Margie McClure, Bob and Penny Fulton, Lonnie Frisbee, Carl Tuttle, Kenn and Joanie Gulliksen, and Carol—to go with him.[60]

He ministered first in Pytches' Saint Andrew's in Chorleywood, a church John described as properly Anglican and largely made up of professionals, including members of the House of Commons, doctors, lawyers, and educators.[61] He ministered twice on both Saturday and Sunday. On the first morning, he spoke about the relationship between the miraculous and church growth, and in the evening service he taught about healing. After each service, he prayed for the sick with only moderate results. At that time, he had no idea the stir he was causing among the members of Pytches' conservative congregation, but when he arrived at the church the next morning, the people were buzzing about the power of God in their midst. After delivering his sermon on Sunday morning, his team once again prayed for the sick, this time with amazing results. Fulton prayed for a woman who was blind in one eye, and she received her sight.[62] Another man who had multiple sclerosis and was confined to a wheelchair was completely healed. Also during these two days of ministry, over a hundred young people committed their lives to Christ.[63]

Wimber's team then went on to minister in David Watson's St. Michael-le-Belfrey Parish in York and again experienced healings, deliverances, and conversions. When Watson took Wimber's team to the train station to see them off, a friend asked Watson what he would record in his report to the bishop regarding this week of ministry. After a pause, Watson replied, "I don't think it will be difficult to write about what happened. I'll report, 'The blind receive sight, the lame walk . . . and the good news is preached to the poor.'"[64]

Following their time in the United Kingdom, Wimber and his team went to South Africa, where they ministered in forty churches to over twenty thousand people, seeing a conservative number of two thousand people healed and an unknown number of salvations.[65] Margie McClure kept a diary of the trip, recording the events at each church meeting. Carol later said the journal "reads like the book of Acts."[66] Numerous accounts were recorded of blind eyes opening, deaf ears hearing, and backs being straightened. Others were healed of cancer, epilepsy, heart problems, arthritis, goiters, skin diseases, and more.[67]

The following year, in 1981, Wimber returned to the United Kingdom, this time with a team of twenty-nine young people from his church, all between the ages of thirteen and twenty-one. Each one had saved money, worked extra hours, and taken vacation leave to pay their own way. Carol said they were just "ordinary" kids—if you could call them that—chewing gum and casting out demons.[68] When they arrived, Eddie Gibbs suggested to John that they try to "tone things down" a bit because of the differences in culture—the "English don't respond as exuberantly" as folks in California, he said. So John met with the young team to prepare them for the meetings. He explained to them that they were in "someone else's church" and they could not expect to do things like they did at home. "We don't want to frighten the people," he said, "so try to be thoughtful of your host." After a long, considerate gaze, Carol said, John stood to leave. But then he turned around and said, "Listen, kids. That wasn't the Lord. That was just me—what I just told you. You go in and be yourselves and listen to what Jesus tells you to do, and you do that. Don't be afraid; just be obedient. That's what the Lord says."[69] With that, they headed into the church.

Tim Wimber, who was on the team of young people, vividly recalled how they were in awe of the church. It had a pipe organ that seemed to take up a quarter of the church, people were buried under the church, and the pews were hundreds of years old with doors on them. Everything felt so strange. But when people lined up to receive prayer, and the team started ministering to them, they suddenly felt at home and like experts. God gave them words of knowledge, and people were healed.[70] David Watson said it was quite interesting "meeting there in front of the beautiful communion rails and having gum-chewing teenagers in jeans laying hands" on people, and when they could not reach someone to pray for them they "simply climbed over the communion rails. . . . That was great. I thought it really lovely."[71] What impressed Watson most was how they experienced the "overwhelming presence of the love of God, and it was in this context of love that spiritual gifts and ministries were released in a healthy way."[72]

During this trip, in addition to visiting the St. Michael-le-Belfrey parish in York and Pytches' St. Andrew's in Chorleywood, the team also went to Sandy Millar's Holy Trinity Brompton church in Kensington. The first night John taught on healing to about eighty of Millar's home group leaders. At the completion of his teaching, he called for a coffee break before moving into ministry time, where he said they would "do some healing."[73] Millar had no idea what "doing healing" meant, so he prolonged the coffee break as long as possible. When the meeting resumed, he assumed a safe position on the back pew, where he could observe from a distance, rather than on the front row where he had sat during the teaching session.

John began the session with a word of knowledge regarding a man with a congenital defect in his back. After he prayed and the man was healed, Wimber then said there was a woman who was having trouble conceiving. Millar was embarrassed, because proper British did not speak of such things as conception in church—oh, they practiced it, he said, but they did not talk about it—and besides, he was sure no one in his congregation met this description. But to his surprise, a well-known young lady came forward. Sarah Wright received prayer, and nine months later the embarrassing moment was vindicated by the arrival of a beautiful baby boy. Later, Millar had the privilege of baptizing the baby and said it was one the most moving experiences of his ministry.[74]

At another meeting during the same visit to Holy Trinity, where two hundred or more were present, the Holy Spirit began to move, and many members of the congregation began to shake and were "overcome" by the Spirit. As one young man, who had previously been skeptical of Wimber's team, was carried out, John prophesied that God would give him the power to tell people about Jesus. This twenty-seven-year-old barrister, Nicky Gumbel, later became the director of the Alpha Course that is used today around the world as an evangelistic program for reaching and teaching new converts.[75]

Worship leader, songwriter, and author Matt Redman was another person touched during this visit.[76] Redman was only seven years old in 1981 when the team came and introduced a new kind of intimate worship. Redman's dad had died two months before, so family members had taken Matt to St. Andrew's to take in some of the meetings. Redman later said that it was in this environment of intimate worship modeled by Wimber that he had grown up and found healing for the wounds in his heart. According to Redman, Wimber brought to England a new theology and practice of worship. He led them in long periods of uninterrupted, intimate worship—something they had never experienced before. Redman said that Wimber had once been challenged about the amount of time he spent in worship during a service, but he defended himself saying that if no one else needed this time of worship, "he personally needed to worship God and spend that time meeting with him."[77]

According to Sandy Millar, Wimber taught them several things. First, he taught that everything flows out of intimacy with God and with one another. Before Wimber came, Millar said, they had never experienced an extended time of worship without being interrupted by a vicar's commentary, but John had taught them the value of extended times of uninterrupted worship to tell God how much they loved him.[78] Second, Millar said, Wimber had a naturally supernatural, laid-back style that the British culture could embrace. Other Americans, Millar said, had come with a similar type of ministry, but the Anglicans could not receive their messages because of their delivery. "We didn't like shouting," Millar said, "and John didn't shout. He spoke peacefully." He just invited the Holy Spirit to come, Millar said, and they loved him for it.[79] In his relaxed and laid-back manner, Wimber overcame the "expert" model and stressed that leadership was about developing and delegating others to join in the work of Jesus.[80] Through Wimber, they also discovered the Gospels were not just stories about Jesus healing the sick; they also provided a model for them to follow, to do what Jesus did. Wimber taught them that demonstration and proclamation went together, and he helped them realize they were to be "an army, not an audience."[81] John believed the purpose of this army was to advance the kingdom of God, and he said that every time a sick person was healed, a lonely person was embraced, a hungry person was clothed and fed, and an oppressed person was set free, the kingdom was advanced.[82] He was careful to avoid saying that healing was in the atonement, thus presenting a model that allowed for suffering.

He demonstrated a model the British could embrace, and they respected him as an expert in church growth. Millar made changes in his own church based on what he learned in subsequent visits to the Anaheim Vineyard.[83] Millar told his wife, "If that is New Testament, we have got to go for it."[84] They went after it, and Holy Trinity in Brompton was never the same.

International Church Planting

From the time he met David Watson in 1980 until the end of his life, John returned to minister in the United Kingdom on an annual basis. Before the Vineyard team's first visit to the United Kingdom, Bob Fulton had received a vision about ministering in the streets of England, where he saw numerous churches popping up. He believed this meant they were to plant Vineyard churches outside the United States. When Wimber arrived in the United Kingdom and shared this vision with Watson, Watson pleaded with him not to plant new churches but to work with them to revitalize and renew the already established churches. Watson believed it would be difficult for Wimber to pursue renewal if he planted churches, because he would be seen as a threat by competing with existing churches. As a result, Wimber called a moratorium on church planting not only in the United Kingdom but also in some other countries where he was invited to minister.

Steve Nicholson, who led the church-planting task force for the Vineyard movement and oversaw the planning of one hundred churches annually, said "the renewal part of John's ministry in the United States was adversely affected by the great increase in church planting, which took place in the years between 1984 and 1987."[85] On the other hand, Wimber was able to maintain positive relationships with churches seeking renewal outside the United States because he had placed a ban on planting churches in these nations. Even after his dear friend and renewal soulmate, David Watson, died following a difficult battle with colon cancer in June 1984, he held firm to his commitment not to plant new churches in the United Kingdom.[86]

The very next year, in 1985, John Mumford, a curate in the Anglican church, and his wife Eleanor were powerfully touched by God in John's meetings and felt called to plant a Vineyard church in England. Wimber refused their request but allowed them to spend two years working with him in the

Anaheim Vineyard. Then, in the spring of 1987, three years after Watson's death, the Vineyard board overruled John's decision, and he found himself in a position of renegotiating his self-imposed moratorium with the churches in England. As a result, in June of 1987, the Mumfords were released to return to their country to start a Vineyard. The church-planting moratorium in Australia and Germany, however, remained in force until after Wimber's death in 1997.[87] In 1998, Bill Jackson reported that there were 449 Vineyard churches in the United States, 370 churches in 52 other nations, with 156 other churches added for a total of 819 Vineyard churches around the world.[88] Wimber's dream of fathering a church-planting movement had become a reality.

Someone once asked John what made his Vineyard grow. He responded, "I just do what God tells me to do."[89] God had promised to show him his ministry, and over the years, Wimber had been an eager and diligent student—applying what he had learned to grow the Vineyard and launch an international ministry. Now he was ready to take what he had learned and teach it to others.

[1] The Vineyard Church, Wheeling, West Virginia "Our Story: How We Got Here," www.vineyardwheeling.com. Accessed on May 11, 2010.
[2] John Wimber, "The Commission," *First Fruits,* May 1994, 8.
[3] Jack Little, "Church Planting: Aggressive and Violent," *First Fruits,* September/October 1985, 13.
[4] Carol Wimber, *John Wimber,* 156–7.
[5] Andrea Hunter, "Ken Gulliksen: Surprised by Grace and Rescued by Love," *Assistant News Service,* http://www.assistnews.net/Stories/2007/s07010146.htm. Accessed on 1/26/07. Gulliksen was referring to 1 John 4: "God is love." Also see Kenn Gulliksen's song "Charity" at http://www.youtube.com/watch?v=m535OdDhFcY.
[6] Jackson, *Quest for the Radical Middle,* 80.
[7] Melody Green, *No Compromise: The Life Story of Keith Green* (Chatsworth, CA: Sparrow, 1989), 74, 84, 88–99, 115–20. Also see Jackson, *The Quest for the Radical Middle,* 81–2.
[8] Jackson, *Quest for the Radical Middle,* 80.
[9] "'This World Is Not My Home': The Wittenberg Door Interview: Larry Norman," *Wittenberg Door,* Issue 33 (October-November 1976), http://www.wittenburgdoor.com/larry-norman-interview. Accessed on 2/11/2011.
[10] Andy Park, *To Know You More* (Downers Grove, IL: IVP Books, 2002), 147.
[11] Jackson, *Quest for the Radical Middle,* 80.
[12] Kenn Gulliksen, "Birthing a Vineyard," *First Fruits,* July 1985, 14.
[13] Gulliksen, "Birthing a Vineyard," 14.
[14] Jackson, *Quest for the Radical Middle,* 85.
[15] Sam Thompson, "A Vineyard Overview," *Vineyard Newsletter,* Winter 1988, 2.
[16] Interview by the author with Carl Tuttle.
[17] Gulliksen, "Birthing a Vineyard," *First Fruits,* July 1995, 15.
[18] Carol Wimber, *John Wimber,* 157.
[19] Miller, *Reinventing American Protestantism,* 49.
[20] Interview by the author with Carl Tuttle.
[21] Carol Wimber, *John Wimber,* 156; Jackson, *Quest for the Radical Middle,* 87–9.
[22] Wimber, "The Way On," cassette tape 6.
[23] Donald E. Miller, *Reinventing American Protestantism,* 46. Miller states that Gulliksen "disagreed with the denominational direction of the Vineyard under Wimber's leadership and left the movement to start a new church called Metrowest, which is independent from the Association of Vineyard Churches."
[24] Lawson, "The Vineyard: Where Spiritual Gifts Blossom," 39.
[25] Lawson, "The Vineyard: Where Spiritual Gifts Blossom," 39.
[26] Pytches, "A Man Called John," 28.
[27] Sam Thompson, "A Vineyard Overview," in *The Vineyard Newsletter* 3, no.1 (Winter, 1988): 2.
[28] Thompson, "A Vineyard Overview," 2.
[29] Wimber, *MC510,* cassette tape 1A.
[30] Interview by the author with Bob Fulton.
[31] Interview by author with Bob Fulton.
[32] Unsigned Article, "VMI Expands," *First Fruits,* Sept/Oct 1985, 11.
[33] See appendix J.
[34] Carol Wimber, *John Wimber,* 143.
[35] John Wimber, "Isn't He," http://www.youtube.com/watch?v=iIMsX1cpSBs.
[36] Carol Wimber, *John Wimber,* 144.
[37] Matt Redman, "Worshipper and Musician," in *John Wimber: His Influence and Legacy,* 64.
[38] Interview by author with Tim Wimber.
[39] John Wimber, "Worship: Intimacy with God," *Equipping Magazine* 7, no. 3 (Summer

1993): 5–6.

[40] Carol Wimber, "A Wife's Tribute," in *John Wimber: His Influence and Legacy*, 303.

[41] Jack Deere, "The Prophet," in *John Wimber: His Influence and Legacy*, 115.

[42] Todd Hunter, "Church Planting: Listen and Obey," *First Fruits*, June 1984, 10; Lawson, "The Vineyard: Where Spiritual Gifts Blossom," 39.

[43] Wimber, "Zip to 3,000," 18.

[44] Carol Wimber, *John Wimber*, 105.

[45] Information obtained from Jill Ridgway-Ball, accountant, Vineyard Christian Fellowship Anaheim, California, via email on August 8, 2010.

[46] John Wright, "Planting a Local Vineyard Christian Fellowship," in *John Wimber: His Influence and Legacy*, 210.

[47] Wimber, "Liberating Women for Ministry and Leadership, *Vineyard Reflections*, March/April 1994, 1–2.

[48] Interview by the author with Bert Waggoner on August 24, 2011.

[49] Julia C. Loren, "Legacy of a Humble Hero," *Charisma and Christian Life* 33 (November 11, 2007): 93.

[50] Carol Wimber, "A Hunger for God," 12.

[51] David Pytches, "Fully Anglican, Fully Renewed," in *Riding the Third Wave* edited by Kevin Springer (Hants, U.K.: Marshall Pickering, 1987), 169. Of Watson, Pytches said, "What David did today we all tried to do tomorrow."

[52] David Watson, *Fear No Evil: Facing the Final Test of Faith* (London: Hodder & Stoughton, 1984), 50.

[53] Watson, *Fear No Evil*, 51.

[54] Watson, *Fear No Evil*, 51.

[55] Watson, *Fear No Evil*, 52.

[56] Watson, *Fear No Evil*, 52–3.

[57] Eddie Gibbs, "The Evangelist," in *John Wimber: His Influence and Legacy*, 72; Williams, "Friend and Encourager," in *John Wimber: His Influence and Legacy*, 55.

[58] Gibbs, "The Evangelist," 71–2.

[59] Wimber, *Kingdom Come: Understanding What the Bible Says about the Reign of God* (Ann Arbor, MI: Servant Publications, 1988), 9.

[60] Carol Wimber, *John Wimber*, 150–1.

[61] Wimber and Springer, *Power Evangelism*, 152.

[62] David Pytches, "Signs and Wonders," in *John Wimber: His Influence and Legacy*, (London: Eagle Publishing, 1998), 135.

[63] Wimber, *Kingdom Come*, 9–10.

[64] Wimber, *Kingdom Come*, 10–11; Pytches, "Signs and Wonders," 135.

[65] Wimber, *MC510*, cassette tape 1A.

[66] Carol Wimber, *John Wimber*, 151.

[67] Margie McClure, "A Diary of the South African Mission, October 1980," unpublished document, John Wimber Special Collections, Regent University, Virginia Beach, Virginia.

[68] Carol Wimber, *John Wimber*, 159.

[69] Carol Wimber, *John Wimber*, 161.

[70] Interview by the author with Tim Wimber.

[71] Wimber, *MC510*, cassette tape 1A.

[72] Wimber, *MC510*, cassette tape 1A.

[73] Sandy Millar, "A Friend's Recollection," in *John Wimber: His Influence and Legacy*, 267. This article was also published in part in *Equipped: A Vineyard Magazine* (U.K.).

[74] Millar, "A Friend's Recollection," 271.

[75] Gibbs, "The Evangelist," 82.

[76] One of Matt Redman's most famous songs, "The Heart of Worship," is available at http://www.youtube.com/watch?v=Tq62ggQKYJY.

[77] Redman, "Worshipper and Musician," 66–7, 69.

[78] Millar, "A Friend's Recollections," 276.
[79] Millar, "A Friend's Recollections," 279.
[80] Wright, "Planting a Local Vineyard," 213.
[81] Millar, "A Friend's Recollections," 273.
[82] Wright, "Planting a Local Vineyard," 214.
[83] Millar said he attended Anaheim Vineyard conferences in 1982, 1983, 1984, and 1985, where they covered such topics as church growth, spiritual warfare, and prayer and healing. Also during this time, they were learning more about ministry and worship.
[84] Millar, "A Friend's Recollection," 271
[85] Nicholson, "Church Planter," in *John Wimber: His Influence and Legacy*, 122.
[86] Anne Watson, "The Third Wave Has Only Just Begun," in *Power Encounters*, 21.
[87] Nicholson, "Church Planter," 124.
[88] Jackson, *Quest for the Radical Middle*, 340.
[89] Lawson, "The Vineyard: Where Spiritual Gifts Blossom," 39.

Chapter 4

MC510: Signs and Wonders and Church Growth

Although Wimber had resigned as director of the Fuller Institute of Evangelism and Church Growth to pastor his Vineyard church, he remained close friends with C. Peter Wagner. Between 1978 and 1980, John lectured with Wagner in his Doctor of Ministry Church Growth II course every August. During this time, Wimber and his church were also learning to pray for the sick and were experiencing amazing healings.

Wagner closely followed what was going on with John and the Anaheim Vineyard, and out of curiosity he periodically visited on Sunday nights. Then in 1981, John told Wagner he had been teaching on healing in his church and he had collected a great deal of material on the relationship between signs and wonders and church growth. He also shared that he had taken teams outside the country and they had seen miraculous healings. John suggested that he share some of his material and experiences during one of the morning sessions of the Church Growth II class at Fuller.[1]

At first, Wagner was a little hesitant. Like Wimber, Wagner was also a man on a spiritual journey, whose theology was in transition. At one time, Wagner described himself as an anti-Pentecostal dispensationalist who carried a Scofield Bible under his arm, had a limited view of power, and held a worldview shaped by secular humanism.[2] While serving as a missionary in Bolivia, he had even warned believers to stay away from faith healers. But over the years, God had been changing his heart. His transformation had begun when a Methodist missionary to India prayed for an open, festering cyst on his neck, and he was healed. This was followed by a series of positive encounters with Pentecostals in Chile, where he witnessed healings, speaking in tongues, and other manifestations.[3] The third contributing factor to his paradigm shift occurred during his travels for Fuller. On numerous occasions, he had the opportunity to work with leaders of the Church of God, a classical Pentecostal denomination in Cleveland, Tennessee, and whenever he left the meetings he felt so refreshed that he found himself wishing he, too, were a Pentecostal.[4] Eventually, he became more accepting of the Pentecostal and charismatic traditions, but at the same time, he remained fully committed to his Congregational church in Pasadena, where he considered himself a "straight-line evangelical."[5] And now that Wimber had come into his life, he was about to experience the fourth and final paradigm shift that would solidify his understanding of healing and the miraculous.

For years, they had traveled together for Fuller and, consequently, had become close friends. At one time, they had both been on the same narrow evangelical track, but now John was praying for the sick with amazing results, and his church was flourishing.[6] If anyone else had asked him to consider teaching a class on church growth and the miraculous, his immediate answer would have been an unqualified no. But because of their history together, he knew John to be a credible man of integrity, so Wagner "gave him the green light."[7]

Wagner was still a bit hesitant about the class content, so he decided to get a second opinion and invited Paul Pierson, academic dean of the School of World Mission, to sit in on the morning session when John made his presentation. Although neither Wagner nor Pierson had ever heard the material Wimber shared, they were both impressed.

After this initial presentation, John told Wagner that he had more material and suggested they consider adding an entire new course to the curriculum. Wagner might have been concerned, but he knew that Donald McGavran—the founding dean of Fuller's School of World Mission who was also recognized worldwide as an expert on the theory of church growth—had been teaching an advanced course on church growth that included divine healing. McGavran had decided to teach this class when students from third-world countries told him things were happening in their churches that theologians and missionaries in the West were ignoring. He later visited Asia and Africa and witnessed firsthand how native evangelists were praying for the sick with amazing success, resulting in conversions and massive church growth. As a result, he returned to Fuller and began teaching an advanced course on healing and church growth. For Wagner, this "was like a papal imprimatur." He decided "if it was alright for Donald McGavran, it was alright for me."[8]

Armed with this knowledge, Wagner believed the idea would be warmly accepted by the administration. At the same time, he knew there would be a couple of hurdles. Adding a class to an approved course was one thing, but adding an entirely new course to the curriculum was something else. This would require the approval of the entire faculty of the School of World Mission—and that was a different matter.

Course Evaluation and Approval

Fuller Theological Seminary, established in 1947 as a multidenominational evangelical institution, was made up of three separate schools. The School of Theology was the initial school, and the Psychology and World Mission Schools were added in 1965.[9] In 1982, the student body represented approximately forty different denominations, with 13 percent from developing nations and a conservative estimate of 30 percent from a charismatic background. The full-time faculty consisted of professors from twenty-three denominations with diverse backgrounds. One thing the faculty of the School of World Mission all had in common, however, was their missionary experiences.

When the faculty met to discuss Wagner's proposed Signs and Wonders and Church Growth class, one by one the faculty shared how they had felt incompetent on the mission field when faced with demons and supernatural powers in the countries where they served.[10] The faculty also recognized that, as valuable as the social sciences and mechanics of church growth were, it was possible that they had placed too much emphasis on these aspects to the exclusion of the work of the Holy Spirit. They all agreed their current curriculum did not entirely address the needs of the third-world students who came from spiritual cultures that depended on the Holy Spirit to validate their claims of the gospel. In their countries, where people were bound by animistic worldviews and where medical resources were scarce, they needed more than intellectual arguments and doctrines regarding the demonic. They had genuine needs that required real solutions. At one point during the meeting, Charles Kraft, professor of Anthropology and Intercultural Communications stated, "We desperately need to develop a theology of power in our school. In this day and age, we no longer can maintain our integrity as a School of World Mission and send out people to minister in the Third World without first training them how to pray for the sick."[11]

Additionally, the Fuller faculty knew Wimber. He had been on campus as a student and then served as the founding director of the Charles E. Fuller Institute of Evangelism and Church Growth from 1975 to 1977. He had also served for several years as a visiting instructor for the School of World Mission. He was well known and respected for his skills as a church growth analyst, and his integrity was without question. During his time at Fuller, he had been a typical evangelical cessationist and dispensationalist. Only recently had he become involved in divine healing. In other words, Kraft later said, the faculty "had known and learned to trust Wimber before he got 'this way.'"[12]

After several weeks of discussion, the Mission faculty voted unanimously that Wimber, with his experience and insight in church growth and the miraculous, was the perfect candidate to teach a course of this nature.[13] The seminary catalog described the new course as "experimental" and stated that it would focus "on understanding the effects of supernatural signs and wonders on the growth of the church. It is approached from biblical, theological, historical, and contemporary perspectives. Special attention [is] given to the ministry of healing. Field experience [is] an important dimension of the course."[14] The new course was officially called The Miraculous and Church Growth, listed in the catalogue as course number MC510. The name was later changed to Signs, Wonders, and Church Growth.[15] Wagner was to be the professor of record, but Wimber would do most of the teaching.

John's heart was always to give away everything that God had given him. From the time he realized healing was for the church today, he never wanted to build a healing ministry for himself; rather, his dream was to train and equip the entire church body to heal the sick and do the miraculous works of Jesus. He had begun by training his own church, and now he was being offered a larger venue that would extend beyond the church walls and train students who would potentially impact nations.

Launching MC510

With great fanfare Fuller announced the inauguration of MC510 for the 1982 fall semester under the jurisdiction of the School of World Mission.[16] According to David Hubbard, Fuller's president, "The course was designed to deal with both the theory and practice of the miraculous in the proclamation of the Good News to non-Christian audiences."[17]

The classes met each Monday night for ten weeks. John would present lecture material from six to nine o'clock, then offer a one-hour optional laboratory session where students could receive hands-on training to pray for the sick. John believed learning how to pray for the sick was better "caught than taught," so for him, the clinic sessions were a critical part of the course.

Since the class was the first of its kind, it immediately attracted attention and broke all previous enrollment records. The seminary had expected forty-five students the first semester, but approximately eighty registered.[18] To everyone's amazement the number of Theology and World Mission students who enrolled was almost equal. The second year the course attracted 279 students, giving MC510 the largest enrollment of Fuller's 400 courses.[19] Robert Meye, dean of the School of Theology, said he knew "of only two seminary courses which have become so famous . . . one was the course on dogmatics taught at Basel by Karl Barth and the other [was] MC510 taught by John Wimber here at Fuller."[20] While MC510 was Fuller's most popular class, little did they know it would also become one of their most controversial.

In October of 1982, just a few weeks after the course was underway, Robert Walker from *Christian Life Magazine* went to Fuller with the intent of writing a short article about the new class. He was so impressed, however, that the magazine decided to dedicate an entire issue to the course. The headline of the magazine read, "MC510 Origin History, Impact: Could This Number Affect Your Faith?" The issue was such a success that it quickly sold out and was subsequently reprinted in book form. It was this publication that launched Wimber and his teaching on signs and wonders into the realm of international notoriety. Hubbard later said that this class might have been the "first time in American history [that] an academic course preempted an entire issue of a national religious magazine."[21]

Course Content and Syllabus

Wimber's assumptions and purpose for the course were as follows:
1. To be a practical application of signs and wonders as they relate to church growth and not a theology or theory course.
2. To provide information concerning signs and wonders and demonstrate their relationship to church growth, thus illustrating their application for the church today.

3. To teach new skills and offer a model for ministry that followed the pattern of Jesus as seen in the Gospels. The emphasis is on spiritual gifts at a perceptual level more than on a conceptual level. It is by "doing" that one experiences the manifest presence of God and learns how healing works.
4. To improve the student's effectiveness in ministry. The purpose is not just healing, but that one learns to heal as it relates to soul-winning and the expansion of the kingdom of God.[22]

The course, from Wimber's perspective, was designed for practitioners. Thus, he encouraged the students to begin applying what they learned in class.[23] He believed that if the students did not begin praying for people to receive their healing, then the class would simply be an academic exercise. Listening to a lecture without actually praying for the sick would, to Wimber, be analogous to reading a book about water skiing without getting into the water. Further, he believed that a lack of such practice was a problem in the evangelical church. "It is not enough to believe and underline it in your Bible," he wrote. "We've got to do it. Jesus called us to be doers of the word, to actualize what he taught, to be disciples and not just hearers." He said the evangelical church, however, was "like an army that has been trained but never gets into the field. We have the manual, the equipment, but we have not done the work or had the experience."[24]

During the four years the course was offered, the syllabus was tested and revised each time the class was taught. The final product became a two-hundred-page document broken down into eight sections, representing each of the eight weeks the class was in session. In each section there was a short proposition, followed by documented evidence supporting the proposition, and then a conclusion. In the expanded syllabus, the propositions were heavily supported by Scripture.[25]

Wimber started the semester by emphasizing the relationship between signs, wonders, evangelism, and church growth, and the difference in the effectiveness of program evangelism and power evangelism as they connected to this topic. Program evangelism was identified as the typical approach to evangelism employed in the Western world and defined as a presentation of the gospel that seeks to "reach the natural mind by rational means and is often a one-way communication."[26] Power evangelism, on the other hand, is a means of presenting the gospel in a way that is "spontaneous and directed by the Holy

Spirit" via supernatural signs and wonders, and it often results in "explosive church growth."[27]

The second week of the course laid a theological foundation for this thesis and was supported by George Ladd's theology of the kingdom of God. Wimber stated that, "The Kingdom of God is the Rule of God that has invaded the kingdom of Satan and is the arena in which *Signs and Wonders* occur."[28] According to Wimber, Jesus proclaimed the arrival of the kingdom and then demonstrated this reality through miracles, healings, and exorcisms. The arrival of the kingdom initiated a battle with Satan over ownership of this world, and Jesus came out the champion. This battle is not a civil war within a kingdom but is a battle between Satan's kingdom and the kingdom of God, in which Jesus binds, plunders, and curbs the power of Satan. This victory, however, is not yet complete. He likened it to Oscar Cullmann's analogy of World War II and the time between D-day and V-day—the victory has been decided, but the battle will continue until Jesus's second coming, when he ushers in the new age or the age to come. Until then, Christians live between times—which Ladd identifies as the "already and not-yet." Wimber believed miracles were a foreshadowing of the age to come and universal redemption. Casting out demons represents God's invasion of Satan's kingdom and that kingdom's imminent doom. Raising the dead gives proof of the fact that, one day, death will be forever done away with. The healings of Jesus bear witness to the truth that there will come a time when all suffering will end, but, until Jesus returns, there will still be suffering, sickness, and death in this present evil age.

He continued his teaching the third week with an explanation of how the Western worldview has presuppositions and blind spots in dealing with the supernatural. Because of this, he said, the power of God has largely been excluded from church theology. John quoted extensively from the writings of Charles Kraft and Paul Hiebert, both professors at Fuller in the School of World Mission, as resident experts supporting his understanding of this subject.

During the fourth week, John presented the scriptural foundations for the gifts of the Spirit, emphasizing the difference between the Gift of the Holy Spirit (the Giver) and the gifts of the Spirit—the charismata or "gracelets."[29] Whereas traditional Pentecostals recognize only the nine gifts of the Spirit listed in 1 Corinthians 12:8-10, John also included the gifts of administration, hospitality, interpretation of dreams, philanthropy, and so forth. He also taught that the baptism of the Spirit occurs at conversion, that the gifts of the Spirit simply need to be activated at some point during the Christian experience, and that continuous fillings were something that should be expected throughout a person's life.

During the fifth week, he conducted an overview of the Gospels, the Acts of the Apostles, and the Epistles, revealing how signs and wonders were at the heart of Jesus's ministry. Jesus had authority and gave it to the church, as seen in the sending out of the twelve and the seventy and in the Great Commission. Wimber taught the rabbinic model Jesus used, where the master taught and demonstrated the power of God as the disciples observed, then the disciples preached and performed healings and miracles as the master watched and guided the process. The early church carried on the word-and-works ministry of Jesus, and the church grew wherever the gospel was preached and signs and wonders followed. Wimber provided students with a list of ten sign phenomena, along with Scripture, that occurred in the book of Acts, which resulted in evangelistic growth in the church.

The material for week six was the most extensive, occupying fifty-two pages in the class syllabus. It included accounts throughout church history where signs and wonders and miracles—especially healings—were evidenced in the church. He revealed how signs and wonders did not cease with the close of either the first century or the New Testament canon, citing over forty examples of movements and people who experienced the miraculous throughout church history.

In week seven, he taught about churches and movements around the world including those in South Africa, South America, India, Korea, China, Indonesia, the Philippines, and Canada, where unprecedented church growth was occurring because signs and wonders were validating the claims of the gospel. He believed the church grew most rapidly where the Western church had the least amount of immediate influence.[30] And he believed this was largely due to the anti-supernaturalistic worldview held by most evangelicals in the West.[31]

The final week of class, he told stories of notable personalities in the early Pentecostal and charismatic movements who had practiced divine healing and the miraculous in conjunction with evangelism. He presented the strengths of these healing evangelists, along with their acknowledged weaknesses, but also emphasized that, in spite of their faults and limitations, "the Pentecostal Evangelists have done more in this century to evangelize the world than any other group. They have been, in church growth terms, the most effective evangelists of this century, and that is the point. The church grows faster where the power of God is evident!"[32]

Throughout the MC510 Signs and Wonders course, Wimber punctuated the material with personal stories and testimonies that served to illustrate his points. In each class session, questions and classroom discussion were always encouraged.[33]

Optional Clinic Time

Karen Ball, a reporter for *Christian Life Magazine*, visited one of Wimber's training sessions to write an article. The following is her observation of the transition between classroom lectures and the optional clinic sessions:

> The lecture is over. The largest lecture room at the seminary is crowded to the walls with students sitting on the floor. Some stand to stretch, but few move for fear of losing their seats. A teacher, a large, rotund man with a lion-like appearance—thick bushy hair, beard and moustache—observes the class with thoughtful eyes. In a calm voice, one easily given to humor, he states that those who wish to leave before the "practical" session of the class may do so. No one does. He nods slightly then proceeds.[34]

To begin the clinic session, he first invited the Holy Spirit to come, to reveal the Father's loving care, and to give them direction. This was important to Wimber because he considered the goal as learning to follow the leading of the Holy Spirit in ministry, to move with the Spirit, and to do what the Spirit does—because the Spirit is the leader. The students were encouraged to wait, relax, not get too religious, and be tolerant, because this was a training situation and a safe place where they could learn and experience the gifts of the Spirit. The clinic sessions normally began either with a word of knowledge or with someone requesting prayer. The students were taught not just to begin praying for people by going down a line but rather to observe who the Spirit was moving on and pray for those people first. Through experience, they learned that, as some people began to receive, others would be stirred up, and their hearts would open, making it easier for them to receive.[35]

For the practical portion of the class, Wimber developed a five-step prayer model that he would one day use in training sessions around the world.[36] For him, it was important for the students to effectively learn the five-step prayer model, but they were also instructed to be open to the leading of the Holy

Spirit. Regarding instructions for the person receiving prayer, he encouraged the recipient to open their hands in a receiving posture. If they became overwhelmed with the Spirit, he led them to sit in a chair. He saw no benefit in being "slain in the Spirit." If the Spirit was working with a person, a team member was instructed to continue praying quietly or to allow the person to sit calmly in the presence of the Lord.

At no time did Wimber declare someone healed. He would stop praying for someone because he believed the work was finished, but he always encouraged people who believed they were healed to seek confirmation from their physician. Throughout all of the healing and training sessions, he maintained a quiet and subdued environment.[37]

People Impacted by MC510

Student and faculty reactions alike gave testament to the impact of Wimber's Signs and Wonder Class. Nancy Tribley, a Fuller student enrolled in the MC510 class, said that in most seminary classes, all of the students who signed up would attend, but by the tenth week of the semester, as the responsibilities of papers and tests became more intense, attendance would gradually dwindle; however, she said it was just the opposite in Wimber's class. Instead of attendance declining, each week more people came. What she enjoyed most about the class was the receptive atmosphere where students could discover their spiritual gifts and then learn to exercise and grow in them without fear or embarrassment.[38]

Nancy McRae, who was the secretary to the dean of the School of World Mission, took the class when she realized how popular it was. She said the class was "wall-to-wall people each week." She believed so many people came because they were able to see God in action firsthand.[39]

Dr. John White, author, psychiatrist, and former missionary in Latin America, audited the MC510 class in 1984. By that time the enrollment had grown so large the classes were moved off campus and into a nearby church. Clinics were scheduled to end at ten p.m., but they rarely ended on time. Students were so involved in discussion and prayer that they often had to be driven from the room.

Regarding manifestations in the classroom, White said that periodically someone would begin to speak loudly in tongues, at which point John would move quietly behind the person, touch him or her gently on the shoulder, and say, "Be at peace," and each time the person would become calm. A faculty member of the School of Theology who had never attended the classes warned his students against the "sensationalism" displayed in Wimber's class. But White, who had attended all of the MC510 classes, said that John was "laid back" and that at no time did he "manipulate emotions or whip up enthusiasm." Criticism of this nature, he said, was not accurate and simply "represent[ed] defectiveness on the part of the critic."[40]

Charles Kraft, Fuller professor of Anthropology and Intercultural Communications, identified himself as "one of many who have been profoundly affected through the ministry of John Wimber."[41] Kraft talked about his own transformation from being a skeptic who stereotyped healers as "nonintellectual, hyperemotional, and often just plain weird" to becoming not only a believer but an active participant in the sessions. Before joining the class, he had held Wimber in high regard, since the two had been acquainted when Wimber was still a cessationist. So, in January 1982, Kraft and his wife Meg started attending the first MC510 classes. Although he felt awkward because of his high visibility as a senior professor and his feelings of inadequacy regarding healing, he quickly became convinced that this was the direction he wanted to move in his own ministry. Kraft's greatest intellectual challenge was the "words of knowledge," but as he listened and observed, he learned that everyone could operate in the gifts and minister healing to others. He watched and learned as John used the Jesus model—teaching, and then demonstrating, and then giving students the opportunity to minister to one another as he observed and gave input. Kraft said he learned so quickly from this model that by the fourth or fifth session, John asked him to lecture on worldviews and then to share with the class the paradigm shift that he was experiencing. By the following year, 1983, Kraft had not only experienced a shift in paradigm but in practice, having launched out to teach on healing in a Sunday school class in his Pasadena Covenant Church and to pray for people, both with amazing results.[42]

Wagner said that, although he was supportive of the course, his plan had been that John would do the majority of the teaching and minister in the laboratory sessions, while he would simply be the professor of record and sit in the back of the class as an observer. He had no intention of participating. But, by the third week, things began to change. For several years, Wagner had been under treatment for high blood pressure. During one of the sessions, John asked the class if anyone needed healing. Before Wagner realized what was happening, he had his hand in the air. He was asked to sit on a stool while John prayed for him, with the class watching. A few days later, Wagner's physician confirmed his healing. This healing was the final event that transformed Wagner from being a skeptic spectator to a healing participant.

In the summer of 1982, after the first Signs and Wonder's course, Wagner decided to start a Sunday school class, which he called *120 Fellowship*, in his five-thousand-member Lake Avenue Congregational Church pastored by Paul Cedar. His goal was to put into practice in his home church what Wimber was teaching in the classroom at Fuller.

Wagner started taking his Sunday school class to visit Wimber's Anaheim Vineyard on Sunday nights, where they would get charged up, and then go back to their home church and "discharge." They simply started doing what they were learning from John and the Vineyard Church, and as a result, Wagner's *120 Fellowship* Sunday school class started praying for the sick with remarkable results. Wagner said that at this point, he had made the transition from theoretician to practitioner. "We had to be careful," Wagner said, "because our church was so large that we had a Sunday School class for disciples of John MacArthur [who taught that the gifts of the Spirit were not functioning in the church today] and here we were disciples of John Wimber, but Cedar knew how to pastor both of us." Wagner continued, "I was very verbal about the fact that we were not charismatic. The pastor and I agreed that we would only pray in tongues quietly as we prayed for people, but corporate messages in tongues was not allowed. We made all kinds of adjustments so as not to split the church." He believed that was what separated his group from the charismatics, who had a track record of splitting churches.[43] Wagner refused to be labeled a charismatic, preferring to be called a third waver.

The first time Wagner used the term "third wave" was when he was being interviewed by Kevin Perrotta of *Pastoral Renewal* magazine in 1983. In the interview, Wagner explained how the Pentecostal Movement was the first wave of the outpouring of the Holy Spirit, at the turn of the twentieth century, and the second wave was associated with the charismatic movement that began in 1960 with Dennis Bennett, an Episcopal priest who announced that he had spoken in tongues. The third wave, Wagner explained, was comprised of evangelicals from Reformed churches with dispensational backgrounds who had experienced a paradigm shift, through exposure to signs and wonders, and had come to believe the gifts of the Spirit were still active in the church today. Perrotta picked up on Wagner's terminology and used it as the title for his article. Wagner continued using this terminology to refer to Wimber and his signs-and-wonders ministry until "third wave" became common currency.[44]

Reflecting on that period, Wagner said that Wimber impacted his life by introducing him to the person and work of the Holy Spirit. "I always believed in the Holy Spirit and the Apostles' Creed," Wagner said, "but I had never experienced any work of the Spirit until Wimber came along. It was John who took me from program evangelism to power evangelism. He took me through that paradigm shift." He also believed this was the same contribution John made to the body of Christ at large.

Wagner recognized Wimber as a practitioner—as someone who could show in practical ways how to get in touch with the person and work of the Holy Spirit. He said that John introduced signs and wonders and demonic deliverance to the body of Christ in a way that was different from Pentecostals and charismatics. According to Wagner, the goal was to remove as many roadblocks as possible, and one of the main points of contention for evangelicals was the use of tongues. "John and I both spoke in tongues," Wagner said, "but we would not allow public tongues in the classroom. People could pray in tongues, but not public tongues." This made it more acceptable for the evangelicals.[45]

Criticism Begins to Surface

While MC510 Signs, Wonders, and Church Growth became Fuller's most popular class, it also became the most controversial. As John's ministry and popularity increased, so did the voices of both his advocates and his critics. After a few years, latent questions began to surface. First, the seminary began receiving phone calls from pastors whose student interns had attended the class and were being "indiscreet or rash" in applying what they had learned—or thought they had learned—in the course. Faculty also received calls from students and family members disillusioned when power healings had not materialized after prayer. Still others complained of suffering "backlash" from the demonic when they attempted exorcisms.

Second, while John was teaching the course, he was also conducting national and international conferences using the same material. As a result, many saw his teaching and ministry outside the classroom as being closely linked to the seminary. In essence, many came to believe he was Fuller's representative on the road, which created internal and external problems for the school.

Finally, people began to question the wisdom of conducting healing sessions in an academic setting. Many believed that while praying for healing was appropriate in the church setting, it did not belong in the classroom. Fuller's president, Allan Hubbard, said that in their desire to meet the needs of their students in the Department of World Mission—to provide them with the experience of working with the Holy Spirit and equip them for ministry—they actually "short-circuited the signals of caution." In other words, he said, "their engineering outran their science."[46]

In the spring of 1985, the Theology school voted to deny theology students credit for the MC510 course. In September of that same year, *Charisma* magazine featured Wimber and the course as its cover story.[47] Around the time of its publication, Hubbard organized a student-faculty task force to review concerns, which continued to cause division among the faculty. By December the School of World Mission offered a revised course hoping the questions and concerns raised by the School of Theology would be adequately addressed. Then in March of 1986, the School of World Mission faculty, who had approved the course four years prior, reluctantly voted to call a moratorium on the course until it could be further reviewed by the faculty of all three Schools of Theology, Psychology, and World Mission.[48] Three students from the task force responded quickly to the cancelation, organizing a rally that attracted about 120 students—all of whom signed a petition in support of the course. The petition, along with a letter, was sent to Larry DenBesten, Fuller's new provost, requesting that the course be reinstated for the fall semester, provided that the School of Theology approve revision of the syllabus.[49]

Polarization had set in between the School of Theology and the School of World Mission, and reports emerged that the course had been canceled in order to preserve unity in the seminary.[50] Many of Wimber's own supporters believed they could win the debate but felt the price was too high in terms of lost camaraderie and unity among the teaching staff.[51]

A Task Force Is Commissioned

In March 1986, DenBesten appointed a task force to address the questions and concerns being raised about the class. Lewis B. Smedes, professor of

Theology and Ethics, was the leader of the group.[52] The committee consisted of eleven other professors.[53]

DenBesten was strongly opposed to charismatic-type ministry, and he appointed professors with the same theological perspective. Consequently, Wagner said he was the only person on the committee to defend Wimber's ministry. He went on to say he was particularly upset when DenBesten bypassed Chuck Kraft, who had attended Wimber's classes, and instead chose Paul Hiebert, another anthropologist who had always kept the MC510 at arm's length. Wagner said that for twelve weeks it was eleven against one—and it was a miserable ordeal.[54]

The task force was to evaluate the biblical, theological, scientific, and pastoral implications of the concerns being raised and present their findings in the fall of 1986. Their final document was published in book form under the title *Ministry and the Miraculous: A Case Study at Fuller Theological Seminary*. They had hoped the book would update the public and explain their decision and present their pastoral and theological concerns regarding the course[55]; however, because MC510 had become such a popular course, through both the religious and secular media, hundreds of questions poured into Fuller regarding the moratorium.

Committee Findings and Conclusion

By the fall of 1986, the twelve faculty members had completed their assignment and submitted their report. Russell Spittler, senior professor of New Testament at Fuller, recalled there being a great deal of respect among the members of the committee as they met and worked through the issues.[56]

The purpose of the committee's discussions, according to the report, was not to evaluate or call into question either the presence of signs, wonders, and healing in church history or the special needs of missionaries. Rather, the purpose was to reflect upon the place and appropriateness of such phenomena in a seminary curriculum as it related to the education of ministers, missionaries, and psychologists. (For an overview of the seven chapters of the committee's report, see appendix E.)

Five months after Fuller canceled the class, *Christianity Today* carried a three-part feature story on Wimber. One article, "Cause for Concern," listed five issues that Fuller's Theology Department had with Wimber's teaching.

First, they believed he had overemphasized the miraculous and healing and had created an unbiblical dualism. Second, they suggested that he had claimed signs and wonders were "the norm" for the church and thus seemed to imply that those who did not have such experiences were not doing the work of God. Third, they believed his deliverance ministry bordered on Christian magic. Fourth, they believed there was too much emphasis on experience while ethical issues were marginalized. And finally, there was pastoral concern for those who were not healed.[57]

Some said that Fuller had gone charismatic, but as Wagner pointed out, "Those who [made] that statement [were] not aware that MC510 was only one course of many hundred taught there, or that the students who took it [were] only a handful among the some twenty-eight hundred enrolled in its three schools. They also [did] not realize that a number of respected Fuller faculty members were not altogether happy that the course was being taught. These professors disagree with a theology which argues that signs, wonders, and miracles as seen in the ministry of Jesus and the apostles are to be expected in today's church."[58]

Faculty members in the School of World Mission were more supportive of Wimber than those in the School of Theology. For example, Kraft stated that John's teaching had changed his entire life. Kraft's *Christianity with Power*, published in 1989, reflected Wimber' influence.[59] Regarding Fuller's rejection of MC510, Kraft stated,

> The rub comes if you begin to practice ministering in power as Jesus did. Those among my academic colleagues who objected to our Signs and Wonders course, for example, made it clear that they would not complain much if we simply offered a course that discussed healing ministries. It is when we insist on practicing what we preach that they get upset. Westerners, especially academics, are really typically a good bit more open to 'talking about' something than to 'doing the works.'[60]

When all was said and done, the committee's final decision was that teaching belongs in the classroom and practice belongs in the local church.[61] The faculty decided the course should be reorganized and offered again as MC550 with Kraft and Wagner teaching the class, but Wimber would no longer be allowed to participate.[62] The reason he was not permitted to teach the course he birthed was never specifically stated; however, from faculty comments, it appeared to be a combination of Wimber's lack of academic credentials, the course's highly controversial content, and the popularity of Wimber's ministry outside Fuller.[63] After the MC510 class was cancelled, one clinic session was later held at the Anaheim Vineyard church, but John was not invited to teach the material he had personally developed.

Ken Blue, Wimber's teaching assistant during the last two years of MC510, offered a fourth possible reason. He said it was sheer jealousy on the part of the Fuller faculty, which created the rub that eventually caused the demise of MC510. For example, John's class was packed with nearly three hundred students and had standing room only, with a waiting list of students wanting to enroll. Meanwhile, Fuller professor Colin Brown had only six students signed up for his Patristics class. The popularity of the class, exacerbated by the fact that John did not hold a terminal degree, in Blue's opinion, was the truthful reason Wimber was removed from his teaching post at Fuller.[64]

The Launching of His Book Ministry

The material Wimber developed for his MC510 class was, however, used to launch his book ministry. The syllabus and class content were condensed into the book *Power Evangelism,* which he co-authored with Kevin Springer in 1986. How could Wimber have known at the time that, twenty years later, *Christianity Today* would publish a list of the "Top 50 Books that Have Shaped Evangelicals." A distinguished panel of 62 editors and authors listed Wimber's *Power Evangelism* as the twelfth most influential book of the twentieth century, just behind Richard Foster's *Celebration of Disciplines* and just ahead of Josh McDowell's *Evidence that Demands a Verdict.*[65]

In 1987, Wimber and Springer co-authored a second book, *Power Healing,* which is laced with Wimber's personal theology and testimony of how he evolved from being an "unlikely healer" to believing that healing is part of the normal Christian life.[66] It was in this book he affirmed that healing was *through* the atonement, and involves the whole person, including physical healing, inner healing (i.e., curing the negative effects of the past), healing of demonization and mental illness (not only in unbelievers but also in Christians), and healing of the dead or dying.[67] *Power Points: Your Action Plan to Hear God's Voice, Believe God's Word, Seek the Father, Submit to Christ, Take Up the Cross, Depend on the Holy Spirit, Fulfill the Great Commission,* released in 1991, was the third and final volume of his power trilogy.[68] Like all of Wimber's books, *Power Points* provides candid and transparent testimonies of his own life and struggle as well as an overview of his practical, hands-on theology. Wimber's theology, which will be covered in the following chapter, differentiated him and put him at odds with many traditional Pentecostals who believed healing is *in* the atonement, that Christians cannot be demonized, and who also have a narrow view on inner healing. But more importantly, his signs and wonders ministry put him at odds with outspoken Evangelical dispensational cessationists—those who believed that the gifts of the Spirit were no longer operational in the church today and had ceased with the last apostles. And it was this latter group, that soon became his most vicious critics.

Healing in the Middle of His Pain

When Fuller announced the cancellation of the MC510 course in March 1986, John was devastated. Three months later, he suffered his first heart attack.[69] Bill Jackson said he believed John just "wanted a place at the evangelical table for the Vineyard," and when Fuller rejected his ministry, a wound was inflicted in his heart that he never got over.[70] This was just the beginning of his heartbreak. For the remainder of his life, he would be afflicted with physical illness, and his critics would dog him unmercifully.

But there was also a period of sweet respite in the middle of John's pain. In October of 1987, over seven thousand charismatic leaders from forty denominations, including Roman Catholic, Baptist, Methodist, Assemblies of God, Church of God in Christ, Presbyterian, and others, gathered in the Louisiana Superdome in New Orleans for the Leader's Congress on the Holy Spirit and World Evangelization. Historian and chairman of the congress, Vinson Synan, told *Charisma*, "We want to give visibility and definition to the charismatic and Pentecostal movements," and "we also want to gather first as leaders to wait upon and hear the Lord."[71] Prominent leaders who were present included Paul Yonggi Cho, the pastor of the largest church in the world, located in South Korea; Jane Hansen of Women's Aglow; Ithiel Clemmons of the Church of God in Christ; and Everett Fullman of the Episcopal Church. In addition, Oral Roberts; Demos Shakarian, president of the Full Gospel Businessmen's Fellowship; Ecumenical leader David du Plessis; and Mennonite renewal leader Nelson Litwiller were honored for their contributions in a special presentation.

The theme of the conference was world evangelism, which speakers affirmed would be accomplished through "the miraculous gifts of the Holy

Spirit—healing, prophecy, speaking in tongues, words of knowledge—collectively known as 'signs and wonders.'"[72] Steve Lawson of *Charisma* wrote, "It was made clear that this evangelism would not rely upon methods and strategies calculated by man, but rather it would come through signs and wonders. To that end, John Wimber was one of the major speakers."[73] Julia Duin of *Christianity Today* wrote, "Without a doubt, the pulse of the conference was John Wimber . . . though recovering from an angina attack he suffered in June, Wimber was at center stage for much of the meetings."[74] Wimber spoke at the Thursday night leaders' session, led three afternoon workshops on signs and wonders, and was one of the speakers at the Saturday night main event, which attracted eleven thousand people.[75]

Following the event, Wimber said he felt vindicated by the fact that his often-criticized signs-and-wonders message had so thoroughly permeated the charismatic renewal. "This conference has been an affirmation for me," he said, "There's a sense that there's now a credibility to what I've been saying."[76]

[1] Wagner, "MC520: Genesis of a Concept," 41–2. In 1982, *Christian Life Magazine* published a complete issue about the MC510 course at Fuller. *Christian Life Missions* later reprinted this publication in conjunction with Wagner under the title *Signs and Wonders Today*. The magazine published in book form was expanded and organized into thirteen sessions with study questions and material added at the end of each session. In 1987, Wagner edited the same material, added three new chapters, and published it through Creation House as a book. It had the same title, but the magazine pictures and study materials were omitted.

[2] Wagner, "God Wasn't Pulling My Leg," 46.

[3] Wagner, *How to Have a Healing Ministry without Making Your Church Sick* (Ventura, CA: Regal Books, 1990), 48. Also Springer, "Applying the Gifts," 26.

[4] Wagner, "God Wasn't Pulling My Leg," 49.

[5] Wagner, "God Wasn't Pulling My Leg," 50.

[6] Wagner, "Signs and Wonders Today," 43.

[7] Wagner, "God Wasn't Pulling My Leg," 51; Wagner, *Signs and Wonders Today*, 43.

[8] Wagner, "Signs and Wonders Today," 44.

[9] "History," Fuller Seminary website, http://www.fuller.edu/about-fuller/mission-and-history/history.aspx. Accessed July 27, 2010.

[10] Wagner, "Signs and Wonders Today," 5, 7, 9.

[11] C. Peter Wagner, "MC510: Signs, Wonders and Church Growth," *Christian Life* 44, no. 6 (October 1982): 48.

[12] Charles Kraft, "Shifting Worldviews, Shifting Attitudes," in *Power Encounters among Christians in the Western World*, ed. Kevin Springer (San Francisco: Harper & Row, 1988), 60.

[13] David Allen Hubbard, Foreword to *Ministry and the Miraculous: A Case Study at Fuller Theological Seminary* ed. Lewis B. Smedes (Pasadena, CA: Fuller Theological Seminary, 1987), 6.

[14] Robert Walker, ed. "Signs and Wonders Today," *Christian Life Magazine* (Wheaton, IL: Christian Life Missions, 1982), 8. These articles were so popular, the magazine sold out and the articles were reprinted in book form, also with the title *Signs and Wonder Today,* and published by *Christian Life Magazine*.

[15] Hubbard, Foreword, 6.

[16] Walker, ed., preface to *Signs and Wonders Today*, 6.

[17] Hubbard, Foreword, 6.

[18] Wimber, *MC510*, cassette tape 2A.

[19] Chandler, "Fuller Seminary Cancels Course on Signs and Wonders," 48.

[20] Wagner, *Third Wave of the Holy Spirit*, 25.

[21] Hubbard, Foreword, 6.

[22] Wimber, *MC510*, cassette tape 1A.

[23] Wimber, *MC510*, cassette tape 1A.

[24] John Wimber, "Signs and Wonders Conference," http://www.youtube.com/watch?v=aFzHHfwX7Xc.

[25] John Wimber, *MC510 Syllabus: Signs and Wonders and Church Growth* (Placentia, CA: Vineyard Ministries International, 1984), John Wimber Special Collections, Regent University Library, Virginia Beach, Virginia. This is a copy of the syllabus Wimber used for his MC510 class, which was later reprinted and used in his Signs and Wonder's conferences. In the original, the pages are not numbered sequentially. For a more complete overview of the syllabus content, see appendix B.

[26] Wimber, *MC510 Syllabus*, 11.

[27] Wimber, *MC510 Syllabus*, 11.

[28] Wimber, *MC510 Syllabus*, 22. Signs and Wonders is italicized throughout the original text.

[29] Wimber, *MC510 Syllabus,* 46. "Gracelets" was a term coined by Russell Spittler, professor in the Fuller School of Theology.

[30] Wimber, *MC510 Syllabus*, 131.
[31] Wimber, *MC510 Syllabus*, 131.
[32] Wimber, *MC510 Syllabus*, 186.
[33] John Wimber, *MC510 Signs and Wonders and Church Growth*, cassette tape 16. John Wimber Special Collections, Regent University Library, Virginia Beach, Virginia. Also, C. Peter Wagner, *Third Wave of the Holy Spirit*, 27.
[34] Karen Ball, "The Student's View," *Christian Life* 44, no. 6 (October 1982): 70.
[35] Wimber, *MC510*, cassette tape 1A.
[36] See Appendix C for the Five-Step Prayer Model.
[37] Wimber, *MC510*, cassette tape.
[38] Ball, "The Student's View," 71.
[39] Ball, "The Student's View," 75.
[40] John White, "MC510: A Look Inside, Part I and Part II," *First Fruits*, July/August, 7–10, and September/October 1985, 23–6.
[41] Kraft, "Shifting Worldviews," 67.
[42] Kraft, "Shifting Worldviews," 60.
[43] Telephone interview by author with C. Peter Wagner, August 10, 2011.
[44] Wagner, "God Wasn't Pulling My Leg," 54. Also, C. Peter Wagner, "Third Wave," in *NIDPCM*, 1141. Wagner, *How to Have a Healing Ministry*, 16–7.
[45] Interview by author with C. Peter Wagner.
[46] Hubbard, Foreword, 7.
[47] Springer, "Applying the Gifts to Everyday Life," 26–34; Wimber and Springer, "John Wimber Calls It Power Evangelism," 35–8; also Lawson, "The Vineyard: Where Spiritual Gifts Blossom," 39.
[48] Hubbard, Foreword, 7; Chandler, "Fuller Seminary Cancels Course on Signs and Wonders," 48.
[49] Chandler, "Fuller Seminary Cancels Course on Signs and Wonders," 48.
[50] Chandler, "Fuller Seminary Cancels Course on Signs and Wonders," 48.
[51] Humphrey Babbage, *Reflections on the Ministry of John Wimber and His Team in New Zealand*, A Discussion Paper (Wellington, NZ: Scripture Union, 1986), 4.
[52] The previous provost, Glen Backer, died suddenly of a heart attack in May 1984, and the position remained empty until Lawrence DenBesten took the post in January 1986. It was not until the Spring of 1986 that DenBesten was able to step in and provide the needed leadership for the MC510 controversy.
[53] Members included James E. Bradley, associate professor of Church History, Foursquare; Colin Brown, professor of Systematic Theology, Episcopal; Arthur Glasser, dean emeritus of the School of World Mission and senior professor of Theology and East Asian Studies, Reformed Presbyterian; Roberta Hestenes, associate professor of Christian Formation and Discipleship, Presbyterian Church U.S.A.; Donald Hagner, professor of New Testament, Presbyterian Church, U.S.A.; Paul Hiebert, professor of Anthropology and South Asian Studies, Mennonite Brethren Church in North America; H. Newton Malony, professor of Psychology, United Methodist; Samuel Southard, professor of Pastoral Theology, Southern Baptist; Hendrika Vande Kemp, associate professor of Psychology, Presbyterian Church U.S.A.; and C. Peter Wagner and Donald A. McGavran, professors of Church Growth, Conservative Congregational Christian Conference (Hubbard, foreword, 9–10).
[54] C. Peter Wagner, *Wrestling with Alligators, Prophets and Theologians: Lessons from a Lifetime in the Church—A Memoir* (Ventura, CA: Regal, 2010), 148.
[55] Hubbard, Foreword, 7–8.
[56] Interview by the author with Russell Spittler on February 8, 2010, in Santa Ana, California.
[57] Ben Patterson, "Cause for Concern," *Christianity Today*, August 1986, 20.
[58] Wagner, *Third Wave of the Holy Spirit*, 26.
[59] Chandler, "Fuller Seminary Cancels Course on Signs and Wonders," 48; Kraft,

Christianity with Power.
60 Kraft, *Christianity with Power*, 94.
61 Smedes, ed., *Ministry and the Miraculous*, 55–8.
62 Chandler, "Fuller Seminary Cancels Course on Signs and Wonders." 49.
63 Jackson, *Quest for the Radical Middle*, 124.
64 Telephone interview by the author with Ken Blue, September 5, 2010. Ken was a doctor of ministry student at Fuller and became Wimber's personal teaching assistant. They became good friends after Blue graduated from Fuller and Blue was sent out from Vineyard to teach intensives. He taught the MC510 material so many times, he eventually authored the book *Authority to Heal,* which reflects Wimber's early teaching.
65 https://www.librarything.com/bookaward/Christianity+Today%27s+Top+50+Books+That+Have+Shaped+Evangelicals (accessed July 13, 2020).
66 Wimber and Springer, *Power Healing*, 23.
67 Wimber and Springer, *Power Healing*, 61–2.
68 Wimber and Springer, *Power Points*.
69 Carol Wimber, *John Wimber*, 167, 168, 177.
70 Interview by the author with Bill Jackson, August 9, 2011.
71 Steve Lawson, "Leaders Unite in New Orleans," *Charisma,* December 1986, 58.
72 Julia Duin, "Signs and Wonders in New Orleans," *Christianity Today,* November 21, 1986, 26.
73 Lawson, "Leaders Unite in New Orleans," 59.
74 Duin, "Signs and Wonders in New Orleans," 26.
75 Lawson, "Leaders Unite in New Orleans," 59.
76 Duin, "Signs and Wonders in New Orleans," 59.

Chapter 5

A Practical Theology

While a complete exposition of Wimber's theology is beyond the scope of this work, this chapter will attempt to provide a overview of some the most significant aspects of his teaching and will draw heavily upon his three power books: *Power Evangelism*, *Power Healing*, and *Power Points*.

Third Wave

As noted earlier, church historian Vinson Synan said the Third Wave of the Spirit had its origin in Wimber's class at Fuller and credits C. Peter Wagner with coining the term "third wave."[1] Wagner first used the term when he was interviewed by Kevin Perrotta of *Pastoral Renewal Magazine* in 1983.[2] In the interview, Perrotta asked Wagner to expound on what was happening in the early 1980s among evangelicals experiencing spiritual power with signs and wonders. Perrotta also asked whether this was something new. Wagner said what was happening among evangelicals was a "third wave of the Spirit" and spoke of the previous two waves being the Pentecostal and charismatic movements respectively. Perrotta subsequently used Wagner's phrase in the title of the article, which was later reprinted around the world.[3] The term "third wave" eventually became the term for the renewal movement that had its origin with Wimber's signs and wonders teaching.

The first wave of the Spirit is identified as the classic or modern Pentecostal movement that began at the turn of twentieth century. It traditionally traces its origin to Charles Parham's Bethel Bible College in Topeka, Kansas, where one of Parham's students was filled with the Holy Spirit and began speaking in tongues. Parham quickly formulated the doctrine that tongues was the "Bible evidence" of baptism in the Holy Spirit, based on accounts in the book of Acts. Parham's experiential pneumatology spread and soon resulted in an outpouring of the Spirit in Los Angeles known as the Azusa Street Revival of 1906, under the leadership of William Seymour, one of Parham's former students.[4] While Pentecostals are Bible-believing evangelicals in their doctrine, what separates them from other conservative, mainline evangelicals is their distinctive doctrine that tongues is the initial physical evidence of the baptism of the Holy Spirit, which they identify as a second and subsequent experience following the believer's new birth.

The second wave of the Spirit was the charismatic movement. The charismatics trace their roots to Dennis Bennett, an Episcopal priest in Van Nuys, California, who announced to his congregation in 1960 that he had been filled with the Holy Spirit and had spoken in tongues. Bennett was the first well-known mainline evangelical to publicly embrace the "initial evidence" of Holy Spirit baptism and remain within his denomination.[5] Charismatics are those who experience the baptism of the Holy Spirit and speaking in tongues, but normally choose to remain within their denomination with a desire to bring renewal to their own people. The Catholic charismatic movement also comes under this umbrella.[6]

The third wave of the Spirit, also known as the neo-charismatics, is associated with Wimber and the Vineyard movement. According to David Barrett and Todd Johnson's global statistics, those involved in the Third Wave movement outnumbered the combined total of Pentecostals and charismatics by over 53 million in the year 2000, with an expected growth increase exceeding 87 million above those involved in the other two movements by the year 2025.[7]

Wimber's understanding of the baptism of the Holy Spirit differs somewhat from both the first and second waves of the Spirit. Wimber was a traditional evangelical who posited that a believer receives the fullness of the Holy Spirit at the time of conversion, which he calls the "consummate Christian experience."[8] For him, when a person is born again, they received the Holy Spirit; therefore, there is no need for a subsequent baptism. However, unlike traditional evangelicals, he also believed that at some point in the believer's life, whether at the time of conversion or sometime later, the gifts of the Spirit need to be activated. Typically, when someone asked him to pray for them to be "filled with the Spirit," he would ask if they were born again, and if the answer was affirmative, he would lay hands on them and say, "speak in tongues or prophesy," and they would. From his perspective, he was simply activating what the Spirit had already given them.[9] He believed there was no need to develop a theology for an additional baptism when, in fact, everything was already included in the first experience. He believed that if the gospel was preached in a way as to expect the recipients to receive everything in one experience, believers would not only receive regeneration at the time of conversion but would also, simultaneously, experience the vitality of empowerment as promised in Acts 1:8.[10]

Wimber acknowledged that there were people—and he was one of them—who testified to the reality of a second experience. How, then, could he square this with his evangelical perspective that a person receives the fullness of the Spirit at conversion? He believed that while there is one filling at the time of conversion, there might, and even should, be many "fillings" throughout a person's life. In his understanding, once a person received the Holy Spirit at conversion, they gained access to all the gifts needed to advance the kingdom of God—they just simply need to be activated in a believer's life by faith.[11]

Wimber held that the Holy Spirit is the gift given to the church, and the gifts of the Spirit are what he called "gracelets," but these gifts, or gracelets, should not be confused with the gift of the Holy Spirit.[12] Once the gifts of the Spirit are released, they are permanent, and people normally mature and grow in their effectiveness at exercising these spiritual gifts in ministry.[13] His perspective was that everyone should expect to operate in any and all of the gifts of the Spirit, depending on the need or situation encountered while ministering; he held that there were also times, however, when a person's gifts could constitute a "job description."[14] In other words, when a person was consistently and effectively used in practicing a gift, it could represent a ministry gift, such as the ministry of healing.

In Wimber's understanding, one baptism at conversion with many subsequent fillings brought into focus the thoughts of both Luke and Paul and also bridged Pentecostal and evangelical theology. This unique perspective of Holy Spirit baptism—or "fillings," as was Wimber's preferred terminology—became the distinctive understanding of the emerging Third Wave movement.[15] Those who study Wimber know he was flexible on this issue. From his reading of Paul and Luke, he realized they used the terms "baptism" and "fillings" differently as it related to the Holy Spirit; therefore, he found it difficult to be "too precise" or dogmatic on this issue.[16] For example, although he taught the traditional evangelical experience outlined above, he also testified to the fact that, at one point in his life, someone had laid hands on him and he was "baptized with the Spirit"—and that this was, for him, a separate event from conversion.[17]

The Paradigm Shift

As we discovered in chapter two, when John became a Christian, he was immediately introduced to Gunner Payne, who taught him a lay-down-your-life type of Christianity and trained him to be an avid and effective soul-winner. From the outset of his Christian walk, he was a receptive vessel to the supernatural, speaking in tongues and receiving words of knowledge that enabled him to bring people quickly to salvation. What he saw Jesus doing in the Bible, he assumed Christians were supposed to do today. But a few years into his Christian experience, things changed. His Quaker church recognized the call of God on his life and sent him off to an evangelical Bible school to be trained for ministry. Through his education and ministry training, he was indoctrinated out of his supernatural worldview and belief in biblical experiences and into the doctrines of cessationism and dispensationalism, both which promote a belief that the gifts of the Spirit and the supernatural ministry of Jesus ceased with the death of the apostles, the canonization of Scripture, and the establishment of the church.

Then a few years later, after John experienced two consecutive spiritual and emotional burnouts in ministry, one as a pastor and the second as a church growth consultant, God promised to show him how to do ministry God's way. Several things happened that served to reshape his spiritual worldview. Carol had a power encounter in her sleep, where she was baptized in the Spirit and spoke in tongues. The total transformation in her life was a dramatic witness that caused John to consider his current outlook on spiritual issues. At the same time, he was exposed to Wagner and other professors in the School of World Mission at Fuller, who had been missionaries in developing countries. They shared testimonies of how the power of the Holy Spirit, manifested through miraculous healings and the expulsion of demons, had resulted in mass conversions and rapid church growth. These credible witnesses, along with similar testimonies of Fuller students from these nations, created a paradigm shift that caused him to seriously question his cessationist perspective. He felt compelled to reinvestigate the Scriptures, especially the accounts of Jesus in the Gospels. What he discovered ultimately became his ministry model and life message.

Jesus: The Gospels and the Kingdom

One of Wimber's greatest contributions may have been to bring the church back to the Gospels and the ministry of Jesus. Historically, Pentecostals and charismatics tend to derive their distinctive doctrine of baptism in the Holy Spirit from the book of Acts. Conservative evangelicals, on the other hand, have traditionally focused on the writings of Paul and the epistles. Wimber challenged both Pentecostals and contemporary evangelicals to reinvestigate Jesus and the purpose of his supernatural ministry.

For evangelicals, the miraculous signs-and-wonders ministry of Jesus was to validate his deity; therefore, once he was recognized as the Messiah and the church was established, miracles were no longer needed. This is the view of traditional dispensational cessationists. Wimber believed that while Jesus was God incarnate, he laid aside his divine attributes through the incarnation and ministered as a man empowered by the Holy Spirit, and in so doing, he became a ministry model for his followers. Wimber believed that Jesus, in his humanity, performed supernatural miracles through the power of the Holy Spirit and that believers, likewise, are empowered by the Holy Spirit to do the same works of Jesus today.[18]

As such, Wimber saw the Bible as a textbook—a manual for ministry. And he discovered in the Gospels that Jesus consistently used a twofold approach to ministry. He would first proclaim the gospel and then demonstrate the power of the Holy Spirit through signs, wonders, and miracles, such as healing the sick, casting out demons, raising the dead, and taking authority over nature.

Just as Jesus empowered and commissioned the twelve and then the seventy to preach the good news and demonstrate the presence of the kingdom with signs and wonders in his name, he calls believers today and commissions them with the power and authority to do the same. "The church," Wimber contended, "is the instrument of the kingdom. As disciples, we are called to proclaim and demonstrate the kingdom of God, which includes healing the sick and casting out demons. As Christ's instruments, we war on satanic strongholds, replacing their dominion with the kingdom of God."[19] In essence, Wimber felt Jesus was *the* ministry model for the body of Christ today and that believers were to continue "doing the stuff" that Jesus did.

Wimber also saw in the ministry of Jesus the challenge for contemporary believers to get out of the church and into the streets to minister to the lost and hurting. One of his catch phrases was, "The meat is in the street." It became his ministry goal to train and equip the body of Christ to operate naturally in the supernatural gifts of the Spirit in the marketplace and streets, among people in need. He challenged the church to get out of their prayer huddles and use the gifts of the Spirit in the marketplace because it was there that the meat of ministry happened.

The Influence of George Eldon Ladd

With this biblical blueprint in place, he also needed a theological framework that would integrate it all. He found that model in George Eldon Ladd.[20] Ladd was a Baptist minister and professor of New Testament and theology who came to Fuller Theological Seminary in its fourth year of existence. He is known for his inaugurated post-tribulation eschatology and his work on the kingdom of God, which became very popular during the 1950s.[21] Though Ladd had already retired from Fuller when Wimber was there, John was profoundly impacted by Ladd's writings, especially his books *Jesus and the Kingdom* and *The Gospel and the Kingdom*.

Wimber discovered Ladd's texts in 1974, and with them, the ministry and message of Jesus seemed to fall into place. Regarding Ladd's influence, Wimber said,

> As I read George Ladd's books and reread the Gospels, I realized that at the very heart of the gospel lies the kingdom of God and that power for effective evangelism and discipleship relates directly to our understanding and experiencing the Kingdom today. This revelation remains for me the most significant spiritual experience since my conversion in 1963.[22]

As he read the Gospels, he saw a direct correlation between Jesus preaching the gospel of the kingdom and healing the sick.[23] Jesus was the "presence of the Kingdom, the Anointed One sent from his heavenly Father," and he brought the rule and reign of God to earth.[24] At the outset of Jesus's ministry, he proclaimed "the Kingdom is near" and called for action—"repent and believe." Every miraculous act was proof that the kingdom had come and people had to decide to accept or reject it.[25]

As proof of Jesus's power and authority, he set about proclaiming and demonstrating the kingdom by casting out demons, healing the sick, taking authority over nature, and raising the dead.[26] He said, "If I drive out demons by the finger of God then the kingdom of God has come to you."[27] In other words, healings and exorcisms were visible signs that the kingdom had arrived. This became Wimber's key for power evangelism.[28]

Wimber saw that when Jesus preached the good news to the poor, healed sick bodies and emotions, freed people from demonic forces, and brought wholeness to the broken, thus liberating people from the clutches of Satan, he was actually expanding the kingdom of God and bringing people into a living and loving relationship with the Father.[29] He understood that through Christ's death and resurrection, he had defeated Satan and established absolute rule and authority over the powers of darkness; the future age had invaded the present age of Satan's kingdom.[30]

He also understood through Ladd that, while Jesus came to inaugurate the kingdom of God, evil in this present age would not be totally eradicated from the world until Christ's second coming, when Satan would be totally destroyed and removed from this earth. Until that time, Satan still reigns as "prince of the world" and "the ruler of the kingdom of the air, the spirit who is now at work in those who are disobedient."[31] Christians today live "in the presence of the future," between the "already and not yet" of the kingdom.[32] The mission of Jesus was to proclaim the rule and reign of the kingdom of God and demonstrate its power and authority over the works of Satan. Jesus saw the souls of humanity as the battleground in which the conflict between the opposing forces raged.[33] Wimber wrote,

> Paul makes much of the fact that Christ is seated 'at his [the Father's] right hand in the heavenly realms, far above all rule and authority, power and dominion, and every title that can be given, not only in the present age but also in the one to come.' (Eph 1:20-21). Christ is now in a place of absolute authority over all other authorities; he is 'the Holy Ruler, the King of kings and Lord of lords.' (1 Tim 6:15). Yes—this is the tension all Christians feel—evil has not been eradicated.[34]

To explain this tension between Jesus's death and resurrection and his second coming or *Parousia*, Wimber found an appropriate analogy in the book *Christ and Time* by Lutheran theologian Oscar Cullman, who compares the present church to that of the allies in World War II after D-day.

Although the Allies had won the victory on June 6, 1944, when they successfully invaded Nazi-occupied Europe on the Normandy beaches, it took another eleven months, until May 8, 1945, for the war to finally end. During these eleven months, some of the bloodiest battles were fought, resulting in thousands of American casualties.[35] Wimber said, "So it is with Jesus; our D-day is Easter Sunday, and our V-day is the second coming. Between the two, the war wages."[36] In this present age, the kingdom of God and the kingdom of Satan are at war, and when a person is healed or delivered of a demon, the powers of darkness are defeated and the kingdom is advanced.[37]

In his earthly ministry, Jesus proved his authority by casting out demons, healing diseases, taking authority over nature, and raising the dead. He then trained and equipped his disciples, giving them power and authority to do the same.[38] The signs and wonders Jesus performed were not just proof that he was the Son of God but that he had brought the presence of the kingdom into the present age.

Whereas, at one time, Wimber believed that the age of miracles had ceased, he came to believe that this aspect of Jesus's ministry remained the commission for the church today. This change came, in part, after a review of church history, where he realized that in every century, there were reliable reports of healing and miracles.[39] He thus came to believe that demonstrating the kingdom through healing and signs and wonders was to be as much a part of the church today as the proclamation of the gospel of salvation. For him, the gifts of the Spirit were power tools God gives the church to be more effective soul-winners. When Jesus had proclaimed and demonstrated the good news of the kingdom, Satan's kingdom had suffered defeat; therefore, it was the responsibility of every believer in the church today to do the works of Jesus and carry on his ministry until he returns.[40] Following his resurrection, Jesus commissioned his followers to continue his work in His name. Wimber realized the key to accomplishing this was the outpouring and empowerment of the Holy Spirit as seen on the day of Pentecost in Acts 2.

Already-and-Not-Yet Eschatology

Another influence Ladd had on Wimber was his inaugurated eschatology or understanding of the already-and-not-yet aspect of the kingdom. It was through Ladd that he was able to reject evangelical dispensationalism, a concept formed by John Nelson Darby, a Plymouth Brethren Bible teacher in the 1800s, whose teaching was advanced through the Scofield Reference Bible. Dispensationalism divides the way God works through church history into different dispensations, with the present dispensation being the existing church age, which looks forward to a pretribulation rapture and embraces a cessationist view of the gifts of the Spirit or charismata.[41]

Wimber also rejected the restorational eschatology of the Pentecostals, which was a modified form of evangelical dispensationalism. This view traditionally held—though many recent scholars now understand it otherwise—that the gifts of the Spirit died out in early church history but were suddenly restored with the outpouring of the Holy Spirit at the turn of the twentieth century. Early Pentecostals, therefore, saw themselves as a restoration movement, in which God restored to the church what had been lost through indifference or disuse in the early church. This restoration eschatological perspective understood that the baptism of the Holy Spirit and tongues was to empower missionary endeavors and enable believers to reach people even at the ends of the earth, thus hastening the return of Christ.[42] Wimber, on the other hand, through reading works like Morton Kelsey's *Healing and Christianity*, discovered that the gifts of the Spirit, especially healing, had been present throughout church history—admittedly often marginalized from mainstream Christianity, but present nonetheless. Therefore, Wimber believed there was no need to restore spiritual gifts but to simply recognize and activate what was in the church from the very beginning.[43]

Ladd's inaugurated eschatology caused Wimber to reject both dispensational and restoration eschatology. He saw, through Ladd, that the end times had been inaugurated in the life, death, and resurrection of Jesus but that the future world would not be fully realized or consummated until Christ's second coming. Jesus was the embodiment of the kingdom, thus the church has been living in the last days since the resurrection of Christ. The future age of the eternal kingdom broke into the present time, bringing with it the power and glory of God's eternal realm through Jesus, by the power of the Holy Spirit. This was Ladd's already-and-not-yet understanding of the kingdom of God, which implied that Jesus gave birth to the church, thus the church was to continue to proclaim and demonstrate the kingdom of God on earth as it was in heaven.[44]

Wimber, however, seemed to take Ladd's eschatological model a step further, believing that the manifestation of gifts, such as healing, deliverance, and signs and wonders, were evidence of the inbreaking of the future age into the present and therefore could be realized in the church today—something Ladd would not necessarily have agreed with.

Power Ministry

Wimber's inaugurated eschatology also gave him a spiritual warfare model and a framework for his concept of "power ministry." He believed that when the kingdom of God came in the person of Jesus Christ, it was a declaration of war on the powers of darkness and Satan's kingdom. Wimber's power ministry concept, explained below, comprised of three main areas: the power encounter, power evangelism, and power healing.

Power Encounters

According to John, the clash of the kingdom of God with the kingdom of Satan constitutes an event called a "power encounter."[45] In this confrontation, a conflict results, where the authority of God overcomes the power of Satan; Jesus is the invader and Satan is on the defense.[46] Wimber found an appropriate model of the power encounter in the story of Elijah in the Old Testament, where Elijah confronted 450 prophets of Baal on Mount Carmel demanding a show of force to prove whose god was more powerful. At God's command, Elijah called fire down from heaven, which consumed the altar of the false prophets. The prophets of Baal were destroyed, and the hearts of the people were turned back to God, who had revealed himself as being more powerful than Baal, who they worshiped.[47] This story, he believed, was an Old Testament representation of the New Testament confrontation between the kingdom of God and the kingdom of Satan. Wimber firmly believed that Satan was a created being who had usurped his authority, and a power encounter was a "visible, practical demonstration that Jesus Christ is more powerful" than Satan and his kingdom.[48]

Wimber also observed that Jesus had used the method of proclamation and demonstration to aggressively confront and overpower the enemy. The ultimate power encounter was Jesus's death and resurrection, where Jesus became the victor, secured salvation for all who placed their faith in him, and sealed Satan's doom.[49] Wimber further expanded on this biblical warfare model by developing concepts he termed "power evangelism" and "power healing."

Power Evangelism

Immediately after John and Carol were introduced to the good news of the gospel, they became ardent soul-winners. From the outset, John noticed a marked contrast between Carol's approach to evangelism and his own, which he attributed to their backgrounds: Carol came from a Christian home and was educated in a parochial school, so her approach took on a more intellectual form than John's. For her, the task of evangelism was to make a clear, logical presentation of the gospel message, in which she answered all the questions, even if the questions were not being asked. Wimber, on the other hand, relied more on intuition and felt that, with only minimal information, a person could enter into a personal relationship with Jesus. He later discovered they both were right. For effective evangelism to take place, a person needed a clear presentation of the gospel; while at the same time, that person's heart had to be ripe and ready to receive.[50]

Wimber believed the approach to evangelism in the Western church was more inclined toward an intellectual approach, such as that used in a formal church service or Billy Graham-type crusade. He identified this approach as "program evangelism," which attempts to reach the natural mind by rational means and is usually a one-way form of communication.[51] Based on his personal experience and on program-evangelism statistics, however, he was not convinced that this was the best or most productive method. Rather, he came to believe the most effective model was in the ministry model of Jesus. Jesus would first preach the gospel of the kingdom and then demonstrate the power and presence of God's rule and reign through a power encounter, such as a healing, demon expulsion, or other miracles. This combination of proclamation and demonstration, he felt, resulted in the conversion of both the mind to understand and the heart to believe and receive—and eventually became what he called "power evangelism."[52]

For Wimber, power evangelism is a clear, rational presentation of the gospel—the finished work of Christ on the cross—with the demonstration of God's power through signs and wonders, which normally results in large groups of people receiving salvation.[53] This type of evangelism not only reveals the reality of God but proves that God knows the needs of people and cares about them personally. When people understand God's desire for a personal relationship, it expedites their discipleship and spiritual growth.[54] Thus, for John, the Holy Spirit and power ministry were intimately tied to the salvation of souls.[55]

Wimber discovered that when a person had a supernatural power encounter that enabled them to see, in a tangible way, the power of God, that person could quickly be delivered from the powers of darkness and brought into the kingdom. Power evangelism employs gifts of the Spirit, such as the word of knowledge, to reveal the secrets of a person's heart in a way that communicates God's love and opens that person's heart to receive the Savior and surrender to his lordship. A vivid example is the time John boarded a plane and saw the word "ADULTERY" written across a man's forehead. Through this word of knowledge, he had insight into the man's spiritual condition, and when John acted by faith and shared with the man what the Spirit had revealed, the man realized God knew his sin and wanted to set him free. As a result, John was able to lead not only the man but also his wife to the Lord. This was a clear situation where the kingdom of God invaded, overpowered, and plundered the kingdom of darkness: two souls were rescued from Satan's grip, thus advancing the rule and reign of God in the earth.[56] Wimber also called events such as these "divine appointments," another term he coined that has since become common usage in the church today.[57]

Power Healing

The primary reason Wimber prayed for the sick was out of obedience to God's word. Jesus healed people every place he went and gave no indication that there was any benefit in people being sick.[58] As we saw in chapter two, Wimber's understanding of divine healing was transformed when he realized Christians were called to heal the sick in the same way they were called to evangelize. The Lord spoke to him through Matthew 9, the healing of the paralytic, and helped him to realize that healing is no more difficult than forgiving sin—in fact, God seemed to imply that healing the sick was actually easier than forgiving sins. He felt the Lord say that most people are hesitant to pray for the sick because they do not understand God's compassion and mercy. When God said this, Wimber immediately realized the reason he had not prayed for the sick was because his theology had denied that God could heal today. The Lord went on to say, "Just as I give authority to preach the gospel of forgiveness of sins, in a similar way I give authority to heal the sick."[59]

John realized from this conversation with the Lord and from what he saw in Scripture that it was not only he who was commissioned to pray for the sick; but, every believer was commissioned to do the same works that Jesus did. After all, when Jesus came, he preached the good news of the kingdom and healed the sick. Later Jesus called and commissioned his twelve disciples and then the seventy to do the same, giving them power and authority to drive out all demons and to cure diseases. And in his post-resurrection appearance, Jesus told his disciples they would place their hands on sick people and the sick would get well.[60] So Wimber became convinced that he had to learn not only to pray effectively for the sick but also to train and equip every member of his congregation to do the same.

After he had prayed for the sick for months with no results, he had become discouraged and wanted to give up. Wimber said, this first healing and the honeycomb vision revolutionized his life more than any other experience. "What made this experience so powerful," he said, "was that it confirmed to my new-found conviction, rooted in Scripture, that God's abundant grace included divine healing, if only we could believe him for it."[61]

Regarding this pivotal moment he went on to say,

> Through the honeycomb vision I also understood that my first healing was only the beginning of my experiencing God's mercy—if I would only choose to believe and to receive it. In the vision, some people rejoiced, freely received, and freely gave away. The more they gave away, the more they received. 'There's plenty for everyone,' the Lord said. 'Don't ever beg for healing again.'[62]

The key, for Wimber, to experiencing God's healing, was simply to believe in the God who heals. With this understanding, he continued to press on, learning and discovering more about healing, knowing it was God's will to heal. He saw this period of failure as a learning experience during which he was purged of pride and self-sufficiency—he was humbled and humiliated. But as he gained a little proficiency, he started training and equipping his small congregation to pray for the sick as well. It seemed he was only a baby step ahead of the people he was training, but as he gained proficiency, his training-and-equipping ministry expanded.

Throughout Wimber's ministry, he trained thousands of believers how to confidently pray for the sick—especially in his *Equipping the Saints* healing seminars. Because of his passion to equip the Body of Christ to do the works of Jesus, when he taught, he rarely prayed for the sick himself. Rather, he would teach the Scriptures and then, during the practical portion of the seminars, he would coach and help others to learn how to effectively pray for the sick. He was convinced that the entire body of Christ was called, commissioned, and anointed by the power of the Holy Spirit to heal the sick. Eventually he developed a five-step healing model that people could follow as they prayed for the sick (see appendix C).[63]

Power Healing, Inner Healing, and Demonization

Wimber realized from Scripture that at least one-third of Jesus's ministry was demon expulsion, and so he saw the casting out of demons as an integral part of Jesus's power ministry. Once, when Jesus was accused of casting out demons by the power of Beelzebub, Jesus declared, "If I drive out demons by the spirit of God, then the kingdom of God has come upon you."[64] Mark's gospel is especially replete with such encounters. Wimber saw Jesus as the "divine invader" who came "to destroy demons and release men and women to eternal life," and "his ministry was marked by continual conflict with Satan and demons for the purpose of establishing God's reign on earth."[65] When Jesus sent out the twelve, giving them authority over the powers of darkness to heal the sick and drive out demons, they came back wide-eyed with excitement that they had this kind of power in his name.[66]

This perspective on demonology also raised the question, could a Christian have a demon? For Wimber, the answer to this question is found in the meaning of the related terminology. The Greek word for "having a demon" in the Bible is *diamonizomenoi* and is more literally translated "demonized," which means to be influenced, afflicted, or tormented in some way by a demonic power.[67] With this, Wimber found biblical grounds for the idea that nonbelievers could give themselves over so completely to sin that they could eventually become totally possessed. On the other hand, he believed Scripture taught that a born again child of God could never be possessed, though they could suffer varying degrees of demonization.[68] He often said,

> Christians can be affected and even controlled by evil spirits if they live in unconfessed and serious sin. Our situation with demons is analogous to our situation with the flesh and the world. We are forgiven and born again in Christ, but if we choose to believe the lies of the world and yield to our flesh, we will live in sin. Demonization works the same way; we have been delivered from the power of demons yet we can still be affected by them.[69]

He believed that if Christians choose to live in sin, they are at risk of being demonized. There is a war going on, he said, and Satan will not be bound until Christ's second coming. The entry points through which the powers of darkness gain access to people, he claimed, are willful, sinful practices; the occult; and sins done against them, including sexual abuse.[70] He further stated that Christians should not however walk in fear, because they have spiritual armor, as seen in Ephesians 6:10-18, that will help them to not only resist but also successfully wage spiritual warfare against these evil forces.[71] For this biblical interpretation, he caught criticism from evangelicals and Pentecostals alike, since neither believe a Christian can be demonized.[72] But he was confident he could support his claim through both Scripture and experience. He also believed the most loving thing he could do for the demonized person was to set them free.

Wimber believed Jesus provided healing for the entire person—spirit, soul, and body—which also included healing from past hurts, or what he called "inner healing." He defined inner healing as, "a process which the Holy Spirit brings forgiveness of sins and emotional renewal to people suffering damaged minds, wills, and emotions. It is a way of bringing the power of the gospel to a specific area of need."[73] Repentance and forgiveness were the primary means for inner healing—they were two sides of the same coin.[74] And however valuable it was to help a person be healed from past hurts, the most important aspect of this process was to teach "people to believe they are a new creation in Christ," because this was the ultimate key to a person's freedom.[75]

Non-Healing and the Atonement

While Wimber was thoroughly convinced that it was God's will to save, heal, and deliver, he was also faced with the reality that not everyone he prayed for was healed.

For example, Wimber prayed hard for his good friend, David Watson, but then Watson died of liver cancer in 1984. Later John wrote,

> I wish I could [tell you] that David Watson is alive today and completely healed of cancer; I also wish I could tell you that I have been healed of the heart problems . . . but if I did it would not be the truth. David Watson's death and my physical problems raise a larger question about divine healing: what about those who are not healed?[76]

Jesus came to establish the kingdom of God and to disarm the kingdom of Satan. He healed the sick, then gave his followers authority over the powers of darkness and commissioned them to likewise heal the sick in his name. Then why were many not healed? As does everyone who believes Christ is the healer, Wimber wrestled with this question.

His first interpretative key came through his understanding of the atonement. The atonement comes through Christ's work on the cross and makes it possible for a person to have his or her sins forgiven and to thereby enter into a right relationship with God.[77] Theologians agree regarding sins being removed through Jesus's finished work, but there are various perspectives of how healing, with regards to the atonement, is received.

A. J. Gordon, in his book *The Ministry of Healing*, was the first to promote the idea that both forgiveness of sins and healing for the body are found *in* the atonement. Holiness leaders such as R. A. Torrey and A. B. Simpson further advanced the idea. This understanding flowed into the emerging Pentecostal movement at the turn of the twentieth century and was embraced to become one of their cardinal doctrines. On the other hand, evangelical theologians, like Colin Brown, made a case that healing was not *in* the atonement, although he believed God does heal today in answer to prayer.

So where was healing? Was it *in* or *not in* the atonement? In evaluating possible responses to this question, Wimber created a third option. For him, healing came *through* the atonement—a concept that he again saw in Ladd's already-and-not-yet kingdom model.[78] While the kingdom of God had come in Jesus, we still live in the presence of the future. So while salvation is guaranteed when a person looks to Jesus and his finished work on the cross, the body continues to be subject to the spiritual battle that is still going on (between D-day and V-day). In this age, between the inauguration and the final consummation at the second coming, humanity will continue to live in fallen bodies, subject to sin and sickness. In the fullness of the age to come, when all evil will be destroyed and sin and suffering will be no more, sickness will also be eradicated. Until then, sickness remains part of the battle Christians fight in this present age.[79] Wimber wrote,

> The body is not redeemed now as it will be after Christ's second coming in the fullness of the kingdom of God. This could explain why not everyone is healed when prayed for. We still live in a time that awaits the fullness of the kingdom of God, what Scriptures calls 'the age to come of the renewal of all things' (Matt. 19:28). In this age we 'know in part,' but we are assured of a time when we 'shall know fully' (1 Cor. 13:12).[80]

When Christ came, he inaugurated the kingdom of God, but the consummation of that kingdom awaits future fulfillment. So if healing does not come in this life, there is the assurance of ultimate healing in the coming age. Until then, we graciously receive the healing God provided through the atonement. "Our part is to pray, 'Thy Kingdom come,' and trust God for whatever healing comes from his gracious hand," Wimber says.[81]

When asked about people who were not healed in his ministry, he would often respond that more people were healed when he prayed for them than when he did not pray for them; therefore, he would continue to pray, and as a consequence, some would be healed. In his understanding, everyone will find ultimate healing in the age to come, but today the ministry of healing will always be partial.[82]

Regarding suffering, Wimber differentiated it from sickness. He said the writers of the New Testament, when referring to "suffering," used the Greek word *pascho,* a term normally limited to persecution from people or demons—therefore, suffering was not the same thing as sickness. In addition, Jesus understood that sickness comes from the enemy—its source is Satan's kingdom. As such, Wimber felt that to think suffering comes in the form of sickness sent by God for our good is not only unbiblical but also makes people resistant to divine healing. These same people, he said, might reason that if they pray for the sick, they would actually be opposing God's will.[83]

On the other hand, he felt there are times a Christian may be called by God to suffer; for example, his friend Gunner Payne, whose daughter was killed and whose son was permanently disabled in a severe automobile accident. Suffering of this nature falls under the category of Ladd's already-and-not-yet understanding that we still live in a fallen world—that while the kingdom of the future has broken into the present church age, there will still be suffering. But for Wimber, this kind of suffering was different from physical sickness.

Scripture and Revelation

In one of his writings, Wimber shared a story about an American soldier who had fathered a daughter with a Vietnamese woman during the Vietnam war. After their daughter's birth, the woman died, and he was forced to flee as the Viet Cong invaded Saigon. Years later, the man saw a photograph in a national magazine that featured Vietnamese children left behind by American soldiers. Although his daughter was now a teenager, he recognized her in the picture because she looked so much like him. It took him two years, but finally he was able to reunite with her. During the two years of diplomatic negotiations as he worked to bring her to the United States, they became acquainted by communicating through letters. Can you imagine, John asked, what these letters must have meant to this young girl as she learned about her father and read his words of love and affection? Comparing this to Scripture, he wrote,

> Of course, for the girl to experience her father's love personally she had actually to meet him. The letters sustained her until she came to America, but what she got from the letters could never be compared to her later personal acquaintance with her father. Scripture is analogous to the father's letters. The Bible is like a series of letters from a heavenly Father to his children, telling us how much he loves us and of his goal that we should know him personally through his Son, Jesus Christ.[84]

For Wimber, the Scriptures were "lifelines to a living relationship," where the Holy Spirit reveals God's love and enables us to experience a personal relationship with our heavenly Father.

In addition to seeing the Scriptures as a book of love letters from God to his children, John also saw the Bible as a training manual. In reading the Gospels, he saw in Jesus's ministry the combination of the proclamation and demonstration of the good news and the works of the kingdom. It became his ministry goal, therefore, to train and equip every Christian, not only to study but also to be doers of the word.

John did not believe that God's communication to us was limited to Scripture. He also believed God spoke to his people through revelations. According to Wimber, there are two kinds of revelation. The first is "general revelation," which bears witness to God through such things as nature. This is what he encountered in the Las Vegas desert in 1961 that caused him to feel he was "in touch with the supernatural."[85] He later realized that general revelation does not offer enough information for a person to receive salvation; it simply serves to make God known to a person and to produce an internal hunger for a personal relationship with the Creator.[86]

The second kind of revelation, "special revelation," is God's self-disclosure through the Scriptures, inspired by the Holy Spirit.[87] This revelation, Wimber said, was what put him on the narrow path to salvation:

When I became convinced the Bible was the word of God and submitted to it, my life was changed. I knew I could no longer stand in judgment upon Scripture, discarding teaching I could not accept and submitting only to those ideas that conformed to *my* idea of truth. I realized the Bible was written in such a manner that to reject one part was to reject it all.[88]

It is important to note here that, in John 1:1, 14, and 18, Jesus is referred to as the "word of God." At the same time, the Bible is also called the "word of God." Wimber differentiated the two by referring to the Bible with a small *w* (word of God) and to Jesus the incarnate with a capital *W* (Word of God).[89] In other words, the Bible is the *word of God*, which reveals Jesus, who is *Word of God* incarnate and the centerpiece of the whole of Scripture.[90]

Many mainline evangelicals, Wimber contended, inadvertently elevated the Bible (the word) above the Holy Spirit. Evangelicals were quick to affirm that God speaks through preaching, teaching, and witnessing but that extrabiblical revelations should be rejected. As such, Wimber believed that what they are actually saying is they believe in "God the Father, God the Son, and God the Holy Book."[91] John, on the other hand, believed God is greater than the book and that God still speaks to people today.[92]

As such, he said the third type of revelation—what he called "divine revelation"—can be seen in both the Old and New Testaments when God spoke to his people through "dreams, visions, inner impressions, angels, tongues, words of wisdom, words of knowledge, discernment of spirits, teaching, preaching, prophesying, circumstances, and even personal appearances."[93] John contended that through such experiences or divine revelations, our paradigm can quickly be shifted away from what we believed was true based on the worldview we were given. This happened for him when Carol had a dream and woke up speaking in tongues—her experience suddenly challenged their theology.

This perspective of divine revelation ultimately became the fodder on which his critics would soon feed, but what they failed to understand was that, though Wimber may have thought the Word was greater than the word, he was still a man of the Scripture. While contending that God still communicates to his people through dreams and visions as seen in Scripture, he was also quick to acknowledge that experiences are subjective and must always be weighed against the true plumb line of the Bible.[94] Indeed, the Bible was the book John staked his life on. Rich Nathan, a good friend and associate of Wimber's, said that he had heard Wimber speak over a hundred times, and every time he would open the Bible and expound on the Scriptures *before* doing ministry.[95] Wimber held to a firm evangelical understanding that the Bible is infallible, inerrant, and inspired—the plumb line against which all must be measured. The bottom line for Wimber, however, was that the proclamation of the Scriptures was only the beginning of ministry. Being a doer of the word—a "word worker"—was the ultimate goal of biblical ministry. See appendix D for more on Wimber's view of the Bible.

Equipping the Saints

Historically, people who are powerfully used in the gifts of divine healing and miracles build a ministry around themselves, but Wimber was different. He never wanted to build a ministry; his goal was to train and equip the saints to carry on the supernatural ministry of Jesus and "do the stuff" that Jesus did.

Although he was a successful soul-winner, pastor, and church growth consultant, from the time he experienced his first healing in 1977, he began to understand his call differently. After experiencing the supernatural power of God, he was convinced his calling and commission was to train and equip the body of Christ based on Ephesians 4:11-13.[96] In fact, he believed leaders were acting negligent if they did all the work and failed to train others to do it.[97] He believed this was a significant problem in the evangelical church, saying, "It [is] not enough to believe and underline it in your Bible. We've got to actually do it. Jesus called us to be doers of the word, to actualize what he taught, to be disciples and not just hearers." The church, however, had become "like an army that has been trained but never gets into the field. We have the manual, the equipment, but we have not done the work or had the experience."[98] Wimber wanted to build not an audience but an army. And he was inspired to train and equip not only the people in his church, but ultimately also the entire body of Christ, to heal the sick.[99]

In relationship to this, Wimber operated on the kingdom principle that the more a person gives away, the more he or she receives from God. As such, it became his goal to give away everything God had given him.[100] If he gave away all his knowledge and experience to equip the saints, more souls would be evangelized than through his individual efforts. The more he invested in training and equipping the saints to do the work of the ministry, the less he prayed for the sick himself, preferring to lead others through the healing process.[101]

Rather than healing conferences, then, where he alone prayed for the sick, he held training conferences centered on teaching believers about the kingdom of God, along with their calling, commissioning, empowerment, and authority to heal the sick. He also employed the rabbinic model common in New Testament times and used by Jesus when he trained and equipped his own disciples.[102]

The rabbinic method used a combination of didactic teaching coupled with hands-on experience. It focused on learning as a way of life more than as the accumulation of knowledge. The rabbi would teach while the disciples observed what the master was doing, and then the disciples would minister, with the master watching their teaching and making corrections as the training moved forward. Finally, the teacher would send his disciples on short mission trips where they would minister on their own and then return to report their experiences. At that point, the teacher would again make corrections and provide further instruction.[103]

In line with the hands-on rabbinic method, Wimber believed that power ministry was better "caught than taught" and that if he could get people *doing* the ministry of praying for the sick, then they could rapidly begin to move in signs and wonders. This was the impetus behind the clinic sessions, which were an integral part of the equipping and training sessions that followed his teaching.[104] Thus, the rabbinic method became the model Wimber used in his training and equipping seminars around the world.

In the end, because Wimber did not aim to build a ministry around himself but aimed instead to equip others, he inadvertently set himself apart from others who have historically practiced the gifts of divine healing and miracles. As such, he became a pioneer in the power ministry. But in history, pioneers are traditionally the ones who catch the arrows—and for Wimber the pioneer, he caught more than his share of the arrows of criticism.

[1] Synan, *Century of the Holy Spirit,* 397; Synan, *The Holiness-Pentecostal Tradition,* 228, 284.
[2] C. Peter Wagner, "A Third Wave?" *Pastoral Renewal,* July-August, 1993, 1–5.
[3] Wagner, *How to Have a Healing Ministry,* 16–7.
[4] Synan, *Century of the Holy Spirit,* 285.
[5] Synan, *Holiness-Pentecostal Tradition,* 228, 284.
[6] Synan, *Century of the Holy Spirit,* 178.
[7] Burgess, *The New International Dictionary of Pentecostal and Charismatic Movements,* xxi, 286.
[8] John Wimber, "Spiritual Gifts," vol. 1, cassette tape 4 (Anaheim, CA: Vineyard Ministries International, 1985).
[9] Wimber and Springer, "John Wimber Calls It Power Evangelism," 35; Wimber and Springer, *Power Healing,* 191.
[10] Wimber, "Spiritual Gifts," vol. 1, cassette tape 4; also Rich Nathan and Ken Wilson, *Empowered Evangelicals: Bringing Together the Best of the Evangelical and Charismatic Worlds* (Ann Arbor, MI: Vine Books, 1995), 212.
[11] Wimber and Springer, *Power Healing,* 189.
[12] Wimber and Springer, *Power Points,* 147. Wimber borrowed the term "gracelets" from Russell Spittler, professor at Fuller Seminary.
[13] Wimber, *MC510,* cassette tape 5B.
[14] Wimber, *MC510,* cassette tape 3B.
[15] Wimber and Springer, *Power Points,* 136, Rich Nathan, *Vineyard Position Paper #5,* 25.
[16] Wimber and Springer, *Power Points,* 136.
[17] John Wimber, "Refreshing, Renewal, and Revival," *Vineyard Reflections,* July/August 1994, 5.
[18] Nathan, "The Bible Teacher," 96–7. Nathan is quick to point out that this teaching "is not meant in any way to take away from Jesus's full divinity or to teach some kenotic theory of the Incarnation. While Jesus was fully human and fully God, Wimber showed from the Gospels that Jesus relied on the promptings of the Spirit for his ministry. Wimber never tired of pointing out Jesus's utter dependence on the Spirit."
[19] Wimber, *Kingdom Come,* 34.
[20] Interview by the author with Bob Fulton.
[21] George Eldon Ladd (1911–1982). Though popular among Reformed theologians, Ladd was not Reformed and rejected Calvin's view of salvation. Ladd carried forth the work of Oscar Cullmann (1902–1999), a Lutheran theologian who suggested the analogy of D-day and V-day to depict the difference between the first coming of Jesus and his second coming, which would inaugurate the final establishment of God's kingdom on earth.
[22] Wimber, *Kingdom Come,* 8.
[23] Wimber, *Kingdom Come,* 8.
[24] Wimber, *Kingdom Come,* 23.
[25] Wimber and Springer, *Power Evangelism* (1986), 1.
[26] Wimber, *Kingdom Come,* 22–3.
[27] Luke 11:20 (NIV).
[28] Wimber and Springer, *Power Evangelism* (1986), xx.
[29] John Wimber, "Ministering the Compassion of Jesus," *First Fruits,* March 1985, 3.
[30] Wimber and Springer, *Power Evangelism* (1986), 5.
[31] Wimber, *Kingdom Come,* 20.
[32] Ladd, *Gospel of the Kingdom,* 21–2.
[33] Ladd, *Theology of the New Testament,* 48–50.
[34] Wimber, *Kingdom Come,* 28.
[35] Wimber, *Kingdom Come,* 28–9.
[36] Wimber, *Kingdom Come,* 29.
[37] Wimber and Springer, *Power Evangelism,* 55

[38] Wimber, *Kingdom Come*, 31; Matthew 4:23-25 and 9:35-36.
[39] Wimber and Springer, *Power Points,* 170.
[40] Wimber, *Kingdom Come*, 41.
[41] William D. Faupel, *The Everlasting Gospel* (Sheffield: Sheffield Academic Press, 1996), 29.
[42] Faupel, *Everlasting Gospel,* 39.
[43] Morton T. Kelsey, *Healing & Christianity* (San Francisco: Harper and Row, 1976).
[44] Ladd, *Presence of the Future*, 33. Ladd uses the term "inaugurated eschatology" from A. M. Hunter's *Introducing New Testament Theology*, 13–51.
[45] Wimber and Springer, *Power Evangelism* (1986), 16.
[46] Wimber and Springer, *Power Evangelism* (2009), 54.
[47] Wimber and Springer, *Power Evangelism*, 50–1; 1 Kings 18:16-45.
[48] Wimber and Springer, *Power Evangelism*, (1986) 49; Wimber and Springer, *Power Healing*, 103–6.
[49] Wimber and Springer, *Power Evangelism* (1986), 20.
[50] Wimber and Springer, *Power Evangelism* (1986), 14–5, 17.
[51] Wimber, *MC510*, 15.
[52] Wimber, *MC510*, 15.
[53] Wimber and Springer, *Power Evangelism* (2001), 78.
[54] Wimber and Springer, *Power Evangelism* (1986), 35.
[55] Wimber, *MC510*, cassette tape 1A.
[29] Wimber and Springer, *Power Evangelism* (1986), 32–4.
[57] Wimber and Springer, *Power Evangelism*, (1986)52, 57.
[58] Wimber and Springer, *Power Healing*, 40.
[59] Wimber and Springer, *Power Healing*, 47–8.
[60] Mark 1:34, Luke 9:1, and Mark 16:18 (NIV); Wimber and Springer, *Power Healing*, xvii.
[61] Wimber and Springer, *Power Healing*, 53.
[62] Wimber and Springer, *Power Healing*, 52–3.
[63] See appendix C for this healing model.
[64] Matthew 12:28 (NIV).
[65] Wimber and Springer, *Power Healing*, 101.
[66] Luke 9:1-6; 10:19-21.
[67] Wimber and Springer, *Power Healing*, 109.
[68] Wimber and Springer, *Power Healing*, 109–10, 114.
[69] Wimber and Springer, *Power Healing*, 116.
[70] Wimber and Springer, *Power Healing*, 118–9.
[71] Wimber and Springer, *Power Healing*, 120–3.
[72] Wimber and Springer, *Power Healing*, 108.
[73] Wimber and Springer, *Power Healing*, 80.
[74] Wimber and Springer, *Power Healing*, 90.
[75] Wimber and Springer, *Power Healing*, 94.
[76] Wimber and Springer, *Power Healing*, 149–50.
[77] Wimber and Springer, *Power Healing*, 153.
[78] Wimber and Springer, *Power Healing*, 157.
[79] Wimber, *Kingdom Come*, 19–21.
[80] Wimber and Springer, *Power Healing*, 157.
[81] Wimber and Springer, *Power Healing*, 157.
[82] Wimber and Springer, *Power Healing*, 37.
[83] Wimber and Springer, *Power Healing*, 13.
[84] Wimber and Springer, *Power Points*, 34–5.
[85] Wimber and Springer, *Power Points*, 17–8.
[86] Wimber and Springer, *Power Points*, 20–1.
[87] Wimber and Springer, *Power Points*, 26.
[88] Wimber and Springer, *Power Points*, 28.

89 Wimber and Springer, *Power Points*, 28, 34.
90 Wimber and Springer, *Power Points*, 34.
91 Wimber, "The Way On," cassette tape 10A.
92 Wimber, "The Way On," cassette tape 4. Wimber and Springer, *Power Points*, 53–4.
93 Wimber and Springer, *Power Points*, 53.
94 Wimber and Springer, *Power Points*, 53–4.
95 Nathan, "Bible Teacher," 102.
96 Wimber, *MC510*, cassette tape 3B.
97 Wimber and Springer, *Power Evangelism*, 178.
98 Wimber, *MC510*, cassette tape 1A.
99 Wimber and Springer, *Power Evangelism*, 50.
100 Wimber and Springer, *Power Evangelism*, 179; also Williams, "Friend and Encourager," 52.
101 Wimber and Springer, *Power Evangelism*, 171.
102 Wimber, *MC510*, cassette tape 7A.
103 Wimber and Springer, *Power Evangelism* (1986), 109.
104 Wimber, *MC510*, cassette tape 12B.

Chapter 6

The Pain of Criticism

The cancelation of the Fuller MC510 Signs and Wonders class in March 1986 was heartbreaking for Wimber, and he suffered physically and emotionally from the devastating blow. Around the same time, adding insult to injury, criticism surrounding his theology and ministry also reached a crescendo.

Just a year before, in 1985, authors David Hunt and T. A. McMahon, in their book *The Seduction of Christianity: Spiritual Discernment in the Last Days,* accused Wimber of using New Age techniques as he practiced inner healing.[1] Then in August of 1986, just a few months after the class was canceled and John suffered his first heart attack, *Christianity Today* carried a cover story titled "Testing the Wine from John Wimber's Vineyard." While its author Tim Stafford provided a balanced overview of Wimber's teaching, he also gave liberal voice to his critics.[2] Finally, in 1988, *Bibliotheca Sacra,* a theological journal published by Dallas Theological Seminary, carried a twenty-five-page article by Ken Sarles, assistant professor of Systematic Theology at Dallas Theological Seminary, titled "An Appraisal of the Signs and Wonders Movement."[3] Sarles's evaluation of Wimber's teaching and ministry was neither fair nor balanced, and it misrepresented him in several areas. Then there was Hank Hanegraaff, the "Bible Answer Man," who was constantly haranguing Wimber on his radio program. (Much later, in 1997, the year of Wimber's death, Hanegraaff also published *Counterfeit Revival,* a book that contained two chapters directly attacking Wimber and the Vineyard.)[4]

"Why I Don't Respond to Criticism"

In the early days of Wimber's ministry, he chose not to respond to his critics, and there were people who questioned the wisdom of his silence. To clarify the matter, Wimber wrote an article "Why I Don't Respond to Criticism," published in the 1988 summer issue of *Equipping the Saints.*[5] An overview of this article was also published in *Christianity Today.*[6] In these two articles, Wimber attributed his silence, first, to his belief that the biblical process to follow when a believer is "suspected of wrongdoing like...teaching error" is to go to that person privately, one on one. Based on Matthew 18:15-17, Galatians 6:1, and 1 Timothy 5:1, Wimber believed this was the recommended course of action as opposed to the use of a public format such as a book or magazine, or a radio or television program. Entering into an open debate, he believed, only created division. What bothered Wimber most about his critics was that they rarely contacted him personally to clarify his teaching or express their concerns before attacking him in the media.[7]

The second reason Wimber said he refused to respond to his critics was based on the prophetic word he had received in 1977, which told him that he should not defend himself against his enemies. The woman who had prophesied his worldwide ministry had also said, "Your brother and your sister are never your enemies."[8] At that time, Wimber had no personal enemies, so the word did not make sense, but as the voices of his critics intensified, he recognized the forewarning in this prophecy.

At the same time, Wimber expressed some measure of empathy toward his critics. He recalled the time he had been called a "reformer" by an interviewer, and he recognized that reformers were "change agents" and that even legitimate change could create "fear, anger, hurt, and accusations from those who don't understand why change is needed." He then went on to say,

> The chance for misunderstanding is multiplied when one attempts to minister to Christians from a variety of denominations. The feeling of many critics is that I am calling for radical change—and they're correct—which in part explains their response.[9]

In other words, because Wimber ministered to Christians from a wide variety of denominations, his call for radical change increased his susceptibility to criticism.

Charles Whitehead, president of the International Catholic Charismatic Renewal, said John had an ability to reach across denominational boundaries through his engaging personality and heart for unity. Whitehead said,

> Pentecostals and charismatics accepted him because of his commitment to the exercise of the spiritual gifts in the healing ministry. Many, but not all, evangelicals accepted his teaching on the supernatural because he always sought a scriptural base for what he said and did. Protestant denominational Christians accepted him because although he was a New Church leader and

founder of the Vineyard, he respected the history and place of the denominations and made no attempt to steal their sheep. Catholics accepted him because of his openness to the mystical, his desire for dialogue and greater understanding, and because we knew he was prepared to pay the price for relationship with us.[10]

It never seemed to matter to Wimber if a person was Anglican, Pentecostal, or Baptist. He treated everyone equally. He was devoted to ecumenism and would say, "Your brother is your brother. He is never your enemy."[11] Therefore, when the criticisms first started, Wimber remain silent.

There were times when Wimber received constructive criticism, however, and he welcomed this and responded positively. He cited one instance in which a book reviewer had raised two specific questions regarding his book *Power Healing*. Wimber wrote the reviewer and asked for more clarification, and the outcome was very positive.[12] On another occasion, when Vineyard music was criticized for not making the cross a central theme of its songs, John gave all the songwriters a copy of Martyn Lloyd-Jones's book *The Cross* and asked them to study the meaning of the cross in Scripture. This exchange resulted in songs such as "Holy and Anointed One," "It's Your Blood That Cleanses Me," "You Gave Your Body," "At the Cross," "The Blood of Jesus," and others.[13]

Carol believed John had the capacity to glean validity from even his most vicious critics. She said he was able to "turn the other cheek" better than anyone she had known: "John never got worried about criticism, never got excited or agitated by it. It was merely the other side of the coin. 'Shall I take good from the Lord and not evil?' Job asked. You can't live in the kind of blessing we existed in and not expect to be hassled by hell."[14]

Reflecting on Carol's assessment, Wayne Grudem said that Wimber had an amazing capacity for self-correction and was eager to listen to people who offered suggestions or criticisms based on Scripture because they wanted to be faithful to the word. On the other hand, Grudem said, Wimber would not back down when he was convinced that the ministry he was doing was biblical and when he was demonstrating it through prayer so that people were miraculously touched and healed.[15]

Indeed, Wimber did not believe it was wrong to respond to criticism. He understood the Bible was filled with such examples—even Jesus and his disciples had defended themselves. But at this time in his life, he believed God was requiring something different from him. He was not trying to avoid his critics and the tough issues; he was simply trying to be obedient. He asked that people read his books and listen to his teachings and then judge for themselves whether his critics were justified in their accusations. After all, Wimber said, "If my teaching is sound and the fruit of it is lasting, that is all the defense I need."[16]

Criticism from Evangelical Scholars

In 1989, a year after Wimber's explanatory article was published, eleven evangelical scholars from a variety of universities and colleges, largely from the Mennonite church in Canada, published the book *Wonders and the Word*.[17] Angered by the fact that Wimber held a nondenominational "signs and wonders" seminar in their area of southern British Columbia and then, after the meeting, planting a Vineyard church, they launched an attack against him and his ministry.[18]

Abraham Friesen compared Wimber with the radical reformer Thomas Müntzer and accused him of overemphasizing the Holy Spirit at the expense of the Word of God.[19] Donald Lewis posited that Wimber espoused a radical Arminianism that ignored the fall; embraced a divine healing model that "leaves no room for sanctification through suffering;" advocated an exaggerated eschatology and restoration model of the church; sensationalized "signs and wonders," which sidetracked people from Jesus; and taught a nonbiblical demonology.[20] In the same book, Paul Hiebert charged that Wimber's teaching on suffering was weak and did not allow for the fact that sickness may be God's will for a Christian and can be used for a person's good.[21] The tenor of the manuscript remained derogatory throughout, but still Wimber chose to remain silent.

Two years later, another vicious attack was unleashed. But this time, two of Wimber's close friends and colleagues believed it was time to speak out.

Criticism in Australia

The criticism began in Australia in March 1990. Wimber was invited by a large committee of evangelical pastors and leaders from various denominations to hold a four-day Vineyard conference in Sydney titled, "What the Holy Spirit is Saying to the Church Today."[22] Before his arrival, Wimber was warned that a few people attending the conference were hostile toward the Vineyard and had openly opposed his coming. After he arrived, along with Paul Cain, Jack Deere, and Dan Armstrong, they agreed to meet with three of the men who had expressed opposition—Phillip Jensen, John Woodhouse, and David Cook, all from the evangelical cessationist community.

Deere said that Wimber's impression had been that they would discuss their theological differences with the goal of clearing up misunderstandings. But when the two groups met, the first thing Jensen said to Wimber was, "We don't want you here. We would like you to go back home." Deere said, "It seemed Jensen had already concluded, without ever having talked to John Wimber, that he was a deceived person and could only have a negative influence on the Christian community in Australia."[23]

The following month, in April 1990, that private meeting and the entire conference was critiqued in a double issue of *The Briefing*, published by Philip Jensen, pastor of St. Matthias Anglican Church in Sydney.[24] The article, "John Wimber: Friend or Foe?" was a direct assault on Wimber, but the publication carried additional articles that also leveled serious attacks against Deere and the other speakers at the conference. Deere said the article was "a serious misrepresentation" of their teaching.[25] Wayne Grudem agreed with Deere, saying the accusations in *The Briefing* were absolutely false. In hindsight, Grudem said he wished Wimber had responded to his critics more quickly and extensively, because he believed the slanderous account did much damage to the Vineyard. Because both Grudem and Deere realized that Wimber's health was failing at the time and that he did not have the strength or energy to respond—they decided to stepped in and help.[26]

Position Paper #1: "Why I Respond to Criticism"

Grudem and Deere, both respected theologians, were instrumental in convincing Wimber it was time to defend his position, and they stood willing to assist.

The first step in responding to the critics was to release a position paper from the Association of Vineyard Churches by Wimber stating why he was now responding to his critics after he had said four years earlier that he would not. In this initial response paper, Wimber said he had changed his thinking about the application of the prophetic word he had received in 1977. He still believed the word was from God, but the application was now different for his life.[27] He said,

> I now sense the Lord is saying that defending and clarifying my *message* in a loving and respectful way against unjust criticism is important for the well-being of people who are confused by the attacks and who sincerely need answers to questions about my teaching. I am now convinced that, according to Scripture, there are occasions that warrant—even *require*—a public response.[28]

Wimber used passages from the Old Testament, the life of Jesus, and the disciples as examples showing it was biblical to defend oneself against critics. He said he believed a public response was biblical when false criticism

- was believed by a significant number of Christians,
- seriously misrepresented the views and practices it was criticizing, and
- when the criticism significantly hindered the work of God.[29]

Based on this understanding, he went on to say that leaders should defend their ministries and personal integrity when falsely accused; take attacks seriously when the lies and slander threaten to hurt, confuse, and undermine the faith of those under their care; and also, publicly acknowledge when criticism is accurate and subsequently repent.[30]

He had finally come to realize that his lack of response had hindered his ministry, and it was time to respond. He said this was the situation they were facing in Australia where,

> Several men published a slanderous report about me and the Vineyard ministry that contained serious and false accusations. It was widely disseminated and significantly hindered the work of the ministry. After much prayer and consultation with other Christian leaders, we sense the Holy Spirit leading us to respond.[31]

Wimber's position paper on "why he now believed the Vineyard could and should respond to criticism" was published in May 1992 and with this, a green light was given to the organization to move forward with other Vineyard's responses. Over the next year, four more position papers were written, one by Jack Deere, one by Rich Nathan, and two by Wayne Grudem.

Position Paper #2: Response to *The Briefing*

The same month Wimber published his position paper on why he was now responding to criticism, Jack Deere wrote *Position Paper #2* titled "The Vineyard's Response to *The Briefing*," which not only defended Wimber's teaching but also addressed the accusation against the Vineyard ministry team and Deere himself.[32] In a thirty-one-page response, Deere said the articles in the scathing double issue by St. Matthias Anglican Church were such a serious misrepresentation of himself, Wimber, and others at the conference that "many people in the body of Christ, including pastors and members of the Christian academic community," asked that the accused leaders respond to the charges.[33]

Five basic issues were at the root of the charges expressed in *The Briefing*. First was the concern regarding "continuing revelation." In one teaching session, Deere had made the comment that "in order to fulfill God's highest purposes for our lives, we must be able to hear his voice both in the written word and in the word freshly spoken from heaven." Deere went on to say that he believed it was a demonic doctrine propagated by Christian theologians that says, "God no longer speaks through the written word." But because Wimber and the Vineyard team believed God continued to speak today, apart from the Bible, Mark Thompson, one of the contributing authors in *The Briefing*, accused them of having "lost confidence in the Scripture itself."[34] In answer to this, Deere clarified the Vineyard position saying,

> We believe that the Scriptures are the primary way that God speaks to his children. We believe in the verbal, inerrant, plenary inspiration of the word of God. We believe that when the Holy Spirit illuminates the heart of man, the Scriptures are sufficient to lead man into salvation and godly living. We also believe that God never intended that his communication with man be exhausted by his written word; such a doctrine is not taught either by example or by precept in the Old or New Testament.[35]

Next, Thompson accused Vineyard leaders of using allegorical interpretation and giving lip service to Scripture. Rather than expounding on Scripture, he said, they constantly appealed to anecdotes and their own experiences or the experiences of others. Deere countered that the underlying hermeneutical principle behind this assumption was that if the Vineyard holds a different interpretation from the authors of *The Briefing* then the views of the Vineyard could not possibly be based on Scripture. Regarding anecdotes and personal experiences, Deere pointed to great preaching orators such as

Spurgeon and Whitefield who saw the value of using "personal experience to illustrate, clarify, support, and confirm the teaching of Scripture; and [this] is why the Scripture is filled with biography and historical writings."[36]

The third issue raised in *The Briefing* questioned the validity of the healings at Vineyard conferences. Philip Jensen wrote, "The evidence so far suggests that John Wimber heals in the 'sugar pill area' . . . to put it bluntly, it is to be seriously doubted that any miraculous healings are taking place at all."[37]

In Wimber's defense, Deere pointed to the book *Healing: Fiction, Fantasy, or Fact?* In this book, David Lewis, a fellow of the Royal Anthropological Institute who had trained at both Cambridge and Manchester universities, documented through exhaustive research the results of a Vineyard conference by Wimber on healing in Harrogate, England, in the fall of 1986. Out of the 2,470 people who had registered for the conference, 1,890 responded to the detailed questionnaire regarding their healing and other experiences. Six months to a year later, 100 of these respondents were randomly selected for an extensive follow-up interview. Dr. Lewis noted that the Vineyard's stated purpose for the conference was to "equip [the attendees] to practice in their home situations what they learned at Harrogate." As such, the 100 follow-up interviewees reported 867 cases of prayer for physical healing after the conference, which involved 621 people. Out of this number, 279 people, or 32 percent, said they received either "a great deal" of healing or "total healing." A total of 222 people, or 26 percent, claimed to have received a "fair amount" of healing, and the remainder said they received either "a little" or "no healing." This, Deere noted, was documented evidence that the healings that occurred in Wimber's ministry and Vineyard conferences were more than simply sugar pill healings.[38]

The fourth accusation was that Vineyard believed the Bible teaches that Christians can be demonized. Deere said that the Vineyard's understanding of "demonized" means "coming under the influence or control of demonic power."[39] He then offered four biblical bases for Vineyard's doctrine of demonization. First, he said, there was no place either in the Old or New Testaments that says a Christian cannot be demonized or have a demon. Deere said people frequently ask how Christ could dwell in a vessel with a demon. He said this can happen in the same way that Jesus can dwell in a person who has sin in his or her life. Jesus comes into the heart of a new believer who is still bound in sin, and if he can dwell there, why could he not dwell in a person who is demonized? Second, Deere said, Saul in the Old Testament was described in language that was appropriate for a believer, and yet he rebelled and God gave him over to an evil spirit to torment him (1 Sam. 16:14 and 18:10-11). Third, there was the crippled woman who Jesus called the "daughter of Abraham" (Luke 13:10-17), yet Jesus said an evil spirit had bound her for eighteen years. Finally, Deere referred to the man in 1 Corinthians 5:1-5 who was delivered over to Satan for the destruction of the flesh, and yet Paul said his spirit would be saved on the day of the Lord Jesus Christ. According to Deere, a Christians can be demonized when they are involved in prolonged, voluntary sin that removes the protection of the Lord and opens them up to some form of demonic influence.[40]

The fifth and final concern addressed in *The Briefing* was Wimber's and the Vineyard's general lack of emphasis on the Cross. Deere said Wimber "acknowledged that he did not do an adequate job in presenting the message of the Cross at the Thursday night meeting" in Sydney, where the authors of *The Briefing* had gathered their fodder. But he continued by saying, "It needs to be pointed out that a failure to mention or stress a particular belief does not mean that one doesn't hold that particular belief in the highest esteem."[41] Deere acknowledged that Wimber took this criticism to heart, however, and went back to California to ask his worship team to study Scripture and other books on the Cross and then to write songs that exalted the Cross. Wimber also rectified this apparent oversight by placing a greater emphasis on the Cross in his revised edition of *Power Evangelism*, published in April 1992.[42]

Position Paper #3: Response to *The Standard*

Vineyard's third position paper came out in June of 1992, just three months after Deere responded to *The Briefing*. This paper addressed a series of articles published in *The Standard,* a journal produced by the Baptist General Conference (BGC). Over a ten-month period, between October 1990 and July 1991, John Armstrong, pastor of Trinity Baptist Church in Wheaton, Illinois, had written ten three-page articles that were critical of Wimber and the Vineyard ministry. In addition, the January issue of *The Standard* carried a critical review of Wimber's book *Power Evangelism*, and in February, an additional article charged that Vineyard-style revival had caused division in a Baptist church. These twelve articles created a total of thirty-four pages of critical material about Wimber and the Vineyard.

Wayne Grudem chose to respond to these criticisms because of his unique relationship with both the BGC and the Vineyard. Before becoming a professor at Trinity Evangelical Divinity School, Grudem had received his ordination in a BGC church in 1974 and then taught systematic theology for four years at Bethel, a BGC college, in St. Paul, Minnesota. Grudem was also friends with John Armstrong and had spoken at his Baptist church in Wheaton several times. During the two years prior to writing the Vineyard position paper, Grudem was also a member of a Vineyard church and an elder in the Vineyard Christian Fellowship of Mundelein, Illinois.[43]

Grudem identified eight areas where Armstrong had criticized Wimber and the Vineyard. Following each area, Grudem used Wimber's three books, *Power Evangelism*, *Power Healing*, and *Power Points,* and the Vineyard's official journal *Equipping the Saints*, to methodically refute each accusation.[44]

First, Armstrong had claimed that the Vineyard did not understand or preach a biblical gospel or preach the Cross of Christ. Grudem said he believed this was Armstrong's most serious accusation. To say that a person did not understand or preach the gospel was tantamount to charging them with heresy, and Grudem took personal offense to this. He said that to accuse the Vineyard movement of heresy was to accuse all of its pastors and leaders of this offense, including Grudem, who was then a Vineyard elder. Grudem employed extensive quotes from Wimber's writings and the Association of Vineyard Churches' statement of faith to soundly repudiate Armstrong's charge.[45]

Second, Armstrong had accused Wimber of refusing to listen or respond to criticism. Grudem defended Wimber on this charge, saying, "From the day I met him in 1988, I have found John Wimber to be genuinely open to criticism and correction, and eager to hear and change if in any way he is being unfaithful to Scripture."[46]

Armstrong's third allegation was that Vineyard exalted experience over Scripture and reason. Grudem pointed out that Armstrong was unable to produce a single example of Wimber "ridiculing or belittling" Scripture as Armstrong had charged. Again, Grudem said, "In many hours of conversation and meetings, I have never heard anything from Wimber but the highest respect and reverence for Scripture. In fact, it was obedience to the Bible that first got him started in praying for people to be healed."[47] Grudem also said that what he appreciated most about the Vineyard was that they combined faithfulness to Scripture with a healthy emphasis on experiences of power and the presence of God in everyday life.[48]

Fourth, Armstrong had charged that Wimber and the Vineyard were teaching unorthodox doctrine. In this case, said Grudem, Armstrong was making Wimber guilty by association. Armstrong had first accused the teachings of such people as C. Peter Wagner, Paul Cain and his association with William Branham, and even the New Age movement, and then somehow connected Wimber with their teachings. Grudem then used supporting documents to show that Vineyard did not hold to or teach any unorthodox doctrine but, in reality, supported a historic Christian orthodox that was "solidly conservative evangelical."[49]

Fifth, Armstrong asserted that Vineyard encouraged strange and highly emotional experiences in worship. Grudem agreed there were times when unusual evidences of the Holy Spirit were present during Vineyard services. But then he pointed out that Armstrong never once mentioned having personally visited a Sunday service at a Vineyard church or having talked to one of its pastors; and yet he felt qualified to speak at length regarding Vineyard church services.[50]

The sixth indictment was that Wimber endorsed a kind of contemporary prophecy that led people astray. In this respect, Armstrong also differed with Grudem, who asserted in his book *The Gift of Prophecy in the New Testament and Today* that "the gift of prophecy in the New Testament consist[ed] of 'reporting something God spontaneously brings to mind.'"[51] In response, Grudem reiterated his position, saying "such 'prophecies' are not equal to Scripture in authority, because they can have mistakes that enter when the speaker is unsure of what God has brought to mind."[52]

Seventh, Armstrong said that Vineyard overemphasized encounters with demonic forces and that its theology seemed to see Satan as being more powerful than the word of God. To contest this, Grudem pointed to Wimber's book *Power Healing*, where he clearly states that, regarding spiritual warfare, while Satan is strong, Christ is stronger.[53]

Finally, Armstrong claimed that Wimber's healing ministry was not effective and said he doubted that any genuine healings had occurred at Vineyard meetings. Grudem countered these viewpoints by pointing out that Wimber kept detailed records of people who had received prayer by the ministry team at his Anaheim Vineyard Fellowship and that, in 1986, their records revealed that 32 percent of all people they had prayed for had been completely healed and 86 percent had testified to receiving a significant healing.

Grudem also referred to Dr. David Lewis's research of the Harrogate, England, conference in 1986, which was published in the book *Healing: Fiction, Fantasy, or Fact?*[54]

Position Paper #4: Response to *Power Religion*

Wayne Grudem wrote the fourth position paper in March 1992 in response to the book *Power Religion: The Selling Out of the Evangelical Church*.[55] The 353-page volume was the combined effort of fifteen authors from pastoral and academic backgrounds. The book is broken into six parts, and the second part titled "Power Evangelism" contained three chapters specifically related to Wimber and the Vineyard movement: "In Search of Spiritual Power" by John H. Armstrong, "The Purpose of Signs and Wonders in the New Testament" by D. A. Carson, and "A Better Way: The Power of Word and Spirit" by James M. Boice. Grudem knew all three authors personally. On several occasions, he had worked with Boice, a Reformed theologian, in mutual efforts for the International Council on Biblical Inerrancy. In addition, Grudem had considered Armstrong a friend for years, having been invited twice to speak at his Baptist church in Wheaten and sharing with him mutual doctrinal convictions. And as for Carson, he had been a faculty colleague at Trinity Evangelical Divinity School where, for eleven years, Grudem occupied an office across the hall from him.[56]

Grudem provided general responses first, starting with his belief that Armstrong, Carson, and Boice had all been "uncharacteristically careless and surprisingly inaccurate in gathering and assessing information about the Vineyard."[57] Second, he said, their criticisms were so significant, and Carson and Boice such "well-known and widely-respected" evangelical scholars, that Grudem believed the majority of scholars would assume their accusations were accurate unless "another viewpoint" was presented.[58] Finally, Grudem stated that most of the concerns raised in these three chapters were concerns others had also articulated about the Vineyard; thus, by responding to *Power Religion*, he was addressing criticism that had already been previously expressed.[59]

Grudem's first specific response was to D. A. Carson, whose criticism, according to Grudem, was so serious and incorrect that Grudem had no choice but to offer an alternative assessment for those interested.[60] Carson had insinuated that the healings seen in Wimber's ministry were of a demonic origin and that the Vineyard had espoused "another Jesus" instead of the true, historical Jesus of the Gospels. He discredited the healings by associating them with healings seen in non-Christian groups such those of Muslims, Hindus, and Buddhists. He then went on to connect Wimber and the Vineyard with the "Jesuses of the Mormons, Muslims, and Jehovah's Witnesses." Grudem said this was "all done through innuendo and unanswered question, but the strong suggestion that will be picked up by readers is that the 'Jesus's being worshipped in the Vineyard is not Jesus Christ the only Son of God but is a false god, a pagan deity, and that the Vineyard is therefore a false religion and not Christian at all." This, Grudem said, "is an extraordinarily serious charge. And it is simply false."[61] Grudem spoke from personal experience, saying that he had been a part of the Vineyard churches for three years and that, during this time, he had worshiped Jesus more deeply and passionately than in any other time in his life. Therefore, for Carson to say that he, his family, and his friends were worshiping some other Jesus was like calling his pure and precious love for Jesus impure and false.[62] According to Grudem, after reading through Carson's accusations, "ordinary readers just won't be able to tell whether the Vineyard is leading people to false gods or not," leaving the impression they need to depend on him, "a respected scholar" who has "more than usual discernment" to keep them safe. This, Grudem says, would frighten people and cause them to distrust the Vineyard, even if they saw no evidence of a false religion.[63]

Carson had also charged that the Vineyard placed too much emphasis on miracles rather than the gospel. With this accusation, Grudem said, Carson had implied that a saving faith that comes about because of a miracle is inferior to faith that is in response to hearing the gospel preached. Grudem argued that the New Testament pattern is to preach the word *and* perform miracles, and he held firmly that there were no New Testament examples in which miracles were performed without the preaching of the gospel; therefore, this too was the belief and practice of the Vineyard.[64]

Carson's other accusations included that the Vineyard had a wrongful emphasis and a mistaken central focus, was arrogant, held a defective view of spirituality, did not call people to self-denial, and skewed their healing reports.[65] In response to all this, Grudem said,

> Carson nowhere quotes John Wimber to support these charges, nor does he quote anyone else in the Vineyard movement (except his inaccurate recounting of my story of the man with headaches), nor does he give any

evidence of ever having visited a Vineyard church or talked with any Vineyard pastor or any other responsible leader within the Vineyard movement.[66]

Grudem, who had spent hundreds of hours in Vineyard churches and talked with several Vineyard pastors and leaders, went on to say that Carson's picture of the Vineyard was so inaccurate that Grudem was unable to "recognize the great majority of his characterizations as accurate or truthful." Grudem then asked that Carson, even if he disagreed with the Vineyard theologically, "at least try to represent their position in a way that they [the Vineyard] would recognize it as accurate."[67] Grudem's final analysis of Carson's article was this:

> If a scholar wants to criticize a movement, no matter how biblical or sound that movement is, he can criticize it for a number of reasons [but if] a respected scholar does not take the time to find out what the facts are, but simply speaks in broad generalizations that make all sorts of accusations without support from any evidence, the criticism can be very damaging whether it is grounded in fact of not."[68]

Grudem then moved on to respond to James Boice. To begin, Grudem addressed the incorrect statements Boice had made regarding Wimber's life and ministry. First, Boice had seemed to diminish Wimber's relationship with Fuller Theological Seminary by saying Wimber had worked only a "short time" at Fuller. In reality, Grudem pointed out, Wimber had worked as a full-time visiting faculty member in the Fuller Evangelistic Association, had co-led the famous the MC510 Signs and Wonders and Church Growth class with C. Peter Wagner, and—even after the class was canceled—continued to function as visiting faculty member in the doctor of ministry program. All of this occurred between 1975 and 1992, a total of seventeen years—hardly a "short time," stated Grudem. Boice also claimed that Kevin Springer was actually the author of Wimber's book *Power Evangelism*. This, Grudem said, was also an incorrect statement. In reality, Springer had used Wimber's lecture notes and teaching tapes to put Wimber's teachings into prose, and he worked closely with Wimber to produce the material. As such, Springer was listed as a coauthor.[69]

Second, Boice claimed that Wimber and the Vineyard taught that evangelism should be done through the working of miracles and *not* by preaching the word. To this charge, Grudem said,

Boice gives no documentation for these claims, in fact he could not do so, because John Wimber has never taught we should work miracles rather than preaching the gospel message. Wimber always argues that Jesus's own ministry *combined* proclamation of the word with demonstration of God's present power in life. It is proclamation of the word *plus* demonstration of God's power, not one or the other, that Wimber is arguing for.[70]

According to Grudem, Wimber had never taught that people should be saved through signs and wonders rather than through the gospel message. These charges were simply false.

Boice also claimed that Wimber denied the values of suffering and that the "signs and wonders movement cheapens suffering." According to Boice, "The religion of signs reduces all those to unnecessary affliction and further burdens us with lacking faith if the demon of suffering cannot be quickly cast out. That is a cruel burden to lay on God's people."[71] Grudem pointed to several examples where Wimber had affirmed the redemptive aspects of suffering. In *Power Healing*, Wimber stated that God uses pain and sickness to break us of our rebellious self, that suffering in sickness plays a part in spiritual growth, and that some types of suffering are marks of the Christian life.[72] It would be more accurate to say Wimber taught that, while God works through evil, that does not mean a believer should passively accept it. Grudem also pointed to the fact that Wimber was always transparent about his own physical conditions, and he mentioned Wimber's good friend, David Watson, who, even after they earnestly prayed for him, still died of cancer. Grudem went on to say that if the Vineyard taught the "cruel doctrine that suffering and sickness are always due to our lack of faith," then he "would have nothing to do with it. These are serious heresies. They are false, unbiblical doctrines of major consequence."[73]

In addition, Boice charged that to desire "signs and wonders [was] sinful and unbelieving."[74] Grudem said Boice would be hard-pressed to prove this statement, because it was not in agreement with the activity of the early church in Acts 4:30, where the believers asked God to stretch out his hand to heal and perform signs and wonders through the name of Jesus. Grudem also quoted Romans 15:18-19, where Paul said he had won the Gentiles to Christ "by word and deed, by the power of signs and wonders, by the power of the Holy Spirit."[75]

Boice next accused Wimber of giving "glory to the Holy Spirit." Grudem questioned why this was problematic since the doxology sang in Boice's own church ended with, "Praise Father, Son, and Holy Ghost!"[76]

Finally, Boice attempted to force an either/or choice upon the Vineyard, when in actuality they taught a doctrine of both/and. Boice declared, "not miracles, but Scriptures," but the Vineyard taught both Scriptures and gifts of the Spirit. Boice writes,

> The signs and wonders movement shifts from the sublime to the ridiculous. It cheapens and overshadows the gospel . . . those alleged wonders are next to nothing in comparison to the message of God's redemptive work in Jesus Christ or the true miracle of the new birth.[77]

According to Grudem, then, Boice would prefer "not healings, but Christ's redeeming work and the new birth." Grudem agreed that the greatest miracles are the incarnation, the atonement, and the new birth, but this did not mean that healing cheapened the gospel. For the person who has suffered in body for years and is healed, healing is not ridiculous. The new birth is important, Grudem affirmed, but physical healing is also important. We need to be thankful for *both* healing people *and* preaching the gospel, which is closer to the New Testament model than one in which *either* healing *or* preaching the gospel must be chosen, as espoused by Boice.[78]

Grudem concluded his response to Boice by asking, "I wonder if Dr. Boice would want his treatment of John Wimber [who Grudem had called a leader of high visibility in the church] to be used as a model for Christians to follow when they speak and write about those with whom they disagree."[79]

Several weeks after Boice died, in June of 2000, Grudem received a personal letter from Boice's daughter saying that, before he died, Boice had asked her to convey to Grudem that he was thankful for Grudem's ministry. The letter did not specifically mention Grudem's response to Boice's 1992 chapter criticizing the Vineyard, but Grudem immediately understood it to be related to that issue.[80]

Leaving Boice's concerns, Grudem turned his last thoughts to John Armstrong, a friend and colleague from the Baptist Conference. In 1990 and 1991, Armstrong had written ten articles, which were printed in *The Standard*, a journal published by the Baptist General Conference. In 1992, Grudem had written the Vineyard's third position paper in response to those articles. That same year, Armstrong submitted a chapter for the book *Power Religion,* which someone sent to Grudem before it went to print. When Grudem discovered the chapter contained a rehash of Armstrong's previous criticisms, even after Grudem had soundly refuted them in the third position paper, he wrote a letter to the editor of Moody Press along with a copy of his critiques of Armstrong's articles. When the book *Power Religion* came out, Grudem was surprised to see that the chapter had been rewritten but contained new charges, which were also without foundational support. Grudem once again had to face his Baptist friend, whom he now believed was on an "apparent crusade to prove that the Vineyard teaches things that it does not."[81]

First, Armstrong quoted numerous non-Vineyard people, accusing them of error, then implied Wimber was guilty by association. Armstrong also made allegations against Wimber using quotes from bits and pieces that were inaccessible to the general public, making it nearly impossible for people to check the accuracy of the material. Grudem's response was to ask Armstrong if he thought this method was an accurate way to bring charges against a major leader in the church today.[82]

Second, Armstrong accused the Vineyard of promoting a paradigm shift from a Western to an Eastern worldview. According to Grudem, Wimber never taught they should shift to an Eastern worldview that promoted religious mysticism, anti-rationalism, or syncretism, as Armstrong implied. Rather, Wimber taught "we should shift from a Western *materialistic, rationalistic* worldview to a *biblical* worldview that includes the supernatural and the spiritual reality of creation."[83]

Armstrong also believed it was inappropriate for the Vineyard to train people how to pray for the sick and do evangelism, saying these were not "learned skills" in the New Testament and therefore to teach such skills degenerated prayer for healing into "superstition and magic." As a seminary professor, Grudem struggled with Armstrong's logic and reminded him of courses that are regularly offered in seminaries to teach people how to preach, evangelize, and counsel.[84]

In conclusion, Grudem said he responded to the criticisms made in *Power Religion* first because truth is important; second because "the ministry and reputation of the Vineyard and John Wimber are important, and they have been damaged by this book"; and finally because "fellowship and trust between Christians are important" and these were damaged through the contents of their work.[85] According to Grudem, he found it difficult to differ with his friends and colleagues, but due to their inaccurate portrayal of Wimber and the Vineyard movement, he felt it necessary to respond and set the record straight.

Position Paper #5: Response to *Charismatic Chaos*

John MacArthur's attack on the Pentecostal and charismatic movements began in 1978 with his book *The Charismatics*.[86] In 1992, MacArthur launched a second attack on the movements in his book *Charismatic Chaos*.[87] In this updated version, MacArthur also criticized the Third Wave movement in general and John Wimber in particular.

MacArthur was a 1970 graduate of Talbot Theological Seminary, the pastor of Grace Community Church in Sun Valley, California, and the host of his own daily radio program "Grace for You." While his entire book was a polemic against the Pentecostal and charismatic movements, chapter six, "What is behind the Third Wave?" was a personal attack against Wimber. Therefore, in April of 1993, Rich Nathan was commissioned by the Association of Vineyard Churches to write a response to *Charismatic Chaos*. Nathan's reply became Vineyard's fifth position paper.[88]

Nathan had been the senior pastor of the Vineyard Church in Columbus, Ohio, since 1987. He held bachelor of arts in religion and history as well as a juris doctorate from Ohio State University School of Law. Before pastoring, he was assistant professor of Business Law at the same university. According to Nathan, the reason Vineyard chose to respond to MacArthur's accusations was that "once a charge has been made and is read by thousands of Christian friends, it demands to be answered."[89]

Nathan accepted the charge and responded to MacArthur's *Charismatic Chaos*, which Nathan said was not only "unquestionably pejorative and unloving" but also "filled with factual and biblical errors."[90] According to Nathan, MacArthur's approach was to build a "straw man" using "examples of the worst or the weakest charismatic proponents" to launch a "wholesale attack on the charismatic movement."[91] In the first thirteen pages of his twenty-four-page reply, Nathan responded to MacArthur's general accusations about charismatics and Pentecostals who were, in MacArthur's opinion, "keen but clueless," "anti-intellectual," "not far removed from existentialism, humanism and paganism," and were "perilously close to neo-baalism."[92] Regarding MacArthur's research on the subject, Nathan pointed out that MacArthur had used spurious quotations from children's Sunday school literature and unpublished tapes rather than quoting from more scholarly material by Pentecostal/charismatic scholars such as Russell Spittler, Gordon Fee, Killian McDonald, or Kevin Ranaghan.[93]

The second half of Nathan's position paper addressed the accusations against the third wave, which MacArthur said was "rolling in like a destructive tsunami, leaving chaos and confusion in its wake."[94] Here Nathan tackled, point by point, MacArthur's "most derisory and virulent attacks against John Wimber, whom he arbitrarily lumps with the third wave" by calling him the leader of the movement which, according to Nathan, "force[d] Wimber to defend a label that he himself is uncomfortable with and only gingerly holds."[95]

MacArthur then charged that the Vineyard movement lacked a written statement of faith, so Nathan produced the eleven-point statement adopted by the Vineyard in 1986—which MacArthur could have readily obtained if he had simply asked either the Association of Vineyard Churches or contacted Wimber personally.[96]

MacArthur also accused the third wave of underemphasizing traditional means of spiritual growth. He wrote:

> Like Pentecostals and charismatics, common third wave adherents aggressively pursue ecstatic experiences, mystical phenomena, miraculous powers, and supernatural wonders—*while tending to under-emphasize the traditional means of spiritual growth: prayer, Bible study, the teaching of the Word, persevering in obedience and fellowship of other believers.*[97]

In response, Nathan again pointed out that MacArthur had not examined Vineyard's Statement of Fundamental Priorities, which included worship, teaching the Bible, prayer, fellowship, ministry, training, and evangelism and world missions as priorities.[98] According to Nathan, the Vineyard's "first leadership requirement is 'a sincere love and pursuit of Jesus Christ demonstrated in regular personal worship, meditation on God's Word, and prayer.'"[99]

Third, MacArthur attacked Wimber's teaching on power evangelism, saying it was "patently unbiblical" and that nowhere in the ministry of Jesus or in the book of Acts was power evangelism practiced.[100] In his book, *Power Evangelism*, Wimber defined what he meant by this term:

> By power evangelism I mean a presentation of the gospel that is rational, but that also transcends the rational (though it is in no way 'irrational' or anti-rational). The explanation of the gospel—the clear proclamation of the finished work of Christ on the cross—comes with a demonstration of God's power through signs and wonders. Power evangelism is a spontaneous, Spirit-inspired, empowered presentation of the gospel. Power evangelism is preceded and undergirded by demonstrations of God's presence, and frequently results in groups of people being saved. Signs and wonders do not save; only Jesus and His substitutionary work on the cross saves. Through these supernatural encounters people experience the presence and power of God. Usually this takes the form of words of knowledge . . . healing, prophecy, and deliverance from evil spirits.[101]

Again, Nathan declared that MacArthur had misrepresented Wimber's teachings related to power evangelism, which in reality holds that "signs and wonders *accredit* the message and messenger of salvation."[102]

Fourth, MacArthur used a statement that Wimber made in an unpublished tape as support for the allegation that Wimber denied the deity of Christ. MacArthur wrote,

> Wimber's teaching regarding the person of Jesus Christ is careless at best, blasphemous at worst, but in any case clearly contradictory of Scripture. In his taped healing seminar, Wimber says, 'Haven't you been taught that Jesus knows all things? There are many times in the Gospel when Jesus doesn't know, and he has to ask questions.'

Nathan questioned why MacArthur did not use Wimber's book *Power Points* and instead used obscure unpublished and oral material. *Power Points*, Nathan said, contained a "well stated and orthodox view of the deity of Christ," and revealed an entire chapter on the subject of Jesus being fully God.[103]

Finally, MacArthur charged Wimber with drifting from biblical orthodoxy as seen in his associations with Catholics, Anglicans, Shakers, and Quakers. As further evidence of this claim, MacArthur quoted the following statement that Wimber had made about the pope:

> The pope . . . by the way is very responsive to the charismatic movement, and is himself a born-again evangelical. If you've read any of his texts concerning salvation, you'd know he is preaching the gospel as clear as anybody is preaching it in the world today.[104]

Because of this and Wimber's ecumenical associations, MacArthur charged that Wimber had abandoned conservative evangelicalism.[105] Nathan defended Wimber by saying, "Celebrating the pope's statements hardly makes Wimber guilty of heresy." Nathan went on to say that Wimber had always declared himself to be a conservative evangelical who spoke in tongues. He never watered down his evangelical beliefs, and the reason he was willing to speak in a variety of church settings was "because he sees a huge need for the message and ministry that God has given him and is willing to declare that message wherever and whenever God gives him an opportunity so long as he can do so without conditions or compromise."[106]

On a personal note, Nathan said he had "heard John Wimber teach on more than one hundred occasions," and knew that . . .

> His public image is no different from the private person that I have come to know and respect. He firmly holds to conservative evangelical beliefs regarding the trinity, the deity of Christ, the substitutionary atonement, Christ's physical resurrection, the inerrancy of the scriptures, both Old and New Testaments, and the personal, visible return of our Lord Jesus Christ.[107]

Nathan's conclusion was that MacArthur's charges against Wimber were unfair and inappropriate, and it was "MacArthur's rancorous, bombastic style that undermines his objectivity and any value [his] book may have had as a necessary corrective to excesses or errors in the charismatic, Pentecostal and Third Wave movements."[108]

In the summer of 1993, J. Rodman Williams, distinguished professor of theology at Regent University in Virginia Beach, Virginia, also brought MacArthur's *Charismatic Chaos* charges to task in his article "Biblical Truth and Experience: A Reply to *Charismatic Chaos* by John F. MacArthur, Jr."[109] Williams stated that his primary concern for writing was "the way MacArthur handle[d] biblical truth in regard to the charismatic renewal."[110] While Williams did not directly defend Wimber, his response served to support and validate Nathan's position paper.

[1] Hunt, *The Seduction of Christianity*, 171–88.
[2] Stafford, "Testing the Wine from John Wimber's Vineyard," 17–22.
[3] Ken L. Sarles, "An Appraisal of the Signs and Wonders Movement," *Bibliotheca Sacra*, January/March 1988, 57–82.
[4] Hank Hanegraaff, *Counterfeit Revival: Looking for God in All the Wrong Places* (Dallas, TX: Word Publishing, 1997).
[5] John Wimber, "Why I Don't Respond to Criticism," *Equipping the Saints*, Summer 1988, 15–6.
[6] Unsigned, "Signs and Wonders," 66–8.
[7] Interview by the author with Bob Fulton.
[8] Wimber, "Why I Don't Respond to Criticism," 15.
[9] Wimber, "Why I Don't Respond to Criticism," 15.
[10] Whitehead, "A Catholic Evaluation," in *John Wimber: His Influence and Legacy*, 219-20.
[11] Millar, "A Friend's Recollections," in *John Wimber: His Influence and Legacy*, 286.
[12] Wimber, "Why I Don't Respond to Criticism," 16.
[13] Carol Wimber, *John Wimber*, 171.
[14] Carol Wimber, *John Wimber*, 172.
[15] Interview by the author with Wayne Grudem on February 23, 2010, at the Phoenix Seminary in Phoenix, Arizona.
[16] Wimber, "Why I Don't Respond to Criticism," 16.
[17] Coggins and Paul G. Hiebert, eds., *Wonders and the Word: An Examination of the Issues Raised by John Wimber and the Vineyard Movement* (Winnipeg: Kindred Press, 1989). The contributing authors include James R. Coggins, editor, a Mennonite with a PhD in history from the University of Waterloo, Waterloo, Ontario; Paul G. Hiebert, editor, professor of mission anthropology in South Asian studies at Fuller Theological Seminary, Pasadena, California; Abraham Friesen, professor of history at the University of California in Santa Barbara, California; Victor G. Doerksen, professor and head of the department of German at the University of Manitoba, Winnipeg; Levi Keidel, head of the missions department at Columbia Bible College, Clearbrook, British Columbia; Don Lewis, assistant professor of church history at Regent College, Vancouver, British Columbia; John Vooys, teacher of New Testament and theology at Columbia Bible College, Clearbrook, British Columbia; John Schmidt, academic dean at Columbia Bible College, Clearbrook, British Columbia; Tim Geddert, assistant professor of New Testament at Mennonite Brethren Biblical Seminary, Fresno, California; J. B. Toews, professor emeritus of history and theology at Mennonite Brethren Biblical Seminary, Fresno, California; and Art Glasser, professor of mission theology at Fuller Theological Seminary, Fresno, California.
[18] Coggins, *Wonders and the Word*, 7.
[19] Friesen, "Wimber, Word and Spirit," 36, 40–1.
[20] Donald M. Lewis, "An Historian's Assessment," 52–61.
[21] Paul G. Hiebert, "Healing and the Kingdom," 123–4.
[22] Jack Deere, "The Vineyard's Response to the Briefing," *Vineyard Position Paper #2* (May 1992), 1. Also, Jackson, *Quest for the Radical Middle*, 154.
[23] Deere, *Position Paper #2*, 3.
[24] Deere, *Position Paper #2*, 2.
[25] Deere, *Position Paper #2*, 2.
[26] Interview by the author with Wayne Grudem.
[27] Wimber, "Why I Respond to Criticism," *Position Paper # 1*, 2.
[28] Wimber, *Position Paper #1*, 2, 3.
[29] Wimber, *Position Paper #1*, 6.
[30] Wimber, *Position Paper #1*, 5.
[31] Wimber, *Position Paper #1*, 6.

[32] Phillip Jensen and Tony Payne, "John Wimber: Friend or Foe?" *The Briefing* 45/46 (April 24, 1990). (Published in Sydney, Australia, by St. Matthias Anglican Church.)
[33] Deere, *Position Paper #2*, 2.
[34] Deere, *Position Paper #2*, 23.
[35] Deere, *Position Paper #2*, 24.
[36] Deere, *Position Paper #2*, 25.
[37] Deere, *Position Paper #2*, 25.
[38] David Lewis, *Healing: Fiction, Fantasy or Fact?* (London, England: Hodder & Stoughton, 1989), 21–2.
[39] Deere, *Position Paper #2*, 26.
[40] Deere, *Position Paper #2*, 26.
[41] Deere, *Position Paper #2*, 28.
[42] Deere, *Position Paper #2*, 28.
[43] Grudem, *Position Paper #3*, 1–2.
[44] Grudem, *Position Paper #3*, 3.
[45] Grudem, *Position Paper #3*, 3.
[46] Grudem, *Position Paper #3*, 8.
[47] Grudem, *Position Paper #3*, 9.
[48] Grudem, *Position Paper #3*, 10.
[49] Grudem, *Position Paper #3*, 12–3.
[50] Grudem, *Position Paper #3*, 14.
[51] Grudem, *Position Paper #3*, 17.
[52] Grudem, *Position Paper #3*, 17.
[53] Grudem, *Position Paper #3*, 19.
[54] Grudem, *Position Paper #3*, 20.
[55] Michael Scott Horton, ed., *Power Religion: The Selling Out of the Evangelical Church?* (Chicago, IL: Moody Bible Institute, 1992).
[56] Grudem, *Position Paper #4*, 1, 47.
[57] Grudem, *Position Paper #4*, 1.
[58] Grudem, *Position Paper #4*, 1.
[59] Grudem, *Position Paper #4*, 1.
[60] Grudem, *Position Paper #4*, 3.
[61] Grudem, *Position Paper #4*, 5.
[62] Grudem, *Position Paper #4*, 8.
[63] Grudem, *Position Paper #4*, 6.
[64] Grudem, *Position Paper #4*, 27.
[65] Grudem, *Position Paper #4*, 8.
[66] Grudem, *Position Paper #4*, 8.
[67] Grudem, *Position Paper #4*, 8.
[68] Grudem, *Position Paper #4*, 28.
[69] Grudem, *Position Paper #4*, 30–1.
[70] Grudem, *Position Paper #4*, 31.
[71] James M. Boice, "A Better Way: The Power of the Word and Spirit," in *Power Religion*, ed. Michael Scott Horton (Chicago, IL: Moody Press, 1992), 130.
[72] Wimber and Springer, *Power Healing*, 13, 15, 16.
[73] Grudem, *Position Paper #4*, 36.
[74] Grudem, *Position Paper #4*, 36.
[75] Grudem, *Position Paper #4*, 37, 38.
[76] Grudem, *Position Paper #4*, 40.
[77] Boice, "A Better Way," 129.
[78] Grudem, *Position Paper #4*, 42.
[79] Grudem, *Position Paper #4*, 46.
[80] Personal email from Wayne Grudem to Connie Dawson, June 28, 2019.

[81] Grudem, *Position Paper* #4, 55.
[82] Grudem, *Position Paper* #4, 50.
[83] Grudem, *Position Paper* #4, 51.
[84] Grudem, *Position Paper* #4, 52.
[85] Grudem, *Position Paper* #4, 56.
[86] John MacArthur, *The Charismatics* (Grand Rapids: Zondervan, 1978).
[87] MacArthur, *Charismatic Chaos*.
[88] Jackson, *Quest for the Radical Middle*, 166.
[89] Nathan, *Position Paper* #5, 24.
[90] Nathan, *Position Paper* #5, 14.
[91] Nathan, *Position Paper* #5, 2, 11.
[92] Nathan, *Position Paper* #5, 6; MacArthur, *Charismatic Chaos*, 21, 40, 41, 43.
[93] Nathan, *Position Paper* #5, 2, 20.
[94] Nathan, 6; MacArthur, *Charismatic Chaos*, 131.
[95] Nathan, *Position Paper* #5, 14, 24.
[96] Nathan, *Position Paper* #5, 15.
[97] Nathan, *Position Paper* #5, 16; italics added by Nathan.
[98] Nathan, *Position Paper* #5, 16.
[99] Nathan, *Position Paper* #5, 16.
[100] MacArthur, *Charismatic Chaos*, 168.
[101] Nathan, *Position Paper* #5, 17.
[102] Nathan, *Position Paper* #5, 17; emphasis added.
[103] Nathan, *Position Paper* #5, 20–1; Wimber, 87–93.
[104] MacArthur, *Charismatic Chaos*, 180.
[105] MacArthur, *Charismatic Chaos*, 181.
[106] Nathan, *Position Paper* #5, 22.
[107] Nathan, *Position Paper* #5, 25.
[108] Nathan, Position Paper #5, 26.
[109] J. Rodman Williams, "Biblical Truth and Experience: A Reply to *Charismatic Chaos* by John F. MacArthur, Jr.," *Paraclete,* Summer 1993, 16–30.
[110] Williams, "Biblical Truth and Experience," 16.

Chapter 7

The Prophetic Years

The early 1980s were glorious for Wimber, but toward the middle of the decade, things began to change. In the larger church arena, the Jim Bakker and Jimmy Swaggart scandals were headlining church news, and Wimber and the Vineyard movement felt the effect of the storm as critics began speaking disparagingly against the supernatural nature of his ministry. In addition to receiving outside criticism, he was suffering from health problems. In October 1985, he went to England for three weeks to speak at various conferences and later reported that many were healed, "one of which was not me."[1] After returning to America, he was diagnosed with angina, ulcers, and high blood pressure. He was overweight and overworked.

At this time, Wimber was also experiencing stress in his family and church. One of his sons, Sean, was away from the Lord and struggling with drug and alcohol addiction.[2] Then in 1986, two of Wimber's key associates fell into sexual immorality. During this time, he was also made aware of pride and carnality in the Vineyard, and he felt the Lord saying that the movement was barren and spiritually dry. Although he prayed and repented, and subsequently preached a sixteen-part series on repentance, he still lacked clarity into where they had gotten off course and how to get back on track.[3]

It was in this context that he was introduced to Mike Bickle, Bob Jones, and Paul Cain—men involved in the prophetic who had a profound impact on Wimber and the Vineyard movement.

Mike Bickle and the Kansas City Fellowship

In his writings on the Holy Spirit, Stan Burgess said that, throughout church history, there has always been a tension between the spirit of order in the mainline church and the spirit of prophecy.[4] Mike Bickle was a man who had dealt with this conflict in his early Christian experience only to find himself pastoring a church full of prophetic people. For about eight years, from 1988 to 1996, Bickle was a key figure in Wimber's life and ministry.

In February 1972, when Bickle was sixteen, he was filled with the Holy Spirit at Evangel Temple, an Assemblies of God church in Kansas City. At first, he did not know what had happened; he was just engulfed by the Holy Spirit and began speaking in tongues, something he had no knowledge of until the people at the Presbyterian church he normally attended explained what had happened to him. When he shared with one of the Presbyterian youth leaders about his powerful experience, he was told that this was a demonic encounter. So Bickle spent the next five years on a mission to warn everyone to avoid all "counterfeit" charismatic experiences.

Then in 1976, at the age of twenty, a rural Lutheran church in Rosebud, Missouri, recruited him to be their pastor. Unbeknownst to him, this little church of about thirty people had just gotten filled with the Holy Spirit, so for a year, God used these precious people to soften his heart to the things of the Spirit. He was still unsure, however, when the pastor of New Covenant Fellowship, the largest charismatic church in the St. Louis area, asked him to be their youth pastor. After he spent two years in this position, in September 1979, New Covenant Fellowship decided to plant a new church on the south side of St. Louis, and they asked Bickle to be the pastor. It was here, in June 1982, that he met Augustine Alcala, a traveling prophet who prophesied that Bickle would move to Kansas City and plant a new church, which he did in December 1982.[5]

Before moving to Kansas City, however, Bickle went to India for a teaching conference with a team of eight pastors and, afterward, took a short trip to Cairo, Egypt. While in Egypt, he had a powerful visitation from the Lord, who said, "I am going to change the understanding of Christianity in the earth in one generation, and I am inviting you to be a part of a work that will be a part of this." The Lord then showed him that this work must be built on four values: night-and-day prayer, holiness of heart, the prophetic, and extravagant giving to the poor. In response, Bickled cried, "Yes, Lord! Yes, Lord!" And the Lord responded, "Many have said yes but did not do it. And you have only said yes, but you have not yet done it."[6]

The Lord impressed upon him the seriousness of this call and the importance of obedience to a number of values seen in the New Testament church, noting that these four values are often neglected.[7] Bickle said the Lord told him that he had to guard his heart lest his brothers try to steal these four particular values from him, and as such, they became the non-negotiables that would hold Bickle steady through the coming decades.[8] Starting with his very first days in Kansas City, Mike emphasized these four values and enforced the authority of Scripture and the first commandment to love Jesus with all of our heart, which overflows into loving people.⁹

Mike and his wife Diane moved to Kansas City in November 1982, where the Lord miraculously provided them with a building on the south side of town. Just before moving to Kansas City, Augustine, the traveling prophet, once again visited Bickle in St. Louis in October and gave him a four-part prophecy. The first two parts were wonderful—the Lord would bring multitudes of young people to this ministry, and at the appointed time, he would see a full manifestation of the gifts of the Spirit. The second two parts were not as positive: there would be a false prophet in their midst from the very beginning, and they would face resistance and much controversy. But Bickle was encouraged not to lose heart.¹⁰

Bob Jones: Helping Bickle Embrace the Prophetic

After being in Kansas City with his new young adult church-plant for only a few months, in February 1983, an older man told Bickle that there was a prophet in Kansas City by the name of Bob Jones who had been talking for several years about a twenty-seven-year-old man who would come to south Kansas City, focused on intercession and revival, and lead a group of young people. At that time, Bickle was twenty-seven, and intercession and revival were his messages. Bickle was skeptical, however, and declined to meet with Jones. Then on March 7, fifty-three-year-old Jones walked into Bickle's office. It was a balmy spring day, and Bickle wondered why Jones was wearing a heavy winter coat. Jones prophesied that God was going to "raise up worldwide a young adult prayer movement led by prophetic singers and musicians in Kansas City."¹¹ A red flag immediately went up in Bickle's mind as he wondered if this was the false prophet Augustine had warned him about. As if reading Bickle's mind, Jones reiterated the four-part prophecy Augustine had given him. As Jones left Bickle's office, he turned and said that on the first day of spring, when the snow melted, they would be sitting around the table and his prophetic ministry would be accepted by Bickle, thus the reason for the winter coat—it was a parabolic symbol.¹²

Two weeks later, Art Katz, an itinerate preacher with a global prophetic burden, came to town. He had heard about a young adult church hosting prayer meetings seven nights a week, believing God for revival in Kansas City. He was curious to see this new church of young people, so he attended Bickle's South Kansas City Fellowship. At the morning meeting, Jones introduced himself to Katz and told Katz the secrets of his heart. Katz became immediately convinced that Jones was a true prophet of God and, later that night, called Bickle to ask if they could meet with Jones. Katz had planned to fly out on Sunday afternoon, but his small four-passenger airplane was snowed in by an unseasonable spring storm.

At nine o'clock Sunday night, Katz, Jones, and a few others met in Bickle's home to talk. This time, Jones shared things from Bickle's life that only Mike himself knew, things that convinced him Jones was a true prophet. There was much weeping, talking, and praying, which lasted until 4 o'clock in the morning. On that early Monday morning, March 21, the first day of spring, they were all sitting around the table, and just before the morning sun came up, the snow was melting.[13] Just as Jones had prophesied, Bickle, who at one time had rejected charismatic teaching, had now welcomed Jones as a prophet. Over the coming years, Jones became Bickle's close friend and ministry colleague.

A month later, Bickle said he had received instruction from the Lord to call the churches of Kansas City to a twenty-one-day fast and that, along with the five hundred people in Bickle's new church-plant, others from Kansas City would join them in the solemn assembly. Because Mike was so young and new in the city, he was concerned he would appear presumptuous, but Jones confirmed the commission, saying he had received the same word. So, on May 7, 1983, the fast began. The first night of the fast, seven hundred people responded, and for the next twenty-one days, they met eighteen hours a day in prayer—from six o'clock a.m. to midnight. About two hundred people came for morning hours and about the same number prayed throughout the afternoons, with about five hundred showing up for the nightly meetings, which lasted until midnight.[14]

At the end of the twenty-one days, on May 28, Jones stood up and said the bad news was that revival would not be coming to the city right then. Bickle said the people were horrified. What did he mean the revival they had been praying and fasting for was not coming? Jones went on to say that there was a spiritual drought in the nation and that the revival they were expecting, one that would eclipse the revival in the book of Acts, would not come until after his death. He said that, to prove this word was true and that God was sovereignly in control, God would send a natural rain in the midst of their current drought on August 23. At the time, they were in the worst drought in Kansas City's one-hundred-year history.

Just as Jones prophesied, on August 23, several thousand people gathered at seven o'clock to pray, and there was a torrential outpouring of rain that lasted for about twenty minutes. While the total volume of rain was small, for those twenty minutes, the downpour was severe. The spiritual parabolic point, Jones said, was this: There would be an outpouring of the Holy Spirit that would come on America, it would be a sovereign move, it would come suddenly, it would end the spiritual drought, and it would even surpass the revival seen in the book of Acts. Jones said, just as surely as this prophetic sign of rain in the natural was given and fulfilled, the spiritual outpouring of the future revival would also come to pass.[15]

In January of 1984, Jones told Bickle that God was going to connect him with a movement located thirty-five miles south of Los Angeles. This group, he said, functioned under a spiritual banner of "compassion and worship," and God wanted them to "cross-pollinate" with the Kansas City spiritual banners of the "prophetic and intercession." Bickle had not heard of Wimber or the Vineyard movement when Jones gave him this word, but in June of 1984, he took a group from the South Kansas City Fellowship to the Anaheim Vineyard to attend Wimber's first public MC510 Signs and Wonders and Church Growth conference.[16] Although Bickle attended the conference, he did not connect with Wimber until four years later, in January 1988.[17]

Introducing Paul Cain

About nine months before they met, in April 1987, Bickle met Paul Cain for the first time. Cain was a man who would have a significant impact on his life and, later, on Wimber.[18]

Bickle had first heard of Paul Cain in June 1984, but it was another three years before he actually met the famous prophet. Cain was a man who seemed to have walked in the realm of the supernatural all his life. Even his birth was miraculous. In 1929, forty-five-year-old Anna Cain was pregnant with a son. She had just returned home from Baylor University Hospital in Dallas, Texas, where she had been diagnosed with three terminal conditions—heart problems, tuberculosis, and malignant tumors in her uterus and breasts. The doctors sent her home to die, but God had other plans. In her eighth month of pregnancy, an angel appeared to her and said, "Daughter, be of good cheer. Be not afraid.

You shall not die, but live to bear this child. The fruit of your womb is a male whom I have anointed to preach my gospel like the apostle Paul of old. Name him Paul. He will be born in perfect health."[19] His mother was instantly healed and lived to be 105 years old. Cain's mother did not tell her son about the divine visitation, but at the age of eight, Cain had his own angelic encounter, at which time he received his call to ministry. He immediately began preaching to his own backyard congregation made up of railroad spikes, which he later said were quite "hard headed." At the age of nine, his Baptist pastor recognized the call of God on his life and started mentoring him. Even in these early years, his pastor realized he could see and hear spiritual things that only God could have revealed. By the time he was eighteen, he had a radio ministry and was traveling and conducting healing meetings. Those were the days of the Pentecostal healing evangelists such as Oral Roberts, T. L. Osborn, Jack Coe, and A. A. Allen, but the one who befriended the young preacher-prophet was William Branham.[20]

Branham was known as the father of the miraculous healing campaigns that followed the Second World War. He was born into poverty, had limited education, and had also experienced an angelic visitation, in which he was promised a divine healing ministry. Branham was recognized as a prophet who operated powerfully in the word of knowledge.[21] Walter Hollenweger, a Swiss theologian and scholar of Pentecostalism, served as Branham's interpreter on one of his trips to Europe. Hollenweger testified that he witnessed Branham "name with astonishing accuracy the sickness, and often also hidden sins, of people who he had never seen" and that he himself was "not aware of any case in which he [Branham] was mistaken in the often detailed statements he made."[22]

In those early days, Cain was perceived as having spiritual gifts that matched Branham's. Though he never worked on the platform with Branham, the older prophet often asked Cain to fulfill Branham's preaching commitments because of his frail health. The two worked together in this capacity and communicated on a regular basis. Branham had a powerful ministry, but in the later years of his life he veered off into heretical teachings, at which time Cain was no longer associated with him.[23] As the post-World War II healing evangelist era began to decline, Cain felt called aside for a season of seclusion. God said to him, "I am going to take you aside into the desert until a new breed of men is raised up. In the days to come this ministry will be taken forward without superstars" and they will be known for their humility, purity, and power.[24] For the next twenty-five years, Cain lived in a modest home in Phoenix, Arizona, cared for his mother, and waited for the new breed of men. In April 1987, God directed Cain to go to Birmingham, Alabama, where he would meet Mike Bickle.[25] His time of waiting had come to an end.

Bickle was a conference speaker, and Cain appeared and introduced himself to the young preacher. Bickle was impressed with Cain and invited him to preach at the South Kansas City Fellowship. When he arrived, Cain was shocked to realize that this was the same facility he had seen in a vision twenty years earlier. In the vision he saw an illuminated billboard that read, "Joel's army in training." When he realized this, he was convinced this was the place God was going to raise up the "new breed" of leaders and teachers who would work for God's glory.[26] Bickle now had two prophetic ministers, Jones and Cain, committed to the vision God had given him. It was at this point that Wimber entered the picture.[27]

Wimber Connects with Bickle

In October 1987, Bob Jones prophesied to Bickle that John Wimber would be calling him in three months and that the "cross pollination" he had earlier spoken of would soon begin. Bickle was incredulous. Wimber had a worldwide ministry! Why would someone of his caliber contact someone like him? However, Jones's words came to pass in January 1988, when Wimber called and invited Bickle to be the speaker at a Vineyard staff retreat they would be having in three days.[28]

Wimber's retreat, designed for the one hundred people on his church staff, lasted three days, with three sessions each day, for a total of nine sessions. Wimber wanted Bickle to speak at all nine. Bickle was stunned, but then he responded—almost from a state of shock—that he would be there. Bickle gathered a few of his pastors from Kansas City to take with him. The meetings were two days away, so there was no time to prepare, but the Holy Spirit moved in a powerful way. Through the process, a friendship developed between Wimber and Bickle, and they felt a spiritual bond. After their time together, unbeknownst to Bickle, Wimber believed God was asking him to mentor the young preacher, but he was so busy, he did not contact Bickle again for over six months.[29]

On June 5, 1988, Jones again prophesied to Bickle that Wimber would soon open three large doors to him. This, he said, would be a "Holy Spirit seminary season" for him that would last three years. Jones told Bickle that he did not know how to minister in the context of large groups, but Wimber would teach him.[30] The next day Wimber called and invited Bickle to go with him on a ministry trip to Edinburgh, Scotland, and the United Kingdom. From this point forward, Wimber began inviting Bickle to travel with him to conferences around the world, and it was during these years that he taught Bickle how to minister through words of knowledge and the power of the Spirit.[31]

Throughout 1987, Wimber also came to realize that the Vineyard was in desperate spiritual condition, and he cried out to God in repentance asking for help. God seemed to respond to his cry by speaking to him through Bickle during the ministry trip to Scotland in 1988. He later said that Bickle had kept "pestering" him to begin accepting full responsibility as the leader of the Vineyard movement, and it was through Bickle's persistence that Wimber's resistance was broken and God was able to speak to him. As a result, Wimber made adjustments. He felt chastised yet reassured by the Lord that help was on the way. And that help came in the form of the prophets.[32]

Wimber Meets Paul Cain

Wimber was introduced to Cain through their mutual friend, Jack Deere. Deere had first met Wimber in 1986 at one of his conferences held at Lake County Baptist Church in Fort Worth, Texas. Deere, then associate professor of Old Testament at Dallas Theological Seminary, had never witnessed anyone being used in the word of knowledge and the gifts of healing the way Wimber had. After the conference, Deere introduced himself to Wimber, and they soon became close friends.

Through his contact with Wimber, Deere became more and more interested in the supernatural ministry of the Holy Spirit, which ultimately resulted in his leaving his Baptist church and being dismissed from his position at the seminary. In the fall of 1986, Deere helped George Mallone start Grace Vineyard Church in Arlington, Texas, and in September, the two of them went to Kansas City for a conference. While there, Bickle told them about Paul Cain and his amazing ministry in the 1940s and 1950s as well as his twenty-five years of seclusion. So once he was back in Texas, Deere contacted Cain and began spending large amounts of time with him. Deere found him to be all that Bickle had said and more.

In the fall of 1988, Deere was packing to leave Texas to join Wimber in ministry at the Anaheim Vineyard, but before leaving he had the opportunity to minister at a conference with Cain. As they ministered together, Deere witnessed Cain's mature prophetic gifting firsthand and believed it to exceed anything he had ever witnessed.[33]

In November of 1988, Cain felt God impressing upon him that he was to meet Wimber, so Deere offered to set up an appointment. Wimber was under a great deal of stress at the time, trying to run three organizations—the Anaheim Vineyard Christian Fellowship, the Association of Vineyard Churches, and Vineyard Ministries International—and he was not too keen on meeting a prophet. But due to Deere's persistence and stories about Cain from Bickle, Wimber finally agreed to a meeting in December.

Deere told Wimber this was a very important contact. For added confirmation, Cain prophesied that there would be an earthquake in the area the day he arrived on December 3, and that on December 7, the day after he was to leave Anaheim, there would be a major earthquake somewhere else in the world. Deere also delivered Wimber a prophetic word from Paul Cain, quoting Jeremiah 33:8: "I will cleanse from them all the sin they have committed against me and will forgive all their sins of rebellion against me." He said God was going to show mercy to the Vineyard with regards to immorality.[34] Wimber wrote,

> He told me that I was close to committing the sins of Eli with my spiritual sons, and that as a result we were very close to judgment as a movement. Paul's opening words to me were, 'Grace, grace, grace.' He then said that the Lord recognized my repentance, and that he was calling me to deal more seriously with sin, especially in the lives of the leaders of the Vineyard. We were in jeopardy of going down in history as a corrupted and immoral people who had started out under God's grace but had drifted far from his plan. I had allowed the sins of a few leaders to continue, thus contaminating the whole movement. (If one sins, all sins.)[35]

After assuring Wimber of God's grace, Cain went on to tell him that if they would repent, God would spare them the judgment of their sins. Wimber said, "I was admonished to no longer tolerate low standards and loose living in the Vineyard, and to discipline and raise up a people of purity and holiness."[36] Cain encouraged Wimber to step up and become a real father to the movement. He also told Wimber that, as a token of appreciation from the Lord for doing this,

his son Sean, who was living in sinful rebellion, would "see a great light before his next birthday and before John addressed the Vineyard again."[37]

At 3:38 a.m. the day Cain arrived, there was indeed an earthquake in Pasadena. Cain told Wimber that the time of the earthquake—3:38 a.m.—was a confirmation of the Jeremiah 33:8 prophecy.[38] According to C. Peter Wagner, the epicenter of this quake was one block from Fuller Seminary. The quake, he said, was so powerful that all of his books were shaken off the shelves, and it took him three days to get them all put away again.[39] Even more significant, on the day after he left, on December 7, just as Cain had prophesied, there was a major earthquake in Armenia that was reported worldwide.[40]

Following this encounter, Wimber immediately began to preach holiness in the Vineyard. Referring to this time, he said:

> The Lord is hard at work putting holiness and purity in the Vineyard. He's showing us that many of our habits and standards are not based on his word, and that his ways are higher than ours. God is taking us onto the 'Way of Holiness,' and the standards of behavior there are much higher than those under which we have lived in the past. Behavior that the Lord once tolerated in us will kill us on this path, for with greater privilege and revelation come greater responsibility and consequence. He's calling us to be careful with our tongues, dedicated in prayer and Scripture study, careful to avoid all evil and even the appearance of evil, upright with our finances, diligent with our time, faithful to our families. God's saying, 'If you're going to walk on my highway, you've got to do it my way.'[41]

This call to holiness became a part of Wimber's conference messages for the remainder of his ministry.

It was on December 3, 1988, when Cain had met Wimber, and the next national Vineyard conference was scheduled for July of the following year. Sean's birthday was in August, and just as Cain had prophesied, Sean came home in June, just before the conference and his twenty-seventh birthday. It was then that God used another prophet, Bob Jones, to speak to Sean's heart.[42]

Out of the blue one day, Jones knocked on Wimber's door. He asked to speak to Sean, but Wimber said Sean neither lived there nor was expected to visit anytime soon. Then suddenly, Sean walked in! Jones spoke words to Sean that opened his heart and caused him to repent and become reconciled to his family. As far as John and Carol were concerned, this was a true miracle.[43]

Up to this point, Wimber had held reservations regarding the prophetic, but after this event, everything changed. He recognized these prophets to be "men of character without fault, men of humility, teachable, submitted to God's word, and modest in lifestyle."[44] He was deeply affected through his new relationship with them. Both men had been involved in his son coming home, and Wimber credited Cain with saving the Vineyard through bringing much-needed spiritual correction.[45]

After this positive encounter with Paul Cain and his time with Mike Bickle, Wimber was ready to introduce the prophetic to the Vineyard movement. In January of 1990, the entire fall issue of *Equipping the Saints* was dedicated to the prophetic ministry. In an editorial, Wimber shared the entire story—his introduction to the prophets, the desperate condition of the Vineyard, and the Vineyard's "quantum leap in holiness and righteousness" as a result of their ministry. He declared that God was rooting out all kinds of sin. People were reading their Bibles as never before and they had been more devoted to prayer, fasting, worship, and spiritual disciplines since the two men's arrival.

He also forewarned the people that there would be a temporary focus on the prophetic that would appear to be out of balance as it was introduced. He said that, traditionally, when God initiated something new, they had a tendency to overemphasize it. He reminded them that when they had started as a movement in 1978, they had learned about worship and would consequently meet and worship for one-and-a-half hours and then often dismiss without much prayer or Bible study. Then tongues were introduced, and for a time that became their major focus. When they started praying for the sick, he said, healing became the center of their attention. Each time God launched them into something new, it was their focal point for a season, but then they eventually grew out of the myopic practice as the new teaching was assimilated into their spiritual DNA. In the same way, he predicted, the prophetic would take center stage for a season, but it would eventually settle into its appropriate place in the church. He also warned people not to elevate prophecy above Scripture and to remember that, in addition to prophecy, God also speaks through Scripture, dreams, visions, counsel, and other means of direct communication.

Wimber encouraged Vineyard pastors to allow the seeds of the prophetic to take root by first teaching on it, then stirring up the gift, and then making room for people to operate in the gift. He predicted that it would take years for the prophetic to mature in the Vineyard and that it could be messy as they grew from the infant stage through adolescence to maturity. He was convinced, however, that God was once again molding them by the Spirit, and he encouraged the people to "take a chance with the prophetic ministry."[46] With this single publication of *Equipping the Saints*, Wimber had initiated the cross-pollination process into the Vineyard movement.

Merging Ministries

In February of 1989, just two months after meeting Cain, Wimber hosted a Spiritual Warfare conference at the Anaheim Vineyard and asked Cain to be one of the speakers. The meetings were so powerful that the conference was extended by two days. At one point, Cain announced he had been given a torch to ignite the last-days ministry and had been instructed to give this torch to the Vineyard. Cain said that Wimber was the leader who would usher in a new move of God, a new wave of the Spirit.[47] Wimber, on the other hand, felt this was presumptuous and was so stunned that he was unable to respond.[48]

A few months later, in August 1989, Cain was invited to the Vineyard pastor's conference in Denver, where he gave several prophetic words calling the Vineyard back to its original commission of "worship and compassion." At one point, Cain also prophesied over John and Eleanor Mumford, pastors of the Southwest London Vineyard in England, saying, "I believe that revival will probably find its starting point somewhere in October there [in England], when the Lord will just start to move throughout London and throughout England."[49] Cain did not give the year, but the Mumfords assumed it would begin in October of that year. This prophecy ignited a blaze of controversy that became increasingly heated over the months ahead and ultimately called into question the integrity of the prophetic ministry on an international level.

In the fall, following the pastor's conference, Wimber conducted a conference on prophecy and invited Mike Bickle, Wayne Grudem, and John C. Blattner to join him as speakers.[50] Then in January of 1990, Wimber held another conference, this time on holiness, where over eight thousand people attended the two weeks of meetings. This event kicked off a second wave of holiness, prophecy, and intercession that spread throughout the Vineyard.[51] For the next decade and more, Wimber traveled around the world, teaching on holiness and calling the church to repentance as the forerunner for revival. By this time, Cain, Jones, and Bickle were traveling on a regular basis with Wimber and sharing his platform. Other prophets from the Kansas City group, such as

John Paul Jackson, Jim Goll, and Larry Randolph, also began traveling on a regular basis as part of the Vineyard team.[52]

In September of 1989, *Charisma* magazine dedicated the entire issue to prophecy and featured prophets including Paul Cain, Bob Jones, and John Paul Jackson. Though not a prophet himself, Mike Bickle was featured as the pastor of the Kansas City Prophets. In one article, Cain was quoted as predicting, "the Lord is raising up a 'new breed' of prophetic ministers whose purity of life will make them fit to channel divine power with integrity."[53] In the article, Cain was declared to be one of these new breed of men. Wimber completely supported Cain's ministry and, in the fall issue of *Equipping the Saints*, stated that "the most satisfying aspect of Paul Cain's ministry . . . is his clarion call—by word and example—to live holy lives that are submitted to God, and thus join the new breed of men and women whom God is raising up in the '90s."[54] It appeared that prophecy was on the front burner of God's agenda and Wimber was right in the middle of the move of the Spirit.

Revival Prophecy Debate

October 1989 found Wimber and Cain sharing the conference platform in England during Wimber's annual ministry trip to the United Kingdom. There were many healings and prophetic words, but it did not meet the Mumford's expectations of a coming revival, based on Cain's prophecy two months earlier. According to Wimber, the Mumfords had assumed revival would come to London in October 1989, but when that date came and went and nothing happened, he began to wonder if Cain had missed it. Wimber said that David Parker, a pastor from Kansas City Metro Vineyard, later pointed out to the Mumfords that Cain was always very precise about dates, and after listening to the recorded prophecy again, they realized no specific year had been given. Parker told them that if Cain had meant 1989, he would have said so. The Mumfords then decided that they had received a correct prophecy from Cain but had attached a wrong interpretation to it.[55]

The following spring, Wimber contacted Sandy Millar, vicar of Holy Trinity Brompton, and asked him to host a three-day conference sometime in July of 1990. The goal was to bring some of the people from the Kansas City Fellowship to the conference to introduce the prophetic. The meetings were not meant to be open to the general public but only to the leaders of the various denominations. As Wimber spoke to Millar, he recalled how seven years earlier,

David Watson had been so excited about introducing Wimber's ministry to the United Kingdom. Wimber had come in the early 1980s with healing and signs and wonders, and the Anglican church in England had never been the same. Now Wimber wanted to introduce them to the prophetic. Millar knew there was controversy surrounding the prophets in the United States, but they had a positive history with Wimber, so when Wimber suggested a conference, the doors were opened.[56]

The meetings were held July 11–13, 1990, and Millar later testified that everyone in attendance was encouraged. Just as God had used Wimber as an instrument to introduce the ministry of healing, he was now using Wimber to teach from the Scriptures about the ministry of intercession and the prophetic.[57] Before leaving the United Kingdom, Cain, Mumford, and other associates met with Wimber to make plans for his next annual October meetings and discuss how they could introduce the prophetic to the entire church body in Britain. During the planning meeting, questions were raised about the prophecy Cain had spoken over the Mumfords—that revival was coming to London. Cain responded, "I stand by every word I prophesied to John Mumford on August 5th." He went on to say, "Thus saith the Lord: Revival will be released in England in October of 1990. . . . *Tokens* of revival will come in October 1990."[58] Wimber was shocked because he had never heard Cain use the phrase "Thus saith the Lord," so he questioned him further. Cain's response was then to confirm that both people and churches would be revived. As a result, Wimber concluded Cain meant that the "first shot" of revival would come to England in October 1990, that the *tokens* would be the first fruits of a greater revival, and that both individuals and churches would feel the effects.[59]

Wimber moved forward with plans to speak at the October 1990 conferences on church growth, holiness, prophecy, and issues facing the nineties. When the time came, he took a three-hundred-member team with him, and conducted five major conferences and thirty-five regional conferences. Over fifty thousand people attended the meetings. Everyone, including Wimber, anticipated "the first shot of revival to begin in England" on this trip.[60] In fact, Wimber was so convinced that revival would break out that he took his entire family. He also scheduled a conference for January in his Anaheim Vineyard with the expectation that they would bring revival back from England and it would be released into his own congregation.

Bill Jackson, a Vineyard pastor from San Diego, was one of the speakers at the Edinburgh conference and also took a team from his church to Britain. Jackson said, "To this day I have never experienced preaching under the anointing of God as I did at the end of my final sermon."[61] Then at the Harrogate conference, which was for "pastors only," hundreds of leaders openly repented of denominational rivalry that had divided and weakened the church. Many people were healed, blessed, and refreshed, but the overall reaction of many was that they did not believe the meetings measured up to their expectations of revival.[62]

Had revival come to England? Wimber attempted to address this question in the winter 1991 issue of *Equipping the Saints*. In his article "Revival Fire," he said he believed that revival comes first to the church, bringing a refreshing and restoring first love. This, he went on to say, results in a call to holiness, repentance, and unity. Then as the church is revived and refreshed, the move flows out into the community, resulting in the salvation of souls, church growth, and social reform. All of this comes in stages, Wimber said, with the first stage beginning in the church. His final analysis was that he believed a "fire of revival" had been lit in England in October 1990 and that families and whole congregations had been touched. He testified that he was personally touched and said, "I've been running like a scalded dog ever since, intent as never before on seeking 'times of refreshing from the presence of the Lord.'"[63] While it was too early to determine which stage of revival England had experienced, he did believe the tokens of revival that Cain had prophesied had indeed come.

But even if it was possible, as Wimber believed, that tokens of revival had come, was this the revival Cain had prophesied? Or was it feasible that, during the October 1990 conferences, they indeed saw tokens of revival but the true revival prophesied by Cain would not be sparked until a few years later, when Mumford returned from the revival called "The Father's Blessing" in Toronto? After all, in April 1984, Bob Jones had heard the audible voice of God say, "In ten years I will begin to release the wine of my Spirit."[64] And in 1994, ten years later, the Toronto Airport Vineyard received an outpouring of the Holy Spirit that moved across North America and around the world. Further, Eleanor Mumford had been among those visiting Toronto during the first few months of the revival, and upon her return to England, revival broke out and swept across the United Kingdom. Was it possible that the prophetic emphasis on holiness and repentance during the October 1990 conferences was a necessary forerunner for revival that would ultimately come four years later?

As the prophetic ministry became more visible, questions and doubts continued. Fortunately, in 1989, the Vineyard family discovered Wayne Grudem, professor of Biblical and Systematic Theology at Trinity Evangelical Divinity School, Deerfield, Illinois, through his article "What Should be the Relationship between Prophet and Pastor?"[65] As it turned out, Grudem had also published the book *The Gift of Prophecy in the New Testament and Today* just the year before; consequently, Grudem, with his book on prophecy, along with Jack Deere, became valuable resources for Wimber during these years.

The Controversies Begin

Everything seemed to be going as planned. The "prophetic and intercession" ministry of Kansas City was cross-pollinating with the Vineyard's "compassion and worship," when suddenly someone seemed to step on a landmine, and a battle was underway.[66] The first shot of the prophecy war was fired by fifty-four-year-old Ernie Gruen, senior pastor of Full Faith Church of Love, the largest charismatic church in the greater Kansas City area. During the Sunday morning church service on January 21, 1990, Gruen preached a passionate message titled, "Do We Keep on Smiling and Say Nothing?" In the sermon, he accused Bickle and the Kansas City Fellowship of promoting false prophecies, primarily through their partnership with Bob Jones, and issued charges of "charismatic heresy." Gruen then duplicated the sermon tape and sent copies around the nation. He later told Lee Grady of *Ministries Today* that these actions came from a growing conviction that something was very wrong. He said he had gone to Bickle in private on two occasions and also had spoken to the leaders of the Kansas City Fellowship, but because he felt his concerns were not adequately addressed, he decided to take the issue before the church at large.[67]

According to Gruen, the relationship between him and Bickle had not always been at odds. When Bickle had first arrived in Kansas in 1982, to pioneer his own church, Gruen offered friendship to the young pastor and even placed him on a steering committee of the citywide Charismatic Pastor's Fellowship. At that point, Gruen had heard strange stories and troubling rumors regarding controversies in the church, but he had never sought to substantiate them. Even when Bickle had boldly called for a citywide, twenty-one-day fast in May 1983, which ruffled the feathers of many pastors in Kansas City, Gruen said he withheld judgment. Then in 1984, Gruen and Bickle had a doctrinal disagreement at a pastor's retreat, after which Gruen became increasingly concerned about what he considered false prophecies being promoted by the Kansas City Fellowship leaders. Finally, Gruen decided to take drastic action.[68]

The Battle Rages

On January 29, eight days after Gruen delivered his "Do We Keep on Smiling?" sermon, thirty-five-year-old Bickle responded with a three-page open letter to Gruen. In it, he was gracious, and he honored Gruen as a man of sincerity and integrity, saying that he did not see Gruen as a man of purposeful malice. Bickle expressed sorrow over their miscommunication. He said he believed they had sufficiently addressed the problem in their previous meetings, and he apologized for being insensitive and mistaken in that evaluation. He then asked Gruen to consider calling a group of men with national ministries to further mediate their communication so that their misunderstandings could be rectified. Bickle believed that many of Gruen's concerns were based on misinformation, because if what Gruen had said were true, then Bickle himself would also be appalled. Bickle asked that they proclaim a three-day period of prayer and fasting from January 24 to 26, to seek God and pray that the destructive powers of darkness not gain any access and harm God's people. He believed that if they humbled themselves, upheld God's word, and lived in holiness and integrity, God would answer their prayers and people would be spared unnecessary pain.[69]

Rather than calm things down, Bickle's call for a fast seemed only to throw more fuel on the smoldering flames. The situation reached a new level in May, when Gruen released a 233-page spiral-bound document titled "Documentation of the Aberrant Practices and Teachings of Kansas City Fellowship (Grace Ministries)."[70] Most of Gruen's accusations in this document were based on excerpts of alleged comments made by Mike Bickle, Paul Cain, Bob Jones, and John Paul Jackson and recorded on tape.[71] Gruen said he believed he was a watchman on the wall and that the Lord had spoken to him, saying, "You are my point guard. You must take the ball and bring it up the court." Gruen said that God had also warned him, saying, "Do not foul; do not step out of bounds . . . and you must know when to pass the ball to the taller players."[72] In the Kansas City area, forty pastors sided with Gruen, and on a national level, Derek Prince and Pat Robertson of Christian Broadcast Network also rallied behind him.[73]

After Gruen went public with his document, Bickle turned to Wimber for help, which led the Kansas City Fellowship to formally come under the covering of the Association of Vineyard Churches. And on May 12, 1990, the Kansas City Fellowship was renamed Metro Vineyard Fellowship of Kansas City—Bickle had fully submitted himself and his church to Wimber for pastoral care, accountability, and direction.[74]

The next month, April 1990, Paul Cain and Jack Deere, then associate pastors of the Anaheim Vineyard, met with Gruen and his staff to evaluate the charges and to seek ways to resolve as many issues as possible. Then on June 28, in an attempt at resolution, Wimber went with Deere and Cain to meet with Gruen and his staff. After several hours of deliberation, Gruen agreed to stop attacking Bickle and the prophets and to turn the matter over to Wimber. At this point, Gruen acknowledged that he had been wrong on three points in his accusations. First, he had used the testimonies of disgruntled people from the Kansas City Fellowship, and, as he said, every church had disgruntled people with negative comments. Second, he apologized to Cain and said that, in his dealings with Cain, he had found him to be a man of integrity. He also conceded to the fact that Cain did not hold to heretical doctrine, recognized that his allegations of Cain communicating with the dead were totally false, and acknowledged that Cain had indeed worked with William Branham (something Gruen had previously adamantly refuted). Finally, he exonerated Cain of charges that he was involved in the occult. In addition, Gruen retracted a story regarding a prophecy involving a woman whose baby died after a home delivery. After the meeting, Gruen told Wimber, "We release the entire situation of Kansas City Fellowship into your hands. We recognize that it is not our responsibility to provide either *correction* or *approval* of the Kansas City Fellowship."[75] Gruen, the point guard, had passed the ball to the taller player.

On the same day Wimber met with Gruen and his staff, he also administered discipline to the Kansas City Fellowship leaders. In a conference before seventy-five hundred leaders in Kansas City, Wimber had Mike Bickle read a list of fifteen errors that Wimber and his staff had discovered through their own investigation into Kansas City Fellowship actions based on Gruen's accusations. The most serious of the charges was that of exaggerating prophecies (specifically the details surrounding the drought Jones had prophesied in 1983). Other charges included exhibiting an elitist spirit and a lack of accountability.

Wimber felt, that with Bickle's public rebuke and confession, the issue had been appropriately dealt with. And in an interview with *Charisma* magazine, Wimber said, "We are not about to lay an axe to anything. Long live the prophetic voice. We need to hear from God."[76] As a result of the controversy regarding the prophets, Wimber issued to the Vineyard a four-page policy written by Jack Deere titled "Vineyard Policy Regarding the Prophetic."

In addition to formal polices, the document included specifics regarding the three prophets named in Gruen's indictments. Paul Cain was exonerated of all charges and was declared free to minister anywhere in the Vineyard. And because approximately 75 percent of Gruen's concerns were charges against Bob Jones, it was acknowledged that Jones was not a gifted teacher.[77] He, therefore, was to travel only under the direction of teachers such as Bickle, and his prophecies would be limited to the back room with leadership. Finally, John Paul Jackson was reassigned to the Anaheim Vineyard, where he would travel principally with Wimber.[78]

Casualties in the Aftermath

After the dust settled, it was discovered that Gruen had been involved in many immoral relationships, and in May of 1993, he resigned as the apostle of Full Faith Church of Love, which he had founded in 1967, and filed for divorce.[79] On May 16, 1993, Gruen and Bickle signed a statement asking the universal body of Christ to forgive them, and came together in the spirit of forgiveness to publicly lay aside all personal animosities, wounds, and misunderstandings between the two churches.[80]

Also shortly after the controversy, Deere announced that he was leaving the Vineyard and would be working with a Dallas-based ministry as his home base for an international teaching ministry.[81] John Paul Jackson relocated to Anaheim where he worked closely with Wimber for three years, then went on to plant a Vineyard church and develop a well-respected prophetic ministry.

One year after the conflict, Bob Jones was charged with sexual misconduct (not adultery) with two women and was sternly disciplined by the Vineyard leaders. As part of his discipline, Jones was not permitted to attend any of the church meetings for six months or to participate in any form of ministry.[82]

Perhaps Paul Cain had more influence on Wimber than any of the others associated with the prophetic. Wimber brought no disciplinary action against him, and in the end Gruen exonerated him of all charges.[83] Then in 1992, Paul Cain left and joined Westminster Chapel in London, where Martyn Lloyd-Jones was once pastor. Wimber said Cain had felt strongly called to preach on end-times and last-days ministries, while Wimber had felt called to equip the saints. Their ministries had two different emphases, and a parting of the ways became inevitable. Wimber acknowledged, however, that through his relationship with Cain, his eschatology had gone through marked revisions from his dispensational roots. He now believed the last-days church would be a "victorious" church rather than a church that simply hangs around waiting for the Rapture.

Bickle's Reflection and Final Separation

Throughout 1989, Bickle traveled extensively with Wimber and spoke regularly to crowds of thousands. Because of his association with the high-profile Wimber, he received an overwhelming number of invitations to preach as well as requests for interviews for magazine articles, television shows, and book publishers. His ego was being stroked, and he was in over his head. In hindsight, he realized that warning signs were going off, but he and Wimber were moving too fast to recognize them. If someone would have told them they had pride, he said, "We would have gone overboard repenting . . . but that's not the same as actually seeing your pride from God's perspective."[84] Then suddenly, "like tripping a bomb wire" they entered into the 1990s, and the attack began.

When it all started, they remembered that, in April of 1984, Jones had prophesied that God was going to bring a new emphasis on humility to the leadership of the church. For Bickle, this meant confronting pride and selfish ambition even if it involved being mistreated and then being required to bless his enemies. Knowing that they were going to be humbled, they realized as they were going through the turmoil that God was in control. In the end, they saw God's redemptive hand and grew in wisdom and humility.

Through the process, there were five specific lessons Bickle said he learned. First, he said he saw their pride and need for humility. Second, he realized their need for other ministries. Third, they gained a greater understanding of the prophetic process. Fourth, they learned the importance of being accountable. And fifth, they learned the necessity of having a balanced ministry team.[85]

Regarding this time in the early 1990s, Bickle later wrote,

We realize now that it was divine discipline of our ministry, though most of what was said by our accusers was inaccurate. They misrepresented our doctrines and practices and fabricated many stories to validate their accusations. It was a difficult season of attack and turmoil for our church. That does not change the fact that there were several important issues in our midst that God was determined to address and correct. He disciplines those He loves so that we grow up in the things that are necessary to receiving our full inheritance.[86]

Bickle worked closely with Wimber and the Vineyard movement for the next five years and was a frequent speaker at their conferences. Then in June of 1996, at the Metro Vineyard's annual conference, he came under conviction and openly repented for having a divided heart and the fear of man.[87] He followed this act of contrition with a fourteen-page letter to the Vineyard executive council saying that, as a result of "a direct prophetic word from Paul Cain, several private dreams, and a growing suspicion that the Vineyard movement did not share his views on intercession and the prophetic," he had repented of the fear of man and recommitted himself to trumpet the four banner themes God had called him to during his visit to Egypt in 1982.[88] Bickle also said he did not believe that the cross-pollination of "worship and compassion" with the "prophetic and intercession" had happened as he had hoped. In addition, he said he was committed to the Vineyard's emphasis of equipping the saints, practicing the fivefold ministry of Ephesians 4:11, and praying for the end-time harvest of souls; in turn, he requested that the Vineyard fully embrace the four banner themes God had commissioned him to trumpet. Finally, Bickle requested that Vineyard leaders revisit their treatment of the Toronto Vineyard (to be discussed in more detail the next chapter).[89]

Wimber responded by saying they had reviewed Bickle's concerns but could not assure him that the Association of Vineyard Churches could comply to his satisfaction. In the end, Wimber did not reject the prophetic and intercession; rather, Bickle felt that if he continued in the Vineyard, he would compromise what God had called him to do. So in August of 1996, Mike Bickle and the Metro Vineyard Fellowship of Kansas City resigned from the Association of Vineyard Churches.[90]

Reflections

From the moment Wimber was introduced to the prophetic, it resonated with his spiritual DNA. Since his conversion, God had spoken to him through words of knowledge, dreams and visions, and personal prophecy; and in his early days of soul-winning, he would receive insight into people's lives that would open their hearts and enable them to be receptive to the gospel. Some, however, said that Wimber rejected the prophetic.

Carol emphatically believed this was not the case. She said he had attempted to correct some of the doctrines of prophetic people, but "he didn't reject the prophetic gifts. He loved and welcomed the whole spectrum of the gifts of the Holy Spirit."[91] John Paul Jackson, who worked closely with Wimber in the years following the Gruen incident, agreed with Carol's statement. In a conversation between the two men during the last part of Wimber's life, Wimber had told Jackson that he regretted the way he had handled the prophetic but had never regretted being involved with it.[92]

Wimber was convinced the prophetic was biblical and theologically correct, that history bore witness to it, and that the church still desperately needed it. He also realized, however, that when he was first introduced to the prophetic, it was so new to him that he did not handle it correctly. If he'd had the opportunity to do it over again, he said, he would do things differently. He would have introduced it more slowly and taken the time to educate everyone about how the prophetic worked. He later realized that the Vineyard board had felt threatened because it had appeared to them that the prophetic was usurping their governing authority and that Wimber was listening only to the prophets and making decisions based exclusively on their input. This assumption was incorrect, however, and Wimber believed that if he had moved more slowly, he could have circumvented these misperceptions. He also wished he had done more to inform and equip the people about the prophetic early in the process. Although he had done some teaching, he realized later that the education he'd provided was very elementary—because at the time, his own understanding of the prophetic was limited.[93]

Those both inside and outside the Vineyard had mixed views of the prophets, and because of the subjectivity of those involved as well as the subjectivity of the writers of their history, the complete truth about the prophetic years may never be known. Some believed the prophets brought much-needed correction to the Vineyard, renewing the spiritual emphasis on prayer and holiness and releasing the gift of prophecy and words of knowledge. Others believed that the prophets moved the Vineyard away from their identity as a movement and created confusion. There were yet others who believed the prophets made a subtle shift in Wimber's theology away from his Calvinistic roots to a more Arminian focus, which emphasized fasting, prayer, and holiness as a necessary prerequisite to revival whereas Wimber in the past had believed renewal was a sovereign move of God.[94]

Along the same line, Wimber had always emphasized equipping the saints—or "everybody gets to play"—but after the introduction of the prophets, he realized the people in his church began to change. He became aware that the "common, ordinary, garden-variety-type believers had pulled back in their own ministering to the sick, the demonized, and the poor" because of the emphasis they had placed on the prophets and the coming great revival. In hindsight, he said they had made an audience out of them, when he had trained them to be an army.[95] This may have been Wimber's deepest regret regarding their involvement with the prophets.

In the aftermath of the prophetic controversy, David Pytches, vicar of St. Andrew's Anglican Church in Chorleywood, England, wrote the book *Some Said it Thundered* as a historical account of the prophetic controversy. Some believed his was a sanitized version of the story that glossed over many of the negative aspects associated with the Kansas City-based group.

Although it was a painful era, Bickle humbly embraced it as a God-directed time of correction that enabled them to emerge as a stronger and legitimate ministry. Wimber also framed the prophetic years in the positive. His son, Sean, had come home and was living for the Lord; the sin and carnality of the Vineyard leaders had been dealt with through a renewed emphasis on holiness and repentance; his own eschatology had shifted; and he now believed they were facing the greatest move of God the church had ever seen.

It seems adjustments were made in both groups, and maybe this was part of the cross-pollination God had intended: they each came out of the prophetic season with a portion of the other and yet with their own identity intact—and fruitful ministry resulted. And as they moved into the 1990s, Wimber continued to call the church to prayer and holiness in preparation for the revival he believed was soon to come.

[1] In Wimber and Springer, *Power Healing*, xv, Wimber states the date was October, 1986, but corresponding information reveals this was in 1985.
[2] Carol Wimber, *John Wimber*, 168, 178–9. Wimber and Springer, *Power Healing*, 30.
[3] John Wimber, "The Way of Holiness," in *Holiness unto the Lord*, lecture notes (Anaheim, CA: Mercy Publishing, 1990), 89. Interview by the author with Tim Wimber.
[4] Stanley M. Burgess, *The Holy Spirit: Ancient Christian Traditions* (Peabody, MA: Hendrickson, 1984), 3.
[5] Interview by the author with Mike Bickle; also see *Growing in the Prophetic* (Lake Mary, FL: Charisma House, 2008), 5–9.
[6] Interview by the author with Mike Bickle.
[7] These four values later became the Four Values of the International House of Prayer Kansas City. https://www.ihopkc.org/resources/blog/four-core-values-ihopkc/ (Accessed June 15, 2020).
[8] Interview by the author with Mike Bickle; also see Pytches, *Some Said It Thundered*, 61.
[9] Interview by the author with Mike Bickle.
[10] Pytches, *Some Said It Thundered*, 64–5; Bickle, *Growing in the Prophetic*, 9, 13.
[11] Bickle, *Growing in the Prophetic*, 13–4.
[12] Interview by the author with Mike Bickle; Pytches, *Some Said It Thundered*, 65–7; Jackson, *Quest for the Radical Middle*, 194–5.
[13] Interview by the author with Mike Bickle; also see Bickle, *Growing in the Prophetic*, 13–4; Pytches, *Some Said It Thundered*, 80–5.
[14] Interview by the author with Mike Bickle.
[15] Interview by the author with Mike Bickle; also see Bickle, *Growing in the Prophetic*, 17–8; Pytches, *Some Said It Thundered*, 86–91.
[16] Jackson, *Quest for the Radical Middle*, 198.
[17] Mike Bickle, "Things I learned from John Wimber," http://mikebickle.org/resources/resource/2974.
[18] Interview by the author with Mike Bickle.
[19] Kevin Springer, "Paul Cain: A New Breed of Man," *Equipping the Saints* 3 no. 4 (Fall 1989): 11–2.
[20] Pytches, *Some Said It Thundered*, 24–7.
[21] David Edwin Harrell Jr., *All Things Are Possible: The Healing and Charismatic Revivals in Modern America* (Bloomington, IN: Indiana University, 1975), 27–40; J. D. Wilson, "William Marrion Branham," in *NIDPCM*, 440–1.
[22] Walter Hollenweger, *The Pentecostals* (London, England: SCM Press), 354.
[23] Kevin Springer, "Paul Cain Answers Some Tough Questions," *Equipping the Saints* 4, no. 4 (Fall 1990): 9.
[24] Pytches, *Some Said It Thundered*, 46; Maudlin, "Seers in the Heartland," 21.
[25] Springer, "Paul Cain: A New Breed of Man" 13.
[26] Pytches, *Some Said It Thundered*, 132.
[27] Interview by the author with Mike Bickle.
[28] Bickle, "Things I Learned from John Wimber," http://mikebickle.org/resources/resource/2974.
[29] Bickle, "Things I Learned from John Wimber," http://mikebickle.org/resources/resource/2974. In a conversation with Carl Tuttle, Bickles said this was the way Wimber worked with the young men he was mentoring. Tuttle said as a team, they would be at an international conference, and it was not unusual for Wimber to turn to one of them during breakfast and tell them they would be taking his place as the speaker for the main session that morning. "It sent waves of fear up our spine," Tuttle recalled, but it also taught them to be prepared in season and out.
[30] Bickle, "Things I Learned from John Wimber."

[31] Bickle, "Things I Learned from John Wimber."
[32] John Wimber, "Introducing the Prophetic Ministry," *Equipping the Saints* 3, no. 4 (Fall 1989): 4.
[33] Jack Deere, *Surprised by the Power of the Spirit* (Grand Rapids, Zondervan, 1993), 37–8.
[34] Wimber, "Introducing the Prophetic Ministry," 4–5.
[35] Wimber, "Holiness unto the Lord," 90.
[36] Wimber, "Introducing the Prophetic Ministry," 5.
[37] Carol Wimber, *John Wimber*, 178.
[38] Interview by the author with Mike Bickle.
[39] Interview by the author with C. Peter Wagner.
[40] Wimber, "Introducing the Prophetic Ministry," 5. The earthquake in Armenia was a magnitude of 6.5. For more information see
http://earthquake.usgs.gov/earthquakes/world/events/1988_12_07_ev.php.
[41] Wimber, "Holiness unto the Lord," 92.
[42] Carol Wimber, *John Wimber*, 179.
[43] Jackson, *Quest for the Radical Middle*, 211.
[44] Wimber, "Introducing the Prophetic Ministry," 5.
[45] Maudlin, "Seers in the Heartland," 21.
[46] Wimber, "Introducing the Prophetic Ministry," 5, 30.
[47] Paul Cain, "Prophecy for the Vineyard," cassette (Vineyard Christian Fellowship: Anaheim, CA, February 1989).
[48] Jackson, *Quest for the Radical Middle*, 204.
[49] John Wimber, "Revival Fire," *Equipping the Saints* 5, no. 1 (Winter 1991): 11. The prophecy was recorded on tape and transcribed for the article. This same article was reprinted in *Renewal Magazine*, no. 184 (September 1991). Wimber also addressed the concerns related to the prophetic in an issue of *Goodnews*, a newsletter for Catholic Charismatic Renewal in England, dated September/October 1990.
[50] John Wimber, "Prophecy Conference," lecture notes (Anaheim, CA: Mercy Publishing, 1989), John Wimber Special Collections, Regent University Library, Virginia Beach, Virginia.
[51] Jackson, *Quest for the Radical Middle*, 211.
[52] Jackson, *Quest for the Radical Middle*, 211.
[53] Paul Thigpen, "How Is God Speaking Today," *Charisma*, September 1989, 52.
[54] Springer, "Paul Cain: A New Breed of Man," 13.
[55] Wimber, "Revival Fire," 11.
[56] Sandy Millar, "Observations on the Prophetic in England," *Equipping the Saints* 4, no. 4 (Fall 1990): 28.
[57] Millar, "Observations on the Prophetic in England," 28–9.
[58] Wimber, "Revival Fire," 11.
[59] Wimber, "Revival Fire," 11.
[60] Wimber, "Revival Fire," 10.
[61] Jackson, *Quest for the Radical Middle*, 224.
[62] Jackson, *Quest for the Radical Middle*, 225.
[63] Wimber, "Revival Fire," 12–3, 21.
[64] Bickle, *Growing in the Prophetic*, 82.
[65] Wayne Grudem, "What Should be the Relationship between Prophet and Pastor?" *Equipping the Saints* 3 no. 4 (Fall 1989): 7–9, 21–2.
[66] Bickle, *Growing in the Prophetic*, 146.
[67] Lee Grady, "Resolving the Kansas City Prophecy Controversy," *Ministries Today*, September/October, 1990, 50.
[68] Ernie Gruen, "What's the Problem?" An open letter by Ernie Gruen, pastor of Full Faith Church of Love, n.d.
[69] Mike Bickle, "Open Letter to Ernie Gruen," January 22, 1990.
[70] Ernie Gruen, "Documentation of the Aberrant Practices and Teachings of Kansas City

Fellowship (Grace Ministries)," http://www.birthpangs.org/articles/kcp/kcp-gruen.html.

[71] In an interview by the author, Mike Bickle stated these were inaccurate quotes and taken completely out of context. They were accused of believing that prophecies were equal to Scripture and that no one could be saved without being a part of their ministry—both horrible accusations were totally false.

[72] Gruen, "Documentation of the Aberrant Practices," 3.

[73] In an interview with Mike Bickle, he said the forty pastors were asked generic questions such as, "If a pastor thinks his prophecies are equal to Scripture, what would you say?" to which they answered that they would think the pastor was a heretic. "But Ernie never mention my name," Bickle said, "nor did he mention the names of pastors who made the comments, because he knew they would be outraged. Many of these pastors were my friends, and they apologized to me for being quoted out of context of speaking against me. They did not know Gruen was actually talking about Mike Bickle; letter from Derek Prince and Al Sarno, "Memo to 700 Club Counselors," April 1990, personal files of Vinson Synan. Also see Grady, "Resolving the Kansas City Prophecy Controversy," 50–1.

[74] Kevin Springer, "KCF Renamed the Metro Vineyard," *Equipping the Saints* 4, no. 4 (Fall 1990): 14.

[75] John Wimber, "A Response to Pastor Ernie Gruen's Controversy with Kansas City Fellowship," *Equipping the Saints* 4, no. 4 (Fall 1990): 5.

[76] "Truce Called in Bickle Controversy," *Charisma*, September 1990, 42.

[77] Grady, "Resolving the Kansas City Prophecy Controversy," 52.

[78] Jack Deere, "Vineyard Polity Regarding the Prophetic," Association of Vineyard Churches, 1990, John Wimber Special Collections, Regent University Library, Virginia Beach, Virginia.

[79] "Kansas City Feud Declared Dead," *Christianity Today*, July 19, 1993, 51; Jackson, *Quest for the Radical Middle*, 219.

[80] See a copy of the letter in Appendix F.

[81] "Wimber Parts with Two Associates," *Christianity Today*, August 17, 1992, 48.

[82] "Kansas City 'Prophet' Disciplined," *Christianity Today*, March 9, 1992, 67.

[83] James Beverly, *Holy Laughter & the Toronto Blessing* (Grand Rapids, MI: Zondervan, 1995), 129.

[84] Bickle, *Growing in the Prophetic*, 143–6.

[85] Bickle, *Growing in the Prophetic*, 150–1.

[86] Bickle, *Growing in the Prophetic*, 141.

[87] Interview by the author with Mike Bickle.

[88] James A. Beverly, "Leading Church Leaves Association," *Christianity Today*, October 7, 1996, 86. Banner themes that Bickle was to trumpet included intercession, holiness, offering (radically giving to the poor), and prayer.

[89] Jackson, *Quest for the Radical Middle*, 336–7.

[90] Jackson, *Quest for the Radical Middle*, 336–7.

[91] Carol Wimber, "John Wimber," 181.

[92] Interview by the author with John Paul Jackson on November 12, 2010.

[93] Interview by the author with John Paul Jackson.

[94] Jackson, *Quest for the Radical Middle*, 231.

[95] Carol Wimber, *John Wimber*, 180–1.

Chapter 8

The Father's Blessing

By the end of 1992, the storm surrounding the prophets seemed to have blown over, but now John faced a different storm—one closer to home. In the middle of the night, in April of 1993, he was jolted from sleep. His immediate response was, "What is it, Lord?" and his first instinct was to wonder if he should be concerned about his children or grandchildren. But in his heart, he sensed they were okay. The uneasiness made his stomach queasy and his mouth dry. There was a sense of dread, like something terrible lay ahead, so he slipped out of bed, went to his favorite place in the living room, and began to pray his crisis prayer: "Oh, God! Oh God! Oh, God!" Although he did not receive a response, he gained enough comfort from Psalm 33 to turn the concern over to the Lord and return to bed.[1]

Over the next few days, he thought he had a sinus infection and was treated with a dose of antibiotics, but after failing to improve, he scheduled an appointment with Dr. Ken Wong, an ear, nose, and throat specialist. Wong, who attended the Anaheim Vineyard church, had had a dream about John's condition and knew exactly where to look when John came in. As a result of the examination, just seven days after being awakened during the night with uneasiness, John was diagnosed with a malignant tumor, approximately 3.2 centimeters in diameter, in his right nasal pharynx. It was a form of cancer common among Chinese but rare in Caucasians. It was too close to the brain to operate, so their only hope was to shrink the tumor through radiation. John immediately began a regimen of twenty-four radiation treatments followed by twenty-two proton treatments at the Loma Linda University Medical Center.[2] The therapy was aggressive, but he was given an 85 percent chance of complete recovery without reoccurrence for five years.[3]

Cancer: Knocked Down but Not Out

Wimber thought it would be easy: just show up for treatments and then fly off for more meetings. But that turned out to be naively optimistic. When treatments started in May, he quickly realized he would need to take a leave of absence from all three of his areas of responsibility: as the pastor of Anaheim Vineyard, the head of Vineyard Ministries International, and the leader of the Association of Vineyard Churches.

To deliver the radiation treatments, the medical team created a head mask and used it to hold his head to the table as they placed him inside the MRI machine. He became so nauseated from the ordeal that they had to stop every few minutes to let him vomit. He also developed a severe oral yeast infection, which was exacerbated by the radiation treatments. The combination irritated his mouth and throat so severely that he could hardly eat, and it made him so nauseous that even the smell of food made him violently ill. Initially he was fed nutrients intravenously, but gradually he was able to drink canned-milk food supplements. In the process, he lost 110 pounds. Wimber, the bigger-than-life, loveable teddy bear, soon became emaciated and frail. His once thick, white hair and bushy beard became thin and brittle. The pain was severe, but he was unable to take pain medications because even the smallest doses caused him to hallucinate. Possibly the worst side effect of the radiation treatment was the scarring of his eustachian tubes, which caused a partial loss of hearing and the destruction of his salivary glands. He had to use a spray can of artificial saliva, or what he liked to call "pig spit," to keep his mouth moist enough to speak.[4]

During this low point in his life, he began to wonder if he could continue to practice what the Scriptures taught regarding healing. He realized, however, that from the outset of his ministry, he had founded his understanding of suffering and nonhealing on Ladd's already-and-not-yet kingdom theology. Now in the midst of his greatest physical suffering, he could experientially embrace his long-held belief that the perfect realization of the not-yet kingdom was still in the future—and that, until Christ returned, Christians would continue to face suffering and would endure by God's grace. Wimber also believed that pain was not only biblical, but that, through it, believers often experienced their greatest advances in spiritual maturity. This had, in fact, been an aspect of his teaching that his critics consistently failed to realize. So through the trial of his own grief, he recommitted himself to teaching the biblical view of healing, regardless of circumstances. And it was out of this painful ordeal, in 1996, that he wrote the book *Living with Uncertainty: My Bout with Inoperable Cancer*.[5]

As he went through treatments from May to August, he was so weak and sick he often felt like he would not live from one day to the next. He was fifty-nine years old and felt like he was ninety.[6] It was during this low point that Carol received an encouraging word regarding his future ministry. In July of 1993, she said the Holy Spirit told her John would be going to the nations. John and Carol both interpreted this to mean he would go to the churches in the nations not to evangelize but to stir them up for renewal. At the time that Carol received this promise, John was sleeping for between twenty and twenty-two hours a day, so she questioned the Lord but received no immediate response. A Vineyard pastors' conference was scheduled for the next day, and leaders would be coming from around the world, but John was so weak he couldn't even stand, much less speak. So Carol asked God to confirm His promise by giving John his voice back so he could minister at the conference. To their amazement, John woke up the next day able to speak and had just enough strength to participate in the meeting.[7]

Season of New Beginnings

By October of 1993, Wimber said God had spoken twenty-seven times to him and Carol, confirming his commission to the nations. He also said God had spoken seventeen times, in the same context, saying this would be a "season of new beginnings." According to John, the Lord also gave him the following promise: "I'm going to start it all over again. I am going to pour out my Spirit in your midst like I did in the beginning."[8] In November, he shared these words with the leaders at the Anaheim Vineyard Church National Board and Council Meeting in Palm Springs. The committee agreed that God was once again calling Wimber to the nations; so they laid hands on him and Bob Fulton, the International Coordinator, and blessed them to go and stir up the international churches for renewal.[9]

By December, John had regained his health enough to resume his leadership responsibilities. At the time, he felt the Holy Spirit leading him to begin to stir up the gifts of the Spirit in the Anaheim Vineyard congregation so that the people would have a deeper hunger for Jesus. And throughout December, he indeed felt an increase in the presence of the Holy Spirit in their meetings.[10]

Then during the 1994 New Year's service at the Anaheim Vineyard, Paul Cain prophesied, "There is coming a fresh release and visitation of the Spirit to John and Carol. This new move will bless the Vineyard." Everyone was excited and praised the Lord, but Cain later pulled Wimber aside and told him that

God had said it was "John and Carol—not Wimber!"[11] Cain said he did not understand the implications of this because he did not know another John and Carol. Wimber, in pondering the prophecy, recognized that the only other John and Carol he knew were the pastors of the Airport Vineyard in Toronto, Canada.

Then on Sunday, January 16, the Holy Spirit gave John the word "Pentecost." As he spent the afternoon considering the significance of this utterance, he had a vision of young people. So, following the Sunday evening service, he asked the young people to come forward for prayer. As they did, the Holy Spirit moved on them in a powerful way, igniting a new fire in the church. Wimber believed this was the initiation of the new beginning that God had promised.[12]

John Arnott Meets Randy Clark

John Arnott had been at the pastors' meeting in November 1993, when the Anaheim Vineyard National Board and Council had laid hands on Wimber to send him to the nations. In that same meeting, Wimber also told the group about the vision God had given him regarding a time of "new beginnings" in the Vineyard movement. Arnott, of the Airport Vineyard in Toronto, Canada, was one of the pastors who had latched onto Wimber's prophetic word.

At the same conference, Arnott had learned from Happy Leman, the Midwest regional overseer of the Vineyard, that the Holy Spirit had moved in an extraordinary way at the regional meeting in Wisconsin. Leman told Arnott that after Randy Clark had shared a testimony of what was happening in his Vineyard church in St. Louis, Missouri, Clark then prayed for the ministers at the meeting to receive a fresh touch from the Holy Spirit, at which point the Spirit of God came upon the pastors, and they suddenly began to run, dance, act drunk, and laugh hysterically. In the past, Leman had not always lived up to his name "Happy" and was better known by his peers as "Mr. Control," so when Arnott heard Happy's story, he was convinced this was a genuine move of God.[13] Arnott had long been hungry for a fresh touch of the Holy Spirit for his church, so he immediately contacted Clark to see if he would come to Toronto and hold four consecutive services from January 20–24. Arnott was hopeful his church would be a part of the season of new beginnings that God had promised to Wimber.

John and Carol Arnott

John and Carol Arnott had been deeply impacted by Kathryn Kuhlman and Benny Hinn's ministry in the 1960s and 1970s, but it was not until 1980, when the Arnotts took a short-term missions trip to Indonesia, that they felt a call to full-time ministry. When they returned from Indonesia, John resigned his business career and pioneered a church similar to the Calvary Chapel model.[14]

The Arnotts had first met Wimber at a Vineyard conference in 1986 in Vancouver and later again in Ohio. At that time, the Arnotts were pastoring a small independent church in Carol's hometown of Stratford, Ontario. From the moment Arnott encountered Wimber, he felt an immediate bond with him and the Vineyard model, so just a few months later, in 1987, Arnott brought his church under the covering of the Association of Vineyard Churches. At the same time, he planted a second church in west Toronto, and for the next four years he traveled between the two cities, pastoring both churches. By the summer of 1992, his original church in Stratford had grown large enough that Arnott installed Jerry Steingard, one of his associate pastors, as the senior pastor. This freed Arnott to devote his full attention to the Toronto church, now located in a warehouse building in a small industrial strip mall at the end of the Lester B. Pearson International Airport runway. Thus he named the church the Toronto Airport Vineyard.[15]

By the fall of 1992, John and Carol were dry and worn out in ministry. At this point, they saw their church as a "hospital" that ministered to the inner hurts of people. They were experiencing some success and deliverances, but the process of seeing people's lives significantly changed was long and arduous, taking two and sometimes three years. Eventually they realized they were more focused on the problems of people than on God, and they knew something had to change. In October of the same year, they attended a Benny Hinn conference. The Arnotts and Hinn had been friends for twenty years, so when they saw the power of the Holy Spirit raise people from wheelchairs, they were challenged once again to seek God for a fresh anointing. Returning home from the meetings, they made a commitment to spend their mornings in prayer, Bible study, and worship. After a year and a half, they said they had fallen in love with Jesus again in ways they could never have imagined, and the hunger for a move of the Holy Spirit in their church increased. Then in June of 1993, while visiting John's daughter in Texas, John and Carol attended a Rodney Howard-Brown meeting.[16]

Howard-Brown was an evangelist from Port Elizabeth, South Africa, who was converted to life in Christ at the age of five, filled with the Holy Spirit at age eight, and imparted with a burden for the lost through a dream at age thirteen. Then in 1979, when he was eighteen, Howard-Brown felt what he called the liquid fire of the Holy Spirit being poured on him, and it consumed him so completely that he began to weep, laugh, and become drunk in the Spirit for three days. In December of 1987, Howard-Brown came to the United States where he started an evangelistic ministry and held extended revival services. At the meetings, the power of God would come suddenly and unexpectedly upon people, causing them to fall out of their seats and to roll on the floor, laughing uncontrollably.[17] As such, Howard-Brown became associated with what the charismatics called the "laughing revival."[18]

The Arnotts received a touch from God at the June 1993 Howard-Brown meeting, but they were still hungry for more. So in November of that year, they took a spiritual journey to Argentina to attend the revival meetings of Claudio Freidzon, an Assemblies of God leader.[19] Freidzon was associated with a second wave of revival in that nation, the first being attributed to the ministry of Carlos Annacondia in the early 1980s. As a struggling pastor, Freidzon had felt he needed a fresh touch of the Holy Spirit. He had attended a Benny Hinn meeting in Orlando, where Hinn prayed that he would receive such an anointing that all of Argentina would be touched through his ministry.[20] When he returned to his country, revival broke out along with unusual manifestations. The previous focus of Freidzon's ministry had been worship and personal holiness that produced a changed lifestyle, but now people were experiencing physical manifestations, such as weeping, laughing, falling under the power, and becoming drunk in the Spirit. The most significant aspect of the revival was that people were receiving a fresh anointing at his meetings to take back to their own churches, where they would then experience the same revival manifestations. As a result, Freidzon's Buenos Aires church grew from a small struggling congregation to over three thousand people in just four years.[21]

When Freidzon prayed for John Arnott in 1993, Arnott remembered falling under the power of the Holy Spirit, but then reasoning soon got the better of him, and he immediately began questioning the experience and stood back up. When he stood, Freidzon asked him if he wanted the anointing. He said, "Oh, yes, I want it all right." So Freidzon slapped his outstretched hands and said, "Then take it!" Something inside Arnott seemed to click, as if the Lord were saying, "For goodness sake, will you take this? Take it, it's yours."[22] Right then, Arnott decided to receive an impartation of the Holy Spirit by faith through Freidzon's ministry.[23] And when Arnott returned to Toronto, the spirit of God began to touch people in the same way it had at Freidzon's meetings.

At the same time, there was some concern in Arnott's heart. This was all new for him, and he wasn't sure how to sustain what they were experiencing. So when Happy Leman told him how God had worked through Randy Clark at the Vineyard Leadership conference, Arnott hoped that if Clark came and held some meetings, the power of God would not only stay, but increase.[24]

Randy Clark: The Match That Ignited the Fire

Randy Clark had been on his own spiritual life journey. At the age of seven, Clark heard a sermon by Jack Haygood in his grandmother's Baptist church. The sermon was about Lot's wife and the necessity of giving your life to Christ and never looking back. Randy wept that night because he knew he wanted to live for God, but it took nine more years for him to make the commitment. It happened on his sixteenth birthday, when his Uncle Reno, who had Down's syndrome, asked him to become a Christian. His heart melted and he found himself at the altar "praying through."[25] Two years later, Clark was severely injured in an automobile accident and then miraculously healed. He saw this as his wake-up call and responded to his commission to preach. He graduated from the Southern Baptist Theological Seminary in Louisville, Kentucky, in 1978 and pastored an American Baptist church in Spillertown, Illinois.[26]

Clark believed in healing, but he had never taught on healing or prayed for the sick. Then one day, he felt impressed by God to begin teaching on healing and to have a healing conference in his church. He contacted Larry Hart, a Baptist friend and associate professor at Oral Roberts University, who suggested he contact John Wimber. He had never heard of Wimber, but the very next day, while watching the Trinity Broadcast Network's *Praise the Lord* show, he witnessed Paul Crouch introduce Wimber to the television audience. To Clark, Wimber looked like a cross between a big teddy bear and Kenny Rogers. Clark was so impressed with what Wimber had to say that he contacted the Anaheim Vineyard and invited him to hold a teaching conference on healing in his church. Wimber's schedule was booked, but he agreed to send a team in March of the following year.[27]

Clark spent the remainder of the year preparing his congregation for the upcoming conference. Then in January of 1984, two months before the meetings were to begin, he took two of his deacons to a James Robison's Bible Conference, where Wimber was one of the special speakers. At the meeting, Clark was able to observe Wimber's ministry firsthand. Wimber also prayed for him and gave him a word of prophecy regarding his future ministry. After this encounter and the subsequent healing conference that Wimber's team held at Clark's church (led by Blaine Cook), Clark decided to join the Vineyard movement.[28] He resigned from his Baptist church and planted a Vineyard church in St. Louis, Missouri.

Wimber and the Vineyard leadership team were very supportive, and although Clark had experienced transformational encounters with the Holy Spirit at Vineyard conferences, it was still a very difficult and humbling journey. Then in 1989 at a Vineyard conference, Clark said God promised him a ministry of evangelism, but it was not until four years later, in 1993, that he began to see the fulfillment of this promise.[29]

Clark had always been an opponent of the Word of Faith movement, but he was dry, hungry, and desperate for a fresh touch from God. So, against his better judgment, he decided to go to Tulsa, Oklahoma, where he attended a Rodney Howard-Brown meeting at the Rhema Bible Church.[30] Forty-five hundred people were packed into the auditorium to hear the evangelist preach and to experience the manifestations of joy and laughter. Clark received prayer several times from Howard-Brown, falling under the power of the Spirit, and then getting up and standing in line for prayer again. He did this over and over. Then he remembered Wimber saying, "You've got to learn to see what the Father is doing," so he started following Howard-Brown around to observe the way he prayed for people. As he watched, Howard-Brown tapped people on the forehead, saying, "Fill! Fill! Fill!" Clark prayed, "Lord, burn this into my mind so I never forget it."[31] The following Sunday, when he returned to his Vineyard church in St. Louis, Clark invited anyone who desired prayer to come forward. He began praying for people just as he had observed at the Howard-Brown meetings, and immediately people began falling under the power of the Spirit. Clark said no one was more surprised than he was that God would do such a thing in his church.[32]

A few weeks after this experience, Clark attended the Vineyard Midwest regional meeting in Wisconsin where Happy Leman asked him to share what God was doing in his church. When Clark spoke, the Holy Spirit came upon the Vineyard pastors with the same manifestations he had seen in the Howard-Brown meetings and in his own church. It was at this meeting that Leman, the regional overseer known as "Mr. Control," became drunk in the Spirit and laughed hysterically. And it was this story that motivated Arnott to invite Clark to Toronto.[33]

The Toronto Blessing Begins

Arnott knew Clark as a casual friend and promptly contacted him to come to Toronto to hold services from January 20–24, 1994. Arnott asked Clark to speak during the four services, but Clark was hesitant and told Arnott that all he had was one sermon and a testimony! Besides, what if God did not show up? Arnott said he was willing to take the risk, so a reluctant Clark agreed.[34]

Just before leaving St. Louis, Clark's friend, Richard Holcomb, called with a prophetic word. He said,

> The Lord says, Randy, test Me now. Test Me now. Test Me now! Do not be afraid. I will back you up! I want your eyes to be opened as Elisha prayed for Gehazi, that you will see into the heavenlies and see My resources for you. Do not become anxious because when you become anxious, you cannot hear from Me.[35]

Clark said this prophetic word filled his heart with faith. Then he remembered that Howard-Brown had told him that if he wanted to see revival, he should go north in the winter.[36] If this was true, then the sub-zero temperature of Toronto in January looked promising.

Just as Holcomb had prophesied, God did back him up, and what started as a four-day preaching engagement turned into forty-two days. After six weeks, Clark returned to his church in St. Louis, and Wes Campbell took over as the primary speaker. Larry Randolph later followed Campbell. Eventually, Clark resigned from his St. Louis church and went on to fulfill his calling to global evangelism.[37] And what he left behind in the Toronto Vineyard was a flame that would become instrumental in igniting revival fires around the world.

The Father's Blessing

According to *Christianity Today*, the name Toronto means "meeting place" in the local Native dialect, and that is exactly what happened as people started flocking to the services to experience the presence of God.[38] The renewal meetings in the Toronto Vineyard ran six nights a week with only Mondays off. Arnott said that the church was a "hospital," but instead of taking months or even years, the healing of emotional and childhood wounds happened quickly, through the outpouring of the Father's love.[39] According to Randy Clark's observation, from the outset of the revival, approximately 30 percent of the people who attended were burned-out pastors needing a fresh touch from God and healing from ministry wounds.[40] Jesus had come to bind up the brokenhearted and set the captive free, and they were witnessing this fulfillment through the outpouring of the Father's blessing.

From the beginning of the revival, the Toronto outpouring was known for its graphic and exotic manifestations. When the Spirit came on people, they laughed, cried, fell under the power, danced, jumped, shook, and rolled on the floor. Such phenomena were not unheard of; as a matter of fact, manifestations like these had been witnessed in revival movements throughout church history. At the outset of the revival, for example, Guy Chevreau, in his book *Catch the Fire: The Toronto Blessing*, framed the manifestations occurring in Toronto in the context of Jonathan Edwards' meetings in the Great Awakening.[41] And Lee Grady of *Charisma* magazine compared Toronto with the Azusa Street Revival at the turn of the twentieth century:

> God used a rented warehouse in Los Angeles to impact the world. Now something similar to Azusa has erupted in another rented warehouse building used by a Vineyard church in Toronto. I am sure this movement in Toronto—like Azusa—has its flaws. There's plenty of emotionalism, along with weird noises and strange body movements. But it's brought renewal to churches in many parts of the world.[42]

Grady went on to say that many who had gone to Azusa were "horrified at the emotional frenzy" and that many stories written about it had not been "flattering"; nonetheless, they served to "get the message out—and visitors from all over the world flocked to the tiny church."[43] Later, he added:

> What happens at the altar at the Toronto church might seem irreverent to anyone unfamiliar with the history of Pentecostalism. But scholars who have studied the Azusa Street Revival of 1906 say what happened in Toronto—will eventually make it into the history books, too.[44]

In addition, Daina Doucet, in a *Charisma* magazine article, said manifestations in worshipers such as being overcome by laughing, weeping, groaning, shaking, and falling were nothing new but were common to Pentecostal revivals of "days gone by," like the ones that once shook the Azusa Street Revival.[45]

The Lion Roars

Possibly the most bizarre manifestation witnessed in the Toronto outpouring was animal noises. People reportedly roared like lions, crowed like roosters, snorted like oxen, and made sounds like eagles. Although these did occur, people who attended the meetings said the publicity surrounding the animal noises was far greater than what actually occurred. Both Arnott and Clark said that while much attention was given to these manifestations, they were actually quite rare. Clark said he could count on one hand the number of meetings where he had heard animal sounds, and although he had heard people talk about other manifestations, the lion's roar was the only sound he had personally heard.[46] He also said that, while he understood the "prophetic" nature of the "four living creatures" in Revelation 4, he was "concerned that the attention would be drawn to the bizarre nature of this new phenomenon and away from the good fruit."[47]

By far, the most common animal sound witnessed at the Toronto outpouring was the roar of the lion, which originated with Gideon Chu. Chu was a Cantonese Chinese pastor from Vancouver who Arnott knew personally. Arnott respected Chu and knew him to be a quiet man of integrity who was given to a great deal prayer and fasting. One night when Arnott asked Chu to give his testimony, this meek and humble pastor suddenly began to roar like a lion and to pace back and forth across the stage. Then, with a word of prophecy based on Amos 3:8, Chu declared: "Let My people go! Let My people go!" He declared that the dragon had deceived the Chinese people for hundreds of years, and now the Lion of the Tribe of Judah was coming to set his people free.[48] As Chu released this prophetic word, the people in the church exploded in praise. From that point forward, Arnott believed that manifestations such as lion-roaring were prophetic in nature. He also decided that, while the manifestations may be offensive to some, as he had previously learned from Wimber, God often offends the mind to get to the heart.[49]

The Toronto outpouring and its unusual manifestations captured the attention of the media, which recorded both positive and negative comments. Hank Hanegraaff, the "Bible Answer Man," said "such fearsome noise suggest[ed] possession by the Devil—and the need for exorcism."[50] Henry Blackaby, Southern Baptist director of prayer and spiritual awakening said, "What I'm hearing about the Toronto Blessing has none of the marks of the Bible."[51]

On the other hand, John Stackhouse, associate professor of modern Christianity at the University of Manitoba, saw things differently: "It seems to me that people are enthusiastic about Jesus, are happy to be Christians, and there doesn't seem to be an oversupply of that in North American Christianity. . . . If you don't like the idea of holy laughter that breaks out in a church service, then what kind of laughter do you believe in?"[52] David Mainse, Canadian Christian TV talk-show host of *100 Huntley Street* also endorsed the Toronto outpouring after falling on the floor and lying motionless for three hours after receiving prayer.[53] And *American Spectator* magazine sounded a positive note, saying that local hotels in Canada were thrilled with what was happening at the Toronto Vineyard. They reported that "some 100 new year-round jobs [had] been created by the Blessing, most in the tourist industry." And as for the chamber of commerce, the article reported, "every day it continues is another blessing."[54]

Renewal Goes International

In May of 1994, Eleanor Mumford visited the Toronto Airport Vineyard and became the agent accredited with carrying revival fire back to England. Mumford was the assistant pastor of the Southwest London Vineyard and the wife of John Mumford, senior pastor and overseer of the Vineyard churches in the United Kingdom. Upon her return from Toronto, she met with friends and church leaders to describe her experience. After her time of sharing, she prayed for the people present, and to their amazement they experienced the same manifestations that were occurring in the Toronto meetings.

Nicky Gumbel, then curate of the Anglican church Holy Trinity Brompton, was one of the people Mumford prayed for.[55] After receiving prayer, he suddenly realized he was late for a staff meeting at his church so he quickly excused himself and left.[56] After arriving late for his meeting, he told the group about what Mumford had shared. At the end of their meeting,

Gumbel was asked to close in prayer. As he prayed, Gumbel asked the Holy Spirit to come and fill them. Immediately people began falling under the power of the Spirit. Even the people walking by in the hallway were being impacted. The influence of that prayer lasted all day, with people either laid out on the floor or drunk in the Spirit. When Sandy Millar, the vicar of Holy Trinity Brompton saw what had happened in the staff meeting, he invited Mumford to come the following Sunday to share about her experience in Toronto with the congregation. Eleanor Mumford came, and at the close of the service she invited anyone who wanted prayer to come forward. When she prayed, the same manifestations she had experienced in Toronto broke out in the Holy Trinity Brompton Anglican church congregation.

News of what happened at Holy Trinity Brompton quickly spread throughout the Christian community.[57] It was not long before the secular press also picked up on what was happening. On June 18, 1994, the *Times* (London) carried an article titled, "Spread of Hysteria Fad Worries Church." The article stated, "A religious craze that originated in Canada and involves mass fainting and hysterical laughter has crossed the Atlantic to cause growing concern in the Church of England." The article went on to say that "one vicar was forced to cancel an evening service of Holy Communion and remove the chairs from the nave because so many in his congregation were laying on the floor after experiencing the 'Toronto Blessing.'" (Importantly, while the secular media in the United Kingdom had dubbed the revival the "Toronto Blessing," Arnott rejected this title and preferred to call it the "The Father's Blessing," since he believed it was from the Father and was for everyone—not just Toronto.)[58] Pastors from around the world, the article declared, were flying to Toronto to investigate the phenomenon.[59] The next day, the *Sunday Telegraph* (London) reported that "British Airways flight 092 took off from Toronto Airport on Thursday evening just as the Holy Spirit landed on a small building 100 yards from the end of the runway."[60]

The Independent, a London newspaper, carried an article on June 21, 1994, titled, "The Holy Spirit Hits South Kensington." The author said,

> When the Holy Spirit hit St. Paul's Onslow Square, SW7, on Sunday morning, I felt it through the floor. There were four heavy thuds as congregants fainted, and then sudden rapid drummings—like the noise that rabbits make to warn one another—when people started to shake uncontrollably and beat their feet against the floor. . . . This was, after all, an Anglican church in the heart of South Kensington, with a well-heeled congregation that had put nearly 4,000

pounds into the collection bag the previous Sunday for Rwanda relief.... The scenes at St. Paul's and a number of other London churches over the past three weeks have led enthusiasts to believe that a real religious revival is underway.[61]

Time magazine (London) article "Laughing for the Lord" reported that while other Anglican churches on Sunday nights had "pathetically tiny flocks of Londoners" attending their services, at Holy Trinity Brompton, people started lining up one and a half hours before services and the church had a "standing-room-only turnout of 1,500."[62] The same article stated that holy laugher was not a new phenomenon but had been common in early Pentecostalism and died out. Why had it resurfaced? The article quoted historian Vinson Synan as saying, "It's a kind of emotional release for a lot of people. It shows there's a spiritual and emotional hunger that's not being met in mainline churches."[63]

Nicky Lee, the pastor of St. Paul's was quoted in the *Independent* as saying that the phenomena of the Toronto Blessing had "spread like the Beijing flu, by contact from person to person."[64] If this was the case, then Eleanor Mumford had been the vector that carried the virus from Toronto to infect England with what many believed to be the early stages of revival—and by December, the Toronto Blessing had impacted more than four thousand churches.[65]

To the United Kingdom and Back Again

The Toronto Blessing was also circuitously connected to the Brownsville revival in Pensacola, Florida, under the leadership of pastor John Kilpatrick. It was evangelist Steve Hill who was credited with igniting this fire on Father's Day, June 18, 1995. Before coming to Brownsville that fateful day, Hill was tired and worn out from his ministry as an international evangelist and church planter. He was in need of a fresh touch from God when he heard of the outpouring of the Holy Spirit at Holy Trinity Brompton. Out of desperation, he asked a friend to make an appointment for him to talk with Sandy Millar to ask for prayer. When Hill arrived at the church, he knew the meeting was more about receiving than talking, so after a short conversation, he asked Millar to lay hands on him and pray. Millar prayed a simple prayer: "Touch him, Jesus. Bless him, Lord." Hill said that as Millar prayed, all the strength seemed to drain from his body, and he fell to the floor. Millar then got down on the floor beside

Hill and said, "You don't have to do anything. He loves you. Rest in that love. Nurture that love. From that will come the harvest. Don't try to do anything. You don't have to prove anything to anybody."[66]

This was the story Hill shared with the Brownsville congregation that Father's Day in 1995. At the close of the service, Hill gave an invitation for people who desired prayer. About a thousand people, approximately half the congregation, came forward. People were slain in the Spirit just as they had been in the Toronto Vineyard and at Holy Trinity Brompton. Even Kilpatrick, who had been a skeptic of such manifestations, was out in the Spirit for several hours.[67] The Toronto revival had traveled from the Vineyard in Canada through the Vineyard in the United Kingdom to the Anglican church and back across the Atlantic to ignite a revival fire in an Assemblies of God church in North America.

Back in Canada, the *Toronto Star* asked, "Why Toronto?" The response was, "Only God knows . . . and possibly Mark Dupont." Dupont, one of the seven Airport Vineyard pastors, told the *Toronto Star* that he "had a prophetic vision two years ago that a wave of water 'the size of Niagara Falls' would wash over Toronto refreshing and renewing its people. It would happen in early 1994 and would be the beginning of a global spiritual revival."[68] Dupont went on to say, "We don't know why. 'Did you pray it in?' Yes, we prayed, and we hoped. But we were just a group of people trying to muddle along and find faith."[69] The article also acknowledged the global impact, reporting that the service the journalist had attended had a roll call of countries including the United States, Britain, Holland, Germany, Switzerland, Norway, South America, Australia, New Zealand, and South Africa.

In 1984, Paul Cain had prophesied over Eleanor Mumford that tokens of revival would begin in October, at which time the Lord would start to move in London and throughout England. Could it be that Wimber's association with the prophets and his subsequent emphasis on holiness and repentance was the forerunner experience needed for this revival to occur? Now the question was being asked if what was happening at Toronto was the season of "new beginnings" God had promised Wimber. But if it was, it seemed to have come at a time and in a place he did not expect.

Wimber's Initial Responses

When Wimber heard about the outpouring of the Spirit at the Toronto Vineyard, he was supportive and even flew to Toronto to experience the meetings firsthand. When he returned, he told Larry Randolph, who was working with John at the Anaheim Vineyard at the time, that he believed the Toronto Vineyard had become the "epicenter" of the work God was doing.[70]

He never questioned whether the Toronto outpouring was a genuine move of God, but he was concerned about the way the manifestations were being pastored. And as time went by, he became increasingly concerned about the negative criticism Toronto was attracting through the media and how this was reflecting on the overall Vineyard movement. As the leader of Vineyard International, Wimber was catching the heat from both inside and outside the organization. This pressure was exacerbated by the fact that he was still sick and struggling with cancer. It had been physically challenging for him just to carry out his daily responsibilities, and now his Anaheim office was being inundated with phone calls from Vineyard pastors and others concerned about what they were hearing about Toronto—especially the laughter and animal sounds, which soon became the focal point of people's concerns and criticisms.[71]

Hank Hanegraaff, the Bible Answer Man, daily used his radio broadcast to hammer Wimber and slander the Toronto Vineyard; however, *Charisma* magazine journalist Lee Grady offered these opinions regarding Hanegraaff and his treatment of Toronto:

> The tough-talking cult specialist believes his life's mission is to protect the church from heresy. But there's trouble in Dodge City. Hanegraaff's critics want to know who elected him to police America's pulpits. They say Hanegraaff is a maverick outlaw who enjoys chasing his Christian brothers with a branding iron. During his daily hour-long program, which is aired from Southern California on 100 Christian stations nationwide, Hanegraaff tells callers how to refute false doctrines of Mormons, Jehovah's Witnesses and New Agers. But since he took the helm of the 37-year-old Christian Research Institute (CRI) in 1988, Hanegraaff has spent as much time scrutinizing other Christians and their beliefs as he has the cults.[72]

Grady went on to say,

Hanegraaff has not labeled the Association of Vineyard Churches a cult, but he regularly warns his audience that Vineyard leaders are promoting aberrant theology because he disagrees with the current 'Toronto Blessing' movement.[73]

Grady said a major problem with Hanegraaff was that he accused Christian leaders of heresy on his radio program without first confronting them in private. For these reasons, many Christians believed Hanegraaff's accusations were unfair and harsh and promoted hurtful divisions in the church.[74]

Hanegraaff's comments wreaked havoc on the Vineyard churches, especially in southern California. One of the hardest hit was John McClure's church in New Port Beach. McClure lost approximately 40 percent of his congregation over the Toronto controversy. Since McClure was on Wimber's church board, he was a constant reminder of how this issue was potentially damaging the entire movement, which only put further pressure on Wimber to address the situation.[75]

Wimber's Attempt to Deal with Toronto

Wimber chose to use the *Vineyard Reflections* newsletter as the primary platform to express to the entire Vineyard organization the concerns surrounding Toronto. Since this circular was addressed to Vineyard pastors, it appears Wimber may have chosen this format with the hope of correcting misperceptions, eliminating confusion, and addressing apprehension. What follows is a summary of these communications.

First Newsletter

The first *Vineyard Reflections* addressing the Toronto renewal was published in the May/June 1994 issue, titled "Season of New Beginnings." In it, Wimber stated,

> In recent months the Holy Spirit has been falling in meetings throughout the Vineyard. This season of visitation began about the same time in Toronto, Canada at the Airport Vineyard and in Anaheim, California, then ripped out across America, Canada, United Kingdom, Australia, New Zealand, and to other parts of the world. . . .[76]

By making this statement, he seemed to want the Vineyard movement to understand that, although Toronto was garnering a great deal of media attention, the outpouring of the Spirit was not unique to that location. At this point, he believed they were in the early stages of an outpouring, but it was not yet revival. True revival, he said, would be "marked by widespread repentance both within the church, and among unbelievers."

In the newsletter, he told how he had forecast in November of 1993, at the National Board and Council meeting in Palm Springs, that a "new beginning" was coming to the Vineyard and that it was this word that prompted Arnott to invite Clark to Toronto to hold special meetings. He also expressed his thoughts regarding the manifestations and referred to Jonathan Edwards' meetings as an example of phenomena consistent with revivals throughout church history. He went on to say, "Laughter will bubble forth. So don't be afraid of it. It indicates the ongoing truth of God's word. . . . It is not people acting weird. But it's appropriate. God just goes about doing things differently than you and I would."[77]

Wimber also offered some pastoral advice for the smaller churches that were experiencing renewal with limited staff and resources. He suggested that rather than having nightly meetings, they schedule weekly or biweekly "seeker" meetings. By "seeker" he was drawing on his Quaker roots and meant they should create an atmosphere where Christians who were seeking more could come and receive. He also encouraged the pastors to invite questions and give clear instructions regarding phenomena and to keep their preaching "Christ-centered."[78]

In the last section of the seven-page newsletter, Wimber addressed issues that related specifically to the practices at Toronto. His first concern was the way they put tape on the floor and lined people up for prayer, and the second was the fact that the prayer team consisted of one person praying while another served as a catcher. He reminded them that everyone can minister in the power of the Spirit and there should be no "superstars." Also, rather than using catchers, he recommended that the person receiving prayer stand at their seats so that if they fell they would go down into their seat. He implied in the newsletter that he had personally spoken to Arnott regarding these concerns and that Arnott had understood and graciously received his suggestions.[79]

Randy Clark later said the idea for catchers and tape on the floor had been his idea. According to Clark, when they prayed for people, people would fall under the power of the Spirit and bodies would pile up on the floor so that it became a chaotic mess. In his attempt to bring organization to the prayer time, he had people stand in single file lines along the tape on the floor. When people were prayed for and they went down under the power of the Spirit, the catchers would line them up side-by-side rather than allowing people to fall over on top of one another. He said they tried to implement Wimber's suggestion of praying for people in front of their seats, but people would fall out of their chairs and this did not remedy the situation.[80]

Inviting Toronto to Anaheim

Wimber recognized that Toronto was the "epicenter" of what God was doing, and he also believed this was a genuine move of the Spirit. So in an attempt to observe the expressions of Toronto on his own turf and among his own congregation, he invited those involved with the Toronto outpouring, including John Arnott, Randy Clark, Wes Campbell, and Lance Pittluck, to speak at the "Let the Fire Fall" conference at the Anaheim Vineyard in July of 1994.[81] Nearly five thousand people were in attendance.[82] During the conference, the story of Gideon Chu, the Chinese pastor, was shared, along with his prophecy that when the Lion of Judah roars, the Chinese, who had been held captive by the dragon, would be set free. Clark said that before this conference he had heard of only a handful of roaring sounds, but when this story was shared in Anaheim, he heard more lion manifestations than at any meeting before or since. He also said that there was a large group of Asians at the conference, and most of the noise was coming from them.[83] Following the conference, the Anaheim Vineyard was inundated with over a thousand phone calls, letters, and notes, both positive and negative, regarding the meetings. Wimber stated that this was the largest response to any meeting or conference they had ever had.[84] By now they were six months into the renewal, and more than a hundred thousand people in the combined churches throughout the Vineyard had been touched.[85]

Second Newsletter

In the July/August 1994 issue of *Vineyard Reflections*, Wimber again expressed his thoughts in an article titled "Refreshing, Renewal, and Revival." He stated that many, including himself, had been profoundly touched at the "Let the Fire Fall" conference. He acknowledged they had received negative reactions but reminded everyone that revivals were like childbirth; they can be messy. He also acknowledged that some people were confused as to what they saw and heard while others questioned whether they had received anything since they experienced no outward manifestation. He assured them that phenomena did not equate to an experience with God. However, there were a variety of ways people can respond to a spiritual encounter, and he was comfortable with making room for these experiences. Others had felt abused by overzealous ministry teams who prayed such things as, "Fall, fall, fall," or "Roar, roar, roar." This, he acknowledged, was out of order. He also believed that most of what was being experienced in the meetings was God, but it was God in humans. He believed what may be allowable in a renewal service may differ from what was acceptable in a typical Sunday morning worship service open to the public. He attempted to refocus people on the Vineyard core values, which were Scripture reading, witnessing, healing the sick, casting out demons, and feeding the poor. He also acknowledged that Toronto had reported an increased number of conversions and was delighted because of this. This, he said, was the fruit he was looking for.

While he had been praying for direction regarding renewal, God gave him a vision, which he shared in the newsletter:

> In the picture he showed me a magnificent mountain lake. Beautiful sunshine reflected off the water that was so fresh and inviting. The water of the lake spilled over a dam and cascaded into a river and came down the sides of a mountain into a large plain. In the plain, there were thousands and thousands of acres of vineyards. I saw men working in the fields, digging irrigation ditches. Then the vision ended. So I said, 'Lord, what does it mean?' In my mind, he gave me, 'The lake is the blessing I'm pouring out. Isn't it beautiful? Isn't it refreshing?' I was so touched, I began crying. He then said, 'The cascading stream is the church. I'm pouring it first into the church.' And I wept more. I just thought, 'Oh thank you Lord. Thank you for blessing the church.' Then I saw again how the water came down the bottom of the mountain into the plain, where the workers were tending the irrigation ditches. I recognized these irrigation ditches as 'Ministry to the poor, ministry to the weak, sick, broken, and lost. There were different kinds of vineyards with different kinds of fruit growing on the vines. Then he said 'That's my people. This blessing can either stay in the church, with great meetings that eventually end. Or we can pull the gates up and let the water begin flowing. If you want, you can direct the water, the blessing, into the fields.' I got the clear impression of a co-laboring. God was pouring out his blessing. But if we don't dig the channels, if we don't go out into the highways and by-ways, if we don't put evangelism forward, if we didn't do these things God calls us to do, revival won't spread.[86]

For Wimber, the goal of renewal was for the church to be blessed so they could be a blessing. He had always believed God had called them to the *doing* of the gospel, and if the blessing stayed in the church, it would soon end; however, if they took it to the streets it would spread. For him the "main and plain things of Scripture" were what they were to focus on.[87]

Third Newsletter

In the third *Vineyard Reflections* leadership letter, dated September/October 1994, Wimber's article "An Unchanging Destination" voiced growing concerns. He reminded the church that Vineyard's earliest commission was to be a church-planting movement for the sake of winning the lost, and all renewal activity must be evaluated in light of whether it contributed or hindered the achievement of this goal. If being "revived" meant empowerment to reach this destination, then it should be humbly and gratefully received. If it was a fleshly manifestation that altered the course, then correction was necessary.

He consulted with historian Vinson Synan regarding the phenomena. Synan confirmed that manifestations had always accompanied revivals in recent church history.[88] However, these are not the *essence* of revival. Wimber believed that the essence of revival consists of mass conversion, changed lives, measurable impact on society, and a response to the Great Commission. Phenomena must never be the focus of church life, rather he encouraged pastors to teach the Word of God, administer the ordinances, pastor the people, equip the saints for ministry, lead the people in worship, and do the work of an evangelist. When the Spirit moves on people for renewal, the focus must be on Holy Spirit baptism, actualizing the gifts of the Spirit, and the Great Commission.[89]

Emergency Board Session

Stories regarding "unbiblical manifestations" continued to raise concern in the evangelical church at large. It seemed the eyes of the world were watching Toronto and waiting to see what Wimber would do. Finally, he called an emergency board meeting and published the results in *The Board Report* dated September/October 1994. The document was signed by Todd Hunter who, because of Wimber's failing health, was the acting director of the Association of Vineyard Churches.

The main concern expressed in the meeting, again, was in regard to the pastoral administration of exotic phenomena, especially animal noises. The board was not prepared to make a blanket statement regarding animal noises, but they did offer a few suggestions. First, their desire was to be known as "evangelists" or "zealous Christian workers" rather than "roarers or shakers."[90] Second, they believed people were not making animal noises but rather sounds that resembled animals; therefore, such manifestations, they advised, should not be referred to in that way. Third, they said church services should not be patterned around renewal meetings; rather, pastors should focus on maintaining the basic infrastructure of caring for the people and programs of their church. In conclusion, the desire of the Vineyard board was to "embrace all that is good about this renewal while correcting that which is excessive." The report went on to say the mission and purpose of Vineyard had always been "committed to 'power *evangelism*' not just 'power' and to 'signs and wonders and *church growth*,' not just 'signs and wonders.'"[91]

Wimber's Response to Phenomena

Wimber also issued a two-page summary of his response to phenomena, which focused primarily on the issue of "roaring." First, he stated that there was no biblical or theological framework through which to evaluate such phenomena, and therefore categorized such manifestations as "nonbiblical" or "exotic." He had, however, received seven or eight testimonies from people who had "roared," and all had believed the manifestation was prophetic in nature. That is to say, these people sensed "God's indignation at the state of the church and the impact of the enemy's presence in the church" and felt the "prophetic roar" was a "sort of 'announcement' of God's intention to take back territory."[92]

He stated that he was aware that there were people in the Vineyard who enthusiastically endorsed such experiences and others who sharply disagreed. He did not believe such phenomena were demonic or divine, but put it in the category of "pondering" or "I don't know." He advised pastors not to showcase manifestations but to encourage the "main and plain things of Scripture."[93]

Wimber Confronts the Toronto Leaders

In October of 1994, John Arnott hosted the Catch the Fire conference at the Toronto Airport Vineyard. Following the conference, Arnott, Clark, and Campbell were invited to Anaheim to meet with Wimber and Todd Hunter. The purpose of the meeting was to deal with concerns raised by Vineyard pastors related to the exotic manifestations at the Toronto meetings, and, according to Clark, there were about twenty items on the agenda, but most of their time and attention was focused on discussing the animal noises. Clark said that while this seemed to be a big deal to Wimber and Hunter, it was not a significant issue for the Toronto team. He went on to say, however, "Apparently I had underestimated the seriousness of the issue, for it would later prove to be the singular cataclysmic event responsible for the disfellowshipping of the Toronto Vineyard."[94]

Clark remembered his year at Toronto as being the most significant time in his life and ministry. He saw thousands of weary pastors and leaders come to Toronto to be refreshed as the Father's love touched and enabled them to go on in ministry. He had been a recipient of this love, and he had also received a fresh commission to the nations and the end-time harvest. He was convinced that God was pouring out his Spirit in "Toronto for just one reason—to equip the church to go!"[95]

Wimber did not disagree that Toronto was a genuine move of God. He was even willing to allow for the fact that the manifestations may be God offending the mind to get at the heart. He told the Toronto leadership team, however, that as the leader of an international movement, he saw the big picture and had to act accordingly.

More specifically, according to Bob Fulton, Wimber's brother-in-law and international coordinator of church planting, John saw Toronto as another power surge in the Vineyard movement. On the other hand, John knew some Vineyard leaders had become troubled by the media attention and global focus on Toronto, and he was concerned Toronto was beginning to take the Vineyard movement in a different direction.[96] In other words, because the Toronto Vineyard had gained attention from around the world, people were beginning to see *it* as the Vineyard model, and, as a result, Toronto was defining Vineyard. As the international leader of the movement, John felt it was his responsibility to bring the areas of concern back into alignment with the Vineyard ethos.[97]

Exacerbating this internal turmoil, Hanegraaff, whose radio station was just a few miles from Wimber's Anaheim Vineyard, aired disparaging commentary on Wimber, the Vineyard movement, and the events at Toronto daily. In addition, many of the Vineyard churches in southern California were losing members, with a large majority of them migrating to Chuck Smith's Calvary Chapel, where Hanegraaff attended. So, while the Toronto leadership thought the issue was insignificant, it was an everyday thorn in Wimber's side. It was Wimber's hope that his meeting with the Toronto leaders would bring the necessary corrections to stop the controversy, stabilize the Vineyard ship, and move the organization forward.

Wimber's Health Continues to Decline

All through 1994, Wimber struggled to regain his health following cancer and radiation therapy. Then on December 18 of that year, he resigned as pastor of the Anaheim Vineyard and installed Carl Tuttle as the senior pastor.[98] It had been a long and difficult year, but with his workload now lightened, he began to sense life returning to normal. Then in January 1995, he suffered a stroke and was confined to a wheelchair.[99] More will be said about this in the following chapter.

Throughout 1995, John was virtually silent in his communication with the Toronto leadership. Between October 1995 and February 1996, there was only one issue of the *Vineyard Reflection*, the newsletter for his leaders that was normally produced four times a year. This five-page newsletter titled "Staying Focused: The Vineyard as a Centered Set," was dated July 1995–February 1996. In it, John reflected on his treatment of Toronto and reaffirmed the essential aspect of the Vineyard movement.

On January 20, 1995, Toronto celebrated the first anniversary of the renewal with a record crowd of four thousand people from around the globe. In September of the same year, *Christianity Today* carried two major stories on the Toronto outpouring, covering thirteen pages. In the cover story, James Beverly relayed how the *Toronto Life* magazine had billed the Toronto Blessing the top tourist attraction of 1994 and said airlines were offering discounts to travelers flying in for the nightly Tuesday-through-Sunday renewal meetings.[100] Everything in Toronto appeared to be going well; however, in Anaheim, trouble was brewing.

The Controversy Escalates

As Wimber's health continued to decline, Todd Hunter began to play a more prominent role as Vineyard's U.S. national director. As such, both Wimber and Hunter contacted Vinson Synan on separate occasions to discuss the concerns continuing to surface regarding Toronto. Synan's phone conversation with Wimber and Hunter lasted an hour and a half. In the conversation, Synan recommended that the Vineyard not separate from Toronto but give it time and see how things go. "These things happen," Synan told him, "but in time things usually settle down." In his conversation with Hunter, however, Synan said that if the Vineyard leadership chose to distance themselves from what was happening at Toronto, they had historical precedence based on the way the Assemblies of God had dealt with the Latter Rain issue in the late 1940s. But in both conversations, Synan counseled the men to move forward cautiously, because this was an important issue and the world was watching to see how they would handle it.[101]

Perhaps the proverbial last straw was Arnott's book *The Father's Blessing*, published in 1995, which contained a chapter about animal noises. In it, Arnott recounted the story of Gideon Chu and the prophecy of the Chinese being set free when the Lion of Judah roared. He also described how a woman in his church, who played the keyboard and had attended for some time, got down on the floor on all fours, snorted while pawing the ground like an angry ox, and then prophesied for an hour about how the Lord was angry at what Satan had done to God's church. He said another woman, a registered nurse, had crowed like a rooster. Then Arnott reminded readers of how God had described the four living creatures around his throne in animal terms such as ox, eagle, and lion. All of this, according to Arnott, could be interpreted as prophetic words being acted out.[102]

Although Arnott had given Wimber a draft of the book so that he could write a review on it prior to publication, Wimber, in his physical frailty, had failed to read the entire manuscript, missing the chapter on animal noises. Consequently, he wrote a positive endorsement to put on the back cover. When the book was published and Wimber saw the chapter on animal noises, he was outraged.[103]

Toronto Disfellowshipped

By December 1995, the board of the Association of Vineyard Churches had decided to withdraw its support from the Toronto Airport Vineyard. The board said the reasons for this decision were that the events in Toronto did not align with the vision and direction of the Association of Vineyard Churches and that Toronto was not operating in agreement with the association's established guidelines and leadership.

On December 5, 1995, Wimber, along with Association of Vineyard Churches international director; Todd Hunter, national director, USA; Gary Best, national director, Canada; and Bob Fulton, international coordinator, flew to Toronto to meet with the leaders of the Toronto Vineyard to announce the association's decision.

Charisma journalist, Lee Grady, reported Wimber's announcement—"John [Arnott], you're out of the Vineyard"—calling it blunt. "It was an icy way to end a 10-year relationship," Grady wrote, "but Wimber was tired of answering questions about the much-publicized Toronto Blessing. . . . Wimber didn't believe Arnott was promoting theological error, but he struggled with the way the Toronto church used Scripture to defend the shaking, falling, laughing and general rowdiness that was occurring during its marathon revival services . . . so he pruned it."[104]

Bert Waggoner, then a member of the Association of Vineyard Churches' board, said that the board had discussed how they would confront Arnott and his staff at the meeting but that when the time came, Wimber failed to execute the agreed-upon plans. Waggoner was unable to comment further, but he said he believed that if Wimber had stuck to the original arrangement, they could have reached the same outcome with less trauma for the Vineyard movement.[105]

Arnott's staff was shocked by Wimber's actions and realized they had underestimated the seriousness of the situation. Toronto assistant pastor Steve Long told the *Alberta Report*, a local newspaper, "the meeting could have lasted two minutes, the decision was already made when they came in the door." In the same article, Gary Best, the Vineyard national director for Canada, said the meeting was "difficult, though not in any way accusatory."[106]

The meeting lasted nearly three hours and ended with a request for the Toronto leadership to meet among themselves to discuss the decision and then to meet with Best. They were to provide a response to the U.S. leaders the next day.[107] According to Fulton, Wimber's bottom line was this:

> I am drawing a line in the sand. Who are your leaders? Who do you look to? Because it is apparent that you don't look to us. We've tried to lead and guide you through the years but you don't listen. If we're not your leaders we need to know that. So we're going to go to our hotel, you guys meet, talk, and pray about it and let us know your decision.[108]

Wimber and his team then left the meeting, and within two hours Arnott called with a response.[109] Arnott also sent a letter to Wimber. In it, he thanked Wimber for taking the "heat" and criticism for the Toronto church and apologized for the stress and hurt it had caused him. He also expressed sorrow for misreading the intent and extent of Wimber's concerns. Arnott recognized Wimber's leadership, acknowledged that some of what was happening at Toronto lay outside the Vineyard model, and agreed that Wimber should not have to continue answering for what was happening in Toronto. He also acknowledged that he did not completely understand all that God was doing but said that, as the pastor of the outpouring, he was called to help facilitate and faithfully steward what God had entrusted to him. Arnott accepted the board's decision to disengage from the Association of Vineyard Churches but asked if they could leave with the board's blessing. Arnott signed the letter on behalf of the church and pastoral staff.[110] (See Appendix G.)

Arnott's Open Letter

One week later, on December 12, 1995, Arnott wrote an open letter for general distribution for anyone interested in Toronto's disengagement from the Vineyard. The separation, he said, would take place on January 20, 1996, at the second anniversary of the outpouring of the Spirit. He said they were surprised at the finality of the decision and felt they had been removed without due process. He went on to say,

> John Wimber felt he could no longer answer questions, including innuendoes and rumors, regarding the renewal services. Rather than ask us to revamp the renewal meetings, they released us to continue on as we believe God is leading us. Wimber agrees that the Holy Spirit is moving in Toronto, it's just that he (Wimber) feels the AVC [Association of Vineyard Churches] Board is not called to shepherd something outside the ministry model God has given them.

While our local fellowship follows closely the Vineyard model, the renewal services, it seems, do not.[111]

Arnott said they had asked several senior leaders from around the world to form an International Renewal Network, which would serve as an advisory council to help steer and facilitate the renewal and act as a temporary leadership covering. He then thanked Wimber and the Association of Vineyard Churches' board, acknowledging that the Toronto outpouring would not have had a worldwide audience without them. He closed by expressing his desire for love and mercy to continue between the two groups.[112]

The next day, Arnott sent an email message to four key supporters, describing the events of the previous night. According to *Christianity Today*, Richard Riss, a church historian at Drew University, released Arnott's email on the internet prior to Arnott's approval and included a note saying that "a precipitous separation of the sheep from the goats" had occurred and that Wimber was "putting himself in the position of [King] Saul" who had waged war against King David, his eventual successor. Arnott's church quickly distanced themselves from Riss, who subsequently issued an apology for prematurely releasing the information and for making the comments he did regarding Wimber.[113]

Todd Hunter's Letter to Vineyard Pastors

The following day, Todd Hunter responded on behalf of Wimber with a three-page letter to the Vineyard pastors. He acknowledged that the Toronto renewal was from God, but he said that he believed the Vineyard core value of equipping the saints had been marginalized as manifestations had taken center stage. This, Hunter alleged, "reveals a significantly different understanding of what renewal is and how it operates within the church."[114]

In the next two *Vineyard Reflection* newsletters, July 1995–February 1996 and July 1996, Wimber himself responded to questions regarding the disfellowshipping of Toronto and attempted to explain the Vineyard's position. Regarding Arnott's concern that he had not been given "due process," Wimber said,

> I confess that given the serious nature of our misgivings of what was transpiring at the Toronto Church, I myself or perhaps Todd Hunter could have called John Arnott personally and made absolutely sure he understood

those guidelines. I acknowledge some degree of failure (possibly on both our parts) and say, 'Let's not allow our differences to hinder our good will or the work we do for the kingdom.'[115]

The After Effects

In January 1996, Toronto conducted a Catch the Fire conference to celebrate the second anniversary of the renewal. Randy Clark ministered and said it was the most powerful service they had experienced since the meetings started. After the conference, Clark flew directly to Anaheim where he ministered to Wimber's congregation. Clark said the power was "off the charts." It was a party atmosphere with people piling on the floor and key leaders being mightily touched.

Knowing Clark was grieved over their disfellowshipping the Toronto Vineyard, Wimber invited Clark to his office to talk after the meeting. During this talk, Wimber asked point blank whether Clark was planning to leave the Vineyard. Todd Hunter later told Clark that they were concerned that if he left, the Vineyard would lose up to one-third of its churches, especially after the controversy with the Kansas City Prophets and now Toronto.[116] (Hunter also later acknowledged that the Vineyard "lost a lot of churches" in the United States over Toronto. He also told *Charisma* that he "agreed in principle with the decision to oust Toronto" but believed "there were 'flaws in the process' of Wimber's brash action—noting that Wimber himself admitted this in 1995.")[117]

Clark responded to Wimber's question by saying that Wimber himself would be the one to decide. Expounding on this, Clark explained that Wimber, during his entire ministry, had primarily focused on bringing renewal to evangelicals. Clark, on the other hand, believed God had called him to minister to the entire body of Christ, including the Pentecostals. Clark went on to share a prophecy that Mark Dupont, at that time a prophet working in the Toronto church, had given him in August 1994—a year and a half prior. Dupont had received a vision that told him Clark's ministry would change and that God would send him to the Pentecostals, Assemblies of God, and even the Word of Faith camp. Up to that point, Clark had not received any invitations from groups outside the Vineyard movement. After the prophetic word from Dupont, however, his invitations suddenly changed from being 100 percent from Vineyard to being 10 percent from Vineyard and 90 percent from Pentecostals, Assemblies, and Word of Faith combined.[118]

Wimber acknowledged that both Clark and Arnott had a good working relationship with the Pentecostals, and he wanted to know why this was so. Clark said he'd been raised Baptist with an Arminian theology. He'd grown up in a poor country church that he thought could best be described as "Bapticostal," so he was comfortable with emotions and manifestations—and because of this, he believed he could better understand the Pentecostals. Wimber, on the other hand, worked from a Reformed theological framework. In addition, Wimber had felt called to the evangelical church, but Clark believed Pentecostals were hungry for a touch of God just as evangelicals were, and he felt called to both groups. With this, he asked Wimber for an Acts 15 agreement and permission to take the model of the kingdom that Wimber had taught for so many years to the Pentecostals. He also asked Wimber to be more lenient because, at this point, as the leader of an international movement, he was too restrictive. Wimber agreed to release the Vineyard message to him and to bless him to take it to the Pentecostals and others outside the Vineyard churches.

Clark said he believed that Vineyard's break from the Toronto renewal was a tremendous loss for the Vineyard movement—that several more large ministries would be part of the Vineyard today if Toronto had not been disfellowshipped. Out of Toronto came Roland and Heidi Baker's work in Mozambique, which now has over ten thousand churches and has seen over 1 million conversions. Leif Hetland was also impacted by Toronto, and his ministry in Pakistan has now seen over a million conversions. A work in Brazil was only three years old with three thousand churches when Toronto was disfellowshipped. At that time, they had already taken the Vineyard name and logo and had planned to join the movement, but when Toronto was rejected, they pulled away, saying the Vineyard exercised too much control. Today this pastor has thirty thousand members in his local church and oversees over half a million people. And this didn't include the several thousand churches now in Arnott's network; or the ministry of Che Ahn, the founder of Harvest International Ministries; or Bill Johnson's ministry; or Clark's network of apostolic leaders with over sixteen thousand churches.

Clark's ministry has influenced many other denominations and churches as well. Beginning around 2015, its doors opened to influence traditional, non-Pentecostal denominations such as Roman Catholic, Baptist, and Reformed. He was asked to help transition a denomination in Europe from its cessationist position to the continuationist position. He has worked with the largest Baptist churches in Argentina, Brazil, and South Africa, through which several hundreds of thousands of people have been saved and discipled after having been touched by the power of God's Spirit. Henry Madava, an apostolic leader in the Ukraine, has seen over a million conversions in his ministry ever since his church was touched through Clark's ministry. All of these ministries, Clark said, had spawned out of the Toronto renewal and were examples of the potential fruit the Vineyard movement lost when they disfellowshipped Toronto.

Finally, Clark said he believed that if Wimber had simply made a statement to the effect that he did not agree with what was happening in Toronto and then taken a wait-and-see position, the controversy would have blown over—that history itself had proven this would be the result. And indeed, the animal sounds did stop, and the Toronto renewal went on for years, bearing tremendous fruit. Even to this day, the church is healthy and productive.[119]

In Retrospect

Reflecting on the Toronto issue, C. Peter Wagner, Wimber's friend and ministry associate for twenty years, said he believed that Wimber was an apostolic leader but his greatest weakness was that he had trouble allowing his followers to grow and to surpass him—whether it be in their skills, ability, or anointing. Wimber had lost good people in the Vineyard when they became influential in their own right, and Wagner believed the way he dealt with Arnott and Toronto was the most public example of this. Arnott and the Toronto Vineyard were growing in international recognition and becoming as influential and powerful as Wimber, so instead of blessing them, he separated from them, due to such "silly things as animal noises," Wagner said. "So when you look at people like Randy Clark, Che Ahn, and others who would be in the Vineyard today," he continued, "they are fallout from Wimber's own leadership weakness. . . . Even if John could not have absorbed them into the Vineyard, at least he could have blessed Arnott rather than disfellowshipping him." Wagner said it may have been that John Arnott was God's chosen replacement to lead the Vineyard movement and spearhead renewal after Wimber's death.[120]

Even Wimber, upon visiting the Toronto Vineyard, acknowledged that the "epicenter" of what God was doing had shifted from Anaheim to Toronto. Could it be that, while he was able to recognize the shift of the Spirit, he was unable to release the reins of renewal into the hands of another—and that this is what caused him to make the ultimate split with Arnott?

More questions can be asked than there are answers regarding this chapter of Wimber's life, but there is one potentially important question to ponder: throughout Wimber's life, his own issue of fatherlessness was significant. As Jack Deere said, "Who would have thought that a fatherless son from Missouri would father hundreds of spiritual sons all over the world?"[121] Eleanor Mumford echoed this thought, saying, "It is a most extraordinary thing that a man whose own father left home on the very day he was born, and whom he never saw again, was later to become a 'father in the gospel' to so many young men and women both within his own family and across the wider church."[122] Indeed, while John Wimber was the father of the Vineyard movement and of a renewal movement that spread around the world, one wonders how well he dealt with the fatherlessness in his own personal life. In the end, it seems a bit ironic that he ultimately disfellowshipped the move of the Spirit known as "the Father's Blessing." Could it be that John's inability to overcome the pain of his own fatherlessness led him to reject the very movement that would have taken the Vineyard into a new phase of renewal and fulfilled his vision of ten thousand Vineyard churches lighting up across America? These are questions that can be answered only in view of eternity. It is worth noting, however, that based on Wimber's own comments, he believed that the disfellowshipping of Toronto may have been the place he stepped out of God's will.

Wimber's Reflections

Just a few weeks before Wimber died, John Paul Jackson went to visit him. During his visit, Wimber confided in him, saying that if God were to allow him to live, he would take a fresh look at the way he had handled Toronto. After all, Wimber said, nothing had happened in Toronto that had not happened in Yorba Linda in their early years. He told Jackson that God had asked him to take a risk with Toronto, but because he'd wanted to protect the Vineyard, he had told God no. He said he believed this was the reason he was dying—because God had asked him three times to take a risk with Toronto, and three times he had looked God in the face and said, "No, I have too much to lose."

"Imagine this," Wimber said, "Here I am, John Wimber, the man who coined the phrase 'you spell faith R-I-S-K,' and now I am in the latter part of my life and ministry, and I looked God in the face and told him I have too much to lose."[123]

When any life is examined in retrospect, it is easy to identify the weaknesses and flaws. John Wimber's life was no exception to this rule. And this final reflection with Jackson—in which Wimber admitted that he had missed it and that, if he had it to do all over again, Toronto would be one area he would like to redo—is evidence that his treatment of the situation was incongruent with the overall tenor of his heart. In other words, although Wimber may have struggled to release the leadership in Toronto or to allow his "sons" to outgrow him, these failures do not define his entire ministry. Those who knew Wimber best knew him as a man who had no desire to build a big ministry or to create a name for himself. In fact, his son Tim said his dad would have been happy to pastor a small church and just play his music.[124] Carol agreed, saying that what a lot of people saw as ambition was just John's deep sense of responsibility and trying to be faithful with what God had given—and that, despite his mistakes, his primary focus was always to be obedient to what God asked him to do and to reach his generation for Christ.[125]

[1] Wimber, *Living with Uncertainty*, 7–8.
[2] Carol Wimber, *John Wimber*, 185.
[3] Jon Panner, "Editor's Note," *Vineyard Reflections*, June/July 1993, 1–2; John Wimber, "Who Are We and Where Are We Going?" Part II, *Vineyard Reflections*, June 1993, 2.
[4] Carol Wimber, *John Wimber*, 186–9.
[5] Wimber, *Living with Uncertainty*, 16, 20.
[6] Wimber, "Season of New Beginnings," 2.
[7] Wimber, "Season of New Beginnings," 2.
[8] Wimber, "Season of New Beginnings," 2.
[9] Wimber, "Season of New Beginnings," 2–3.
[10] Wimber, "Season of New Beginnings," 3.
[11] Wesley Campbell, *Welcoming a Visitation of the Holy Spirit* (Mary Lake, FL: Creation House, 1996), 44.
[12] Wimber, "Season of New Beginnings," 3.
[13] Randy Clark, *Lighting Fires: Keeping the Spirit of Revival Alive in Your Heart and the Hearts of Others around You* (Lake Mary, FL: Creation House, 1998), xv, 82.
[14] Guy Chevreau, *Catch the Fire: The Toronto Blessing: An Experience of Renewal and Revival* (Toronto: HarperCollins, 1994), 21. Chevreau's controversial book is filled with testimonies and experiences of people who encountered the early days of the Toronto outpouring. The revival ministry of Jonathan Edwards in the eighteenth century was used as a precedence to validate the bizarre and, at times, extrabiblical manifestations seen in the Toronto meetings. Chevreau's book later became fodder for Hank Hanegraaff's book *Counterfeit Revival*.
[15] Chevreau, *Catch the Fire*, 22.
[16] Chevreau, *Catch the Fire*, 23.
[17] Richard Riss, "Rodney Howard-Brown," in *NIDPCM*, 774. Also, Richard Riss, *A History of the Awakening of 1992–1995*, online book, available at http://www.revival-library.org/catalogues/pentecostal/riss.html.
[18] Joe Maxwell, "Is Laughing for the Lord Holy?" *Christianity Today*, October 24, 1994, 78.
[19] John Arnott, *The Father's Blessing* (Lake Mary, FL: Creation House, 1995), 57–8.
[20] Geoff Waugh, *Flashpoints of Revival: History's Mighty Revivals* (Shippensburg, PA: Destiny Image, 1998), 107. Also Chevreau, *Catch the Fire*, 23.
[21] Richard Riss, *A History of the Renewal of 1992–1995*, http://www.grmi.org/renewal/Richard_Riss/history/intro.html.
[22] Arnott, *The Father's Blessing*, 58.
[23] Arnott, *The Father's Blessing*, 58.
[24] Arnott, *The Father's Blessing*, 58–9.
[25] Clark, *Lighting Fires*, 5–6.
[26] Clark, *Lighting Fires*, 28, 34, 38, 61.
[27] Clark, *Lighting Fires*, 41–2. Randy Clark, *There is More: Reclaiming the Power of Impartation* (Mechanicsburg, PA: Global Awakening, 2006), 20.
[28] Clark, *Lighting Fires*, 54, 60.
[29] Clark, *Lighting Fires*, 76.
[30] Clark, *There is More*, 30.
[31] Clark, *Lighting Fires*, 80.
[32] Clark, *Lightning Fires*, 76–82.
[33] Clark, *Lighting Fires*, 82–3.
[34] Clark, *Lighting Fires*, 83.
[35] Clark, *Lighting Fires*, 85.
[36] Clark, *Lighting Fires*, 83.
[37] Interview by the author with Randy Clark.
[38] Maxwell, "Is Laughing for the Lord Holy?" 78.

[39] Arnott, *The Father's Blessing*, 59.
[40] Interview by the author with Randy Clark.
[41] Chevreau's controversial book is filled with testimonies and experiences of people who encountered the early days of the Toronto outpouring. The revival ministry of Jonathan Edwards in the eighteenth century was used as a precedence to validate the bizarre and at times, what some believed to be, extrabiblical manifestations seen in the Toronto meetings. Chevreau's book later became fodder for Hank Hanegraaff's book *Counterfeit Revival*.
[42] J. Lee Grady, "God Can Use Warehouses," *Charisma*, February 1995, 4.
[43] Grady, "God Can Use Warehouses," 4.
[44] J. Lee Grady, "Toronto's Afterglow," *Charisma*, December 1998, 73.
[45] Daina Doucet, "What Is God Doing in Toronto?" *Charisma*, February 1995, 20.
[46] Arnott, *The Father's Blessing*, 169. Confirmed in an interview with Randy Clark.
[47] Clark, *There is More*, 43.
[48] Arnott, *The Father's Blessing*, 169. Arnott's statement was confirmed by Randy Clark.
[49] Arnott, *The Father's Blessing*, 182.
[50] Kenneth L. Woodward and Jeanne Gordon, "The Giggles Are for God," *Newsweek* 124, issue 8 (February 20, 1995): 54; also Doucet, "What Is God Doing in Toronto?" 25.
[51] "Toronto Blessing: Is It a Revival?" *Christianity Today*, May 15, 1995, 51.
[52] Maxwell, "Is Laughing for the Lord Holy?" 78.
[53] Daina Doucet, "Mainse Endorses 'Toronto Blessing,'" *Charisma*, June 1995, 68–9.
[54] David Aikman, "All Fall Down," *The American Spectator*, 28 (November 1995): 68.
[55] Gumbel is now the vicar of Holy Trinity Brompton and is known around the world for his work with the Alpha course. The Holy Trinity church website may be accessed at http://www.htb.org.uk/.
[56] This is the same Nicky Gumbel that Wimber had prophesied would have a powerful ministry and became the director of the famous Alpha course.
[57] Riss, *A History of the Renewal*, http://www.revival-library.org/index.php/catalogues-menu/pentecostal/a-history-of-the-awakening-of-1992–1995.
[58] Arnott, *The Father's Blessing*, 8.
[59] Ruth Gledhill, "Spread of Hysteria Fad Worries Church," *Times*, June 18, 1994, 12.
[60] Sunday Telegraph, June 19, 1994; James Beverly, *Holy Laughter and the Toronto Blessing: An Investigative Report* (Grand Rapids, MI: Zondervan, 1995), 11.
[61] Andrew Brown, "The Holy Spirit Hits South Kensington," *The Independent*, June 21, 1994, 2.
[62] Richard N. Ostling and Helen Gibson, "Laughing for the Lord," *Time* 11 no. 7 (August 15, 1994): 2–3.
[63] Ostling and Gibson, "Laughing for the Lord," 3.
[64] Brown, "The Holy Spirit Hits South Kensington," 2.
[65] Campbell, *Welcoming a Visitation of the Holy Spirit*, 45.
[66] Steve Hill, *The Pursuit of Revival* (Lake Mary, FL: Creation House, 1997), 73.
[67] Hill, *Pursuit of Revival*, 74.
[68] Lynda Hurst, "Laughing All the Way to Heaven in the Church at the End of the Runway with its 'Toronto Blessing,'" *Toronto Star*, December 3, 1994, A1.
[69] Hurst, "Laughing All the Way to Heaven," A1.
[70] Larry Randolph interviewed by Randy Clark in Mechanicsburg, Pennsylvania, http://www.globalawakening.com/Articles/1000050986/Global_Awakening/Media/Video_Podcast/Episode_67_Larry.aspx. Accessed October 26, 2010.
[71] Interview by the author with Tim Wimber.
[72] J. Lee Grady, "Does the Church Need Heresy Hunters?" *Charisma*, May 1995, 47.
[73] Grady, "Does the Church Need Heresy Hunters?" 48.
[74] Grady, "Does the Church Need Heresy Hunters?" 48.
[75] Jackson, *Quest for the Radical Middle*, 313.
[76] Wimber, "Season of New Beginnings," 1.

77 Wimber, "Season of New Beginnings," 5.
78 Wimber, "Season of New Beginnings."
79 Wimber, "Season of New Beginnings," 1–7; John Wimber, "Visitation of the Spirit," *Ministries Today*, September/October 1994, 8–9.
80 Interview by the author with Randy Clark.
81 Campbell, *Welcoming a Visitation of the Holy Spirit*, 26.
82 Wimber, "Refreshing, Renewal, and Revival," 1.
83 Interview by the author with Randy Clark.
84 Wimber, "Refreshing, Renewal, and Revival," 1.
85 Wimber, "Refreshing, Renewal, and Revival," 7.
86 Wimber, "Refreshing, Renewal, and Revival," 6–7.
87 Wimber, "Refreshing, Renewal, and Revival," 1–7; this is a summary of the article.
88 Interview by the author with Vinson Synan.
89 Wimber, "An Unchanging Destination," 1–6; this is a summary of this article.
90 Todd Hunter, *Board Report*, September/October 1994, 2. Special Collections, Regent University Library, Virginia Beach, Virginia.
91 Hunter, *Board Report*, 4.
92 Wimber, "John Wimber Responds to Phenomena."
93 Wimber, "John Wimber Responds to Phenomena."
94 Clark, *Lighting Fires*, 98; Clark confirmed this in a later interview.
95 Clark, *Lighting Fires*, 98.
96 Interview by the author with Bob Fulton.
97 Interview by the author with Bob Fulton.
98 John Wimber, "Fulfill Your Ministry: John Wimber's Installation of Carl & Sonja Tuttle as Senior Pastor of the Anaheim Vineyard, Sunday, Dec. 18, 1994," *Equipping the Saints*, Fourth Quarter, 1994, 16–9.
99 Carol Wimber, *John Wimber*, 189–91.
100 James Beverly, "Toronto's Mixed Blessing" and "The Surprising Works of God," *Christianity Today*, September 11, 1995, 23.
101 Interview by the author with Vinson Synan, June 21, 2010, Chesapeake, Virginia.
102 Arnott, *Father's Blessing*, 168–83.
103 Interview by the author with Tim Wimber.
104 J. Lee Grady, "The Pruning of the Vineyard," *Charisma*, December 1998, 72.
105 Interview by the author, August 24, 2010, with Bert Waggoner, current national director of Vineyard USA.
106 Joseph K. Woodard, "John Wimber Giveth and Taketh Away," *Alberta Report*, February 5, 1996, 37.
107 James A Beverly, "Vineyard Severs Ties with 'Toronto Blessing' Church," *Christianity Today*, January 8, 1995, 66.
108 Interview by the author with Bob Fulton.
109 Beverly, "Vineyard Severs Ties with 'Toronto Blessing' Church," 66.
110 John Arnott, "Letter to John Wimber." (See Appendix G)
111 Arnott, "An Open Letter for General Distribution." (See Appendix G)
112 Arnott, "An Open Letter for General Distribution." (See Appendix G)
113 Beverly, "Vineyard Severs Ties with 'Toronto Blessing' Church," 66.
114 Todd Hunter, "Letter to Vineyard Pastors."
115 John Wimber, "Staying Focused: The Vineyard as a Centered Set," *Vineyard Reflections*, July 1995–February 1996, 5.
116 Interview by the author with Randy Clark.
117 Grady, "The Pruning of the Vineyard," 72.
118 Interview by the author with Randy Clark. Clark did not leave the Vineyard until after Wimber's death, when many of his new friends and leaders were not in the Vineyard. A major reason for leaving and resigning from the Vineyard church he had planted with his wife was

not to plant a new church but to focus on the ministry of Global Awakening. Clark felt that the Vineyard model, or philosophy of ministry, at the time had become seeker-sensitive after the death of Wimber. Another issue was the way the Vineyard government was set up, which didn't allow for governance based on relationships and agreement on the philosophy of ministry. This manner of governance had been allowed in Vineyard through the "Columbus Accords" but had been rescinded under the leadership of Bert Waggoner. Clark had asked to be allowed to be under an area overseer in the Vineyard who was pro-renewal when Waggoner and Clark met at Clark's home. The meeting had been arranged at the suggestion of Vineyard's regional leader, Happy Leman, who oversaw Clark. Clark and Leman have a good relationship to this day.

[119] Interview by the author with Randy Clark.
[120] Interview by the author with C. Peter Wagner.
[121] Deere, "The Prophet," 115.
[122] Mumford, "Father Figure and Pastor," 84.
[123] Interview by the author with John Paul Jackson.
[124] Interview by the author with Tim Wimber.
[125] Carol Wimber, "A Wife's Tribute," 298–9.

Chapter 9

The Closing Years and a Tribute

Between the Kansas City Prophets and the Toronto Blessing, Wimber had dealt with his share of difficult issues. Now he was about to face a battle for his own life. For most of his adult years, Wimber had lived on the ragged edge of health problems. He struggled constantly with his weight. And at the age of twenty-four, he was diagnosed with high blood pressure and warned that if he did not get it under control, he would not live to see twenty-seven. Still alive after that fateful year had come and gone, he continued to feel as though he were living on borrowed time.[1] "Everyone dies of something, I know," Carol would later write. "Cancer, hypertension, stroke, a bad heart or a broken heart, but never has any one man died of so many things at the same time!"[2]

Struggling with Health

In 1993, Wimber was diagnosed with inoperable cancer and began the long and painful ordeal of radiation treatments, which made him so violently ill that he could not eat. Although he drank milk supplements, he lost 110 pounds and became thin and frail. One of the worst side effects of the radiation was his partial hearing loss, which continued to deteriorate until, by the end of his life, he was nearly deaf. The second worst effect was the destruction of his salivary glands, which required him to spray artificial saliva into his mouth in order to speak.[3] From this point on, Wimber also could no longer sing.

Regarding this low point in his life, Wimber said,

> Some Christians believe we should never struggle with doubt, fear, anxiety, disillusionment, depression, sorrow, or agony. And when Christians do, it is because they're not exercising the quality of faith they ought to; periods of disillusionment and despair are sin. If those ideas are true, then I'm not a good Christian. Not only have I suffered physically with health problems, but I also

spent a great deal of time struggling with depression during my battle with cancer.[4]

Wimber said he coped with his depression by becoming addicted to television. He had quit reading his Bible, because his eyes hurt from the radiation treatments, and turned to watching TV instead. And according to Wimber, since he developed an appetite for whatever he "ate," by putting his energy and effort into TV rather than God, his appetite grew in that direction. In his book *Witnesses for a Powerful Christ*, he wrote about the time he realized that if we make something else a "god" in our life, the way to freedom is to go back to the true God, his people, and the Bible. Upon facing this realization, Wimber went to church and confessed his sin, then he began feeding on the Bible to quench the appetite he had developed for TV. It worked: gradually, he increased the amount of time he spent reading the Bible and decreased the time he spent watching TV—and within weeks he had weaned himself from his addiction and regained a healthy appetite for the things of God.[5]

Another struggle he faced while battling cancer was being forced to reexamine his long-held beliefs regarding healing and the kingdom of God. Early in his ministry, when he had first started believing and teaching healing from the Scriptures, he often wondered if he was crazy to keep teaching something with no visible results. He was convinced by Scripture, however, that when Jesus had come, he had brought the kingdom with him, had demonstrated it through healing the sick, and, further, had commissioned his followers to do the same. Thus Wimber humbly obeyed the biblical principle to pray for the sick, even when no one was healed. For years, he prayed for people who did not receive healing, and now, locked in his own battle with incurable cancer, he personally faced the tension between believing God's will is to heal and suffering when healing does not come. In his book *Living with Uncertainty: My Bout with Inoperable Cancer*, Wimber articulated his understanding of this tension between divine healing and nonhealing this way:

> Suppose a father dies and leaves, as part of his will, an unbelievably huge fortune to his children. His heirs are rich—with just one caveat—they can't touch the money until they come of age. They are stuck, in a sense, between the *already* of the inheritance and the *not yet* of their age. What if, however, they had the ability to borrow from their inheritance? They would be borrowing what is already theirs—they would just be getting it early. That is our situation. It is a fact that ultimately we will all be healed and freed from everything that oppresses us. So when we ask God to heal the sick or free the

demonized, we are simply asking that God do now what he has promised to do in the future. Jesus's model prayer, 'Give us today our daily bread' (Matt. 6:11) can also be translated, 'Give us tomorrow's bread today.' We are asking, in essence, to borrow today from the Lord what is guaranteed to us tomorrow. To better cope with adversity that is part of our Christian lives, we need to understand that while tomorrow's bread is available to us today when we ask, God is sovereign. He determines whether or not to grant us what we ask for now—or later. In the end, we will experience liberation from every pain, tragedy and ailment. The age to come will see the fulfillment of all that the reign of God means. Jesus brought the kingdom of God with him, but not in its full realization—that will come when this age is over and the new age begins. Until that time, we live with disease, pain, suffering and inexplicable tragedies. In short, God will not grant miracles to everyone who prays—not yet.[6]

During his battle with incurable cancer, Wimber remained committed to his understanding of the already-and-not-yet theology of the kingdom and of suffering. In fact, at some point, someone asked him if he still believed in healing now that he'd had cancer. He wrote back, saying that he not only believed in healing, but

> I also believe in pain. Both are found in the Word of God. In the year I spent battling cancer God purged me of a lot of habits and attitudes that weren't right, and through it I grew stronger as a Christian. Some of my greatest advances in spiritual maturity came as I embraced the pain—as each day I had to choose to allow God to accomplish his work in me by any method, even adversity.[7]

He wrote that, in his battle with cancer, he wept as he faced fear of the unknown and utter dependence on God. "I discovered what it was like to walk through the valley of the shadow of death," he wrote, and "what I discovered is that the view from the valley isn't so bad. In fact, it gives you a focus on Christ that you can't get any other way."[8] At times, Wimber said, God answers and rescues us from our pain and heals us, and at other times, God allows the tragedy to "achieve some other end." Our focus, he went on to say, is not to be on our circumstances but rather on God, who is ultimately in control.[9]

Dealing with inoperable cancer meant Wimber was also faced with the reality of his own mortality. He believed that God has a plan for when a person is to be born and to die, and that death was the last and worst thing we all face. But, he often quipped, going to heaven is not so bad; after all that's what he signed up for—the reason he became a Christian. Death is just graduation day.[10]

Releasing the Reins

After Wimber's first heart attack, he took steps to lighten his workload in order to ease the stress in his life. At that time, he was the pastor of the Anaheim Vineyard, the head of the Association of Vineyard Churches, and a leader for Vineyard Ministries International. His plan was to turn the responsibilities of senior pastor over to Sam Thompson, who had worked as his associate for several years, but this plan was thwarted when Carol had a dream warning against it. A year and a half later, Wimber once again tried to install Thompson, this time as the national director of the movement, when Paul Cain stepped in with a verbal warning. Wimber stalled his plan again, which permanently severed his relationship with Thompson.[11]

Weak and tired, he struggled to carry on with his responsibilities while trying to regain his strength following cancer and radiation therapy. Then in the latter part of 1994, he was released to turn the pastoral duties of the Anaheim Vineyard over to Carl Tuttle. Wimber had led Tuttle to the Lord when Tuttle had been eleven, and he had grown up like a son in Wimber's home. Wimber had recognized the leadership and pastoral calling on Tuttle's life when Tuttle was a teenager and had mentored him in the ensuing years. Carl was a musician, pastor, and teacher who had worked closely with Wimber and had planted a Vineyard church.[12] Confident that Tuttle was the man for the job, Wimber installed him during the Sunday morning church service at the Anaheim Vineyard on December 18, 1994. His charge to the new pastor revealed the issues closest to Wimber's pastoral heart.

Wimber admonished Tuttle to "Seek the Lord," and to never be a "people pleaser, [or] you'll go under. . . . Be a man who listens and obeys him." Wimber also advised him to remember that the "ways of God are more caught than taught," as your actions speak louder than your words. Then Wimber encouraged Tuttle to give himself to prayer. "Ask daily for things that are bigger than your imagination . . . for things bigger than your nature to do. You know that God gave much greater than anything I ever asked for. Ask big. You have a big God who will do even more than you ask. Settle for nothing less than God. If you haven't found God, you have nothing to give." He encouraged Tuttle to stay fresh in the Lord no matter the cost and to let the word of God dwell in him richly through a daily and deep devotional life. Wimber said that when he personally had "allowed circumstances, people, or problems to rob" him of his time with God, he had become "superficial and insensitive."

He charged Tuttle to guard his heart and to maintain love, faith, and purity, and he told him if he lacked these things, he should go to God to get them. Regarding preaching, he said that it should carry a prophetic sense, as a fresh word from God, and he advised Tuttle to wait upon God daily for fresh bread and to discipline himself to study the Scriptures. Wimber also reminded Tuttle of the Vineyard vision to "lead the saints into becoming a true spiritual army, equipped for life and ministry in Christ." As their pastor, Tuttle's role was to be a trainer. The key to Vineyard's success, Wimber said, was that they modeled kingdom ministry and then stepped aside to allow others to do it. Wimber's last charge was to obey the Spirit. "Following the Spirit," Wimber said, "has been the most difficult thing I have ever done." He went on to say,

> It seems to me people give lip service to it, yet they obey a culturally derived perception of what is proper, what is appropriate, and what is of God. But I believe the Holy Spirit is in the Trinity of God. I believe he is every bit as much God as the Father and the Son. And I believe he is here with us today, and that he has directed us to this place. And if I believe less than that, I couldn't be doing what I am doing."[13]

At the conclusion of these words from the heart of a father to his spiritual son, Wimber transferred the reigns of his leadership of Anaheim Vineyard, the church he had founded and pastored for seventeen years.

Suffering a Stroke

It had been a long and difficult year, and now with his workload lightened and fewer pressures, it was time for life to go back to normal. But just one month after resigning from the church, Wimber was hit with another blow. In January of 1995, John and Carol sold their home in Yorba Linda and moved into a small condominium next to a golf course, which they hoped Wimber could use to get some exercise, to help him regain his strength. After only three weeks in their new home, a blood clot broke loose from his weakened heart and lodged in his brain, causing a stroke. This left Wimber with a spinning sensation, nausea, continual pain, and tingling on the left side of his face and body. He was now confined to a wheelchair.[14]

While Wimber was still in the hospital recovering, Peter Jennings, a television journalist from ABC who was filming a documentary titled "In the Name of God," called to talk with him.[15] Since the Anaheim Vineyard was one of the featured churches, Jennings offered to fly Wimber to New York to film an interview. Although he was still weak, Wimber agreed to go because he believed it was "a good opportunity for the Lord." Their oldest son Chris and Chris's wife Debby flew with him to New York a few weeks later. Still confined to a wheelchair, Wimber was unable to walk, but Chris cared for his dad's every need, which at times meant carrying him like a baby in his arms. And when the video aired, Wimber looked strong. Viewers never guessed he was in a wheelchair, recovering from a recent stroke. His eyes were bright, and it was evident he was in love with Jesus.[16]

Cancer Strikes Again

When Wimber was still recovering from his stroke, there was yet another blow—this time to his son. In May 1990, three years prior to his dad's cancer diagnosis, Chris was diagnosed with melanoma. He was only thirty-two at the time and had two children, Sean and Devon. Chris had labored closely with his dad in the Anaheim Vineyard, starting out as a custodian and working his way up to become the vice president and general manager of Vineyard Music Group.[17]

The cancer was surgically removed, and his prognosis was good. Doctors told him that if he remained cancer-free for five years, he would be pronounced clean. Then while celebrating his fifth-year anniversary, more lumps appeared along with the grim diagnosis that the cancer was not only back but had spread. His lymph nodes were removed and he was placed on a new drug, but when that did not work, they tried Interferon. He became terribly nauseated and weak but continued his work at Vineyard Music Group. Through the months of cancer therapy, John and Carol went with Chris and Debbie to the Cancer Research Center in Santa Monica. Carol remembered their trips as being some of the happiest times for John and Chris, as they sat in the front seat and talked about Chris's favorite subject—Vineyard music.[18]

Then on Christmas 1996, John and Carol received a call from Debbie. Chris had been to the doctor for a checkup and more tests, and they found the cancer had spread to his brain. Chris told his mother that he knew he was dying but that he did not want to talk about it. He preferred to live until he died. His brothers Sean and Tim moved back to Anaheim from Colorado, and John canceled most of his ministry engagements to spend as much time as possible with his son.[19]

Retirement and Reflection

By now, Wimber had resigned as both senior pastor of the Anaheim Vineyard and as board president of the U.S. Association of Vineyard Churches. The only position he continued to hold was that of the international director of the Association of Vineyard Churches. Then in the third quarter of 1996, Wimber announced in *Equipping the Saints* that he was retiring in full and would transition from the role of warrior to that of counselor. Wimber said the decision to retire was based largely on health issues, and he assured those in the Vineyard movement that he would still be there to guide and counsel the anointed spiritual authorities that would take his place. He said he had the utmost confidence in the godly men that would assume these leadership positions and that "if a crisis were to happen, I would rather have it happen now when I can give counsel rather than later when I am with the Lord."[20]

Following his announcement, *Christianity Today* interviewed Wimber, asking him to reflect on his thirty years of ministry. The article declared, "An era is ending at the Vineyard—the Anaheim, California, church and the worldwide movement. John Wimber, charismatic founder and leader of the movement is retiring."[21] In the interview, they posed several questions to Wimber. First, they asked about the critics he faced during his ministry—a ministry that, as a combination of Reformed theology and charismatic practices, bridged traditional evangelical Christianity and Pentecostalism but also made him a target of controversy. In regard to his ministry, Wimber replied that he had once told Walter Kaiser, Old Testament scholar and former president of Gordon-Conwell Theological Seminary, "I believe everything you believe. I just believe a little bit more in terms of pneumatology. I've got some ideas that, yes, are foreign; but they're not unprecedented in church history; nor are they non-biblical." In regard to his critics, Wimber said, "I have known from the outset that what I was going to do would not be popular. It's never wise to wake up sleeping people."[22]

Wimber was also asked if the Vineyard had become all he had hoped it would be, to which he answered, "We never became the evangelistically effective church I wanted to be. That's a failure." On the other hand, Wimber said, he believed he had laid a foundation that would enable the younger generation taking over to be successful. In addition, he gave the Vineyard a high grade for worship, saying, "We've introduced intimacy, which is probably our primary contribution to the church worship scene."

Regarding church planting, Wimber pointed out that the Vineyard had started with approximately 380 churches and grown more than 1,000 percent in its first decade. He then asked, "Do you know of any other denominations that have increased by that percentage in the United States recently?" In this area, he rated the Vineyard a nine out of ten.

He said that unity was the hardest biblical principle he had tried to follow, saying, "How do you love your brothers who don't like you?" When asked about his split with the Toronto Blessing, Wimber said, "Our decision was to withdraw endorsement; their decision was to resign. Toronto was changing our definition of renewal in Vineyard." He went on to say that he had no objection to manifestations, that it's messy when babies are born, but that when it's "fleshly" or "promoted by somebody on stage, that's abysmal."

As for the Kansas City Prophets, Wimber said he had advised them to withdraw from the Vineyard six years before they finally separated, but they had refused, saying they felt called to be a part of Vineyard. He then assumed full responsibility for the prophets being in the Vineyard, saying, "I loved the gifts the prophets exercised; I didn't like the package." Wimber explained further.

> The package involved the presupposition that a gift in itself authenticates you. I don't care if you're the finest communicator around, the finest expositor, the most brilliant theologue—if you can't commit yourself to a board, if you can't commit yourself to the leadership of others, if you can't commit yourself to collegiality and relationship, if you can't be inspected as well as teach, I don't want to play.'[23]

Problems in the Vineyard

In June 1997, just three years after Wimber had installed Tuttle as the senior pastor at Anaheim, John and Carol were at their mountain cabin when news came: Tuttle had fallen under the weight of the responsibility. Marital and other issues were involved, and Wimber had to remove him from the position.[24] Once again, Wimber was responsible for the eight-thousand-member church. Devastated, he responded by having a severe angina attack that landed him in the hospital. It was at this point that John confided in Carol that he believed the Lord had told him he would die before the new year.[25]

Looking back on this time in their life, Carol said there was so much going on that it seemed John would not have time to die.[26] And on top of being busy, he was weak and tired. Still, he worked diligently to get everything in place before his death. He installed Todd Hunter as the national director of the Vineyard Association U.S.A. and Bob Fulton as the international director.[27] Then, once again faced with finding a senior pastor for his Anaheim church, he decided Lance Pittluck was his first choice.

Pittluck had grown up on Long Island, New York, and was the son of a businessman. When he was eighteen, his family moved to Los Angeles, where Pittluck soon encountered the Lord. He was radically changed, accepted a call to ministry, studied Bible at Pepperdine University in Malibu, and went on to get his master of divinity at Fuller. After graduation, he felt a call to return to New York to pastor. In preparation, he spent a year on staff with Wimber. In May 1984, he moved to New York to pastor a Vineyard church.

Pittluck pastored the New York Vineyard for thirteen years. Then just three months before he was to receive Wimber's invitation to pastor Anaheim, Pittluck's son, John, died. The little boy, who had been named after Wimber, had developed a fever.[28] The doctor had advised them just to put John to bed, but he died during the night. Their hearts were broken. Three months later, when Wimber called, Pittluck agreed to take the position but said he could not come until November.

Wimber, as sick and weak as he was, would have to pastor the church until Pittluck arrived. Still, it gave John peace to know that help was on the way.[29] The question of who would care for the Anaheim Vineyard after his death seemed to be settled. Now all that was left to be determined was what direction the Vineyard movement would take.

Wimber's Final Conference

On July 14–18, 1997, just four months before his death, Wimber held his last annual pastors' conference at Anaheim Vineyard, which was attended by three thousand Vineyard pastors and leaders. Wimber invited Richard F. Lovelace, professor of church history at Gordon-Conwell Theological Seminary, and Vinson Synan, academic dean and professor of Pentecostal and charismatic studies at Regent University, to be the main speakers. Wimber asked Lovelace to present the history and theology of the straight-line evangelical church and Synan to present the traditional Pentecostal/charismatic perspective. When he arrived, Synan said he felt overdressed. He and Todd Hunter were the only ones wearing long pants—everyone else had on Bermuda shorts and sandals.

Synan said that just before he spoke, Wimber asked him what he thought were the Vineyard's greatest strengths and weaknesses. Synan told him,

> The greatest strength of Vineyard is that the leader is still alive—John Wimber, the man who created the movement. It is as if I am attending a conference when John Wesley was present. The greatest asset the Methodist had was John Wesley himself, and the greatest asset the Vineyard has is John Wimber.[30]

Synan went on to say that the greatest weakness of the Vineyard was that it had experienced too much undue outside influence in the past. By "outside influence," Synan was referring to Bickle's church and to Paul Cain—who appeared to Synan to be running the Vineyard with his prophecies. Synan then told Wimber that no one knew the vision of the Vineyard church better than John Wimber.

When Synan took the platform, he spoke about the worldwide growth of the Pentecostal and charismatic movements, the baptism of the Holy Spirit, and the way in which these movements had changed history. Following his presentation, he gave an altar call for Vineyard pastors who wanted to be baptized in the Holy Spirit and had never received tongues. About thirty to forty came forward, and Synan, Wimber, and Hunter laid hands on them. Many spoke in tongues for the first time. In hindsight, Synan said it seemed Wimber had wanted him and Lovelace each to make a case for his own denomination, so that Vineyard leaders could choose which trajectory the Vineyard would take after his death: follow Wimber's lead and continue to embrace signs, wonders, and the miraculous with a Pentecostal/charismatic focus, or be absorbed into the mainline evangelical church?[31]

John Paul Jackson made similar observations while reflecting on his last conversation with Wimber, just prior to Wimber's death. Knowing Wimber was gravely ill, John Paul had flown to Anaheim to spend a few minutes and to pray with him. Jackson said Larry Randolph and Paul Cain had already been there, but Wimber had been so frail, they'd only stayed a few minutes. But when Jackson arrived, Wimber was having a good day and wanted to talk. Wimber opened up and shared his concerns over the direction the Vineyard would take after he was gone. Wimber said he believed the Vineyard movement would take on a post-modern philosophy and approach to how they did church, with less emphasis on the supernatural than before. He also believed the Vineyard would seek to become more mainstream, with less emphasis on the supernatural, which, for Wimber, meant it would become just another boring church. He understood there would be exceptions, but as a whole, that is what he predicted would happen. Jackson said Wimber also predicted that Bert Waggoner would eventually take over the Vineyard, saying that if someone else assumed the leadership role, it would be temporary, but eventually Waggoner would take the helm. Wimber believed Waggoner would also move the headquarters to Texas, and this concerned John, because he believed Anaheim was the geographic location God had called them to and southern California was where the headquarters needed to stay.[32]

Waggoner had never heard Wimber make these comments, and nothing to this effect appeared in Vineyard's historical archives. But from Waggoner's perspective, there was never an either/or for the Vineyard; rather, it had always been a both/and movement—evangelical in theology and Pentecostal and charismatic in the experience of the Spirit. Waggoner also said that, after Wimber's death, Todd Hunter had become the national director and had clearly led the movement in a post-modern direction. Waggoner believed this was to enable the Vineyard to engage with a post-modern world.

He went on to say that, in Wimber's last board meeting, he told them to "take the best and leave the rest," and "don't build a shrine and look to the past." Wimber had also reminded them that they were "empowered evangelicals." Waggoner believed Wimber had grown very dissatisfied with just conferencing and had felt they were not producing genuine disciples. He said Wimber seemed to be disenchanted with church growth techniques and wondered if they had placed too much emphasis on techniques and not enough emphasis on the Spirit.

In regard to moving the headquarters to Texas, Waggoner said that Todd Hunter was the national director from 1997 until 2000. Waggoner assumed the role of national director in September 2000 and moved the headquarters to Texas the following year. When asked why, Waggoner's first response was because Texas was where he lived. But the more important reason was that the

Vineyard movement needed its own identity, one separate from the Anaheim church, because the Anaheim location was centered around John and his family. So, with the input and advice of several national leaders who understood church growth, they made the decision to move to Texas. They believed the movement needed a clean break between the entities of the past and the mission God had given them for the future.[33]

Heart Surgery

Having completed his last Vineyard pastor's conference, Wimber resumed running the day-to-day operations of the ministry until Pittluck arrived in November. These last few weeks of Wimber's life were extremely difficult as he led staff meetings and took care of the daily operations of the church. His hearing was now so poor that people had to write notes to communicate with him.

Carol remembered the last task he performed at the church. It was a videotape of him addressing his congregation for the church's Benevolence Sunday. His voice was so weak and hoarse, he could hardly speak. In the video, he reminded the people of their covenant with the poor and how they had always responded with generosity. According to Carol, it was the "sweetest, most heartbreaking, loving and inspiring videotape he had ever made."[34]

At the end of the day, Carol drove to the church office to pick him up. When she arrived, he was walking slowly down the hall away from her, leaning against the wall every few steps to steady himself. She called out to him, but his hearing was so poor he did not hear. Carol came up beside him, put her arms around him, and helped him to the car. He slumped into the seat and immediately fell asleep from exhaustion.[35] They did not know it at the time, but this would be his last day of work in his Vineyard church.

He was scheduled for a doctor's visit and angiogram the next day, and Carol had to transport him in a wheelchair because he was too weak to walk.[36] Tests revealed an enlarged heart with 90 percent blockage, so the surgical team was instructed to prepare for emergency surgery. But to everyone's surprise, John told them there would be no surgery, that he had planned to go home—until Chris came in and talked to him. "Dad, I'm out of here in a few months, and I don't have a choice," he said, referring to his own prognosis from cancer. "You have a choice. Who's going to take care of Debbie and Sean and Devon if we're both gone? What about VMG [Vineyard Music Group]? Who's going to run it?"[37] Reluctantly, John agreed, and he had a successful quadruple bypass on Thursday, September 25, 1997.

The road to recovery was bumpy, but by mid-November, he was up—wobbly, but walking. Then on Sunday morning, November 16, Wimber fell while trying to dress himself for church. Carol heard the crash and ran to the bedroom to find him on the floor, looking stunned. His only complaint was that his shoulder hurt. Carol could not get him up, so she called their son, Sean, for help. Sean checked his dad over, and he seemed to be okay, so Carol went on to church with plans to meet John and Sean and the rest of the family at a restaurant after the service. At the restaurant, Wimber complained of a headache and asked for Tylenol. Then Carol noticed him leaning against her and immediately knew something was wrong. They called an ambulance, and by the time he reached the hospital, he was not breathing. He was immediately intubated and placed on a ventilator. The doctor ordered x-rays, which revealed a massive brain hemorrhage. As it turned out, he had hit his head when he fell that morning, which caused his brain to begin bleeding. John was now unconscious.[38]

He passed away at eight o'clock the next morning, Monday, November 17, 1997. He was sixty-three years old. Funeral services were held Friday, November 21, at six p.m., at the church Wimber founded and pastored for seventeen years. His wife Carol; his sons Chris, Tim, and Sean; his daughter Stephanie; and his eleven grandchildren survived him.

[1] Carol Wimber, *John Wimber*, 175.
[2] Carol Wimber, *John Wimber*, 177.
[3] Carol Wimber, *John Wimber*, 186–9.
[4] Wimber, "Signs, Wonders, and Cancer," 49–51.
[5] Wimber, *Witness for a Powerful Christ*, 21–2.
[6] Wimber, *Living with Uncertainty*, 13.
[7] Wimber, "Signs, Wonders, and Cancer," 50.
[8] Wimber, *Living with Uncertainty*, 25.
[9] Wimber, *Living with Uncertainty*, 22.
[10] Wimber, *Living with Uncertainty*, 34, 41, 46.
[11] Carol Wimber, *John Wimber*, 178; interview by the author with Tim Wimber, February 10, 2010.
[12] Wimber, "Fulfill Your Ministry," 16–9.
[13] Wimber, "Fulfill Your Ministry," 19.
[14] Carol Wimber, *John Wimber*, 189–91.
[15] Peter Jennings, "In the Name of God," *ABC Documentary*, 1995, http://www.youtube.com/watch?v=9I9YCue3Fkk&feature=related.
[16] Carol Wimber, *John Wimber*, 191.
[17] Jimmy Stewart, "Vineyard Music's Wimber Dies," *Charisma*, April 1998, 36.
[18] Carol Wimber, *John Wimber*, 193–5.
[19] Carol Wimber, *John Wimber*, 192–4.
[20] John Wimber, "Leaving but Not Quitting," *Equipping the Saints*, Third Quarter 1996, 23.
[21] Tim Stafford and James Beverly, "God's Wonder Worker," *Christianity Today*, July 14, 1997, 46.
[22] Stafford, "God's Wonder Worker," 46.
[23] Stafford, "God's Wonder Worker," 47.
[24] Carol Wimber, *John Wimber*, 197; interview by the author with Tim Wimber.
[25] Carol Wimber, *John Wimber*, 197.
[26] Carol Wimber, *John Wimber*, 197–8.
[27] Carol Wimber, *John Wimber*, 197.
[28] Interview by the author with Tim Wimber.
[29] Carol Wimber, *John Wimber*, 198; interview by the author with Tim Wimber.
[30] Interview by the author with Vinson Synan.
[31] Interview by the author with Vinson Synan.
[32] Interview by the author with John Paul Jackson.
[33] Interview by the author with Bert Waggoner.
[34] Carol Wimber, *John Wimber*, 198.
[35] Carol Wimber, *John Wimber*, 198.
[36] Carol Wimber, *John Wimber*, 199.
[37] Carol Wimber, *John Wimber*, 199.
[38] Carol Wimber, *John Wimber*, 203.

Chapter 10

Celebration of Wimber's Life and Legacy

Lance Pittluck, Todd Hunter, Bob Fulton, and Carol Wimber paid tribute to Wimber during his memorial service. What follows is a brief overview of their comments.[1]

Lance Pittluck's Tribute

Pittluck said that John had done everything he was supposed to do, and now that he had finished his work on this earth, he was going home. Pittluck recalled that several years before, while pastoring a small church not far from Wimber's, he had called John and asked for an appointment to visit with him. Pittluck had never met John, so he showed up in a three-piece suit. John, on the other hand, was wearing old Birkenstocks, a Hawaiian shirt, and shorts that looked as if they had been worn for many days. When Wimber invited Pittluck to come back to the church on a Sunday night, to see what they were all about, he suggested Pittluck "dress down a little bit" when he came.

When Pittluck thought of John, he said, he thought of a spiritual father who had birthed so many things in the Vineyard movement because they were things he loved. Wimber loved worship, and the Vineyard movement learned to love worship. He loved the Word, and he always wished that he himself were a better teacher. John was unique in that he not only wanted to know the Scripture; he also wanted to experience it and do it—which Pittluck thought was unfortunately rare in the church. John loved people, and he structured the church in a way that the church could practice loving one other in small groups. He believed in the priesthood of all believers and "released us all to play." He believed the church should give away what God gives us, so he taught the Vineyard to give to the poor, share the good news with the lost, and plant churches where they were needed. Although Wimber was known all around the world, Pittluck saw him as a humble man, who often referred to himself as a "fat man just trying to get to heaven." Wimber was also a very generous man, he said, commenting that the two had never been out to dinner together when John had not picked up the check. He remembered how pastors would come to visit John and leave with their arms full of books and tapes, which Wimber gave them to help with their ministries. Wimber was focused to the point of being obsessed, Pittluck said, adding that he believed this was the reason John accomplished what he did—in the church, in the Vineyard movement, and around the world. Pittluck also considered John a balanced man: very spiritual and, at the same time, extremely practical—knowing how things worked but also knowing who God was. Wimber had run his race, Pittluck said, and had passed his baton on to the people—and now he was part of the cloud of witnesses watching them, as they carried on his vision to "do the stuff" that he had taught them to do.

Todd Hunter's Tribute

Hunter called John an incredible God-pleaser and said he would feel constantly rebuked and challenged for the rest of his life by John's incredible tenacity to do the will of God in the face of whatever opposition. He said that John was a leader who was willing to please God and not man, accepting the heat that came his way. John had seemed to know from the beginning of his ministry, Hunter affirmed, that his life would be marked with reproach; but he was always willing to accept it, and because of this, he was effective. Hunter said he respected John immensely as a leader, that John never pointed the way but, rather, as a true leader, always went first and led the way. Hunter went on to say that John had the strength and principle to do what he believed God wanted him to do and that he had the incredibly rare combination of being a spiritual thinker and spiritual feeler.

Hunter also believed that John was willing to make people feel uncomfortable if he believed it was for the common good. He said Wimber had "the mind of a scholar, the heart of a child, and the hide of a rhinoceros—and you don't lead without any of these." Hunter also saw John as a change agent who was after results, not popularity, and who refused to bow to pressures that went against what he felt God wanted him to do.

"He was generous to me," Hunter said. "He taught me to lead and to think and to pray, all at the same time." Hunter believed Wimber's sense of humor was something that endeared him to people, saying he was fun to play with. Finally, Hunter said that John was known around the world as a renewal agent and, as such, if John could be there that night, perhaps the question he would ask would be in regard to the state of their renewal.

Bob Fulton's Tribute

Fulton said that when John became a Christian, he became like a crazy man, going everywhere he could and telling everyone he could about how God loved them and what God could do for them. Fulton believed that when most people thought of John, they saw him as the man on stage ministering to thousands of people, but when he thought of John, he remembered what it was like in the beginning—what God did to make the man—the things God put into him.

In the early days, when John had taught Bible studies, Fulton said, sometimes only three people would show up, but John was faithful with the little God gave him. During that time, God put something into him that later made it possible for John to be obedient when he started ministering to thousands. He was not a prideful man nor was he caught up with himself. Fulton said he had followed John through the 28 years of ministry because he was a man who knew how to repent. Fulton saw Wimber as a leader who was quick to repent. When he made a mistake, he would repent, make adjustments, and move on, and this was one of the most formable characteristics Fulton believed a leader should have.

Through all those years, Fulton said, he never saw Wimber try to hype up a group. He was a risk taker who was willing to follow the leading of the Holy Spirit, while at the same time being very conservative. His approach to ministry was very practical. He just read the Book to figure out what Jesus would do and try to do it. John was a man who would simply teach the Scriptures then he was the first in line to try to understand how to live it out.

Through the years, Fulton observed John as a person who, when he thought he heard from God, would act on it without looking for the approval – even if no one followed. John was a father figure to many in the Vineyard, but to him, he was like a big brother. By observing his life, he learned what it meant to be a man of God, not so much by what John taught but through the consistent and biblical life he lived. John never sought to live longer, he just sought to be obedient to the work God gave him to do, and although he received international notoriety, when he came home he was just John. He did not talk about his exploits, he just came home to his family and friends. He always felt that others were better theologically, more astute biblically, and better teachers so he always marveled that people wanted him to come and do seminars. Who was John Wimber? Fulton said Wimber liked to refer to himself as just a fat saxophone player trying to get to heaven, and in closing, he recounted John's famous line, "I am a fool for Christ, whose fool are you?"

Carol's Tribute

In her tribute, Carol said John would never have allowed her to refer to him as a king, because he always said he had dibs on the servant's role. After all, she recalled, John had said that when Jesus turned the water into wine at the wedding feast, nobody except the servants knew where the wine had come from—so John had always coveted the position of a servant. In fact, Carol said, his only ambition had been to one day come before the Father and hear the words, "Well done, thou good and faithful servant."

What may have looked like driving ambition to many, Carol said, was nothing more than John's sense of responsibility. He felt that what God had given him belonged to the whole church, and he did not want to waste any time getting it to them. That is what drove him: he had a message that people needed to hear.

So even though John would not want to be referred to as a king, since he was not there, Carol said, she could compare him to whomever she wanted—and she had always thought of him as a king, like Hezekiah or Josiah. Carol said that John "did what was right in the eyes of the Lord and he tore down the high places," and she said that by "high places," she was referring to where the religious spirits dwelt and where worship is served.

The first high place he sought to destroy, she said, was exclusiveness. John loved the whole church, from the low church like Vineyard to the high, liturgical church. He loved it all. He never thought of the Vineyard as anything more than one vegetable in the whole stew. He did not think the Vineyard was necessarily the best, but he did believe it was planted by the Lord, and all that John wanted was to be what God had created them to be. This was something he was unwavering about.

The second high place John destroyed was hype: he did not care for theatrics or pretentiousness; he took the church beyond the walls and helped the people take it to the streets; and he never tried to make anything happen—he just looked for what Jesus was doing, lent his hands to that, and encouraged everyone else to do the same.

The third high place John sought to destroy, Carol recounted, was the monopoly of the Holy Spirit by the pastor, priest, or star on the stage. "Everybody gets to play" was his motto. He believed that the ministry of the Holy Spirit was for everyone and that any Christian who was willing to take the risk could do what Jesus did. The ministry of Jesus was his guideline, and Ephesians 4:11-12 was about equipping the saints—not about the stars on the stage. He took great delight in people getting to do what God had called them to do, and he helped all to have a part in the ministry of the Holy Spirit, where for years it seemed reserved only for holy men.

Carol believed that the fourth high place he tried to pull down was false piety. He would not let anyone call him a king, put a robe on him, crown him, or call him an apostle, though he never put down other groups with that kind of hierarchical structure. For John, it was important that people be treated with dignity and respect, and he would not allow people's emotions to be exploited. When the presence of the Spirit would increase to the point that people could hardly stand, John would call for a coffee break. Then when they returned from break still munching on cookies, he would quietly say, "Come, Holy Spirit," and God would break loose—no music, just cold turkey. John believed worship music was only to worship God and should never be used as a vehicle to stir emotions, warm up a congregation before preaching, or soften people for an offering.

She then referred to Todd Hunter's statement that Wimber had "hide like a rhinoceros" and said that was not true. Rather, she said, he just put up with it, because he knew it was part of the job. She said she deeply respected him for keeping on even when his own heart and body were breaking. "I respected that man who lived in that body," Carol said. "I am thankful that I had the privilege to be his wife."[2]

On the cover of the program for Wimber's memorial service was a picture of John. (Carol's book *John Wimber: The Way it Was* would later feature this same photo on its cover.) Beneath his picture, it read "JOHN," in large letters, and overlaying it were the words "Equipper of the Saints." On the back of the program was one of John's favorite Scripture passages:

> For I am already being poured out like a drink offering, and the time has come for my departure. I have fought the good fight, I have finished the race, I have kept the faith. Now there is in store for me the crown of righteousness, which the Lord, the righteous Judge, will award to me on that day—and not only to me, but also to all who have longed for his appearing. (2 Tim. 4:6-8)

Chris Follows His Dad

Three months after Wimber's death, his son, Chris, succumbed to his battle with cancer. Chris, just forty years old, was survived by his wife Debbie; his son Sean, aged ten; his daughter Devan, eight; and his mother, sister, and two brothers.[3] Chris said he was not afraid to die and knowing his dad was there waiting on him made it easier.[4] True to form, Wimber the leader had gone ahead to show the way.

After Chris's death, Jeremy Cook took over the Vineyard Music Group and moved it to the United Kingdom. After two years, it was brought back to the United States and relocated in Houston, Texas, where it continues today under the name of Vineyard Worship.[5]

Later Tributes

The year after Wimber's death, David Pytches edited the book *John Wimber: His Influence and Legacy*, comprised of tributes to Wimber's life and ministry by twenty-three contributors. What follows are just some of the descriptions and memories of Wimber found in this collection.

Wimber was a shy man who did not like small talk. He had unfailing courtesy, irresistible charm, and a strong work ethic yet managed to remain relaxed and never seemed too hurried or busy to laugh at a good joke. He was able to tolerate high levels of "orderly chaos" and spelled "faith" R-I-S-K. On the other hand, he was conservative and even cautious in his temperament.[6] Because of his spiritual zeal, he could be rigid, autocratic, and seemingly stubborn, but some believed this was part of what made him trustworthy in God's eyes.[7]

Concerning success, John defined it as "simply rendering humble service to the Lord." As such, Wimber was a guileless man of humility who "simply did not know how to be pompous."[8] When someone asked him how he stayed humble, John replied, "God gives me enough failure, difficulty, criticism and misunderstanding to keep me humble."[9]

He did not seek personal success, was not a people pleaser, and sought to live for the audience of one—Jesus Christ. His frequent prayer was, "Oh, God! Oh, God!" because he knew he could not do anything on his own. He waited on God for direction and could not be manipulated.[10]

In line with this humility, Wimber did not seek status or try to make a name for himself; he simply wanted to serve and to empower the body of Christ to do the work of the ministry.[11] He had intuitive leadership abilities, but wherever he went, he also left leaders behind. "It was his instinct to equip others to lead, rather than to shine himself."[12] He taught by his actions that great leaders do not do the work of ten people but get ten people to do the work.

In addition to humility, openness and transparency were Wimber's hallmarks. He realized he was not a perfect boss, but he tried his best, and when he made mistakes, he openly admitted them, made corrections, and moved on.[13] He understood that mistakes were part of the package.

As such, he also had a "reluctance and gentleness in correcting those he thought wrong."[14] As an equipper, he thrived in the learning environment and had a high degree of tolerance for people who made mistakes, as long as they learned from them. His goal was to lift people to a higher level and to help them mature to their fullest potential.

As an only child, John was uniquely prepared for the loneliness that exists at the top. He really did not care about how many people followed him. He would often say, "I'm just driving a bus. If you want to go where I'm going, get on and let's go! If you don't want to go where I'm going, it's okay."

As a leader, he was open-minded and kind, and he saw things that other people did not; he was always looking forward and did not seem to have a rear-view mirror.[15]

Ian Prichard, who worked with Wimber at the Anaheim Vineyard as the conference director for Vineyard Ministries International for seven years, talked about Wimber's financial integrity and generosity:

> Many attendees of Vineyard conferences have asked what happened to the profits. Let me go on record and say that not one cent went to John Wimber.

He took no honorarium or payment from the conferences. Yet at the same time he gave honorariums—some very generous ones—to the other speakers and worship leaders. He was an enormously generous person. He saw ministry as a life of giving. Hundreds of thousands of dollars went to the poor and missions. But it did not stop there. He constantly looked for ways to give away those things that God had blessed him with. Pastor after pastor, church leader after church leader went through our warehouses to get as many tape series, books, manuals and music tapes as they could carry. 'Take it all,' John would say, 'and use it in any way that will be beneficial to the Kingdom.' John had no time for empire building. There were no enormous salaries. He drove modest secondhand cars. He lived in a modest house. At the age of fifty-five he took pleasure in letting us know he'd finally paid off his mortgage. Soon after his last son got married, he downsized his living arrangements. 'After all,' he said, 'you can only sleep in one bedroom or use one bathroom at a time!' He gave away the excess.[16]

Bert Waggoner said he believed Wimber's greatest strength was that he lived his life for an audience of one. He was wholly devoted to Jesus and was willing to go wherever he led. Waggoner saw John as a man of great integrity, who had no pretense, and was honest about both his weaknesses and his strengths. He did not like religion, pretense, or hype. Waggoner said he was the most gifted man he had ever known—gifted in terms of the prophetic, words of knowledge, and healing; he was a gifted administrator, leader, and communicator; and he was gifted in worship. He brought a wealth of resources to the Vineyard. Waggoner concluded by saying, "Knowing and working with John Wimber was one of the greatest blessings of my life."

Wimber's Legacy

In C. Peter Wagner's memoirs, he remembered the day he learned of Wimber's death. He wrote,

> I walked into the kitchen of our home, [and] I saw on the island a note that someone had jotted down from a telephone message. It said, 'John Wimber has died. Details to come.' It wasn't 30 seconds until the whole thing sank in and suddenly I began to weep. I don't mean a tear or two coursing down my cheek, but loud sobs! And for a long time! I was embarrassed at myself. Fortunately, I was alone. After I had used a substantial supply of Kleenex, I began to think. The truth is that I hadn't cried when my mother died, nor had I cried when my father died. I can't recall any episode of tears after hearing about anyone else's death, as far as that goes. What was happening? I knew

that John Wimber had influenced my life as few others had, but this grieving must have meant that he had influenced it even far beyond what I had realized.[17]

Wagner's grief echoes the feelings of multiplied thousands around the globe as they said good-bye to the father of a movement, the founder of a denomination, and a man who spearheaded a renewal movement in the twentieth century that carried a fresh wave of the Spirit around the world. Thank you, John Wimber, for touching our lives—you were truly the molder of a generation.

> *"The signs of a true apostle were performed among you*
> *with utmost patience,*
> *by signs and wonders and miracles."*
> *II Corinthians 12:12*

> *"I'm a fool for Christ, whose fool are you?"*
> ~ *John Wimber*

[1] John Wimber Memorial Service, Anaheim, California, November 21, 1997, video cassette recording. A special thanks to Randall Pannell, associate chief academic officer of Regent University and Vineyard pastor, for making this tape available.

[2] All comments taken from the John Wimber Memorial Service video cassette recording.

[3] Stewart, "Vineyard Music's Wimber Dies," 36.

[4] Carol Wimber, *John Wimber*, 195.

[5] Interview by the author with Bert Waggoner, August 24, 2011.

[6] Mumford, "Vineyard Movement Founder," 202–4.

[7] Hunter, "The Leader," 191–2.

[8] Mumford, "Vineyard Movement Founder," 198–9.

[9] John Mumford, "Vineyard Movement Founder," 204.

[10] Pritchard, "The Businessman," 164–5, 173, 177.

[11] Gerald Coats, "The Ecumenist," 154.

[12] Mumford, "Vineyard Movement Founder," 202.

[13] Prichard, "The Businessman," 162, 172.

[14] Hunter, "The Leader," 183.

[15] Hunter, "The Leader," 185–7; Mumford, "Vineyard Movement Founder," 195.

[16] Pritchard, "The Businessman," 176.

[17] Wagner, *Wrestling with Alligators, Prophets, and Theologians*, 113.

Appendix A

A Timeline of Wimber's Life and Ministry

Dates differ in Wimber writings and other sources but attempts have been made to present an accurate timeline on comparative information.

February 25, 1934: Born in Kirksville, Illinois.
1946: Wimber was twelve when his family moved to California.
1949: At age fifteen, played his first professional gig at Dixie Castle, Orange, California.
1955: Won Best Composer and Arranger title at the Light House All Stars Jazz Festival.
December 23,1955: Met Carol in May, and in December they married.
1957: First son, Chris, was born.
1958: Second son, Timothy, was born.
1961: Sean was born.
1962: John introduced Bobby Hatfield and Bill Medley and set up their first job together at the Black Derby in Orange County, California. Contract was signed with the Righteous Brothers. Wimber became their saxophone player and composed their musical arrangements.
1962: Soaring career and diving marriage.
November 1962: John and Carol reacquainted with Dick and Lynn Heying, who introduced them to Gunner Payne.
April 1963: John and Carol began attending Gunner Payne's Bible Study.
May 1963: John and Carol accepted Christ.
1963: Stephanie was born.
1964: John was baptized in the Holy Spirit.
1963–1970: Led several hundred people to Christ under "normal circumstances" (in contrast to leading someone to Christ through power evangelism).
1970: Joined the staff at Yorba Linda Friends Church.
1970: Led eleven Bible studies a week with over five hundred in attendance.
1970: Started his degree in Biblical studies at Azusa Pacific University.

1974: A young man in church came to him with a problem, and God asked, "John, would you go to this church if you weren't paid to?"
1974: Kenn and Joanie Gulliksen move to Los Angeles from Calvary Chapel, Costa Mesa, to plant a church that they eventually name the Vineyard.
1974: C. Peter Wagner offered Wimber the position of founding director of the Department of Church Growth (now Fuller Institute of Evangelism and Church Growth).
1974: Wimber discovered the "Engel Scale," describing the various stages of thinking a person goes through to conversion.
1975: Kenn Gulliksen combined two Bible study groups (Chuck Girard's and Larry Norman's) to form a church.
September 1976: "God is crying over you" and "When are you going to walk in your authority?"
October 1976: Carol and some leaders of their Quaker church started a home meeting.
January 1977: Carol had dream and woke up speaking in tongues.
1977: Gulliksen noted the name *vineyard* while reading Isaiah.
1977: Carol placed John's hand on her shoulder while he was asleep and was healed of rheumatoid arthritis.
March 1977: Carol's Bible study group had grown to over fifteen.
1977: A burned-out Wimber cried out to God, and the Lord responded, "I've seen your ministry. Now let me show you mine." Lutheran pastor gave him a note that said, "Go home."
1977: John started attending Carol's Bible study.
April 1977: Carol's Bible study had grown to one hundred, and John had become the leader.
May 8, 1977: Wimber and the forty members of the Bible study were asked to leave Yorba Linda Friends Church.
May 1977: On Mother's Day, John preached his first sermon as the pastor of their newly formed church.
1977: John discovered that the key to effective evangelism was "proclamation with demonstration of the gospel." He taught healing for nine months before seeing the first person healed.
1978: Wimber met his first demon.
Fall 1979: Todd and Debbie Hunter planted a church in Wheeling, West Virginia.
Mother's Day 1980: Lonnie Frisbee, "Come, Holy Spirit."
1980: The church, now three years old, met in Canyon High School and had approximately fifteen hundred in attendance.
1981: Published his first album.
1981: Took his first ministry trip to England after being invited by David Watson and David Pytches.
1981: First grandchild, Christian Wimber, born.

January 1982: Began teaching the MC510 Signs and Wonders and Church Growth class at Fuller Seminary.
Spring 1982: Met Sandy Miller at Holy Trinity Brompton.
April 1982: Calvary Chapel of Yorba Linda was asked to leave Calvary Chapel affiliations and joined Kenn Gulliksen's group of Vineyard churches.
May 8, 1982: Wimber's church became Vineyard Christian Fellowship.
May 1982: John became the head of the Vineyard movement.
May 1983: Vineyard Ministries International formed.
September 1983: Wimber moved the church from Yorba Linda to Anaheim, California.
1983: *Signs and Wonders Today* was published; positive articles published in *Christian Life Magazine*.
1984: Wimber taught a sixteen-part series on repentance and holiness.
February 18, 1984: David Watson died.
1984: Carl Tuttle planted a church in Santa Maria.
May 1984: The first issue of *First Fruits Magazine* (the Vineyard publication) was circulated.
June 1984: MC510 went public, soon to become worldwide.
1984: Mike Bickle took a group to Wimber's MC510 class at Fuller.
1985: Wimber and Springer's first book *Power Evangelism* was published in England.
1985: The Association of Vineyard Churches was incorporated.
1985: Wimber taught the sixteen-tape series *Repentance in the Body of Christ*.
1985: Mercy Records (worship music) and Mercy Media (teaching material) were formed. Wimber's daily radio broadcast *Walk in the Word* started airing on over five stations. Chris Wimber became the studio engineer and manager of Mercy Media.
October 1985: John taught three weeks of conferences in London, Brighton, and Sheffield, England.
November 1985: Diagnosed with heart disease.
1985: The Vineyard had grown to two hundred churches.
September 1985: *Charisma* featured Wimber in its cover story "Applying the Gifts to Everyday Life."
1986: Wimber and Springer coauthored *Power Evangelism*.
January 1986: Fuller called a moratorium on MC510.
June 1986: Wimber suffered his first heart attack.
Fall 1986: Harrogate (U.K.) International Conference and Exhibition Center.
1987: *Equipping the Saints* magazine replaced *First Fruits*.
1987: Wimber and Springer coauthored the book *Power Healing*.
Spring 1987: Wimber reluctantly released John Mumford to plant a Vineyard church in United Kingdom.
June 1987: *Renewing Australia* magazine featured Wimber.
1987: Bakker and Swaggart scandals exposed.

1987: *Ministry and the Miraculous: A Case Study at Fuller Theological Seminary* was published.
1987: Wimber authored the booklet *Kingdom Mercy*.
1987: Wimber authored the booklet *Kingdom Ministry*.
1987: Wimber authored the booklet *Kingdom Living*.
1988: The beginning of the prophetic era.
1988: Wimber authored the booklet *Kingdom Come*.
1988: Wimber authored the booklet *Kingdom Suffering*.
1988: *Power Encounters among Christians in the Western World* by Kevin Springer was published.
December 1988: Cain prophesied to Wimber that he was close to committing the sin of Eli with his spiritual sons. Wimber repented and began preaching.
February 7–10, 1989: Spiritual Warfare Conference in Anaheim (Equipping, Fall 1988).
1990: Carl Tuttle returned to the Anaheim Vineyard.
March 1990: Four-day "What the Holy Spirit is Saying to the Church Today" conference held in Sydney, Australia.
1990: Ernie Gruen, charismatic pastor in Kansas City, preached the sermon "Do We Keep on Smiling and Say Nothing?
1990: Gruen released a 233-page document accusing Kansas City Fellowship prophets of abuses and calling for correction.
1990: Wimber offered the Vineyard as a spiritual covering for the Kansas City Fellowship.
February 1990: The Holiness Conference was held in Anaheim with nine thousand in attendance; Cain prophesied of a great revival in England with Wimber's next October visit.
October 1990: Wimber and Cain spoke to one thousand leaders at Holy Trinity Brompton to introduce them to the prophetic at the October meetings.
1991: Wimber and Springer coauthored the book *Power Points*.
1991: The Vineyard Christian Fellowship moved into its new facility in Anaheim.
March 9, 1992: Wimber announced the end of self-imposed silence against his critics.
May 1992: First Vineyard position paper, "Why I Respond to Criticism" was produced.
May 1992: Second Vineyard position paper, "The Vineyard Response to the Briefing" was produced.
June 1992: Vineyard's third position paper, "The Vineyard's Response to *The Standard*" was produced.
1993: Wimber diagnosed with a malignant brain tumor.
March 1993: Vineyard's fourth position paper, "Power and Truth: A Response to Power Religion" was produced.

April 1993: Vineyard's fifth position paper, "A Response to Charismatic Chaos: The Book Written by John F. MacArthur" was produced.
January 20, 1994: The "Toronto Blessing" began.
September/October 1994: A board report published a paper expressing pastoral concerns regarding phenomena in the Toronto Vineyard.
December 18, 1994: Wimber installed Carl Tuttle as senior pastor of his Vineyard church in Anaheim.
January 1995: Wimber suffered a stroke.
July 1995: "Let the Fire Fall" Conference held in Anaheim.
December 5, 1995: Wimber and the Association of Vineyard Churches team met with the Toronto leadership team.
December 5, 1995: Arnott wrote a letter accepting the board's decision to disfellowship the Toronto Vineyard and asked for their blessing.
December 12, 1995: Arnott wrote an open letter stating his position regarding the disfellowshipping of the Toronto Vineyard.
December 13, 1995: Todd Hunter (for John Wimber) wrote a four-page letter to Vineyard pastors stating the Vineyard position regarding the disfellowshipping of the Toronto Vineyard.
January 1996: Toronto Association of Vineyard Churches conducted a "Catch the Fire" conference to celebrate its second anniversary.
1996: Authored the booklet *Beyond Intolerance*.
1996: Authored the booklet *Living with Uncertainty*.
1996: Authored the booklet *Witnesses for a Powerful Christ*.
1997: Authored the booklet *Prayer: Intimate Communication*.
Spring 1997: *Voice of the Vineyard* magazine replaced *Equipping the Saints*.
July 1997: Wimber installed Todd Hunter as the national director of the Association of Vineyard Churches (USA).
July 1997: Carl Tuttle crumbled under the weight of pastoring Anaheim Vineyard.
September 25, 1997: Wimber had open heart surgery.
November 17, 1997: Wimber died of a massive brain hemorrhage while recuperating from open heart surgery.
February 6, 1998: Wimber's son Chris died after a long struggle with brain cancer.
1998: *John Wimber: His Influence and Legacy* was published.
1999: Carol Wimber authored the book *John Wimber: The Way It Was*.

Appendix B

An Overview of the MC510 Syllabus

Section One: Introduction to Thesis: Program or Power Evangelism

Proposition: There is a relationship between signs and wonders, evangelism, and church growth.

Documentation: There are two types of evangelism emphasized by the church. First is Program—or Method—Evangelism, which "attempts to reach the mind by natural means. . . and is most often characterized by one-way communication." There are three kinds of Program Evangelism.[1] The first is *Crusade Evangelism*, which is an organized outreach using crowd-gathering techniques. The second is *Saturation Evangelism*, which emphasizes the need for everyone to know the message of salvation and is often done through door-to-door contact. Third is *Personal Evangelism*, which is associated with a Christian-lifestyle witness. In addition to Program Evangelism, Wimber suggested a more effective form of evangelism, which he termed *Power Evangelism*. Power Evangelism also includes the rational presentation of the gospel, but it transcends the rational in that it is spontaneous, is directed by the Spirit, and demonstrates the deity and power of God through signs and wonders. Dr. Paul Yonggi Cho's church in Seoul, Korea, was cited as an example of church growth through signs and wonders.[2] Six passages were used from the book of Acts and the Great Commission in which signs and wonders were evidenced and disciples were commissioned.

Conclusion: The Western church has functioned in Program Evangelism and used this method around the world, resulting in the Westernization of believers in other nations. Power Evangelism was the approach used in the New Testament church and is still the most effective means of evangelism that produces church growth.

Section Two: Theological Foundation: The Kingdom of God

Proposition: "The kingdom of God is the Rule of God (the age to come) which has invaded the kingdom (rule) of Satan (this present evil age), and is the arena in which *Signs and Wonders* occur.[3] They are the 'marks' (signs) of the kingdom. Understanding about the kingdom of God is fundamental to understanding the ministry of Jesus; the kingdom of Satan was his real enemy. There is a war on! Jesus was sent by God to shatter the strongholds of Satan. His one purpose was Satan's defeat. Jesus accomplished this through his death, resurrection, and ascension. This demonstrated that Jesus was the victor, but Satan is not yet cast out and will not be until Christ returns to establish his kingdom forever. The Church is God's army in the continual fight, which goes on with Satan as the church lives 'between the times.'"

Documentation: The power of God is for today because it is the reality of the kingdom of God that was evidenced by Jesus. If people miss the significance of the kingdom, they fail to understand the life, work, and teachings of Jesus, because the kingdom was his message. New Testament people knew what Jesus meant when he spoke of the kingdom because it was an understood Old Testament concept. George Ladd's work on the kingdom reveals the presence of the future, with the church now living "between the inauguration and the consummation of the Kingdom." Jesus's first coming initiated a battle between the kingdom of God and the kingdom of the devil. Jesus bound Satan, plundered his house, and curbed his power but did not render him completely powerless. Jesus's mission to bring the reign of God was also given to the disciples and the church, which has been empowered to carry on this mission. There are seven signs of the kingdom: Jesus himself, the preaching of the gospel, exorcism, healing and miracles over nature, the miracle of conversion and new birth, the transformation of people into Christlike qualities, and suffering.

Conclusion: The words and works of Jesus (miracles such as signs, exorcisms, the raising of the dead, the healing of the sick, the miraculous provision of food to meet human need, and miracles over nature) are all signs of the beginning of the new age of the kingdom and the presence of the age to come.

Section Three: Today's Tension with the Miraculous: Worldview

Proposition: A worldview is a set of presuppositions held about the basic makeup of the world, which influences the way one theologizes and participates in a signs-and-wonders ministry. Westerners have a blind spot in dealing with the supernatural, identified by Paul Hiebert as "The Flaw of the Excluded Middle."[4]

Documentation: John MacArthur is cited as an example of a popular author who has been influenced by a worldview that believes the sign gifts—such as miracles, healings, tongues, and the interpretation of tongues—ceased with the apostles and the biblical canon. MacArthur is said to force "a hermeneutical system called 'Dispensationalism' upon the Biblical text." In such situations, a person needs a "paradigm shift" to see things differently. Hiebert's model of the excluded middle suggests that Christians in the Western world fail to recognize spirits; ghosts; ancestors; demons; earthly gods and goddesses who live within trees, rivers, hills, and villages; supernatural forces; the Holy Spirit; angels; demons; signs and wonders; and gifts of the Spirit that are recognized in the greater two-thirds of the world. Westerners are taught to ignore these and to deal exclusively with the empirical world. Western missionaries who minister in other parts of the world, therefore, are often incapable of meeting the needs of people in developing countries. This forces Christians in third-world countries to turn to magicians for cures instead of to Christ.[5]

Conclusion: Westerners "have excluded God and his power from our theology and thus from our churches," which renders missionaries incompetent to meet the needs of people in cultures that daily encounter the excluded middle of the Western worldview.

Section Four: The Expression of God's Power: Spiritual Gifts

Proposition: "Spiritual Gifts are the expression of God's power at work in the world (church) today. A believer does not possess spiritual gifts; rather, a believer receives gifts from God to be used at special times for special occasions. Gifts are the attestation of the empowering of the Holy Spirit and are vital in a Signs and Wonders ministry. Spiritual empowerment equips one for service. The gifts are the tools that enable one to fulfill the ministry of Jesus. The gifts of the Spirit are received by impartation. The gifts (except for the private use of tongues) are given to us and through us to use for others, and are developed in a climate of risk-taking and willingness to fail."

Documentation: God gives the gifts of the Spirit through the Holy Spirit to the body of Christ for the purpose of edifying the body, equipping the saints, and glorifying God. These gifts operate through the motive of love and include the gifts of the Spirit, ministry gifts, and functional offices. Conversion is the baptism in the Spirit, and all that is needed is the actualization or activation of the gifts. Believers are encouraged, however, to expect many "fillings" throughout their life.[6] Spirit baptism is therefore both initiatory and repeatable as empowerment for Christian service. The gift of the Holy Spirit should not be confused with the gifts of the Spirit, which are tools that empower for ministry. Gifts, or gracelets, are given sovereignly through the laying on of hands and/or through falling upon a person (a scriptural illustration is given for each). Gifts of the Spirit are developed through risk-taking and a willingness to fail. The following were listed as spiritual gifts: Administrations, Apostles, Discerning of Spirits, Effects of miracles/powers, Evangelist, Exhortation, Faith, gifts of healings, Giving, Interpretation of Tongues, Kinds of Tongues, Pastor-Teacher, Prophecy, Prophets, Service, Teachers, Teaching, Word of Knowledge, Word of Wisdom. Other possibilities listed include Celibacy, Craftsmanship, Hospitality, Interpretation of Dreams, Judge, Philanthropy, Intercessory Prayer, Missionary/Cross Culture Ministry, Music, and Worship Leading.

Conclusion: None listed in this section.

Section Five: The Biblical Record: Signs and Wonders in the Gospels, Acts, and the Letters

Proposition: Signs and Wonders were seen as the heart of the ministry of Jesus. In the Great Commission, the *authority* of God was imparted to the church, and at Pentecost the *power* of God was imparted. Jesus began his ministry after he was empowered by the Spirit at his baptism. The disciples, who made up the embryonic church, were empowered to do the same works Jesus did. The result was *Signs and Wonders*, which occurred throughout the book of Acts. Wherever the gospel was preached with Signs and Wonders, the church grew. The miraculous is seen as an emblem of God's compassion toward his people.

Documentation: There are forty-one instances of Jesus healing in the four Gospels, which constitutes one-fifth of his ministry. Three pages of graphs provide a matrix of the healing ministry of Jesus from each of the four Gospels. Key aspects of Jesus's ministry included the following: he began healing after his water baptism and his anointing by the Holy Spirit; he healed and delivered everyone who came to him; he was motivated by compassion; he was limited by unbelief; he was always willing to heal; he used many patterns and methods; and he often healed in public but also withdrew at times. Additional aspects of Jesus's ministry included the following: He was the eternal Son of God who became flesh and had an intimate and childlike relationship with the heavenly Father. He always did the will of the Father and did nothing on his own. The Holy Spirit was Jesus's sole source of supernatural power and the key to his effectiveness in ministry. His prayer life directly related to his healing power and ministry. He was motivated by both love for people and his hatred of the forces that bound them. He was opposed to anything that bound or enslaved people. Sometimes he had to pray more than once for a person to be healed. Jesus came not only to heal and bring the kingdom of God; he also came to impart his healing ministry to others. His method was first to minister while the disciples watched, and then to have them minister while he watched, and finally to release them to minister on their own. Jesus transferred his ministry to committed people, commissioning them and giving them power to do the work. They had freely received and they were to freely give. And they should expect persecution, especially from the religious leaders of their day. In doing this, Jesus's ministry expanded from one to many, and the kingdom of darkness suffered defeat. This healing ministry is also valid for today. Two pages of charts listed the power evangelism events in the book of Acts. Luke and Acts are companion volumes where Jesus was seen teaching and doing the works of the kingdom and then doing and teaching through his disciples as they were empowered by the Holy Spirit.[7]

Conclusion: None listed in this section.

Section Six: The Historical Testimony: Signs and Wonders in Church History

Proposition: "*Signs and Wonders* did not cease with the close of the first century or with the completion of the canon. They have continued to occur in each of the three major historical periods (patristic, medieval, and reformation-modern). When the ones in authority endorsed the gifts, they occurred openly and widely within the church. When those in authority no longer endorsed the gifts, there appears to have been a decline in their usage and their occurrence. The gifts usually became manifest among the pietistic God-seekers and more frequently among the lesser educated, although not always so. When anything happened outside the norm that tended to threaten the structure or status quo, the institution (power base) would try to put a stop to it. Almost every major personality of church history had some exposure to and acceptance of *Signs and Wonders*."

Documentation: This is the longest chapter in the syllabus. Fifty-two pages, dedicated to people and movements, are taken from primary sources that reveal the existence of Signs and Wonders throughout the three periods of church history. J. Sidlow Baxter cites four attitudes associated with healing and miracles that have existed in the church. These four beliefs are that Signs and Wonders

- ceased with the end of the Apostolic age,
- ceased because they belonged to the earlier centuries,
- gradually faded out, as the condition of the church deteriorated, and/or
- have never ceased among true Christian believers.[8]

In earlier years, authorities attempted to banish anything that occurred outside the organized church; then in the Age of Enlightenment, the miraculous acts of God were often discarded as scientifically unproven. Wimber cited no fewer than fifty-two primary sources supporting his thesis that Signs and Wonders never ceased but that they continued throughout church history.

Conclusion: "God has never ceased to work *Signs and Wonders* in his church, where he can find open, willing people through whom he could be God. He is still looking for people today who are open to his Holy Spirit and through whom he can continue to act."

Section Seven: Studies in the Miraculous: Case Histories

Proposition: "*Signs and Wonders* are still occurring in this century. There has been a tremendous gain in the church because of their continuation. They are occurring often both in and out of the immediate supervision of the Western church and its agencies. Early indications are that the church seems to be growing most rapidly where we (the Western church) have the least immediate influence. God's primary tool for expanding the church today is *Signs and Wonders*."

Documentation: Documented, randomly selected cases were presented where Signs and Wonders are still occurring today and have resulted in church growth. These cases occurred in South Africa, the Ivory Coast, South America, Chile, India, Asia, Korea, China, Indonesia, Canada, the Philippines, Kenya, and the United States. In many of these situations, power encounters occurred where there was a visible, practical demonstration that Jesus is more powerful than the false gods or spirits worshiped by the members of a people group.

Conclusion: God still empowers people to break through with the gospel message, but it always involves risk-taking faith. The result is normally church growth. However, there are mitigating circumstances at times, such as a lack of leadership to nurture new converts or a negative backlash that hinders the work.

Section Eight: Some Notable Personalities in the Pentecostal and Charismatic Movements: Their Practices and Pitfalls

Proposition: "Signs and Wonders take place through men and women who will venture out and attempt to minister in them. These people come from all walks of life, both inside and outside of historic church structures. While higher theological education is essential for maintaining balance, in the long run it does not seem to be a primary requisite for one becoming a minister in *Signs and Wonders*. This may be the reason that those who minister in this area have had such skyrocketing careers often ending in disaster."

Documentation: The past two hundred years of church history was reviewed, and documentation of individuals and movements that had an emphasis on Signs and Wonders, especially the ministry of healing, was provided. The early healers included Johann Christoph Blumhardt, Dorothea Trudel, Olga Worrall, and Samuel Zeller. The contemporary charismatic healers were Dennis Bennett, Father Ralph Diorio, Dennis and Matthew Linn, Francis MacNutt, Father Edward McDonough, Sister Briege McKenna, and Agnes Sanford. Pentecostal healers included A. A. Allen, F. F. Bosworth, William Branham, Roxanne Brant, Morris Cerullo, Jack Coe, Jean Darnell, Alexander Dowie, William Freeman, W. V. Grant, Kenneth Hagin, Franklin Hall, H. Richard Hall, Tommy Hicks, O. L. Jaggers, Leroy Jenkins, Kathryn Kuhlman, John G. Lake, Aimee Semple McPherson, David Nunn, T. L. Osborn, Charles S. Price, Oral Roberts, R. W. Schambach, Smith Wigglesworth, Maria Woodworth-Etter, and Lillian B. Yeomans. For each person, a brief biography was presented followed by a comparison and contrast of their childhood, calling, early ministry, models and mentors, personality traits, growth, successes and failures, and doctrinal errors or other aspects of failure. It was recognized that many of their ministries ended prematurely due to scandals, exaggerated claims, misappropriated funds, and/or objectionable lifestyles.

Conclusion: While acknowledging their weaknesses, the text added that "with all their faults and limitations, the Pentecostal Evangelists have done more in this century to evangelize the world than any other group. They have been, in church growth terms, the most effective evangelists of this century, and that after all, is the point. The church grows faster where the power of God is in evidence!"

---

[1] Wimber, *MC510 Syllabus*, Section One, 9. Reference is also made to C. Peter Wagner's book *Frontiers in Missionary Strategy* (Chicago: Moody Press, 1972). Wagner offers 3-P Evangelism: Presence Evangelism – we must be there; Proclamation Evangelism – we must proclaim; and Persuasion Evangelism – we must make disciples. Then adds the forth – Power Evangelism which demonstrates God's power.

[2] Wimber, *MC510 Syllabus*, Section One, 8. Although Wimber focuses primarily on Cho's church, he lists five additional churches that have adopted this model. They include: St. Paul's Episcopal, Darien, Connecticut; Campus Church, Minneapolis, Minnesota; Gateway Baptist Church, Boswell, New Mexico; Crenshaw Christian Center, Crenshaw, CA; and Our Lady of Perpetual Help, Boston, Massachusetts.

[3] Italics and brackets are in the original text.

[4] Paul Hiebert, "The Flaw of the Excluded Middle," *Missiology: An International Revie*, American Society of Missiology Vol X, no. 1 (January 1982): 35–47.

[5] Hiebert, "The Flaw of the Excluded Middle," 37–9.

[6] Russell Spittler, *Perspectives on the New Pentecostalism* (Grand Rapids: Baker Book House, 1976), 1986.

[7] In this section, Wimber did an extensive teaching on every account in the gospels and Acts where Jesus and his disciples performed healings, miracles, and signs and wonders. He discussed the outcomes of these events and correlated them with proclamation and demonstration of the good news of the kingdom.

[8] J. Sidlow Baxter, *Divine Healing of the Body* (Grand Rapids: Zondervan, 1979).

Appendix C

A Five-Step Healing Model

1. Interview: Ask the questions "Where does it hurt?" "What can I pray with you about?" and "What do you want/need God to do for you?"

The interview is conducted on both the natural and supernatural planes. The natural plane sorts the information according to present and/or past experiences, and on the supernatural level, a sorting occurs as the Holy Spirit leads with such things as a word of knowledge, a distinguishing of spirits, and so forth. This is not a medical interview; therefore, a medical history is not necessary. Just find out where the person hurts. The interview is complete when it is discerned whether the cause of the condition is natural, supernatural, social, emotional, or sin, or if God told them what to do.

2. Diagnostic Decision: Answer the question "Why does this person have this condition?"

First investigate the natural realm. Do they have a disease or did they hurt themselves? Was sin, such as a social or transmitted disease, involved? Was a sin committed by them or against them? Is this an emotional or psychosomatic problem? Is it a social problem, such as unforgiveness, anger, or resentment? Is it a familial issue such as family spirits or generational sin? The second area to investigate is the supernatural realm. Is the problem demonic oppression or demonization? Is a curse such as black magic, white magic, or curses spoken over the person by authority figures involved?

3. Prayer Selection: Answer the question "What kind of prayer will I need to pray to help this person?"

Prayer begins by *petitioning God for the Spirit's presence and healing power*. First, pray a prayer of intercession with your mind and then pray in the Spirit. Finally pray the prayer they received from God, either a command prayer of faith or a pronouncement of faith. If necessary, address the demons by rebuking (breaking their power), binding (containing their power), or expelling (eliminating their presence).

4. Prayer of Engagement: Answer the question "How are we doing?"

Watch for physical manifestations in the person being prayed for, such as warmth, tingling, heat, muscle spasms, shaking, deep breathing, and so forth, as these can be visible signs of the Spirit's presence. Because some people are not in tune with their bodies and some are programmed for failure, the person praying should ask questions as the session moves forward. Stop praying when the person receiving prayer indicates the prayer session is over, when the Spirit indicates that it is time to stop; when you can no longer think of anything to pray, or when you have prayed everything and are not gaining ground.

5. Post-Prayer Directions: Ask the question "What should they do to keep their healing?"

Depending on the source of the sickness, they may need to be instructed to "go and sin no more." At other times, they may receive supernatural leading or special direction. The general counsel given to everyone is to read the Scriptures, pray, and so on.[1]

---

[1] Wimber, "Five Steps in the Healing Procedure."

Appendix D

Critical Characteristics of the Bible

Wimber identified eight terms that captured the "critical characteristics" of the Bible:

1. The Bible is *infallible* in that Scripture will never deceive us and never lead us astray. It is wholly trustworthy and wholly reliable. It contains no mistakes and is incapable of error.
2. The Bible is *inerrant* in that it is wholly true. What the Bible says, God says.
3. It is *plenary*, in that the Bible is fully inspired in all parts.
4. The Bible is *verbally inspired*, an inspiration that extends to the words of Scripture themselves and not only to the ideas contained in Scripture.
5. It is *confluent*, which means the Bible is the work of both human authors and God. It has dual authorship. God spoke through human authors, using their unique personalities, and their words are the words of God. People have no right to stand in judgment upon Scripture.
6. The Bible is *clear* enough to be read and understood. The Bible is written for ordinary believers and not just experts.
7. The Bible is *sufficient* and contains enough light to save sinners and direct the church. It does not reveal everything there is to know about God or exhaust every revelation of God, and this does not mean additional revelations from God are to be placed on a level equal with Scripture. In other words, any source of "revelation" that contradicts or exalts itself above Scripture is to be rejected. Personal experience and private revelation need the checks and guidance that only the Bible can provide. Private revelation cannot be normative over the Bible, but this does not mean that all private revelation is false. Here

Wimber quotes Clark Pinnock, who states, "To deny the possibility of private revelation would be to imply that God is now silent."

The Bible is *effective* in bringing people to a personal relationship with Christ. The word of God generates eternal life.[1]

---

[1] Wimber, *Power Points*, 38–42.

Appendix E

An Overview of the Fuller Committee Report

1. The Coming of God's Kingdom and the Ministry of Healing: Although healings and exorcisms were frequent in Jesus's ministry, they are not the only signs of the kingdom. Too much emphasis on the miraculous takes away from helping ordinary people to bear the cross of their suffering. The disciples' mandate to heal is not necessarily the same mandate as the church's mandate; therefore, a seminary should not be required to include healing and the miraculous in its curriculum.[1]

2. The Faith and Practice of the Early Church: It was agreed that the early church expected and experienced the miraculous and that the gift of healing was seen throughout church history. The Reformers, however, emphasized the preaching of the gospel and believed that healing should always be subordinated to the development of moral character.[2]

3. Our Views of God and His World: All healing comes from God; therefore, there should not be a dichotomy between healing through medical science and supernatural healing. Those who train ministers are responsible for teaching them how to have a biblical worldview of all the instruments of healing and how to wisely minister to those who do not receive healing.[3]

4. The Place of Suffering in Christian Experience: Christians are not guaranteed a life void of sickness or guaranteed exemption from suffering, which may be God's invitation to spiritual growth. Therefore, a seminary must equip ministers to help people who suffer and to give them hope for their ultimate healing.

5. Credibility and the Miraculous: Those who minister to the sick must be trained in how to report healings with credibility so that no reproach is brought onto the ministry of the miraculous.[4]

6. The Distinctives of Fuller Seminary: Fuller was defined as being "an evangelical, multidenominational, international, and multiethnic community dedicated to the preparation of men and women for the manifold ministries of Christ and his Church. . . through graduate education, professional development, and spiritual formation." Fuller faculty members were responsible for preventing distortions to and distractions from the seminary's purpose.

Two statements in this chapter seemed particularly pointed toward Wimber:

- Those who teach courses who are not full-time members of the Fuller faculty must be accountable to their colleagues for the content and tenor of their teaching.[5]
- Faculty members are accountable for what happens in the courses they approve, and they must be able to support or defend any course approved for academic credit. If this is true of the faculty as a whole, it is acutely true of the professor of record. No assigned teacher of any course, and especially of a course that has become a public event, may surrender his or her accountability to a guest, particularly when the guest teacher also carries on a widely publicized and critically debated form of ministry within the classroom.[6] The faculty was under no obligation to approve a course simply because it was popular. They had a solemn responsibility to critically evaluate every course to ensure the protection of the churches they served as institutions.

8. **Miraculous Healing and Responsible Ministry:** This chapter dealt with the problems of demon expulsion, the necessity of having controls to protect the people being exorcised, and the necessity of reporting healings with honesty and integrity.[7]

[1] Smedes, ed., *Ministry and the Miraculous*, 14–24.
[2] Smedes, ed., *Ministry and the Miraculous*, 25–9.
[3] Smedes, ed., *Ministry and the Miraculous*, 30–9.
[4] Smedes, ed., *Ministry and the Miraculous*, 46–50.
[5] Smedes, ed., *Ministry and the Miraculous*, 57.
[6] Smedes, ed., *Ministry and the Miraculous*, 58.
[7] Smedes, ed., *Ministry and the Miraculous*, 60–7.

Appendix F

Joint Statement from the Leadership of the Full Faith Church of Love Ministries and the Metro Vineyard Fellowship of Kansas City

May 16, 1993

This is a joint statement from the leadership of
Full Faith Church of Love Ministries and Metro Vineyard Fellowship of Kansas City.

Now there are varieties of gifts, but the same Spirit. And there are varieties of ministries, and the same Lord. And there are varieties of effects, but the same God who works all things in all persons...For even as the body is one and yet has many members, and all the members of the body, though they are many, are one body, so also is Christ.

I Corinthians 12:4-6, 12 (NASV)

Ernie Gruen and Mike Bickle have forgiven each other of all offenses. Their senior leadership has come together in a spirit of forgiveness; we also ask the Body of Christ to forgive us of any offenses that we have caused the Church universal. We feel it is time to bring to a close the events of the past. We believe it is time to go on and to seek to heal past wounds. We want to publicly lay down any personal animosities, wounds or misunderstandings between the two churches. Under the Lordship of Jesus Christ as one Body, we want to be joined and knit together in His love, *"being diligent to preserve the unity of the Spirit in the bond of peace."* (Ephesians 4:3, NASV) We desire the Body of Christ represented by our churches to flow together in the love and mercy of God and begin to rebuild relationships and friendships.

Appendix G

Letters Regarding Toronto

Toronto Airport Vineyard

December 5, 1995

John Wimber
International Director
Vineyard Ministries Int'l

Dear John:

We so appreciated you taking the time to visit us in Toronto. While the meeting was challenging for all parties concerned, I do believe we heard each others' hearts.

John, thank you for taking so much "heat" and criticism for us. We sincerely apologise for the stress and hurt we have caused you. We are sorry that we misread the intent and extent of your concerns. We were not fully aware of the challenges that the move of God's Spirit in Toronto was causing you. We understand your position and we agree that the Toronto Airport Vineyard is not called to speak for the entire Vineyard movement. We acknowledge God's call on your life to pastor the entire Vineyard movement and we acknowledge that some of what is happening in Toronto is outside the Vineyard model. We agree that you and the Vineyard movement should not have to continue answering for the move of God's Spirit in Toronto.

We don't understand all of the Lord's plans but we believe that we are called to help facilitate this particular move of His Spirit. We understand that the long-term implications of this move of God may diverge from what He is doing within the Vineyard movement. That is His prerogative. We are doing our best to be faithful stewards of what God has entrusted to us, as are you.

John, we accept the Board's decision to have our church disengage from the Association of Vineyard Churches. Would you allow us to leave with your blessing? We ask you to take this action to minimize serious hurtful repercussions for the Body of Christ. We think very highly of you and the Vineyard, and we have so appreciated the times we have shared. We want to continue fellowshipping with all who love Jesus and to continue ministering God's love to the whole Body of Christ. We too want to focus on preaching the Cross of Christ to all who come for refreshing.

Thank you for your years of ministry that provided such a wonderful environment for this current move of God.

On behalf of our church and our pastoral staff,
Sincerely in Christ,

John Arnott
Senior Pastor

cc Gary Best

AN OPEN LETTER FOR GENERAL DISTRIBUTION
FROM JOHN ARNOTT
Senior Pastor, Toronto Airport Vineyard
DECEMBER 12, 1995

As you probably know by now, the Toronto Airport Vineyard (TAV) will be disengaging from the Association of Vineyard Churches (AVC). This will officially take place on January 20, 1996, at which time we will announce our new church name, etc. It is also the second anniversary celebration of the outpouring of God's Spirit at the Toronto Airport Vineyard.

This decision to separate was initiated by the US AVC Board. John Wimber, Todd Hunter, Bob Fulton and Gary Best from the Board personally visited Toronto Airport Vineyard on December 5, 1995, to announce their decision to our senior staff. We were surprised at the finality of the decision. We had hoped to have some input into the process. We thought the Board was not getting an accurate picture of what was taking place at the renewal meetings and that any issues could be explained and resolved. The Board, we were told, thought otherwise and we were offered no opportunity for discussion. We were removed without due process.

The bottom line, we were told, is that the Board felt Toronto Airport Vineyard renewal services were not mirroring the Vineyard model. As well, John Wimber felt he could no longer answer questions, including innuendoes and rumours, regarding the renewal services. Rather than ask us to revamp the renewal meetings, they released us to continue on as we believe God is leading us. Wimber agrees that the Holy Spirit is moving in Toronto, it's just that he (Wimber) feels the AVC Board is not called to shepherd something outside the ministry model God has given them. While our local fellowship follows closely the Vineyard model, the renewal services, it seems, do not.

In a letter drafted after the meeting, we apologized to the AVC Board for mis-reading the intent and extent of their concerns (see attached letter of December 5, 1995). They have accepted our apology. We will be parting on friendly terms. We still have the same Saviour and the same enemy. We realize that God is Sovereign over everything, including any mistakes His children might make.

We have asked several Senior leaders from around the world to form an International Renewal Network. They would act as an Advisory Council to help steer and facilitate this renewal. In addition they will act as a temporary leadership covering for our church until such time as new alliances are formed. We hope that those inside and outside the Association of Vineyard churches will feel free to fellowship with us and continue to flow in this move of God. Please pray that God will give wisdom to all those involved. Our heart's desire is to facilitate and pastor this renewal movement according to the Father's Heart. Our meetings are still open to the whole body of Christ. The Cross of Christ remains our central message.

We do want to publicly thank John Wimber and the AVC Board. This current move of God's Spirit would not have achieved its world-wide reach and impact without them. They have modelled Christ to us; they have been ministers of healing to us – we cannot thank them enough. We are not saying goodbye. We simply recognize that the Sovereign Lord is moving this stream of the Holy Spirit along a new tributary. The major difference this decision makes is that if anyone wants to know "What's going on in Toronto?", they now need to ask the leadership in Toronto. Other than that it is onward and upward for us. We hope that all discussions in media and cyberspace will reflect the continuing good will between AVC and the Toronto Airport Vineyard. We hope that all will continue to practice the love and mercy of Jesus that we have preached for so many years. "Beloved, let us love one another." (1 John 4:7)

Sincerely in Christ's Service

John Arnott for the Toronto Airport Vineyard Christian Fellowship

Appendix H

Wimber's Conference Schedule

(As recorded in *First Fruits* and *Equipping the Saints* magazines)

May 8–11, 1984:	Spiritual Warfare Seminar, So Cal. Regional Vineyard Conf.
May 14–16, 1985:	Healing Seminar, Waco, TX
June 18–22, 1984:	Signs and Wonders (MC510), Anaheim Vineyard, Anaheim, CA
July 5–7, 1984:	Worship Seminar, Los Osos, CA
Aug 20–21, 1984:	(No content listed), Garden Grove Crystal Cathedral, CA
Aug 22–23, 1984:	Signs and Wonders, Oral Roberts University
Sept 3–7, 1984:	Annual Vineyard Pastors Conf., Costa Mesa, CA
Sept 27–29, 1984:	Healing Seminar, Detroit, MI
Oct 15–17, 1984:	James Robinson Restoration Conf., Dallas, TX
Oct 19–Nov 4, 1984:	(No content listed), London, England
Nov 7–10, 1984:	Spiritual Gifts Seminar, New York, NY
Feb 12–15, 1985:	Signs, Wonders, and Church Growth, Anaheim, CA
March 5–8, 1985:	Signs, Wonders, and Church Growth, Pt. I, Dallas, TX
March 21–23, 1985:	Healing, Columbus, Ohio
March 28–30, 1985:	Healing, San Antonio, TX
April 11–12, 1985:	Healing, Tulsa, OK
April 24–27, 1985:	Spiritual Warfare Conf., Denver, CO
May 2–4, 1985:	Power Evangelism, Kansas City, MO—James Robertson Assoc.
May 9–11, 1985:	Healing I, Tucson, AZ
May 21–24, 1985:	Signs, Wonders and Church Growth I, Vancouver, Canada
June 9–12, 1985:	Church Growth Leadership, Columbus, OH
June 11–15, 1985:	Spiritual Warfare/Healing II, Houston, TX
June 19–22, 1985:	Spiritual Warfare, Denver, CO
July 25–27, 1985:	Healing I, Oklahoma City, OK
July 29–30, 1985:	(No content listed), James Robinson Evangelical Assoc., Dallas, TX
Aug 6–9, 1985:	(No content listed), Lutheran Renewal, Minneapolis, MN
Aug 20–23, 1985:	Signs, Wonders, and Church Growth, Kansas City, MO
Sept 2–6, 1985:	Vineyard International Pastors Conf., San Diego, CA
Sept 16–18, 1985:	Healing I, Baltimore, MD
Sept 19–21, 1985:	Kingdom of God, Ann Arbor, MI
Oct 14–17, 1985:	Healing in the Church, Brighton, England
Oct 22–25, 1985:	Signs, Wonders, and Church Growth II, Sheffield, England
Oct 28–31, 1985:	Signs, Wonders, and Church Growth I, Sheffield, England
Nov 3–6, 1985:	Women's Aglow International, Anaheim, CA
Jan 28–31, 1986:	Signs and Wonders and Church Growth I, Seattle, WA
Feb 18–21, 1986:	Church Growth Leadership, Anaheim, CA
April 28–May 2, 1986:	Signs and Wonders and Church Growth II, Dallas, TX
May 20–23, 1986:	Teach Us to Pray, Vancouver, BC
June 9–12, 1986:	Church Growth Leadership, Columbus, OH
June 13–14, 1986:	Celebration of the Kingdom of God, Chicago, IL

June 23–27, 1986:	Signs and Wonders and Church Growth I, Baltimore, MD
July 20–26, 1986:	Acts '86, Birmingham, England
July 28–Aug 2, 1986:	Healing in the Church, Belfast, Northern Ireland, and Dublin, Ireland
Oct 27–31, 1986:	Teach Us to Pray, Brighton, England
Nov 1, 1986:	Celebration of the Kingdom, Wembley, England
Nov 3–7, 1986:	Signs, Wonders, and Church Growth II, Harrogate, England
Nov 20–22, 1986:	Power Evangelism, Pasadena, CA
Feb 9–14, 1987:	Signs, Wonders, and Church Growth II, Anaheim, CA
Mar 13–14, 1987:	Pastoral Renewal Leaders' Seminar, Anaheim, CA
June 5–6, 1987:	Power Healing Celebration, Chicago, IL
June 22–25, 1987:	Power Evangelism Conference, Belfast, Northern Ireland
June 19–July 1, 1987:	Prayer Conference, Dublin, Republic of Ireland
July 13–16, 1987:	Healing 1987, Vineyard Christian Fellowship, Anaheim, CA
July 22–26, 1987:	Power Evangelism Workshop, New Orleans, LA
Sept 21–24, 1987:	Power Evangelism Conference, Edinburgh, Scotland
Sept 30–Oct 5, 1987:	Power Evangelism Conference, Frankfurt, Germany
Nov 2–5, 1987:	Signs and Wonders Conference Part II, Auckland, New Zealand
Nov 10–13, 1987:	Signs and Wonders Conference Part I, Canberra, Australia
May 30, 1987:	Power Evangelism Celebration, Irvine, CA
June 5–6, 1987:	Power Healing Celebration, Chicago, IL
June 22–25, 1987:	Power Evangelism Conference, Belfast, Northern Ireland
June 29–July 1, 1987:	Teach Us to Pray, Dublin, Republic of Ireland
July 13–16, 1987:	Healing '87 (with Francis MacNutt), Anaheim, CA
July 22–26, 1987:	Power Evangelism Workshop, New Orleans, LA
Aug 26–28, 1987:	Worship '87, Anaheim, CA
Sept 21–24, 1987:	Power Evangelism Conference, Edinburgh, Scotland
Sept 30– Oct 4, 1987:	Power Evangelism Conference, Frankfurt, Germany
Nov 2–5, 1987:	Signs and Wonders Conference Part II, Auckland, New Zealand
Nov 10–13, 1987:	Signs and Wonders Conference, Canberra, Australia
Feb 8–11, 1988:	Kingdom of God and the Last Days, Anaheim, CA
March 1–4, 1988:	Power Evangelism, Birmingham, AL
April 18–21, 1988:	Spiritual Warfare, Brighton, England
April 26–29, 1988:	Power Evangelism, Johannesburg, South Africa
May 23–26, 1988:	Power Evangelism, Gothenburg, Sweden
Sept 20–23, 1988:	Power Healing, Columbia, SC
Oct 31–Nov 3, 1988:	Power Healing, Edinburgh, Scotland
Nov 11–13, 1988:	Kingdom of God and Healing, Bern, Switzerland
Nov 16–20, 1988:	Power Healing, Frankfurt, Germany
Feb 7–10, 1989:	Spiritual Warfare Conference, Anaheim, CA
Feb 22–25, 1989:	Spiritual Warfare and the Kingdom of God, Auckland, New Zealand
Feb 28–March 3, 1989:	Power Evangelism, Melbourne, Australia
March 7–10, 1989:	Power Evangelism, Perth, Australia
April 11–14, 1989:	Teach Us to Pray, Denver, CO
April 20–22, 1989:	Intercessory Prayer Seminar, Anaheim, CA
May 16–19, 1989:	Power Evangelism, Edmonton, Canada
July 6–8, 1989:	Prophesy II Seminar, Anaheim, CA
Oct 3–6, 1989:	Prophecy Conference, Hempstead, NY
Oct 9–13, 1989:	Worship, Brighton, England
Oct 17–20, 1989:	Kingdom of God and Healing, Paris, France
Nov 7–10, 1989:	Worship Conference, Anaheim, CA
Nov 11–12, 1989:	Enjoying God's Grace, Anaheim, CA
Feb 6–9, 1990:	Holiness unto the Lord Conference, Anaheim, CA
Feb 13–16, 1990:	Holiness unto the Lord, Anaheim, CA

March 6–9, 1990:	Spiritual Warfare, Sydney, Australia
March 13–16, 1990:	What the Holy Spirit is Saying to the Church Today, Perth, Australia
March 20–23, 1990:	Power Evangelism, Singapore
March 27–30, 1990:	(No content listed), Hong Kong
May 7–10, 1990:	What the Holy Spirit is Saying to the Church Today, Chicago, IL
May 14–17, 1990:	Keys to Dynamic Church Life in the '90s, Ann Arbor, MI
June 25–29, 1990:	Grace Ministries Leadership Conf., Kansas City, MO
Sept 18–21, 1990:	Holiness unto the Lord, Edmonton, Alberta, Canada
Oct 5–7, 1990:	Emergence of the Victorious Church, Wales
Oct 8–11, 1990:	A Prophetic Word for the Church Today, Edinburgh, Scotland
Oct 12–14, 1990:	A Prophetic Word for the Church Today, Belfast, Ireland
Oct 15–18, 1990:	Church Growth and the Kingdom of God, Harrogate, England
Oct 19–20, 1990:	Regional Conference, Sheffield, England
Oct 22–25, 1990:	Holiness unto the Lord, London, England
Oct 1990:	(No content listed), Cardiff, Wales
Jan 28–31, 1991:	Revival Fire, Anaheim, CA
March 21–23, 1991:	Revival Fire, Hempstead, NY
March 25–28, 1991:	Revival Fire, Arlington, TX
April 9–12, 1991:	Power Evangelism, Brunswick, Canada
April 16–19, 1991:	Revival Fire, Denver, CO
April 29–May 2, 1991:	Facing the '90s, Tacoma, WA
June 17–20, 1991:	Holiness/Revival, Stockholm, Sweden
Aug 28–31, 1991:	Steps to Revival, Bern, Switzerland
Sept 2–5, 1991:	Church in the '90s, Zwolle, Holland
Sept 30–Oct 3, 1991:	Holiness unto the Lord, Ottawa, CA
Oct 15–18, 1991:	Revival Fire, Perth, Australia
Oct 22–25, 1991:	Holiness unto the Lord, Sydney, Australia
Oct 29–Nov 1, 1991:	Holiness unto the Lord, Wellington, New Zealand
Feb 4–7, 1992:	Healing '92, Anaheim, CA
March 31–April 3, 1992:	Worship '92, Anaheim, CA
May 6–9, 1992:	Revival, Holiness, and Intercession, Hamburg, Germany
June 16–19, 1992:	Healing '92, Brighton, England
June 23–27, 1992:	Doin' the Stuff National Youth Conf., Anaheim, CA
Aug 31–Sept 3, 1992:	Equipping the Saints, Zwolle, Holland
Sept 7–10, 1992:	Equipping the Saints, Manchester, England
Jan 26–29, 1993:	Kingdom Warfare, Anaheim, CA
Jan 31–Feb 3, 1994:	Equipping the Saints Healing, Anaheim, CA
June 2–4, 1994:	The Mission Summit, Kansas City, MO
Aug 3–6, 1994:	Worship and Unity, Anaheim, CA
Aug 2–23, 1994:	Pastoral Leadership Training, Anaheim, CA
Sept 20–23, 1994:	Church Planting and Leadership, London, England
Sept 27–30, 1994:	Healing the Oppressed, Lancashire, England
Oct 3–4, 1994:	Pastoral Leadership Training, Anaheim, CA
Oct 5–8, 1994:	Healing 2, Berne, Switzerland
Aug 29–Sept 1, 1995:	Let Your Glory Fall Worship and Revival Conf., Anaheim, CA
Oct 3–4, 1995:	Leadership Seminar, Anaheim, CA
Nov 6–9, 1995:	Healing '95, Brighton, England
Nov 13–16, 1995:	Healing '95, Harrogate, England
Jan 23–26, 1996:	Let the River Flow, Anaheim, CA
July 22–23, 1996:	Winds of Worship and Evangelism, Anaheim, CA
Sept 17–18, 1996:	Leadership Seminar, Anaheim, CA
Jan 21–24, 1997:	Expanding the Kingdom, Anaheim, CA

Appendix I

Ministry Emphasis and Themes

(As seen in Vineyard publications)

First Fruits Magazine

July 1985:	Signs and Wonders (MC 510 and Church Planting Part I)
Sept/Oct 1985:	Learning to Wait, Signs and Wonders, Church Planting, MC520 Part II
Jan/Feb 1986:	Doin' the Stuff, KOG Establishing God's Rule
Sept/Dec 1986:	Family Relationships

Equipping Magazine

Jan/Feb 1987:	Worship: Intimacy with God
March/April 1987:	Fellowship Groups
May/June 1987:	Signs/Wonders is God's Love in Action, Jackie Pullinger
July/Aug 1987:	Training: A Key to Strong Character and Ministry
Sept/Oct 1987:	Harvest Field, Church Planting, Evangelism
Nov/Dec 1987:	Prayer: Intimacy with God; Dreams
Winter 1988:	Why Christians Suffer
Spring 1988:	The Cross
Summer 1988:	Fallen Leaders, Taking Sin Seriously, Fallen Pastors
Fall 1988:	Confronting New Age, Taking the "Preach" out of Preaching
Winter 1989:	The Bible: The Battle over the Bible, God's Will and the Bible
Spring 1989:	The Lamb's War, Social Justice, The Poor
Summer 1989:	Facing the '90s, Conversation with Mike Bickle
Fall 1989:	Introducing Prophetic Ministry, Paul Cain
Winter 1990:	Holiness in the '90s

Spring 1990:	Intercession, Spiritual Warfare, Binding the Strongman, Praying for Leaders
Summer 1990:	Building Strong Families
Fall 1990:	Prophecy Today
Winter 1991:	Revival Fire
Spring 1991:	Rearing Fruitful Children
Summer 1991:	Missions, Muslims, Japan
Winter 1992:	Kingdom Currency, Money, Get Out of Debt
Spring 1992:	Church Planting, Social Evangelism
Summer 1992:	Unleashing Youth into Ministry
Fall 1992:	Brokenness
Winter 1993:	Arming One Another for Spiritual Warfare
Spring 1993:	Sanctification
Summer 1993:	Vineyard Priorities
Fall 1993:	Spiritual Gifts
Winter 1994:	Small Groups

-Documented dates changed from seasons to quarters-

First Quarter 1994:	Ministry of Jesus and Mission of the Church
Second Quarter 1994:	Following Christ into His Harvest
Fall 1994:	Times of Refreshing
Fourth Quarter 1994:	Living Free with Jesus
First Quarter 1995:	From Vision to Vehicle
Second Quarter 1995:	Fishing, Farming, and Evangelism
Third Quarter 1995:	Building toward the New Millennium
Second Quarter 1996:	Generation X—Hope for Hopeless
Third Quarter 1996:	Witness for a Powerful Christ

Appendix J

Songs Written by Wimber

1. Praise Song
2. Your Love
3. Trust in His Love
4. I Will Live Forever
5. Strangers Here
6. Sweet Perfume
7. Covered in Your Love
8. To Seek Your Face
9. I Sing a New Song
10. No One But You
11. Together
12. We Believe You, Lord
13. Worthy Is the Lamb
14. When You Return
15. Spirit Song
16. Isn't He

Bibliography

Primary Sources

Magazine and Journal Articles

Aikman, David. "All Fall Down." *The American Spectator*, 28 (November 1995): 68.

Armstrong, John. "Signs and Wonders: The Arrival of the Third Wave." *The Standard* 80 (October 1990): 26-28.

_____. "Power Encounters and Modern Evangelism." *The Standard* 80 (November 1990): 26-28.

_____. "World Views and The Phenomena of Revival." *The Standard* 80 (December 1990): 18-20.

_____. "Power Healings: Healthy Questions Needed." *The Standard* 81 (January 1991): 29-31.

_____. "Bearing Fruit for the Kingdom." *The Standard* 81 (February 1991): 36-38.

_____. "A New Generation of Prophets." *The Standard* 81 (March 1991): 20-22.

_____. "A New Breed." *The Standard* 81 (April 1991): 28-30.

_____. "A Supernatural Walk." *The Standard* 81 (May 1991): 20-22.

_____. "Nagging Concerns." *The Standard* 81 (June 1991): 19-21.

_____. "Solutions and Conclusions." *The Standard* 81 (July 1991): 20-22.

_____. "A Brief Reply to the Gift Theology of Dr. John Piper." *The Standard* 81 (December 1991): 31-32.

Andrews, Collin. "Winds of Worship: Live From Toronto." *Charisma* (April 1995): 83.

Arnott, John. "Overwhelmed by His Love." *Charisma* (November 1995): 60-2, 64.

Babbage, Humphrey. "Reflections on the Ministry of John Wimber and His Team in New Zealand." 31. *Wellington: Scripture Union*, 1986.

Ball, Karen. "The Student's View." *Christian Life* 44, no 6 (October 1982): 70.

Benn, Wallace and Mark Burkill. "A Theological and Pastoral Critique of the Teachings of John Wimber." *Churchman* 101, no. 102 (1987): 101-13.

Beverly, James. "Toronto's Mixed Blessing." *Christianity Today* 39, no. 10 (1995): 6.

_____. "Dental Miracle Reports Draw Criticism." *Christianity Today* 40, no. 1 (1999): 1.

_____. "Leading Church Leaves Association." *Christianity Today* (October 7, 1996): 86.

_____. "Vineyard Severs Ties with 'Toronto Blessing' Church." *Christianity Today* (January 8, 1995): 66.

Bickle, Mike. "Administering Prophecy in the Church." *Equipping the Saints* 3 (Fall 1989): 23-27.

Bird, Brian. "Fuller Releases Signs and Wonders Study." *Charisma* (March 1987): 78-9.

Boulton, Wallace. "John Wimber Remembered." *Renewal* Issue 261 (February 1998).

Blattner, John. "Pitfalls of Prophecy and How to Avoid Them." *Equipping the Saints* 3, no. 4 (1989): 14-15, 19-20.

Brown, Andrew. "The Holy Spirit Hits South Kensington." *The Independent* (June 21, 1994): 2.

Brown, Mick. "Unzipper Heaven, Lord Ha-Ha, Ho-Ho, Hee-Hee." *Telegraph Magazine* (n.d.): 26-8-30.

Bruce, Bill. "Vineyard Founder John Wimber Remembered for Legacy." *Charisma* (January 1998): 17.

Cain, Paul. "The Victorious Church." *Equipping the Saints* 4 (Fall 199: 10-11.

Chandler, Majorie Lee. "Fuller Seminary Cancels Course on Signs and Wonders." *Christianity Today* 30, no. 3 (February 1986): 48-49.

Chandler, Russell. "Vineyard: Fellowship Popular With 'Baby Boomers'." *Los Angeles Times* (Friday, October 5, 1990): A34-5.

Deere, Jack. "Vineyard Polity Regarding the Prophetic." Association of Vineyard Churches, 1990. Special Collections, Regent University Library, Virginia Beach, Virginia.

Doucet, Daina. "Renewal Excites Canadian Churches." *Charisma* (June 1994): 53.

_____. "What is God Doing in Toronto." *Charisma* (February 1995): 20.

_____. "Blessings Sweeps the Globe." *Charisma* (November 1995): 63.

_____. "Mainse Endorses 'Toronto Blessing.'" *Charisma* (June 1995): 68-9.

Drammer, Donald. "The Perplexing Power of John Wimber's Power Encounters." *Churchman* 106, no. 1 (1992): 45-64.

Duin, Julia. "Signs and Wonders in New Orleans." *Christianity Today* (November 21, 1986): 26-27.

_____. "An Evening with Rodney Howard-Brown." *Christian Research Journal* 17 (Winter 1995): 43-45.

Duncan, Denis. "Healing is Wholeness: Impact of John Wimber." *Health & Healing* no 15 (May 6 1987): 1-2.

Engleman, Phil. "Deceiving Appearances: Vineyard-style Diversion Squelches Revival in This Church." *The Standard 81* (February 1991): 39-40.

Feinberg, Margaret. "Vineyard Leaders Press on After Wimber's Death." *Charisma* (April 1998): 18-9.

Ford, Marcia. "The Blessing Spreads Worldwide." *Charisma* (July 1997): 54-6, 58-9.

Francis, Vic. "Stroke Fails to Sideline Wimber." *Charisma* (May 1995): 60-2.

Gibb, David. "Look Back in Wonder? Reviewing the Power Evangelism of John Wimber." *Vox Evangelica* 26, (1996): 23-42.

Gledhill, Ruth. "Spread of Hysteria Fad Worries Church." *The Times* (June 18, 1994): 12.

Grady, J. Lee. "Making Adjustments at the Metro Vineyard of Kansas City." *Equipping the Saints* 4, no. 4 (1990): 7.

_____. "Resolving the Kansas City Prophecy Controversy." *Ministries Today* (September/October 1990): 48-54.

_____. "Vineyard Revival Spreads." *Charisma* (September 1994): 74.

_____. "God Can Use Warehouses." *Charisma* (February 1995): 4.

_____. "Does the Church Need Heresy Hunters?" *Charisma* (May 1995): 47-9, 50, 52.

_____. "Kansas City Churches Mend Rift." *Charisma* (September 1995): 32, 34.

_____. "Classical Pentecostals Wary of the 'Toronto Blessing.'" *Charisma* (November 1995): 41-2.

_____. "Toronto's Afterglow." *Charisma* (December 1998): 70-78, 123.

_____. "The Pruning of the Vineyard." *Charisma* (December 1998): 72.

Grudem, Wayne. "What Should Be the Relationship between Prophet & Pastor?" *Equipping the Saints* 3, no. 4 (Fall 1989): 7-9, 21-2.

_____. "Prophecy in the Church." *Faith and Renewal* (July/August 1991): 3-8.

Gulliksen, Kenn. "Birthing a Vineyard." *First Fruits* (July 1985): 14-16.

Hall, David. "Signs and Wonders." *Today* (October 1984): 19-21.

Hiebert, Paul. "The Flaw of the Excluded Middle." *American Society of Missiology* X, no. 1 (1982): 35-47.

Higher, John. "The Devil, Demons & Spiritual Warfare: A Panel of Experts Answer to Often-Asked Questions About the Church's Battle against the Forces of Darkness." *Charisma* (February 1994): 52-7.

Hunter, Todd. *Board Report* (September/October 1994): 2-4.

_____. "Church Planting: Listen and Obey." *First Fruits* (June 1984): 10.

Hurst, Lynda. "Laughing All the Way to Heaven in the Church at the End of the Runway with its 'Toronto Blessing'." *The Toronto Star* (December 3, 1994): A1.

Jensen, Phillip and Tony Payne. eds. "John Wimber: Friend and Foe?" *The Briefing* (April 1990): 4-48. (Reprinted: Ontario, Canada: Canadian Christian Publications, 1994).

Johnson, Peter. "Wimber Responds to Vineyard Critics," and "Changes Within Vineyard Ministries." *Charisma* (August 1992): 52-3.

Kammer, Donald. "The Perplexing Power of John Wimber's Power Encounter." *Churchman* 106, no. 1 (1992): 45-64.

Kelly, Brian. "John Wimber's Healing Message." *New Creation* Vol 3, no. 9 (n.d.): 19-20.

Lawson, Steven. "The Vineyard: Where Spiritual Gifts Bloom." *Charisma* (September 1985).

_____. "Leaders Unite in New Orleans." *Charisma* (December, 1986): 58.

Little, Jack. "Church Planting: Aggressive and Violent." *First Fruits* (September/October 1985): 13.

Loren, Julia C. "Legacy of a Humble Hero." *Charisma* (November 2007): 89, 91-3.

MacNutt, Francis. "Excerpts from Prophecies Given by Bob Jones and John Paul Jacksons for Francis and Judith on July 12, 1990 at Holy Trinity Brompton Anglican Church, London, England." *Christian Healing Ministries* 4, no. 8 (November 1990): 1-4.

Malone, George. "Signs and Wonders Canadian Style." *First Fruits* (July 1985) 11-13.

Mauldin, Michael G. "Seers in the Heartland: Hot on the Trail of the Kansas City Prophets." *Christianity Today* (January 1991): 18-22.

Maxwell, Joe. "Is Laughing for the Lord Holy?" *Christianity Today* (October 24, 1994): 2.

Millar, Sandy. "A Friend's Recollections." *Equipped: A Vineyard Magazine* (October 1997): n.d.

_____. "Observations on the Prophetic in England." *Equipping the Saints* 4, no 4 (Fall, 1990): 28-9.

Mills, John. "Releasing the Oppressed: An Interview with John Wimber." *Renewal Magazine* (n.d.) n.p. (Wimber Collection, Regent University Library).

Newman, Josie. "Charismatic Revivalists Launch Church Network." *Charisma* (May 2008): 25.

Ostling, Richard N. and Helen Gibson. "Laughing for the Lord." *Time* 11, no. 7 (August 15, 1994): 2-3.

Panner, Jon. "Editor's Note." *Vineyard Reflections: John Wimber's Leadership Letter* (June/July 1993): 1-2.

Patterson, Ben. "Cause for Concern." *Christianity Today* (August 1986): 20.

Poloma, Margaret. "The 'Toronto Blessing': Charisma, Institutionalization, and Revival." *Society for the Scientific Study of Religion* 36, no. 2 (1997): 257-71.

_____. "The 'Toronto Blessing': A Holistic Model of Healing." *Journal for the Scientific Study of Religion* 37, no. 2 (1998): 257-72.

Price, Clive. "Revival Without Walls." *Charisma* (November 1995): 54-8.

_____. "When God Came to England." *Charisma* (November 1997): 48-50, 52, 54, 118.

_____. "'Alpha' Booms in England and Beyond." *Charisma* (November 1997): 53.

Rickards, Raymond R. "Supernatural? Naturally!" *On Being* (March 1987): 5-8, 10-12.

Saines, Don. "The Risk of Faith in Practice." *On Being* (February 1988): 5, 7-8.

Salter, Owen. "A New Toronto Blessing is Spreading in Australia." *Charisma* (September 1995): 21-2.

Sarles, Ken L. "An Appraisal of the Signs and Wonders Movement." *Bibliotheca Sacra* (January/March 1988): 57-82.

Smith, Kevin B. "Picking the Vineyards Fruit." *On Being* (February 1989): 8-12.

Springer, Kevin. "Paul Cain: A New Breed of Man." *Equipping the Saints* (Fall 1989): 11-13.

_____. "Paul Cain Answers Some Tough Questions About His Relationship with William Branham." *Equipping the Saints* 4, no. 4 (Fall 1990): 8-12.

_____. "Applying the Gifts to Everyday Life." *Charisma* (September 1985): 26-34.

_____. "KCF Renamed the Metro Vineyard." *Equipping the Saints* 4, no 4 (Fall 1990): 14.

Stafford, Tim. "Testing the Wine from John Wimber's Vineyard." *Christianity Today* (August 1986): 17-22.

Stafford, Tim and James Beverly. "God's Wonder Worker." *Christianity Today* (July 14, 1997): 46-7.

Stewart, Jimmy. "Vineyard Music's Wimber Dies." *Charisma* (April 1998): 36.

Thigpen, Paul. "How Is God Speaking Today?" *Charisma & Christian Life* (September 1989): 50-6.

Thompson, Sam. "A Vineyard Overview," *The Vineyard Newsletter* (Winter 1988): 2.

Unsigned. "Seaside Hosts 4,000 at Prayer." *Evening Argus*, Tuesday, October 30, 1985.

Walker, Andrew. "Pentecostalism Goes Middle Class." *New York Times*, Monday, April 15, 1985.

Wagner, C. Peter. "MC510: Signs, Wonders and Church Growth." *Christian Life* 44, no. 6 (October 1982): 48.

_____. "A Third Wave? Part 1." *First Fruits* (March 1985): 14.

_____. "A Third Wave?" *Pastoral Renewal* (July/August 1993): 1-5.

White, John. "MC510: A Course in Signs and Wonders." *Renewing Australia: The Wimber Edition* (June 1987): 8-10.

_____. "MC510: A Look Inside, Part I and Part II." *First Fruits* (July/August and September/October 1985): 7-10 and 23-26.

Williams, J. Rodman. "Biblical Truth and Experience: A Reply to Charismatic Chaos by John F. Macarthur, Jr." *Paraclete* (Summer 1993): 16-30.

Wimber, Carol. "A Hunger for God: A Reflective Look at the Vineyards Beginnings." *The Vineyard Newsletter* 2, no.3 (Fall 1987).

Wimber, John. "Zip to 3,000 in Five Years." *Christian Life* 44, no. 6 (October 1982): 13-21.

_____. "Ministering the Compassion of Jesus." *First Fruits* (March 1985): 3.

_____. "John Wimber Calls it Power Evangelism." *Charisma* (September 1985): 35.

_____. "A Time to Die." *Renewal* 127, (1986): 13-4.

_____. "Power Healing and a Vision of God's Compassion." *Renewal* no. 127 (December 1986): 9.

_____. "Spiritual Gifts: The Evangelicals' Neglected Inheritance." *Renewing Australia: The Wimber Edition* (June 1987): 4-7.

_____. "No Short Cuts to Maturity," *Equipping the Saints* 1, no. 4 (July/August 1987): 2.

_____. "Utter Obedience." *Pastoral Renewal* 12, no. 12 (September 1987): 12.

_____. "Sent into the Harvest Field." *Equipping the Saints* 1, no. 5 (September/October 1987): 2.

_____. "I Just Loved It." *Renewing Australia* (December 1987): 4-6.

_____. "The Cross." *Equipping the Saints* 2, no. 2 (Spring 1988): 2.

_____. "Why I Don't Respond to Criticism." *Equipping the Saints* 2 no. 1 (Summer 1988): 15-16.

_____. "Introducing Prophetic Ministry." *Equipping the Saints* 3, no. 4 (Fall 1989): 4-6, 30.

_____. "The True Call of the Church is the Cross." *Jesus Lifestyle no. 1* (Fourth Quarter 1989): 9.

_____. "Hearing God's Word: Scripture Provides Safeguards to Ensure That We Are Not Led Astray by So-Called 'Prophetic' Words." *Equipping the Saints* 3, no. 4 (Fall 1990): 22, 27.

_____. "A Response to Ernie Gruen's Controversy with Kansas City Fellowship." *Equipping the Saints* 4, no. 4 (Fall 1990): 4-7, 13-14.

_____. "Flowing in the Spirit: Risks and Rewards." *Charisma* (September 1990): 78, 80, 83.

_____. "Truce Called in Bickle Controversy: Accusers Agree to Turn Matter over to John Wimber and Vineyard Team." *Charisma & Christian Life* (September 1990): 42.

_____. "Were We Healed at the Cross?" *Charisma* (May 1991): 75-8.

_____. "Revival Fire." *Equipping the Saints* 5, no 1 (Winter 1991): 11.

_____. "Signs and Wonders: Wimber Breaks Silence to Answer Vineyard Critics." *Christianity Today* (March 1992): 66-68.

_____. "Kansas City 'Prophet' Disciplined." *Christianity Today* (March 9, 1992): 67.

_____. "Wimber Parts with Two Associates." *Christianity Today* (August 17, 1992): 48.

_____. "The Gift of Prophecy." *Charisma* (December 1992): 53-5.

_____. "Who Are We and Where Are We Going?" Part II. *Vineyard Reflections* (June/July 1993): 1-5.

_____. "Worship: Intimacy with God." *Equipping Magazine* 7, no. 3 (Summer 1993): 5-6.

_____. "Kansas City Feud Declared Dead." *Christianity Today* (July 19, 1993): 51

_____. "Liberating Women for Ministry and Leadership." *Vineyard Reflections* (March/April 1994): 1-2.

_____. "Seasons of New Beginnings." *Vineyard Reflections: John Wimber's Leadership Letter* (May/June 1994): 1-2.

_____. "Refreshing, Renewal, and Revival." *Vineyard Reflections: John Wimber's Leadership Letter* (July/August 1994): 5.

_____. "Visitation of the Spirit." *Ministries Today* (September/October 1994): 8-9.

_____. "Fulfill Your Ministry: John Wimber's Installation of Carl & Sonja Tuttle as Senior Pastor of the Anaheim Vineyard Sunday, Dec. 18, 1994." *Equipping the Saints* (Fourth Quarter 1994): 16-19.

_____. "Vineyard Leader Suffers Stroke." *Charisma* (March 1995): 81.

_____. "Toronto Blessing: Is It a Revival?" *Christianity Today* (May 15, 1995): 51.

_____. "Leaving But Not Quitting." *Equipping the Saints* (Third Quarter, 1996): 23.

_____. "Signs, Wonders, and Cancer." *Christianity Today* (October 1996): 51.

_____. "Staying Focused: The Vineyard as a Centered Set." *Vineyard Reflections: John Wimber's Leadership Letter* (July 1995-February 1996): 5.

_____. "When Cancer Strikes the Healer." *Christianity Today* (November 1996): 38-40.

_____. "Miracles are Not Complicated." *Charisma* (November 2007): 90-1.

_____. "Spiritual Warfare." *Spiritual Warfare*. Sydney, Australia, n.d.

Wimber, John and Kevin Springer. "John Wimber Calls It Power Evangelism." *Charisma* (September 1985): 35-38.

_____. "The Hardest Healing." *Charisma* (June 1987): 30-1, 34.

Woodward, Kenneth L. and Jeanne Gordon. "The Giggles are for God." *Newsweek* 124, no. 8 (February 20, 1995): 54

_____. "John Wimber Giveth and Taketh Away." *Alberta Report* (February 5, 1996): 37

Books

Armstrong, John, D. A Carson and James M. Boice. *Power Religion: The Selling Out of the Evangelical Church?* Chicago, IL: Moody Press, 1992.

Arnott, John. *The Father's Blessing*. Lake Mary, FL: Creation House, 1995.

_____. *Keep the Fire: Allowing the Spirit to Transform Your Life*. London: Marshall Pickering, 1996.

_____. *Experience the Blessing*. Ventura, CA: Renewal/Regal Books, 2000.

_____. *By Their Fruits: The Lasting Impact of Toronto in the U.K.* Milton Keynes, England: Word, 2001.

Beverly, James. *Holy Laughter and the Toronto Blessing: An Investigative Report*. Grand Rapids, MI: Zondervan Publishing House, 1995.

_____. *Revival Wars: A Critique of Counterfeit Revival*. Canada: Evangelical Research Ministries, 1997.

Bickle, Mike. *Passion for Jesus*. Lake Mary, FL: Creation House, 1993.

_____. *Growing in the Prophetic*. Lake Mary, FL: Creation House, 1996.

Boice, James M. "A Better Way: The Power of the Word and Spirit." In *Power Religion*, ed. Michael Scott Horton, 119-136. Chicago: Moody Press, 1992.

Blue, Ken. *Authority to Heal*. Downers Grove, IL: InterVarsity Press, 1987.

Brown, Harvey R. and John Arnott. *When God Strikes the Match: Igniting a Passion for Holiness and Renewal*. Shippensburg, PA: Revival Press, 1997.

Campbell, Wesley. *Welcoming a Visitation of the Holy Spirit*. Orlando: Creation House, 1996.

Chevreau, Guy. *Catch the Fire: The Toronto Blessing: An Experience of Renewal and Revival*. Toronto: HarperCollins, 1994.

_____. *Pray with Fire: Interceding in the Spirit*. London: Marshall Pickering, 1995.

_____. *Share the Fire: The Toronto Blessing and Grace Based Evangelism*. Shippensburg, PA: Revival Press, 1997.

Clark, Randy. *Lighting Fires: Keeping the Spirit of Revival Alive in Your Heart and the Hearts of Others around You*. Orlando, FL: Creation House, 1998.

_____. *There is More: Reclaiming the Power of Impartation*. Mechanicsburg, PA: Global Awakening, 2006.

Coates, Gerald. "The Ecumenist." In *John Wimber: His Influence and Legacy*, ed. David Pytches, 154-160. Surrey: Engle, 1998.

Coggins, James R. and Paul G. Hiebert, eds. *Wonders and the Word: An Examination of Issues Raised by John Wimber and the Vineyard Movement*. Winnipeg: MB: Kindred Press, 1989.

_____. "The Man, the Message and the Movement." In *Wonders and the Word: An Examination of Issues Raised by John Wimber and the Vineyard Movement*. Winnipeg, MB: Kindred Press, 1989.

Cray, Graham. "The Communicator." In *John Wimber: His Influence and Legacy*, ed. David Pytches, 127-143. Surrey: Eagle, 1998.

Deere, Jack. *Surprised by the Power of the Spirit*. Grand Rapids, Zondervan, 1993.

_____. *Surprised by the Voice of God: How God Speaks Today through Prophecies, Dreams, and Visions*. Grand Rapids: Zondervan, 1996.

_____. "The Prophet." In *John Wimber: His Influence and Legacy*, ed. David Pytches, 105-116. Surrey: Engle, 1998.

Doyle, Robert, John Woodhouse, Paul Barnett, and John Reid. *Signs & Wonders and Evangelicals: A Response to the Teachings of John Wimber*. Randburg: Fabel Distributors, 1987.

Enroth, Ronald M., Edward Erickson, and C. Breckenridge Peters. *The Jesus People: Old-Time Religion in the Age of Aquarius*. Grand Rapids, MI: Eerdmans, 1972.

Erickson, Douglas. *Living the Future: The Kingdom of God & the Holy Spirit in the Vineyard Movement*. United States, Independent Publishing, 2016.

Frisbee, Lonnie, Roger Sachs. *Not by Might Nor by Power: Book One*. Santa Maria, CA: Freedom Crusade, 2012.

Friesen, Abraham. "Wimber, Word and Spirit." In *Wonders and the Word*, eds. James R. Coggins and Paul G. Hiebert, 35-47. Winnipeg, MB: Kindred Press, 1989.

Fulton, Bob and Penny. "The Family Man." In *John Wimber: his Influence and Legacy*, ed. David Pytches, 40-49. Surrey: Eagle 1998.

Gibbs, Eddie. "The Evangelist." In *John Wimber: His Influence and Legacy*, ed. David Pytches, 71-83. Surrey: Eagle, 1998.

Graham, Billy. *The Jesus Generation*. Grand Rapids, MI: Zondervan, 1971.

Green, Melody and David Hazard. *No Compromise: The Life Story of Keith Green*. Eugene, OR: Harvest House, 1996.

Greig, Gary S. and Kevin N. Springer. *The Kingdom and the Power: Are Healing and the Spiritual Gifts Used by Jesus and the Early Church Meant for the Church Today?* Ventura, CA: Regal, 1993.

Grudem, Wayne. *The Gift of Prophecy in the New Testament and Today*. Westchester, IL: Crossway Books, 1988.

_____. ed. *Are Miraculous Gifts for Today? Four Views*. Grand Rapids, MI: Zondervan, 1996.

Gunstone, John. "An Anglican Evolution." In *John Wimber: His Influence and Legacy*, ed. David Pytches, 224-236. Surrey: Engle, 1998.

Hanegraaff, Hank. *Christianity in Crisis*. Eugene, OR: Harvest House Publishers, 1993.

_____. *Counterfeit Revival: Looking for God in All the Wrong Places*. Dallas: Word, 1997.

Hiebert, Paul. "Healing and the Kingdom." In *Wonders and the Word*, eds. James R. Coggins and Paul G. Hiebert, 123-4. Winnipeg: Kindred Press, 1989.

Hill, Steve. *The Pursuit of Revival*. Lake Mary, FL: Creation House, 1997.

Horton, Michael Scott. ed. *Power Religion: The Selling Out of the Evangelical Church?* Chicago: Moody Bible Institute, 1992.

Hubbard, David Allen. "Foreword." In *Ministry and the Miraculous: A Case Study at Fuller Theological Seminary* edited by Lewis B. Smedes (Pasadena, CA: Fuller Theological Seminary, 1987): 6.

Hummel, Charles. *Fire in the Fireplace: Charismatic Renewal in the Nineties.* Downers Grove, IL: InterVarsity, 1993.

Hunt, Dave and T. A. McMahon. *The Seduction of Christianity Spiritual Discernment in the Last Days.* Eugene, OR: Harvest Home, 1985.

Hunter, Todd." The Leader." In *John Wimber: His Influence and Legacy*, ed. David Pytches, 180-193. Surrey: Engle, 1998.

Jackson, Bill. *Quest for the Radical Middle: A History of the Vineyard.* Cape Town, South Africa: Vineyard International, 1999.

Jackson, John Paul. *Needless Casualties of War.* Ft. Worth, TX: Streams, 1999.

Kraft, Charles H. *Christianity in Culture.* Maryknolls, NY: Orbis, 1979.

_____. "Shifting Worldviews, Shifting Attitudes." In *Power Encounters Among Christians in the Western World*, ed. Kevin Springer, 57-68. San Francisco: Harper & Row, 1988.

_____. "Spiritual Warfare: A Neo-charismatic Perspective." In *The New International Dictionary of Pentecostal and Charismatic Movements*, eds. Stanley M. Burgess and Eduard M. Van Der Mass, 1091-96. Grand Rapids, MI: Zondervan, 2002.

_____. "Vineyard Christian Fellowship." In *The New International Dictionary of Pentecostal and Charismatic Movements*, eds. Stanley M. Burgess and Eduard M. Van Der Mass, 1177. Grand Rapids, MI: Zondervan, 2002.

_____. *Christianity with Power: Your Worldview and Your Experience of the Supernatural.* Manila: OMF Literature, 1989.

_____. *Communicate with Power: Jesus the Model for Contemporary Communication.* Manila: OMF, 1991.

_____. *I Give You Authority.* Grand Rapids, MI: Chosen Books, 1997.

Kuglin, Robert J. *The Toronto Blessing: What Would the Holy Spirit Say?* Camp Hill, PA: Horizon Books, 1996.

Lewis, David. *Healing: Fiction, Fantasy, or Fact? A Comprehensive Analysis of Healing and Associated Phenomena at Wimber's Harrogate Conference.* London: Hodder & Stoughton, 1990.

Lewis, Donald M. "An Historian's Assessment." In *Wonders and the Word*, eds. James R. Coggins and Paul G. Hiebert, 52-61. Winnipeg: Kindred Press, 1989.

MacArthur, John F. *The Charismatics.* Grand Rapids, MI: Zondervan, 1978.

_____. *Charismatic Chaos.* Grand Rapids, MI: Zondervan, 1992.

Master, Peter. *The Healing Epidemic.* London: Wakeman Trust, 1988.

Millar, Sandy. *"A Friend's Recollection."* In John Wimber: His Influence and Legacy edited by David Pytches (Surrey, UK: Eagle, 1998) 269-287.

Mitton, Michael. *The Heart of Toronto: Exploring the Spirituality of the Toronto Blessing.* Cambridge: Grove Books, 1995.

Mumford, Eleanor. "Father Figure and Pastor." In *John Wimber: His Influence and Legacy*, ed. David Pytches, 84-94. Surrey, UK: Engle, 1998.

Mumford, John. "Vineyard Movement Founder." In *John Wimber: His Influence and Legacy*, ed. David Pytches, 194-205. Surrey, UK: Engle, 1998.

Nathan, Rich and Ken Wilson. *Empowered Evangelicals: Bringing Together the Best of the Evangelical and Charismatic Worlds.* Ann Arbor, MI: Vine Books, 1995.

Nathan, Rich. "The Bible Teacher." In *John Wimber*, ed. David Pytches, 96-7. Surrey, U.K.: Engle, 1998.

Nicholson, Steve. "Church Planter." In *John Wimber: His Influence and Legacy*, ed. David Pytches, 117-126. Surrey, UK: Engle, 1998.

Oakland, Roger. *New Wine or Old Deception? A Biblical Perspective of Experience Based Christianity.* Costa Mesa, CA: The Word for Today, 1995.

Park, Andy. *To Know You More.* Downers Grove: IVP Books, 2002.

Pawson, David. *Is the Blessing Biblical? Thinking Through the Toronto Phenomenon.* London: Hodder & Stoughton, 1995.

Packer, J. I. "The Intellectual." In *John Wimber: His Influence and Legacy*, ed. David Pytches, 257-268. Surrey, UK: Engle, 1998.

Payne, Tony. *No Laughing Matter: The Toronto Blessing & Real Christianity.* New South Wales, London: St. Matthias Press, 1995.

Percy, Martyn. *The Toronto Blessing.* Oxford: Latimer House, 1996.

Piorek, Ed. *The Father Loves You: An Invitation to Perfect Love.* Cape Town, South Africa: Vineyard International, 2013.

Poloma, Margaret. *The Charismatic Movement: Is There a New Pentecost?* Boston: Twayne, 1982.

_____. *The Toronto Report: A Preliminary Sociological Assessment of the Toronto Blessing.* Bradford-on-Avon: Terra Nova, 1996.

_____. *Main Street Mystics: The Toronto Blessing and Reviving Pentecostalism.* Walnut Creek, CA: AltaMira Press, 2003.

Pritchard, Todd. "The Businessman." In *John Wimber: His Influence and Legacy*, ed. David Pytches, 161-179. Surrey, UK: Engle, 1998.

Pytches, David. "Fully Anglican, Fully Renewed." In *Riding the Third Wave* ed. Kevin Springer (Hants, U.K.: Marshall Pickering, 1987), 169-76.

_____. "A Man Called John." In *John Wimber: His influence and Legacy*, ed. David Pytches, 9-39. Surrey, UK: Engle, 1998.

_____. "Signs and Wonders." In *John Wimber: His Influence and Legacy*, ed. David Pytches, 127-43. Surrey, UK: Engle, 1998.

_____. *Some Said It Thundered*. Nashville, TN: Oliver Nelson, 1991.

_____. ed. *John Wimber: His Influence and Legacy* by Carol Wimber and Church Leaders. Guildford, Surrey, UK: Eagle, 1998.

Redman, Matt. "Worshipper and Musician." In *John Wimber: His Influence and Legacy*, ed. David Pytches, 63-70. Surrey, UK: Engle, 1998.

_____. "Rodney Howard-Brown." In *The New International Dictionary of Pentecostal and Charismatic Movements*, eds. Stanley M. Burgess, and Eduard M. Van Der Mass, 774. Grand Rapids, MI: Zondervan, 2002.

_____. *Images of Revival: Another Wave Rolls In*. Shippensburg, PA: Destiny Images, 1997.
Roberts, Dave. *The Toronto Blessing*. Eastbourne, U.K.: Kingsway, 1994.

Scotland, Nigel. "Quo Vadis?" In *John Wimber: His Influence and Legacy*, ed. David Pytches, 305-320. Surrey, UK: Engle, 1998.

Smedes, Lewis B., ed. *Ministry and the Miraculous: A Case Study at Fuller Theological Seminary*. Pasadena, CA: Fuller Theological Seminaries, 1987.

Smith, Chuck. *Charisma Vs. Charismania*. Costa Mesa, CA: The Word for Today, 1993.

_____. *Calvary Chapel Distinctives*. Costa Mesa, CA: The Word for Today, 1993.

Springer, Kevin, ed. *Riding the Third Wave*. U.K.: Marshall Morgan and Scott, 1987.

_____. *Power Encounters* (San Francisco: Harper and Row, 1988).

Tuttle, Carl. *Reckless Mercy: A Trophy of God's Grace*. United States: Coaching Saints, 2017.

Twelftree, Graham. "Fresh Outpouring of the Holy Spirit." In *The Impact of Toronto*, ed. Wallace Boulton, 29-31. Sussex: Monarch, 1995.

Virgo, Terry." A House Church Evaluation." In *John Wimber: His Influence and Legacy*, ed. David Pytches, 237-243. Surrey, UK: Engle, 1998.

Wagner, C. Peter, ed. *Signs & Wonders Today*. Altamonte Springs, FL: Creation House, 1989.

Wagner, C. Peter and David Cannistraci. *Apostles and the Emerging Apostolic Movement*. Ventura, CA: Regal Books, 1998.

Wagner, C. Peter and F. Douglas Pennoyer. *Engaging the Enemy: How to Fight and Defeat Territorial Spirits*. Ventura, CA: Regal Books, 1991.

Wagner, C. Peter and Pablo Deiros. *The Rising Revival*. Ventura: Renewal Books, 1998.

Wagner, C. Peter. "God Wasn't Pulling My Leg." In *Power Encounters Among Christians in the Western World*, ed. Kevin Springer, 43-55. San Francisco: Harper & Row, 1988.

_____. "Vineyard Christian Fellowship." In *The New International Dictionary of Pentecostal and Charismatic Movements*, ed. Stanley M. Burgess and Eduard M. Van Der Mass, 1177. Grand Rapids, MI: Zondervan, 2002.

_____. "John Wimber." In *The New International Dictionary of Pentecostal and Charismatic Movements*, ed. by Stanley M. Burgess and Eduard Van Der Mass, 1199-2000. Grand Rapids: Zondervan, 2002.

_____. "A Third Wave." In *The New International Dictionary of Pentecostal and Charismatic Movements*, ed. Stan Burgess and Eduard Van Der Maas, 1141. Grand Rapids: Zondervan, 2002.

_____. *Look Out! The Pentecostals Are Coming*. Carol Streams, IL: Creation House, 1973.

_____. *Spiritual Power and Church Growth: Lessons from the Amazing Growth of Pentecostal Churches in Latin America*. Altamonte Springs, FL: Strang Communications, 1986.

_____. *Another 100 Years: Which Way for Pentecostal Mission?* South Plainfield, NJ: Bridge Publishing, 1986.

_____. "MC520: Genesis of a Concept." In *Signs and Wonders Today*, ed. C. Peter Wagner, 41-2 (Altamonte Springs, FL: Creation House, 1987).

_____. *The Third Wave of the Holy Spirit: Encountering the Power of Signs and Wonders Today*. Ann Arbor, MI: Vine Books, 1988.

_____. *How to Have a Healing Ministry without Making Your Church Sick*. Ventura, CA: Regal Books, 1990.

_____. *Wrestling with Dark Angels*. Ventura, CA: Regal Books, 1990.

_____. *Breaking Strongholds in Your City*. Ventura, CA: Regal Books, 1993.

_____. *Confronting the Enemy*. Ventura, CA: Regal Books, 1996.

_____. *The New Apostolic Churches*. Ventura, CA: Regal Books, 1998.

_____. *Wrestling with Alligators, Prophets and Theologians: Lessons from a Lifetime in the Church – A Memoir*. Ventura, CA: Regal Books, 2010.

Walvoord, John F. *The Rapture Question*. Grand Rapids: Zondervan, 1957.

Warner, Rob. *Prepare for Revival*. London: Hodder and Stoughton, 1995.

Watson, Anne. *"The Third Wave Has Only Begun."* In Power Encounter, ed. Kevin Springer, 15-24. San Francisco: Harper & Row, 1988.

Watson, Anne. "The Third Wave Has Only Just Begun." In *Power Encounters*, 15-24.

Watson, David. *I Believe in Evangelism*. Grand Rapids, MI: Eerdmans, 1976.

_____. *I Believe in the Church*. Grand Rapids, MI: Eerdmans, 1979.

_____. *Called and Committed*. Wheaton, IL: Harold Shaw, 1982.

_____. *Fear No Evil: Facing the Final Test of Faith*. London: Hodder & Stoughton, 1984.

Waugh, Geoff. *Flashpoints of Revival: History's Mighty Revivals*. Shippensburg, PA: Destiny Image, 1998.

White, John. *When the Spirit Comes with Power: Signs & Wonders among God's People*. Downers Grove, IL: InterVarsity, 1988.

Whitehead, Charles. "A Catholic Evaluation." In *John Wimber: His Influence and Legacy*, ed. David Pytches, 218-223. Surrey: Engle, 1998.

Williams, Don. *Signs, Wonders and the Kingdom of God*. Ann Arbor, MI: Vine Books, 1989.

_____. "Friend and Encourager." In *John Wimber: His Influence and Legacy*, ed. David Pytches, 40-9. Guildford, Surrey, UK: England, 1998.

Williams, J. Rodman. "Biblical Truth and Experience: A Reply to *Charismatic Chaos* by John F. MacArthur, Jr.," *Paraclete* (Summer 1993): 16-30.

Wimber, Carol. *John Wimber: The Way It Was*. London: Hotter & Stoughton, 1999.

_____. "A Hunger for God." In *Power Encounters Among Christians in the Western World*, ed. Kevin Springer, 3-14. San Francisco: Harper & Row, 1988.

_____. "A Wife's Tribute." In *John Wimber: His Influence and Legacy*, ed. David Pytches, 302-3. Guildford, Surrey, UK: England, 1998.

_____. "Coping with Controversy and Suffering." In *John Wimber: His Influence and Legacy*, ed. David Pytches, 288-297. Surrey, UK: Engle, 1998.

Wimber, Christy, ed. *Everyone Gets to Play: John Wimber's Writings and Teachings on Life Together in Christ*. Boise, ID: Ampelon, 2008.

Wimber, John. *MC 510 Syllabus: Signs and Wonders and Church Growth*. Vineyard Ministries International Placentia, CA: Vineyard Ministries, 1984. Wimber Collection: Special Collections, Regent University Library, Virginia Beach, Virginia.

_____. *Kingdom of God*. Placentia, CA: Vineyard Ministries International, 1985.

_____. *Kingdom of Mercy: Living the Power of Forgiveness*. Ann Arbor, MI: Servant Publications, 1987.

_____. *Kingdom Ministry: Walking in the Power of Service*. Ann Arbor, MI: Servant Publications, 1987.

_____. *Kingdom Suffering: Facing Difficulty and Trial in the Christian Life*. Ann Arbor, MI: Servant Publications, 1988.

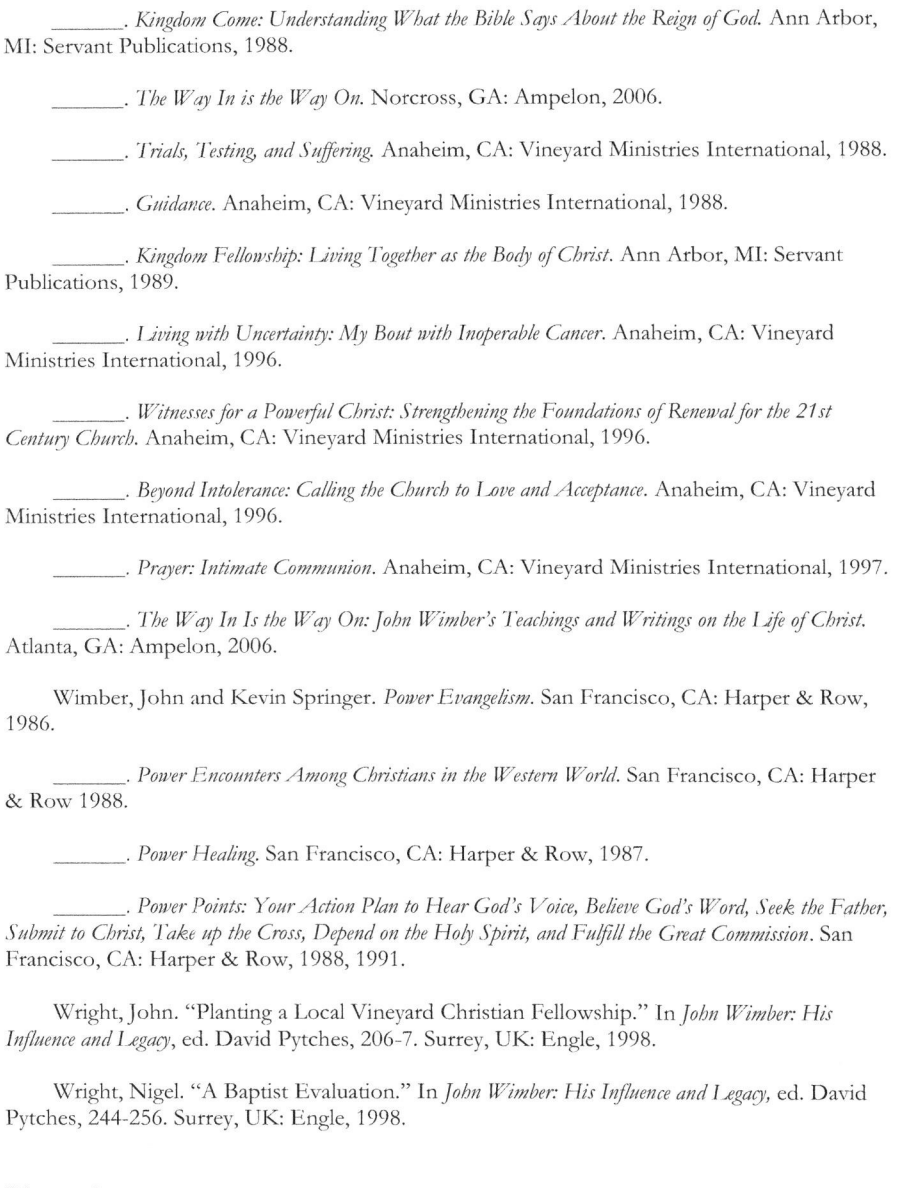

_____. *Kingdom Come: Understanding What the Bible Says About the Reign of God.* Ann Arbor, MI: Servant Publications, 1988.

_____. *The Way In is the Way On.* Norcross, GA: Ampelon, 2006.

_____. *Trials, Testing, and Suffering.* Anaheim, CA: Vineyard Ministries International, 1988.

_____. *Guidance.* Anaheim, CA: Vineyard Ministries International, 1988.

_____. *Kingdom Fellowship: Living Together as the Body of Christ.* Ann Arbor, MI: Servant Publications, 1989.

_____. *Living with Uncertainty: My Bout with Inoperable Cancer.* Anaheim, CA: Vineyard Ministries International, 1996.

_____. *Witnesses for a Powerful Christ: Strengthening the Foundations of Renewal for the 21st Century Church.* Anaheim, CA: Vineyard Ministries International, 1996.

_____. *Beyond Intolerance: Calling the Church to Love and Acceptance.* Anaheim, CA: Vineyard Ministries International, 1996.

_____. *Prayer: Intimate Communion.* Anaheim, CA: Vineyard Ministries International, 1997.

_____. *The Way In Is the Way On: John Wimber's Teachings and Writings on the Life of Christ.* Atlanta, GA: Ampelon, 2006.

Wimber, John and Kevin Springer. *Power Evangelism.* San Francisco, CA: Harper & Row, 1986.

_____. *Power Encounters Among Christians in the Western World.* San Francisco, CA: Harper & Row 1988.

_____. *Power Healing.* San Francisco, CA: Harper & Row, 1987.

_____. *Power Points: Your Action Plan to Hear God's Voice, Believe God's Word, Seek the Father, Submit to Christ, Take up the Cross, Depend on the Holy Spirit, and Fulfill the Great Commission.* San Francisco, CA: Harper & Row, 1988, 1991.

Wright, John. "Planting a Local Vineyard Christian Fellowship." In *John Wimber: His Influence and Legacy*, ed. David Pytches, 206-7. Surrey, UK: Engle, 1998.

Wright, Nigel. "A Baptist Evaluation." In *John Wimber: His Influence and Legacy,* ed. David Pytches, 244-256. Surrey, UK: Engle, 1998.

Electronic

Bickle, Mike "Things I learned from John Wimber." http://mikebickle.org/resources/resource/2974. Accessed December 10, 2010.

Cain, Paul. "Prophecy for the Vineyard." Anaheim, CA: Vineyard Christian Fellowship, 1989, Audio Cassette.

Frisbee, Lonnie. "Mother's Day Service." Anaheim, CA, May 1980. Audio Cassette.

Fuller Seminary History. http://www.fuller.edu/about-fuller/mission-and-history/history.aspx. Accessed on July 27, 2010.

Gruen, Ernie. "Documentation of the Aberrant Practices and Teachings of Kansas City Fellowship," (Grace Ministries). http://www.birthpangs.org/articles/kcp/kcp-gruen.html. Accessed March 10, 2010.

Hunter, Andrea. "Ken Gulliksen: Surprised by Grace and Rescued by Love," Assistant News Service. http://www.assistnews.net/Stories/2007/s07010146.htm.

Jackson, Bill. "What in the World is Happening to us?" www.champaign.vineyard.org/papers/witw/witw.text/ (A defense of the Toronto Blessing phenomena).

Jennings, Peter. "In the Name of God," ABC Documentary, 1995. http://www.youtube.com/watch?v=9I9YCue3Fkk&feature=related

Randolph, Larry. Interview with Randy Clark, April 2009. http://www.globalawakening.com/Articles/1000050986/Global_Awakening/Archive/Video_Podcast/Episode_67_Larry.aspx

_____. A History of the Awakening of 1992-1995, http://www.revival-library.org/catalogues/pentecostal/riss.html

Sabatino, David. Frisbee: *The Life and Death of a Hippie Preacher*. Truly, CA: Jester Media and KQED, 2006. DVD.

Tuttle, Carl. "Vineyard Worship—The Early Years – Part 1" http://www.carltuttle.com/wimber-years/2009/1/31/vineyard-worship-the-early-years-part-1.html. Accessed 1/05/10.

Wimber, Carol. *Back to Our Roots: Stories of the Vineyard*: Vineyard Music, USA, 2006. DVD.

Wimber, John. *Spiritual Gifts: Part 1 and 2*. Anaheim, CA: Vineyard Ministries International, 1985, Audio Cassettes (12).

_____. *Prayer: Intimate Communication*. Anaheim, CA: Vineyard Ministries International, 1985, Audio Cassettes (6).

_____. "Walk With Him in Holiness." In *Equipping the Saints Series: The Way on Repentance in the Body of Christ*. Anaheim, CA: Vineyard Ministries International, 1985, Audio Cassettes Vol. 2, Tape 5.

_____. *The Way On: Repentance in the Body of Christ*. Anaheim, CA: Vineyard Ministries International, 1985, Audio Cassettes Vol. 1 and 2 (16).

_____. *Healing: A Biblical and Historical Perspective*. Anaheim, CA: Vineyard Ministries International, 1986, Audio Cassettes (8).

_____. *The Cross*. Anaheim, CA: Vineyard Ministries International, 1986, CD (13).

_____. *I'm a Fool for Christ, Who's Fool Are You?* Vineyard Music, USA, 1987, DVD.

_____. "Spiritual Warfare", Stafford, TX: Vineyard Music Group, 2004, CD, Vol. 2, no. 3.

_____. "Signs and Wonders and Church Growth Conference." http://www.youtube.com/watch?v=gygnuTpTg7E&feature. Accessed February 4, 2010.

_____. "Signs and Wonders Conference," Anaheim CA,1985. https://www.youtube.com/watch?v=wGkob0n363A. Accessed July 10, 2019.

_____. *Kingdom of God*. Anaheim, CA, n.d. Audio Cassette.

_____. *Wimber's Personal Testimony*. Original audio cassette: Special Collections, Regent University, Virginia Beach, Virginia.

Wimber, John and Bob Fulton. *Church Planting: God's Heart for Expansion Vol. 1*. Anaheim, CA: Vineyard Ministries International, 1985. Audio Cassettes (6).

_____. *Church Planting: God's Heart for Expansion Vol. 2*. Anaheim, CA: Vineyard Ministries International, n.d., Audio Cassettes (6).

Wimber, John and C. Peter Wagner. *MC510: Signs, Wonders and Church Growth*. Recorded in Pasadena, CA, 1982. Original audio cassettes (16): Wimber Collection: Special Collections, Regent University, Virginia Beach, Virginia.

Letters

John Arnott. "Letter to John Wimber." Special Collection, Regent University Library, Virginia Beach, Virginia.

_____. "An Open Letter for General Distribution." Wimber Collection: Special Collections Regent University Library, Virginia Beach, Virginia.

Bickle, Mike. Letter addressed to Ernie Gruen, pastor Full Faith Church of Love, Shawnee, KA. (April 29, 1990).

_____. "Open Letter to Ernie Gruen." Wimber Collection: Special Collections, Regent University Library.

Gruen, Ernest J. "What's the Problem?" An Open Letter by Ernie Gruen, Pastor Full Faith Church of Love. (January 22, 1990).

_____. Letter addressed to Mike Bickle, pastor Kansas City Fellowship, Kansas City, MO. (April 4, 1990).

Deere, Jack. "Vineyard and Polity Regarding Prophetic." Wimber Collection: Special Collections, Regent University Library, Virginia Beach, Virginia.

Hunter, Todd. "Letter to Vineyard Pastors." Special Collections Regent University Virginia Beach, Virginia.

Derek Prince and Al Sarno. "Memo to 700 Club Counselors." (April, 1990). Personal files of Vinson Synan.

Interviews

Bickle, Mike. Telephone interview with the author, September 9, 2019.

Blue, Ken. Telephone interview with the author, October 5, 2010.

Clark, Randy. Telephone interview with the author, October 16, 2010.

Fulton, Bob. Personal interview with the author, February 11, 2010.

Griffin, Winn. Telephone interview with the author, June, 2016.

Grudem, Wayne. Personal interview with the author, February 23, 2010.

Jackson, Bill. Telephone interview with the author, August 29, 2011.

Jackson, John Paul. Telephone interview with the author, November 12, 2010.

Poloma, Margaret. Personal interview with the author, June 28, 2007.

Spicer, Linda. Telephone interview with the author, January 14, 2010.

Spittler, Russell. Personal interview with the author, February 9, 2010.

Suffi, Tino. Personal interview with the author, February 10, 2010.

Synan, Vinson. Personal interview with the author, August 23, 2011.

Tuttle, Carl. Personal interview with the author, February 8, 2010.

Wagner, C. Peter. Telephone interview with the author, August 10, 2010.

Waggoner, Bert. Telephone interview with the author, August 24, 2011.

Wimber, Tim. Personal interview with the author, September 13, 2008.

_____. Personal interview with the author, February 10, 2010.

_____. Telephone interview with the author, February 3, 2010.

Lecture/Conference Materials and Unpublished Manuscripts

McClure, Margie. "A Diary of the South African Mission." Special Collections, Regent University Library, Virginia Beach, VA

Wimber, John. "Kingdom of God." Paper presented at the Pastoral Renewal Leaders Seminar, 1987.

_____. "Kingdom of God" Vol. 1-2. Pastoral Renewal Leaders Seminar. (March 13-14, 1987).

_____. "School For Prophecy." Anaheim, CA: Mercy Publishing, 1988.

_____. "Prophecy Conference," Lecture notes. Special Collections, Regent University Library, Virginia Beach, Virginia. (Anaheim, CA: Mercy Publishing, 1989).

_____. "The Way of Holiness." In *Holiness Unto the Lord* conference notes. Anaheim, CA: Mercy Publishing, 1990.

_____. "Strategic Level Spiritual Warfare: John Wimber Responds." Lecture 1: Kingdom Warfare Conference. Anaheim, CA (January 1993): 1-13.

_____. "Kingdoms in Conflict: Spiritual Warfare and the Spirit of the Age." Lecture 2: Kingdom Warfare Conference. Anaheim, CA (January 1993): 1-14.

_____. "The Weapons of our Warfare: The Sword of the Spirit, the Word of God." Lecture 3: Kingdom Warfare Conference. Anaheim, CA (January 1993): 1-15.

_____. "Kingdoms in Conflict: Spiritual Warfare and the Age of the Spirit." Paper presented at the Kingdom Warfare Conference, Anaheim, CA, 1993.

_____. "The Weapons of Our Warfare: The Sword of the Spirit, the Word of God." Paper presented at the Kingdom Warfare Conference, Anaheim, CA, 1993.

_____. "Thoughts on C. Peter Wagner's Lecture on Strategic Level Spiritual Warfare: A Biblical Rationale." (April 8, 1994): 1-7.

_____. "Equipping the Saints." Paper presented at the Vineyard Conference, n.d.

_____. "Five Steps in the Healing Procedure." Wimber Collection: Special Collections, Regent University Library, Virginia Beach, VA. n.d.

_____. "Equipping the Saints: The Vineyard Conference." (Anaheim, CA) n.d.

_____. "Spiritual Warfare" A four-part teaching. Sydney, Australia. n.d.

_____. "John Wimber Responds to Phenomena." Wimber Collection, Special Collections, Regent University Special Collections, Virginia Beach, Virginia.

Unsigned. *Memorial Service of John Wimber*, 1997. Original, unpublished copy. VCR.

Position Papers

Deere, Jack. "The Vineyard's Response to the Briefing," 1-31: *Vineyard Position Paper 2*, 1992.

Grudem, Wayne. "The Vineyard's Response to the Standard," 1-37: *Vineyard Position Paper 3*, 1992.

_____. "Power & Truth: A Response to the Critiques of Vineyard Teaching and Practice by D. A. Carson, James Montgomery Boice, and John H. Armstrong in Power Religion," 1-62: *Vineyard Position Paper 4*, 1993.

Nathan, Rich. "A Response to Charismatic Chaos: The Book Written by John F. MacArthur, Jr.," 1-27: *Vineyard Position Paper 5*, 1993.

Wimber, John. "Why I Respond to Criticism," 1-7: *Vineyard Position Paper 1*, 1992.

Vineyard position papers available on: www.vineyardusa.org/publications/positionpapers.aspx.

Vineyard Journals

First Fruits (1984-1986)

Equipping the Saints (1987-1996)

The Vineyard Newsletter (1986-1988)

Vineyard Reflections (1993-97)

Voice of Vineyard (1997-2000)

Cutting Edge (2000 – Present)

Secondary Sources

Magazine and Journal Articles

Albrecht, Daniel E. "Pentecostal Spirituality: Looking through the Lens of Ritual." *PNEUMA* 14, no. 2 (Fall 1992): 107-25.

Anderson, Gordon. "The Baptism in the Holy Spirit, Initial Evidence, and a Model." *Paraclete* (Fall 1993): 1-10.

Archer, Kenneth J. "Pentecostal Hermeneutics: Restoration and Prospect." *Journal of Pentecostal Theology* 8, (April 1996): 63-81.

_____. "Early Pentecostal Biblical Interpretation." *Journal of Pentecostal Theology* 18, (2001): 32-70.

_____. "Early Pentecostal Biblical Interpretation." *Journal of Pentecostal Theology* 8, (2001): 32-70.

Benn, Wallace and Mark Burkill. "A Theological and Pastoral Critique of the Teachings of John Wimber." *Churchman* 101, no. 102 (1987): 101-13.

Boone, Jerome R. "Community and Worship: The Key Components of Pentecostal Christian Formation." *Journal of Pentecostal Theology* 8, (1996): 129-42.

Carter, Steve. "Demon Possession and the Christian." *Asian Journal of Pentecostal Studies* (January 2000): 19-31.

Dempster, Murray. "Christian Social Concern and Biblical Mandate of Social Justice." *PNEUMA* 9, (Fall 1987): 222-52.

Higher, John. "The Devil, Demons & Spiritual Warfare: A Panel of Experts Answer to Often-Asked Questions About the Church's Battle Against the Forces of Darkness." *Charisma* (February 1994): 52-7.

Johnson, J. E., "Society of Friends." *Evangelical Dictionary of Theology*, ed. Walter A. Elwell, 470-1. Grand Rapids, MI: Academics, 2001.

Kammer, Donald. "The Perplexing Power of John Wimber's Power Encounter." *Churchman* 106, no. 1 (1992): 45-64.

Kay, William K. "Three Generation On: The Methodology of Pentecostal History." *European Pentecostal Theological Association Bulletin* 11, no. 1-2 (1992): 58-70.

Loren, Junia C. "Legacy of a Humble Hero." *Charisma and Christian Life* Vol 33 (November 1, 2007): 89, 91-93, 112.

Lovelace, Richard F. "The Surprising Works of God: Jonathan Edwards on Revival, Then and Now." *Christianity Today* 39, no. 10 (1995): 5.

Macchia, Frank D. "Sighs Too Deep for Words: Towards a Theology of Glossolalia." *Journal of Pentecostal Theology* (October 1992): 47-73.

McDonnell, Killian and George Montague. "The Determinative Doctrine of the Holy Spirit." *Theology Today* 39, no. 2 (1989): 142-61.

Pluss, Jean-Daniel. "Initial Evidence or Evidential Initials? A European Point of View on a Pentecostal Distinctive." *Asian Journal of Pentecostal Studies* (July 2003): 213-22.

Powers, Janet Evert. "Missionary Tongues?" *Journal of Pentecostal Theology* (2000): 38-55.

Pratt, Thomas. "The Need to Dialogue: A Review of the Debate on Signs, Wonders, Miracles, and Spiritual Warfare Literature of the Third Wave Movement." *PNEUMA* (Spring 1991): 7-32.

Sarles, Ken L. "An Appraisal of the Signs and Wonders Movement." *Bibliotheca sacra*, 145 no. 577 January/March (1988): 57-82.

Wacker, Grant. "Wimber and Wonders: What About Miracles Today?" *The Reformed Journal* 37, no. 4 (1987): 4.

Books

Albrecht, Daniel E. *Rites in the Spirit: A Ritual Approach to Pentecostal/Charismatic Spirituality*. Sheffield: Sheffield Academic, 1999.

_____. "An Anatomy of Worship: A Pentecostal Analysis." In *The Spirit and Spirituality: Essays in Honor of Russell P. Spittler*, ed. Wonsuk Ma and Robert Menzies. London: T & T Clark International, 2004.

Anderson, Alan. *An Introduction to Pentecostalism*. Cambridge, U.K.: Cambridge University Press, 2004.

Anderson, Robert Mapes. *Vision of the Disinherited: The Making of American Pentecostalism*. Oxford: Oxford Press, 1979.

Arrington, F. L. "Hermeneutics, Historical Perspectives on Pentecostal and Charismatic." In *Dictionary of Pentecostal and Charismatic Movements*, ed. Stanley M. Burgess and Gary B. McGee, 376-89. Grand Rapids: Zondervan, 1988.

Barclay, Robert. *Barclay's Apology in Modern English*, ed. Dean Freiday. Second ed. Elberon, NJ: Sowers, 1967.

Bartleman, Frank. *Azusa Street: An Eye Witness Account*, ed. Vinson Synan. Gainesville: Bridge-Logos, 1980.

Barrett, David B. "Global Statistics." In *The New International Dictionary of Pentecostal and Charismatic Movements*, ed. Stanley M. Burgess and Gary B. McGee, 284-302. Grand Rapids: Zondervan, 2002.

Baxter, J. Sidlow. *Divine Healing of the Body*. Grand Rapids: Zondervan, 1979.

Bennett, Dennis. *Nine O'clock in the Morning*. Gainesville, FL: Bridges-Logos, 1970.

Bosworth, F. F. *Christ the Healer*. Grand Rapids: Fleming H. Revell, 1973.

Bright, John. *The Kingdom of God*. Nashville: Abingdon, 1953.

Burgess, Stanley. *The Holy Spirit: Ancient Christian Traditions*. Peabody, MA: Hendrickson, 1984.

_____. "Cutting the Taproot." In *Spirit and Renewal: Essays in Honor of J. Rodman Williams*, ed. Mark W. Wilson, 56-66. Sheffield: Sheffield Academic Press, n.d.

_____. "Proclaiming the Gospel with Miraculous Gifts in the Post-Biblical Early Church." In *The Kingdom and the Power*, ed. Gary S. and Kevin N. Springer Greig, 277-88. Ventura, CA: Regal Books, 1993.

_____. "Introduction." In *The New International Dictionary of Pentecostal and Charismatic Movements*, ed. Stanley M. Burgess and Gary B. McGee, 284-302. Grand Rapids: Zondervan, 2002.

Colson, Charles, ed. *Power Religion: The Selling Out of the Evangelical Church?* Chicago, IL: Moody Bible Institute, 1992.

Cullmann, Oscar. *Christ and Time*. Philadelphia: Westminster Press, 1964.

Dayton, Donald. *Theological Roots of Pentecostalism*. Peabody, MA: Hendrickson Publishing, 1987.

DeArteaga, William. *Quenching the Spirit: Examining Centuries of Opposition to the Moving of the Holy Spirit*. St. Mary's, FL: Creation House, 1992.

Dempster, Murray A., Byron D. Klaus, and Douglas Petersen. *Called and Empowered: Global Mission in Pentecostal Perspective*. Peabody, MA: Hendrickson, 1981.

Dempster, Murray A. *The Globalization of Pentecostalism*. Carlisle, CA: Peternoster, 1999.

Dixon, Patrick. *Signs of Revival*. Eastbourne, U.K.: Kingsway, 1994.

Dobson, James. *When God Doesn't Make Sense*. Wheaton: Tyndale House, 1993.

Ewart, Frank. *The Phenomenon of Pentecost*. Hazelwood, MO: Word Aflame Press, 1947.

Faupel, William D. *The Everlasting Gospel: The Significance of Eschatology in the Development of Pentecostal Thought*. Sheffield: Sheffield Academic Press, 1996.

Gohr, G. W. "Kansas City Prophets." In *The New International Dictionary of Pentecostal and Charismatic Movements*, ed. Stanley M. Burgess and Eduard M. Van Der Maas, 816-7. Grand Rapids: Zondervan, 2002.

Fish, Melinda. *The River Is Here*. Grand Rapids, MI: Chosen, 1996.

Green, Michael. *Evangelism in the Early Church*. Grand Rapids, MI: Eerdmans, 1970.

_____. *I Believe in the Holy Spirit*. Grand Rapids, MI: William Eerdmans, 1975.

Harrell, David E. *All Things Are Possible: The Healing and Charismatic Revivals in Modern America*. Bloomington, IN: University Press, 1975.

Hocken, P. D. "Charismatic Movement." In *The New International Dictionary of Pentecostal and Charismatic Movements*, ed. Stanley M. Burgess and Eduard M. Van Der Maas, 477-519. Grand Rapids, MI: Zondervan, 2002.

Hollenweger, Walter J. *The Pentecostals*. Peabody, MA: Hendrickson, 1988.

_____. "Pentecostals and the Charismatic Movement." In *The Study of Spirituality*, ed. C. Jones and G. Wainwright, 549-54. London: SPECK, 1986.

_____. "Rethinking Spirit Baptism: The Natural and the Supernatural." In *Pentecostals after a Century: Global Perspectives on a Movement in Transition*, eds. Alan and Walter J. Hollenweger Anderson, 164-172. Sheffield: Sheffield Academic Press, 1999.

Hopkins, S. F. "Glossolalia." In *The New International Dictionary of Pentecostal and Charismatic Movements*, ed. Stanley M. Burgess and Eduard M. Van Der Maas, 670-76. Grand Rapids, MI: Zondervan, 2002.

Horton, Stanley M. *What the Bible Says About the Holy Spirit*. Springfield, MO: Gospel Publishing House, 2002.

Hovenden, Gerald. *Speaking in Tongues: The New Testament Evidence in Context*. New York: Sheffield Academic Press, 2002.

Hunter, A.M. *Introducing New Testament Theology*. Naperville, IL: SMC Book Club, 1957

Jacobsen, Donald. *Thinking in the Spirit: Theologies of the Early Pentecostal Movement*. Indianapolis, IN: Indiana University Press, 2003.

Kellas, James. *The Significance of the Synoptic Gospels*. Greenwich: Seabury Press, 1961.

_____. The Satanward View: *A Study in Pauline Theology*. Philadelphia: Westminster, 1966.

_____. *Jesus and the Power of Satan*. Philadelphia, PA: Westminster Press, 1968.

_____. *The Real Satan*. Minneapolis, MN: Augsburg Publishing, 1975.

Kelsey, Morton. *Healing and Christianity*. New York: Harper & Row, 1976.

Kreeft, Peter. *Making Sense out of Suffering*. Ann Arbor, MI: Servant Books, 1996.

Kydd., R.A.N. "Healing in the Christian Church." In *The New International Dictionary of Pentecostal and Charismatic Movements*, ed. Stanley M. Burgess and Eduard M. Van Der Maas, 701. Grand Rapids, MI: Zondervan, 2002.

Ladd, George Eldon. *Crucial Questions About the Kingdom of God*. Grand Rapids: Eerdmans, 1954.

_____. *Jesus and the Kingdom*. Waco, TX: Word Books, 1964.

_____. *The Pattern of New Testament Truth*. Grand Rapids: Eerdmans, 1968.

_____. *Gospel of the Kingdom*. Grand Rapids, MI: Eerdmans, 1973.

_____. *The Presence of the Future*. Grand Rapids, MI: Eerdmans, 1974.

_____. *A Theology of the New Testament*. Grand Rapids, MI: Eerdmans, 1975.

_____. *The Last Things*. Grand Rapids, MI: Eerdmans, 1978.

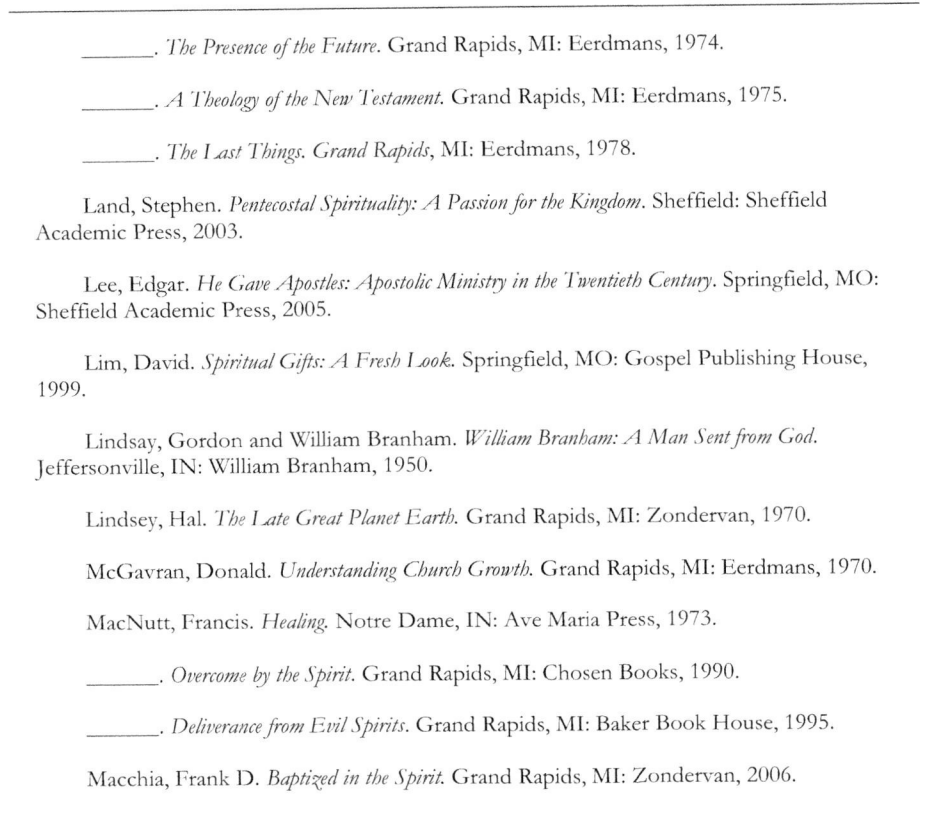

Land, Stephen. *Pentecostal Spirituality: A Passion for the Kingdom*. Sheffield: Sheffield Academic Press, 2003.

Lee, Edgar. *He Gave Apostles: Apostolic Ministry in the Twentieth Century*. Springfield, MO: Sheffield Academic Press, 2005.

Lim, David. *Spiritual Gifts: A Fresh Look*. Springfield, MO: Gospel Publishing House, 1999.

Lindsay, Gordon and William Branham. *William Branham: A Man Sent from God*. Jeffersonville, IN: William Branham, 1950.

Lindsey, Hal. *The Late Great Planet Earth*. Grand Rapids, MI: Zondervan, 1970.

McGavran, Donald. *Understanding Church Growth*. Grand Rapids, MI: Eerdmans, 1970.

MacNutt, Francis. *Healing*. Notre Dame, IN: Ave Maria Press, 1973.

_____. *Overcome by the Spirit*. Grand Rapids, MI: Chosen Books, 1990.

_____. *Deliverance from Evil Spirits*. Grand Rapids, MI: Baker Book House, 1995.

Macchia, Frank D. *Baptized in the Spirit*. Grand Rapids, MI: Zondervan, 2006.

Martin, F. "The Gift of Healing." In *The New International Dictionary of Pentecostal and Charismatic Movements*, ed. Stanley M. Burgess and Eduard M. Van Der Maas, 694-98. Grand Rapids, MI: Zondervan, 2002.

Mason, Mike. *The Gospel According to Job: An Honest Look at Pain and Doubt from the Life of One Who Lost Everything*. Wheaton, IL: Crossway Books, 1994.

Masters, Peter. *The Healing Epidemic*. London: Wakeman Trust, 1988.

McClung, Grant L. *Azusa Street and Beyond: Pentecostal Missions and Church Growth in the Twentieth Century South*. Plainville, NJ: Bridge Publishing, 1986.

McDonnell, Killian. *Baptism in the Holy Spirit and the Rites of Initiation: Evidence from the First Eight Centuries*. Collegeville, MN: Michael Glazier Book Publisher, 1994.

McGee, Gary B. *Initial Evidence: Historical and Biblical Perspectives on the Pentecostal Doctrine of Spirit Baptism*. Peabody, MA: Hendrickson, 1991.

McGee, Gary and B. A. Pavia. "Charles Peter Wagner." In *New International Dictionary of Pentecostal and Charismatic Movements*, ed. Stanley M. Burgess and Eduard M. Van Der Maas, 1181. Grand Rapids, MI: Zondervan, 2002.

Menzies, Robert P. *Empowered for Witness: The Spirit in Luke-Acts*. Sheffield: Sheffield Academic Press, 2001.

Menzies, William and Robert Menzies. *Spirit and Power: Foundations of Pentecostal Experience*. Grand Rapids, MI: Zondervan 2000.

Menzies, William. *Anointed to Serve*. Springfield, MO: Gospel Publishing House, 1971.

Miller, Donald E. *Reinventing American Protestantism: Christianity in the New Millennium*. Berkley, CA: University of California Press, 1999.

Palma, Anthony D. *The Holy Spirit: A Pentecostal Perspective*. Springfield, MO: Gospel Publishing House, 2001.

Pink, Dandelion. *An Introduction to Quakerism*. Cambridge: Cambridge University Press, 2007.

Purdy, Vernon. "Divine Healing." In *Systematic Theology*, ed. Stanley M. Horton, 49-523. Springfield: Legion, 2007.

Quebedeaux, Robert. *The New Pentecostals Two: How a Christian Renewal Movement Became Part of the American Religious Mainstream*. San Francisco: Harper & Row, 1983.

Reddin, Opal. *Power Encounter: A Pentecostal Perspective*. Springfield, MO: Central Bible College Press, 1999.

Riss, Richard. *A Survey of Twentieth Century Revival Movements in North America*. Peabody, MA: Hendrickson, 1988.

Robeck, Cecil M. "Calvary Chapel." In *The New International Dictionary of Pentecostal and Charismatic Movements*, ed. Stanley M. Burgess and Eduard M. Van Der Maas, 453. Grand Rapids: Zondervan 2002.

Sandford, Agnes. *The Healing Light*. Plainfield, NJ: Logos International, 1947.

Spittler, Russell P. *Perspectives on the New Pentecostalism*. Grand Rapids: Baker Book House, 1976.

_____. "Pentecostal Spirituality." In *The New International Dictionary of Pentecostal and Charismatic Movements*, ed. Stanley M. Burgess and Eduard M. Van Der Maas, 1096-102. Grand Rapids: Zondervan, 1988.

Synan, Vinson. *In the Latter Days: The Outpouring of the Holy Spirit in the Twentieth Century*. Ann Arbor: Servant Books, 1991.

_____. *The Holiness Pentecostal Tradition: Charismatic Movements in the Twentieth Century*. Grand Rapids: Eerdmans, 1997.

_____. *Century of the Holy Spirit*. Nashville: Thomas Nelson, 2001.

Twelftree, Graham. "The Holy Spirit Hits Hope Valley." In *Fresh Outpourings of the Holy Spirit: The Impact of Toronto*, ed. Wallace Boulton, 29-31. Crowborough, U.K.: Monarch, 1995.

Williams, Morris. "Can a Christian Have a Demon?" In *Power Encounter: A Pentecostal Perspective*, ed. Opal Reddin, 160-173. Springfield: Central Bible College Press, 1999.

———. "Can Demons Invade Believers?" In *Power Encounters: A Pentecostal Perspective*, ed. Opal Reddin, 160-72. (Springfield, MO: Central Bible College Press, 1999).

Wright, Eric E. *Strange Fire: Assessing the Vineyard Movement and the Toronto Blessing*. England: Evangelical Press, 1996.

Wright, Nigel. "The Theology and Methodology of 'Signs and Wonders.'" In *Charismatic Renewal*. London: SPEC, 1995.

Wright, Nigel. "The Theology and Methodology of 'Signs and Wonders'." In *Charismatic Renewal: The Search for Theology*, eds. Tom Smail and Andrew Walker. London: Society for Promoting Christian Knowledge, 1995.

Yancy, Philip. *Disappointment with God: Three Questions No One Asks Aloud*. New York: Harper, 1988.

———. *Where Is God When It Hurts?* New York: Harper, 1997.

Dissertations

Bogen, Egil. "The Holy Spirit's Role in Initiating Missions in Acts and the Vineyard." PhD Dissertation, Fuller Theological Seminary, 2006.

Chrasta, Michael James. "Jesus People to Promise Keepers: A Revival Sequence and Its Effect on Late Twentieth-Century Evangelical Ideas of Masculinity." PhD Dissertation, University of Texas, 1992.

Chung, Soon. "The Holy Spirit's Work in the Preaching Ministry of John Wimber." DMin Dissertation. Gordon-Conwell Theological Seminary, 2004.

Downs, David Rutherford. "A Biblical Evaluation of John Wimber's Concept of Power Evangelism." ThM Dissertation, Dallas Theological Seminary, 1989.

Hawking, Allen. "Perpetuating the Charisma of the Spirit in a Local Church Movement: Case Study on the Vineyard USA." DMin Dissertation, United Theological Seminary, 2015.

Horton, Kenneth Frank. "The Vineyard Movement and Eschatology: An Interpretation." PhD Dissertation, Dallas Theological Seminary, 1999.

Jackson, Robert Ernest. "An Evaluation of the Evangelistic Emphasis of the North American Power Evangelism Movement, 1977-1997." PhD Dissertation, The Southern Baptist Theological Seminary, 1999.

Lee, Edward Ming. "A Biblical Evaluation of the Physical Healing Passages as Taught by John Wimber." ThM Dissertation. Dallas Theological Seminary, 1990.

Percy, Martyn. "Signs, Wonders and Church Growth: the theme of power in contemporary Christian fundamentalism, with special reference to the works of John Wimber." PhD Dissertation, Kings College, London, 1993.

Perrin, Robin Dale. "Signs and Wonders: The Growth of the Vineyard Christian Fellowship." PhD Dissertation, Washington State University, 1989.

Shephard, David H. "A Critical Analysis of 'Power Evangelism' as an Evangelistic Methodology of the Signs and Wonders Movement." ThD Dissertation, Mid-America Baptist Theological Seminary, 1991.

Symmons, Roderic Paul. "Charismatics at the Crossroads." DMin Dissertation, Fuller Theological Seminary, 1997.

Warrington, Keith. "The teaching and praxis concerning supernatural healing of British Pentecostals, John Wimber and Kenneth Hagin in the light of an analysis of the healing ministry of Jesus as recorded in the Gospels." PhD Dissertation, University of London, 1999.

Printed in Great Britain
by Amazon